GUN CONTROL AND
GUN RIGHTS

GUN CONTROL AND GUN RIGHTS

•

A READER AND GUIDE

•

Edited by Andrew J. McClurg, David B. Kopel,
and Brannon P. Denning

NEW YORK UNIVERSITY PRESS
NEW YORK AND LONDON

NEW YORK UNIVERSITY PRESS
New York and London

Library of Congress Cataloging-in-Publication Data
Gun control and gun rights : a reader and guide / edited by
Andrew McClurg, David Kopel, and Brannon Denning.
p.   cm.
Includes bibliographical references and index.
ISBN 0-8147-4760-4 (pbk. : alk. paper)
ISBN 0-8147-4759-0 (cloth : alk. paper)
1. Gun control—United States. 2. Firearms ownership—
United States. 3. Firearms—Law and legislation—United States.
I. McClurg, Andrew J., 1954– II. Kopel, David B. III. Denning,
Brannon P.
HV7436 .G84 2002
363.3'3'0973—dc21   2001008620

New York University Press books are printed on acid-free paper,
and their binding materials are chosen for strength and durability.

Manufactured in the United States of America

10 9 8 7 6 5 4 3 2 1

CONTENTS

PREFACE

Few issues generate as much emotion and passion as gun control and gun rights. As with other issues where the emotional stakes are high (e.g., abortion and affirmative action), the arguments and judgments we make about guns often occur in a fog of rhetorical fallacies and misinformation.

Discussions about guns usually follow one of two courses. Dialogues among persons who share similar views—whether pro-rights or pro-control—tend to be smug, unchallenging events in which, rather than think critically about their own beliefs, many people are content to smear the other side with *ad hominem* labels such as "gun nuts" or "gun phobes." Discussions about guns with persons of opposite views quickly turn into debates, often heated ones, in which the participants are much more concerned with persuasion than with listening to, and perhaps learning from, the other side.

Even most academic literature regarding firearms policy is one-sided "advocacy" scholarship. While partisan literature is common in other areas, what is striking about the gun debate is that many scholars have failed even to attempt a balanced analysis of the issues.

"Balance" is what makes this book unique. Balance was our goal from day one. We think we achieved it, not because we're any wiser or less biased than other scholars in the area but because we compiled it together. We are in one sense an unlikely trio of coeditors. Kopel and Denning are strong supporters of gun rights. McClurg is an equally fervent supporter of gun control. Each of us has written extensively about guns, clearly staking out his position. Had any one of us attempted to write this book, it is doubtful he could have achieved true even-handedness despite his best-faith efforts. Like everyone else involved in the debate, we are colored by our own values and beliefs.

We learned this lesson time and again during the writing process. Sending or receiving a chapter draft would set off a flurry of e-mailed additions, deletions, and alterations as we all worked hard at keeping one another honest. Sometimes a chapter would zip back and forth among the three of us several times in a single day. While it was frustrating at times to watch a sentence be rewritten ten times until everyone was satisfied with it, the tension in our opposing views generated intense creative energy. This energy helped us shape a firearms policy textbook that we believe is not only balanced but fresh, exciting, and provocative. We hope you enjoy teaching and learning from this book as much as we enjoyed working on it.

FORMAT AND TEACHING TIPS

This text is designed to be user-friendly for both teachers and students. Because the book is intended for use in both law school and undergraduate courses, we took great care to ensure that legal principles are explained lucidly, in terms understandable by laypersons.

The book has six chapters. Each chapter addresses a broad issue in the gun control debate. Chapter 1 analyzes the benefits of guns to individuals and society; chapter 2 assesses the costs of guns. We put these chapters first because of our belief that people's views about gun control ultimately are grounded in their subjective weighing of the relative costs and benefits of firearms to individuals and society. Chapter 3 traces the early historical development of a right to bear arms in organized societies, providing a foundation for analyzing the three principal philosophical justifications offered in support of such a right: self-defense, defense against invasion, and defense against tyranny. Chapter 4 examines the controversial and misunderstood Second Amendment and similar state constitutional provisions and analyzes the extent to which legal restrictions on guns are or are not constitutional. Chapter 5 examines the disparate effects that guns and gun violence have on persons of different races, sexes, classes, and cultures. Chapter 6 addresses an issue that, while relatively new in the gun control debate, has generated intense controversy and attention: attempts to use our system of civil tort law—or "personal injury" law—to seek redress for victims of firearms violence and, ultimately, to change the course of firearms policy in the United States. This chapter is a fitting one with which to close the book because it presents for consideration many of the specific modern proposals sought by gun control advocates for regulating guns, such as changes in firearm design and in the distribution and marketing practices of gun manufacturers.

Each chapter consists of a series of excerpts from academic articles (and, in some chapters, judicial opinions), followed by extensive "Discussion Notes." The notes are designed to force students on both sides of the debate to go beyond their affective, gut reactions and to confront and reason through their own biases. We purposefully call them "Discussion Notes" rather than "Questions" or just "Notes." The issues of gun control and gun rights provide rich fodder for spirited classroom debate, and we encourage teachers to take advantage of this built-in benefit of the subject matter. A large body of educational research shows that active learning is more effective than passive learning. Moreover, only through open, reasoned, and informed exchange can we hope to make progress in a policy area so fraught with intransigent disagreement.

Whenever possible, excerpts were selected and set up to form a point-counterpoint regarding specific issues: that is, a "pro-control" viewpoint is followed immediately by a "pro-rights" viewpoint or vice versa. The goal of this format is to compel students to consider simultaneously reasoned arguments on both sides of an issue. The Discussion Notes frequently follow a similar point–counterpoint pattern.

A fundamental lesson learned from teaching is that students think better about a topic when they know exactly what it is they're supposed to be thinking about. In this vein, rather than ask broad questions such as "What do you think about the excerpt you just read?" we have tried to make each note sufficiently complete and self-contained to enable students to focus on and think through the specific issue raised.

Several of the Discussion Notes include classroom exercises of various types. We highly recommend that teachers make use of them. Exercises are valuable because they facilitate the inclusion of all students in classroom dialogues. Everyone has opinions on the issues of gun control and gun rights. Many students, however, are reticent about expressing their opinions openly in class, particularly if a few strong personalities tend to dominate the discussion. The exercises provide a tool for getting the entire class involved.

The Discussion Notes are quite extensive, so it might be helpful for teachers to study them in advance and select particular notes or exercises they want students to focus on in reading their assignments and preparing for class discussion.

This book is designed so that it can be used as either a supplemental reader in courses related to criminal justice, social or legislative policy, or constitutional law; or as a primary textbook in courses devoted specifically to firearms policy, firearms violence, or the Second Amendment. Coverage of the material can be adjusted to fit the needs of the instructor and the course by placing either greater or lesser emphasis on the Discussion Notes and exercises therein. As an example, an instructor teaching a criminal justice course who wants to devote only an hour of class time to discussing the constitutional right to bear arms could assign chapter 4 in its entirety and select a couple of key issues to focus on. In contrast, an instructor teaching a course in firearms policy could easily fill an hour (or more) of class time by assigning the exercise in Discussion Note 7, page 212, which directs students to redraft the Second Amendment as they think it should have been written originally, and to come to class prepared to defend their positions.

We have tried to provide reliable documentation for the many statistics and other facts referred to in this book. Some citations are Web links that may have been changed or may no longer be active.

ACKNOWLEDGMENTS

Andrew J. McClurg is grateful for the research assistance of Debby Vickers, April Minor, and Jessica Vaught, students at the University of Arkansas at Little Rock William H. Bowen School of Law. McClurg dedicates this book to his daughter, Caitlin, whom he has been lecturing about guns and many other topics, much to her dismay, since she was three.

David B. Kopel would like to thank Ronald K. Noble, professor of law at New York University and director of Interpol. This book was Noble's brainchild, growing out of the "Gun Control and Gun Rights" seminar that Noble and Kopel taught together at New York University School of Law in the fall of 1998. Kopel dedicates this book to his wife, Deirdre.

Brannon P. Denning is grateful to Tara Crane and Jennifer Gill for first-rate research assistance, and to Dean Thomas F. Guernsey for his support, financial and otherwise. Denning dedicates this book to Alli, Gram, and Meg for their unequivocal love and support, and to Glenn Reynolds for introducing him to the subject and to a new profession.

CHAPTER I

THE BENEFITS OF GUN OWNERSHIP

It is estimated that Americans own between 200 and 250 million firearms, if not more. Approximately one-third of these are handguns. The remaining two-thirds are long guns (rifles and shotguns). Pollsters estimate that guns are present in approximately 40 percent of U.S. households—although the true figure could be higher, given the reluctance of some gun owners to disclose personal information to pollsters. It is obvious that a large percentage of the American population sees benefits to owning firearms, despite the fact that guns also present obvious risks. This chapter explores the benefits of gun ownership to both individuals and society. The next chapter examines the costs of gun ownership to individuals and society.

The immediate benefits of gun ownership to individuals can be broken down into two basic categories: recreational use and personal defense. (Various forms of community protection, including the prevention of tyranny or genocide, are discussed in chapter 4.) A majority of gun owners acquire their arms for hunting or other sporting use, such as target shooting. In a 1994 national poll, 60 percent of gun owners stated they acquired their firearms primarily for hunting/sporting purposes. Millions of persons also acquire guns primarily for collecting. The various uses often overlap. For example, a person who buys shotguns for trap and skeet shooting (shooting at flying clay disks) may also enjoy building a collection of finely engraved shotguns. A woman who received a rifle as a family heirloom may use it mainly for deer hunting but also consider the rifle as a weapon to be used for defense in an emergency.

A large percentage of gun owners rely on their firearms for personal defense. The 1998 National Gun Policy Survey conducted by the National Opinion Research Center showed that approximately 40 percent of people in households with firearms acquired their guns at least in part for protection against crime. The percentage is larger for those who own handguns only. Sixty-five percent of handgun owners mentioned protection against crime as a reason for owning a gun.

The benefits of guns for personal defense are controversial and difficult to quantify. Gun rights advocates assert that guns are an effective way to ward off criminals and cite statistics that citizens use guns for defensive purposes about 2.5 million times each year. Gun control advocates dispute both points. They argue that introducing a gun into a violent encounter increases the risk of harm and cite figures that purport to show that defensive gun uses occur at far lower rates.

The protective benefits of gun ownership to society are also hotly disputed. Gun rights supporters assert that gun ownership plays a substantial role in deterring criminal conduct. The deterrence theory holds that criminals are reluctant to burglarize or assault armed citizens out of fear for their own lives. Because criminals do not know who is armed, non–gun owners also enjoy the benefit of this deterrent effect. Gun control supporters counter that higher gun prevalence creates higher risks of overall gun violence, including greater risks that guns will fall into the hands of unauthorized users such as irresponsible children, potential suicides, and criminals.

As with most issues in the gun debate, there is merit in both sides of the arguments. Guns confer both benefits and costs. It is true that gun owners use guns in self-defense, to protect lives and property. It is also true that some criminals are deterred from committing crimes because of a fear of confronting armed victims. Moreover, hunting, sport shooting, and gun collecting provide recreational enjoyment to tens of millions of people. Gun misuse, however, also imposes tremendous human and financial costs, as covered in chapter 2.

With truth on both sides, how does one decide which position is correct? Most people probably engage, at least intuitively, in some kind of cost-benefit analysis. We ask ourselves: Accepting that guns present both benefits and costs to society, do the benefits outweigh the costs or do the costs outweigh the benefits? Keep an open mind regarding this question until you have read this chapter and the next chapter. As you weigh the benefits and costs, think about whether laws can be constructed that will protect or enhance the benefits while reducing the costs.

In reading this chapter and chapter 2, you will see that advocates on both sides have staked many of their arguments on statistical analyses. You will also see that there is wide disagreement on the reliability of the methodologies employed and conclusions reached. Statistics and statistical analyses, like everything else in life, run the gamut in quality from shoddy to outstanding. Even well-constructed statistical analyses, however, conducted by well-intentioned researchers, may be subject to error and flawed construction. Use your common sense as a compass to help guide you through the statistical forest.

A. The Benefits of Guns for Personal Self-Defense

The benefit of guns for self-defense is one of the most contentious issues in the gun debate—for good reason. On the one hand, if guns are recognized as validly possessed for purposes of self-defense, some types of gun control, including gun prohibition or other measures that significantly restrict the availability of guns, are logically precluded. On the other hand, if a right to possess guns for self-defense is denied, virtually all avenues of gun control are at least open for consideration (setting aside constitutional considerations). Britain, for example, has extremely severe gun laws. Handguns are banned. Citizens can own shotguns or rifles, but the licensing system in the United Kingdom is very stringent, and guns must be locked in safes, inhibiting their use for defensive purposes. Whereas most types of recreational gun use can still be engaged in with long guns, the British system is intentionally hostile to the use of guns for personal defense. Some gun control advocates in this country would like to see U.S. law follow the path of Britain and some other countries that refuse to recognize self-defense as a valid purpose for owning a firearm. As one of the most important cards in the gun-debate deck, personal defense receives most of the attention in this chapter. Recreational uses are discussed at the end.

Basic Self-Defense Principles

The concept that one enjoys a right to use force for personal defense is virtually unchallenged, although, as noted above, there is disagreement about whether that right carries with it a right to use and possess firearms. The morality of using force in self-defense derives from natural law. Natural law is a philosophy of law that holds some rights are so basic and fundamental to human existence that they would exist even in a state of nature, regardless of whether they had been set down as written law in the form of cases, statutes, or constitutions. Self-preservation, it is sometimes said, is the first law of nature. Chapter 4 explores these philosophical issues in more detail.

In the United States, both criminal law and civil tort law recognize a right to use force to defend one's person. Although legal rules vary among jurisdictions, it is generally recognized that a person has a right to use force to prevent a threatened harm when she reasonably believes the use of force is necessary, even if it turns out she was mistaken. For example, if Mr. Smith has vowed to kill Ms. Jones on sight, and Ms. Jones sees Mr. Smith approaching her at night carrying what appears to be an ax, Ms. Jones may be legally privileged to use force to protect herself—even if it turns out Smith was carrying only a theater prop and had no hostile intent. If a reasonable person in Ms. Jones's shoes would have believed the use of force was necessary for self-defense, Ms. Jones will not be subject to either criminal or civil liability.

The amount of force used in self-defense must also be reasonable, in light of the relevant circumstances. The allowed defensive force is based on the threat against the actor. Generally speaking, persons are entitled to use deadly force (meaning force likely to cause death or serious bodily injury) in self-defense only when they reasonably believe that no lesser force will suffice and that they are threatened with deadly force or certain violent felonies.

Depending on state law, citizens have similar legal rights to use force to protect others, such as family members or even strangers. (Some states do not allow deadly force to protect a stranger.)

Force can be used to protect property as well as life. However, the amount of force that can be used to protect property is more limited. In most jurisdictions, one may not use deadly force to protect property. This rule is based on the common-law judgment that life is more valuable than property. ("Common law" is the judicially created law of the Anglo-American legal system.)

Some jurisdictions allow deadly force to be used to protect property, but these laws tend to be based on the close association of certain property crimes with violence. Thus, the line in these situations between protecting property and life is blurred. For example, Colorado's "Make My Day" law allows the use of deadly force against violent home invaders, regardless of whether lesser force would suffice (*Colo. Rev. Stats.* § 18-1-704.5). In 1997, Louisiana passed a controversial law labeled in the popular press as the "Kill the Carjacker" statute, which authorizes an occupant of a car to use deadly force against any person who attempts unlawfully to enter the vehicle, without any requirement that the occupant reasonably fear for his or her life (*La. Rev. Stat. Ann.* § 14:20 [3]–[4]).

The right of self-defense is a right only to prevent imminently threatened harm. It is not a right to retaliate, nor is it a right to inflict punishment.

DISCUSSION NOTES

1. Under what circumstances would you use deadly force against a person in self-defense? In defense of a child or other relative? In defense of a stranger? Take a class poll. How many students would use deadly force in self-defense to resist deadly force threatened against them? To resist sexual assault? To resist a nondeadly, nonsexual assault? To resist a robbery (taking of property by force)? To resist a theft (e.g., a pickpocket or shoplifter)? Would you not kill in self-defense for any reason?

2. As noted above, it is a generally accepted rule of law that one cannot use deadly force to defend property only. Do you agree with this rule? Do you think a person should be permitted to shoot a person who, for example, is attempting to steal his or her unoccupied car?

3. Should a person be permitted to shoot a fleeing criminal? Suppose Homeowner wakes up to find Felon in his house. Felon flees the house. Should Homeowner be permitted to shoot Felon while he is fleeing? If so, for what purpose? To prevent escape? To punish? State laws vary widely about the use of deadly force against felons. Some states allow deadly force (when lesser force is insufficient) for any felony committed in one's presence; other states specify only particularly dangerous felonies; while others are more restrictive still. If you were an elected prosecutor, would you bring charges against the homeowner in the above example? If you were on a criminal jury, would you vote to convict a homeowner who shot a fleeing burglar? If you were on a civil tort jury, would you award damages to the injured burglar if he sued the homeowner?

4. Some states bar most felons from suing for injuries they incur in the course of their crimes (e.g., *Colo. Rev. Stats.* § 13-80-119). But in one famous tort case, a burglar was permitted to recover substantial damages against an elderly couple who set up a shotgun booby trap to protect their unoccupied farmhouse. Marvin Katko, the plaintiff, broke into an abandoned farmhouse owned by Ed and Bertha Briney in search of old jars that he considered to be valuable antiques. When he entered the bedroom, a shotgun wired to the door discharged, blasting away a substantial portion of his leg. Katko sued the Brineys and a jury awarded him both compensatory and punitive damages. The Brineys had to sell 120 acres of their farm to get the money to pay the judgment. The Iowa Supreme Court upheld the jury verdict on the principle that life (even the life of a criminal) is more valuable than property. Do you agree with this result? (See *Katko v. Briney*, 183 N.W. 2d 657 [Iowa 1971].)

The Effectiveness of Guns for Self-Defense

Do guns provide owners with real security against crime, or only psychological security? Whether guns are truly effective for purposes of self-defense is an important question in the self-defense debate.

POINT BLANK: GUNS AND VIOLENCE IN AMERICA
(121–24 [1991])

Gary Kleck

Doubts about the defensive utility of guns . . . appear to rest on any of three beliefs: (1) civilians do not need any self-protective devices, because they will never confront criminals, or at least will never do so while they have access to a gun, or (2) they can rely on the police for protection, or (3) they are not able to use guns effectively, regardless of need.

There is certainly some merit to the first belief. Most Americans rarely face a threat of serious physical assault, and some will never do so. Nevertheless, National Crime Survey (NCS) estimates indicate that 83% of Americans will, sometime over the span of their lives, be a victim of a violent crime, all of which by definition involve direct confrontation with a criminal. Further, the most common location for such a confrontation is in or near the victim's home, i.e., the place where victims would be most likely to have access to a gun if they owned one. Although it cannot be stated what share of these incidents will transpire in a way that would allow the victim to actually use a gun, it is clear that a large share of the population will experience such an incident.

The second idea, that citizens can depend on police for effective protection, is simply untrue. It implies that police can serve the same function as a gun in disrupting a crime in progress, before the victim is hurt or loses property. Police cannot do this, and indeed do not themselves even claim to be able to do so. Instead, police primarily respond reactively to crimes *after* they have occurred, questioning the victim and other witnesses, in the hope that they can apprehend the criminals, make them available for prosecution and punishment, and thereby deter other criminals from attempting crimes. Police officers rarely disrupt violent crimes or burglaries in progress; even the most professional and efficient urban police forces rarely can reach the scene of a crime soon enough to catch the criminal "in the act. . . ."

The third idea, that civilians are not generally able to use guns effectively, requires more extended consideration. Gun control proponents sometimes argue that only police have the special training, skills, and emotional control needed to wield guns effectively in self-defense. They hint that would-be gun users are ineffectual, panic-prone hysterics, as likely to accidentally shoot a family member as a burglar. Incidents in which householders shoot family members mistaken for burglars and other criminals do indeed occur, but they are extremely rare. Studies . . . indicate that fewer than 2% of fatal gun accidents (FGAs) involve a person accidentally shooting someone mistaken for an intruder. With about 1400 FGAs in 1987, this implies that there are fewer than 28 incidents of this sort annually. . . . It has been claimed that many people who attempt to use guns for self-protection have the gun taken from them by the criminal and used against them. Although this type of incident is not totally unknown, it is extremely rare. In the 1979–1985 NCS sample, it was possible to identify crime incidents in which the victim used a gun for self-protection and lost a gun to the offender(s). At most, 1% of defensive gun uses resulted in the offender taking a gun away from the victim. . . .

Preventing Completion of the Crime

It has been argued that resistance by crime victims, especially forceful resistance, is generally useless and even dangerous to the victim. Although evidence supports this position as it applies to some forms of resistance, it does not support the claim as it applies to resistance with a gun. Yeager and his colleagues (1976) examined data from victim surveys in eight large U.S. cities, which included information on the fraction of robberies and assaults that was completed against the victim and on victim use of self-protection measures. They did not report results separately for victims resisting with a gun but analyzed a category including victims using any weapon to resist. For robbery, the completion rate was 37% in crimes where the victim resisted with a weapon, a rate lower than that of any other form of self-protection, and far lower than among those who did not resist in any way. Because guns are regarded as more intimidating and deadly weapons than knives and other lesser weapons, one would expect gun-armed resisters to experience lower completion rates than victims resisting with other weapons. Therefore, had gun resisters been separately analyzed by Yeager et al., the results should have indicated even greater effectiveness of gun resistance relative to other forms of self-protection.

This is confirmed by the national data . . . which break out gun-armed resistance from other armed resistance. [The author analyzes a data set of 180,000 sample crime incidents reported to the NCS for the period of 1979–1985.] Respondents were asked if they had been a victim of crime in the previous 6 months, if they used any form of self-protection, if they were attacked, if they suffered injury, and if the crimes were completed. . . . [R]obbery victims who resisted with a gun or with a weapon other than a gun or knife were less likely to lose their property than victims using any other form of self-protection or who did not resist at all.

The remarkably successful outcomes of defensive gun uses might seem surprising if one imagines the incidents to involve shootouts between criminal and victim. This, however, does not describe most gun uses. Among the 1979–1985 violent incidents reported in the NCS, 70.4% of defensive gun uses were against offenders who did not even have a gun (or at least none visible to the victim). . . .

Avoiding Injury

. . . Robbery and assault victims who used a gun to resist were less likely to be attacked or to suffer an injury than those who used any other methods of self-protection or those who did not resist at all. Only 17.4% of gun resisters in robberies, and 12.1% in assaults, were injured. The misleading consequences of lumping gun resistance in with other forms of forceful resistance are made clear by these data, since other forms of forceful self-protection are far more risky than resisting with a gun. After gun resistance, the victim course of action least likely to be associated with injury is doing nothing at all, i.e., not resisting. However, this strategy is also the worst at preventing completion of the crime. Further, passivity is not a completely safe course either, since a quarter of victims who did not resist were injured anyway. This may be because some robbers use violence preemptively, as a way of deterring or heading off victim resistance before it occurs. Thus they may use violence instrumentally to ensure victim compliance, against those victims for whom this seems to be a safe course of action. Other robbers may simply enjoy assaulting victims for its own sake, using violence expressively.

Some analysts of robbery data have uncritically assumed that where crimes involve victims who resisted and were also injured, resistance must somehow have led to the injury. Although it is tempting to assume that resistance to a robber provokes attack, the reverse may also be true. That is, victims otherwise reluctant to resist may do so out of desperation or anger after being attacked by the robber—injury may provoke victim resistance. . . .

DISCUSSION NOTES

1. Defensive firearms instructors emphasize that a gun is not a talisman to ward off criminals; rather, the gun should simply be one element of an integrated defensive strategy. Massad Ayoob, a leading writer for popular gun magazines, states in an article on home defense tactics:

"Understand that the gun won't keep you safe by itself. Far too many citizens have fallen into the trap of thinking, 'I have a gun, so I'm automatically safe'" (Massad Ayoob, *Strategies and Tactics for Home Defense*, Guns and Ammo: Handguns for Home Defense, [1994] at 35, 37). Do you think most gun owners are mentally, physically, and emotionally able to use their guns effectively in self-defense? What is your basis of knowledge about gun owners?

2. Many gun owners acquire informal firearms training from friends and relatives. Some gun owners take formal courses (usually four to fourteen hours) in safe gun handling. These courses are required in a few states to buy a handgun and are required by many states to obtain concealed handgun carry permits. A much smaller number of gun owners take more advanced classes (six days or more) in defensive combat techniques (e.g., how to take cover; strategies for placing defensive shots). Many of these latter courses exceed the amount of firearms training that is legally required for police officers. Most experts agree that the sophistication of the training needed depends on the complexity of the problem to be faced. Should some or all gun owners be required by law to obtain gun use training? How much? Critics of mandatory training argue that imposing government tests on constitutional rights (e.g., literacy tests for voters) is wrong. Do you agree?

3. Have you ever needed a gun in self-defense? Think about incidents in your own life where you were frightened by the possibility that you were in danger of being the victim of a crime. Did you have a gun? Did you use it? Did you wish you had a gun at the time? Do you feel the same way in hindsight? Looking back, do you believe having a gun would have helped the situation, made it worse, or made no difference? Kleck cites data that 70 percent of all defensive uses of guns occur against criminals without guns. Does this suggest that many situations in which people brandish guns defensively could be handled by other means? Or, since criminals tend to be young males who may be adept at street fighting, is the average unarmed citizen at an inherent disadvantage against unarmed criminals?

4. Instead of using guns, should citizens instead learn martial arts or other unarmed combat techniques? (The martial arts originated in East Asia in response to government weapons bans.) Defensive pepper sprays and

the like are legal in most, but not all, states. Should gun owners be encouraged to rely on chemical sprays instead? For what kinds of situations and crime victims are martial arts or chemical sprays a good, or inadequate, substitute for guns? What about knives? Kleck's data, from the
U.S. Department of Justice, suggest that people who use knives for defense against criminals tend to have higher injury rates than people who
use guns, people who resist by shouting for help, or people who submit
to the attacker. Could this be because effective knife fighting requires
close contact with the attacker (unlike a gun, which can project force at
a distance) and street-fighting skills, which most crime victims do not
possess? (By the way, don't take this chapter—or this book—as the last
word in your own strategy for crime prevention or resistance; individuals must make decisions based on their particular circumstances. For example, while using a knife for protection may be dangerous in general,
it might be the only hope against a criminal obviously intent on homicide. Note too that some countries that prohibit defensive gun ownership have also outlawed defensive carrying or use of knives and have imposed very strict rules against carrying a knife in public for any reason.)

5. Is there a danger that gun owners will get "itchy trigger fingers" in tense
situations and shoot when they should not shoot? On October 17, 1992,
Yoshi Hattori, a sixteen-year-old Japanese exchange student living in
Louisiana, rang the doorbell at the home of Rodney and Bonnie Peairs.
Hattori was looking for a Halloween party. He wore a tuxedo jacket and
white-ruffled shirt, like the character John Travolta played in Saturday
Night Fever. Hattori went to the Peairs house by mistake because the address was similar to the one he was looking for and the house was deco-
rated for Halloween. Bonnie Peairs answered the garage door instead of
the front door. When Hattori quickly came around from the front, she
became frightened, slammed the door, and yelled for her husband to get
his gun. Peairs came to the door with a .44 caliber revolver. When he saw
the teen, he shouted "Freeze." Hattori, who was not wearing his contact
lenses and spoke only limited English, kept moving forward. Peairs shot
him in the chest, killing him. A Louisiana jury acquitted Peairs of
manslaughter, apparently accepting his argument that he had reason to
be frightened enough to kill in self-defense. After the verdict, Peairs said
he would no longer use guns. (See *Japanese Student's Killer Is Acquitted,*

Orlando Sentinel, May 24, 1993, at A1.) Note that Kleck estimates the number of accidental shootings resulting from mistaking an innocent for a criminal comprises fewer than 2 percent of annual accidental shootings, or approximately twenty-eight fatal incidents per year.

6. Do you think widespread gun ownership for personal defense might have the adverse effect of encouraging more criminals to carry guns? Is this analogous to the argument that during the Cold War the United States should have unilaterally disarmed its nuclear weapons, so as not to encourage an arms race? Would criminals (or the Soviet Union) just respond more aggressively to disarmed adversaries? Or might robberies increase while victim injuries from robberies decreased?

7. Kleck cites a Department of Justice statistic (from the 1980s) that 83 percent of all Americans will be victims of a serious violent crime at some point in their lives. Take another class poll. How many persons in the class have been the victim of a violent crime? What was the nature of the crime? Was it serious or minor? If one person pushes another, that is technically a "violent crime" (a misdemeanor assault). Should citizens be encouraged to use guns to defend against all "violent crime"? Would you rather lose your wallet or purse to a mugger, or shoot him?

How Many Defensive Gun Uses (DGUs)?

One issue in the self-defense debate is how often citizens actually use guns to defend themselves. If people use guns only infrequently for self-defense, then this would diminish the benefits of guns, thereby helping tip the cost-benefit scales toward greater gun regulation. In contrast, the more frequently people use guns in self-defense, the greater the utility of guns for that purpose and the more the scales tip in favor of protecting widespread private gun ownership.

Of course, quantifying defensive gun uses (DGUs) is not necessarily *the* solution to the gun control debate. For example, if a person thinks defensive gun use is immoral (or that all gun ownership is immoral), statistics that DGUs are frequent probably will not make him support gun rights. Conversely, if a person has used a firearm for personal protection, he is unlikely to support gun prohibition even if statistics prove that DGUs by other people are rare.

Further, whatever the number of DGUs (in the millions or in the tens of thousands), it is apparent that they occur with some frequency. Accordingly, a person might logically support gun policies that she expects will enhance, or at least not diminish, DGUs, while also reducing the number of gun misuses.

Much of the debate on DGU quantification revolves around two studies offering wildly different numbers. Every six months the U.S. Bureau of the Census conducts the National Crime Victimization Survey (NCVS). The NCVS is designed to estimate the number of citizens victimized annually by crime. It also, however, asks persons who have identified themselves as crime victims whether they did anything to protect themselves from the criminal, and if so, how. From these questions, the NCVS estimates that DGUs occur nationally at the rate of sixty-five thousand to eighty-two thousand per year. At the other end of the DGU-counting spectrum lies the National Self-Defense Survey conducted by Gary Kleck and Marc Gertz in 1993. This survey concluded that individuals defend themselves with guns as many as 2.5 million times per year. Several other surveys of varying quality have also estimated greatly higher DGU rates than the NCVS. These figures range from the hundreds of thousands into the millions.

Not surprisingly, gun control advocates often rely on the NCVS results in discussing DGUs, while gun rights advocates cite the Kleck-Gertz figures. Which figures are more accurate? What accounts for such an incredible disparity—a more than thirty-fold difference—between the U.S. government's NCVS figures and the Kleck-Gertz figures? Set forth below are excerpts from the Kleck-Gertz study and, after the Discussion Notes, a response from three firearms researchers.

ARMED RESISTANCE TO CRIME: THE PREVALENCE AND NATURE OF SELF-DEFENSE WITH A GUN
(86 Journal of Criminal Law and Criminology 150 [1995])

Gary Kleck and Marc Gertz

However consistent the evidence may be concerning the effectiveness of armed victim resistance, there are some who minimize its significance by insisting that it is rare. This assertion is invariably based entirely on a single source of information, the National Crime Victimization Survey (NCVS).

Data from the NCVS imply that each year there are only about 68,000 defensive uses of guns in connection with assaults and robberies, or about 80,000 to 82,000 if one adds in uses linked with household burglaries. These figures are less than one-ninth of the estimates implied by the results of at least thirteen other surveys. . . .

[T]hose who take the NCVS-based estimates seriously have consistently ignored the most pronounced limitations of the NCVS for estimating DGU frequency. The NCVS is a nonanonymous national survey conducted by a branch of the federal government, the U.S. Bureau of the Census. Interviewers identify themselves to Rs [respondents] as federal government employees, even displaying, in face-to-face contacts, an identification card with a badge. Rs are told that the interviews are being conducted on behalf of the U.S. Department of Justice, the law enforcement branch of the federal government. . . . [I]t is made very clear to Rs that they are, in effect, speaking to a law enforcement arm of the federal government, whose employees know exactly who the Rs and their family members are, where they live, and how they can be recontacted.

Even under the best of circumstances, reporting the use of a gun for self-protection would be an extremely sensitive and legally controversial matter for either of two reasons. As with other forms of forceful resistance, the defensive act itself, regardless of the characteristics of any weapon used, might constitute an unlawful assault or at least the R might believe that others, including either legal authorities or the researchers, could regard it that way. Resistance with a gun also involves additional elements of sensitivity. Because guns are legally regulated, a victim's possession of the weapon, either in general or at the time of the DGU, might itself be unlawful, either in fact or in the mind of a crime victim who used one. More likely, lay persons with a limited knowledge of the extremely complicated law of either self-defense or firearms regulation are unlikely to know for sure whether their defensive actions or their gun possession was lawful.

It is not hard for gun-using victims interviewed in the NCVS to with-hold information about their use of a gun, especially since they are never directly asked whether they used a gun for self-protection. They are asked only general questions about whether they did anything to protect themselves. . . .

Further, Rs in the NCVS are not even asked the general self-protec-tion question unless they already independently indicated that they had been a victim of a crime. This means that any DGUs associated with crimes the Rs did not want to talk about would remain hidden. It has been estimated that the NCVS may catch less than one-twelfth of spousal assaults and one-third of rapes, thereby missing nearly all DGUs associated with such crimes. . . .

The Gun Surveys

[The authors discuss thirteen previous gun-use surveys. Some of the sur-veys were sponsored by pro–gun control organizations, some by anti-control organizations and some by neutral organizations. Eleven of these surveys contained enough information to allow the authors to compute estimates of DGU frequency. Each of the eleven surveys yielded results that implied more than seven hundred thousand DGUs per year. Table 2, included below in the Discussion Notes, summarizes these surveys. The authors note various flaws in the prior DGU surveys.]

It was the goal of the research reported here to remedy those flaws, to develop a credible estimate of DGU frequency, and to learn something about the nature of DGU incidents and the people who defend them-selves with guns.

The National Self-Defense Survey

Methods. The present survey is the first survey ever devoted to the sub-ject of armed self-defense. It was carefully designed to correct all of the known correctable or avoidable flaws of previous surveys which critics have identified. We use the most anonymous possible national survey format, the anonymous random digit dialed telephone survey. We did not know the identities of those who were interviewed, and made this fact clear to the Rs. We interviewed a large nationally representative sample covering all adults, age eighteen and over, in the lower forty-eight states and living in households with telephones. . . .

Each interview began with a few general "throat-clearing" questions about problems facing the R's community and crime. The interviewers then asked the following question: "Within the past five years, have you yourself or another member of your household used a gun, even if it was not fired, for self-protection or for the protection of property at home, work, or elsewhere? Please do not include military service, police work, or work as a security guard." Rs who answered "yes" were then asked: "Was this to protect against an animal or a person?" Rs who reported a DGU against a person were asked: "How many incidents involving defensive uses of guns against persons happened to members of your household in the past five years?" and "Did this incident [any of these incidents] happen in the past twelve months?" At this point, Rs were asked: "Was it you who used a gun defensively, or did someone else in your household do this?"

All Rs reporting a DGU were asked a long, detailed series of questions establishing exactly what happened in the DGU incident. . . .

Questions about the details of DGU incidents permitted us to establish whether a given DGU met all of the following qualifications for an incident to be treated as a genuine DGU: (1) the incident involved defensive action against a human rather than an animal, but not in connection with police, military, or security guard duties; (2) the incident involved actual contact with a person, rather than merely investigating suspicious circumstances, etc.; (3) the defender could state a specific crime which he thought was being committed at the time of the incident; (4) the gun was actually used in some way—at a minimum it had to be used as part of a threat against a person, either by verbally referring to the gun (e.g., "get away—I've got a gun") or by pointing it at an adversary. We made no effort to assess either the lawfulness or morality of the Rs' defensive actions.

An additional step was taken to minimize the possibility of DGU frequency being overstated. The senior author went through interview sheets on every one of the interviews in which a DGU was reported, looking for any indication that the incident might not be genuine. A case would be coded as questionable if even just one of four problems appeared: (1) it was not clear whether the R actually confronted any adversary he saw; (2) the R was a police officer, member of the military or a security guard, and thus might have been reporting, despite instructions, an incident which occurred as part of his occupational duties; (3) the interviewer did not properly record exactly what the R had done with the gun, so it was possible that he had not used it in any meaningful way; or (4) the R did not state or the interviewer did not record a specific crime that the R thought was being committed against him at the time of the incident. There were a total of twenty-six cases where at least one of these problematic indications was present. It should be emphasized that we do not know that these cases were not genuine DGUs; we only mean to indicate that we do not have as high a degree of confidence on the matter as with the rest of the cases designated as DGUs. Estimates using all of the DGU cases are labeled herein as "A" estimates, while the more conservative estimates based only on cases devoid of any problematic indications are labeled "B" estimates. . . .

Results. [The authors offered a table displaying the results of their study. Their table included data on estimated DGUs broken down by individuals and households; by all types of guns and by handguns only; and by a one-year recall period and a five-year recall period. Table 1, set forth below, is a simplified version of the original table, presenting only the data for persons (rather than households), for all types of guns (rather than handguns only), and for a one-year recall period (rather than a five-year period). The authors assert that the estimates reproduced below are the most reliable ones. The key figures are those for "Annual Uses": 2,549,862 in the "A" category (all DGUs included) and 2,163,519 in the "B" category (the more conservative estimate, which excluded from the calculation process any type of questionable DGU reported to interviewers). These are the figures giving rise to the widely quoted claim that DGUs occur at a rate of from 2.2 million to 2.5 million per year.]

The most technically sound estimates presented in [Table 1] are those based on the shorter one-year recall period that rely on Rs' first-hand

TABLE I Results of Kleck-Gertz National Self-Defense Survey[a]

Recall Period		Past year
Base		Persons
Gun Types		All guns included
Weighted Sample Cases	A[c]	66
	B[c]	56
% Used[b]	A	1.326
	B	1.125
Persons	A	2,549,862
	B	2,163,519
Annual Uses	A	2,549,862
	B	2,163,519

Population Bases: Estimated resident population, age eighteen and over: 190,538,000; estimated households: 97,045,525 (U.S. Bureau of the Census 1993).

[a] Defensive uses of guns against humans by civilians (i.e. excluding police officers, security guards, or military personnel). All figures are based on weighted data.

[b] Percent of persons with at least one defensive gun use during the one year preceding the interview.

[c] A estimates are based on all reported defensive gun uses reported in the survey. B estimates are based on only cases with no indications that the case might not be a genuine defensive gun use.

accounts of their own experiences. . . . They indicate that each year in the U.S. there are about 2.2 to 2.5 million DGUs of all types by civilians against humans. . . .

Are these estimates plausible? Could it really be true that Americans use guns for self-protection as often as 2.1 to 2.5 million times a year? The estimate may seem remarkable in comparison to expectations based on conventional wisdom, but it is not implausibly large in comparison to various gun-related phenomena. There are probably over 220 million guns in private hands in the U.S., implying that only about 1% of them are used for defensive purposes in any one year—not an impossibly high fraction. . . .

One natural standard of comparison by which the magnitude of these numbers could be judged is the frequency with which guns are used for criminal purposes. The highest annual estimate of criminal gun use for the peak year of gun crime is the NCVS estimate for 1992, when there were an estimated 847,652 violent crime incidents in which, according to the victim, at least one offender possessed a gun. This NCVS figure is not directly comparable with our DGU estimates because our DGU estimates are restricted only to incidents in which the gun was actually used by the defender, as opposed to incidents in which a victim merely possessed a gun. Many of the "gun crimes" in the NCVS, on the other hand, do not involve the gun actually being used by the criminal. . . .

Our estimates of DGUs are probably . . . too low, partly because, unlike the NCVS, our survey did not cover adolescents, the age group most frequently victimized in violence. Furthermore, our use of telephone surveying excludes the 5% of the nation's households without telephones, households which are disproportionately poor and/or rural. Low income persons are more likely to be crime victims, while rural persons are more likely to own guns and to be geographically distant from the nearest police officer. Both groups therefore may have more opportunities to use guns for self-protection and excluding them from the sample could contribute to an underestimation of DGU.

Both parameters also are subject to underestimation due to intentional respondent underreporting. It is also probable that typical survey Rs are more reluctant to tell interviewers about questionable acts that they themselves have committed, such as threatening another person with a gun for purportedly defensive reasons, than they are to report criminal acts that other people have committed against them. . . .

The only known significant source of overestimation of DGUs in this survey is "telescoping," the tendency of Rs to report incidents which actually happened earlier than the recall period, such as reporting a six-year-old incident as having happened in the past five years. It is likely that telescoping effects are more than counterbalanced by Rs who actually experienced DGUs failing to report them. . . .

The Nature of Defensive Gun Use

[M]uch like the typical gun crime, many of these cases were relatively undramatic and minor compared to fictional portrayals of gun use. Only 24% of the gun defenders in the present study reported firing the gun, and only 8% report wounding an adversary. This parallels the fact that only 17% of the gun crimes reported in the NCVS involve the offender shooting at the victim, and only 3% involve the victim suffering a gunshot wound. Low as it is, even an 8% wounding rate is probably too high, both because of the censoring of less serious cases, which in this context would be cases without a wounding, and because the survey did not establish how Rs knew they had wounded someone. We suspect that in incidents where the offender left without being captured, some Rs "remembered with favor" their marksmanship and assumed they had hit their adversaries. If 8.3% really hit their adversaries, and a total of 15.6% fired at their adversaries, this would imply a 53% (8.3/15.6) "incident hit rate," a level of combat marksmanship far exceeding that typically observed even among police officers. In a review of fifteen reports, police officers inflicted at least one gunshot wound on at least one adversary in 37% of the incidents in which they intentionally fired at someone. A 53% hit rate would also be triple the 18% hit rate of criminals shooting at crime victims. Therefore, we believe that even the rather modest 8.3% wounding rate we found is probably too high, and that typical DGUs are less serious or dramatic in their consequences than our data suggest. In any case, the 8.3% figure was produced by just seventeen sample cases in which Rs reported that they wounded an offender. . . .

Guns were most commonly used for defense against burglary, assault, and robbery. Cases of "mutual combat," where it would be hard to tell who is the aggressor or where both parties are aggressors, would be a subset of the 30% of cases where assault was the crime involved. However, only 19% of all DGU cases involved only assault and no other crime where victim and offender could be more easily distinguished. . . .

Another way of assessing how serious these incidents appeared to the victims is to ask them how potentially fatal the encounter was. We asked Rs: "If you had not used a gun for protection in this incident, how likely do you think it is that you or someone else would have been killed? Would you say almost certainly not, probably not, might have, probably would have, or almost certainly would have been killed?" . . . 15.7% of the Rs stated that they or someone else "almost certainly would have" been killed, with another 14.2% responding "probably would have" and 16.2% responding "might have." Thus, nearly half claimed that they perceived some significant chance of someone being killed in the incident if they had not used a gun defensively.

It should be emphasized that these are just stated perceptions of participants, not objective assessments of actual probabilities. Some defenders might have been bolstering the justification for their actions by exaggerating the seriousness of the threat they faced. . . .

If we consider only the 15.7% who believed someone almost certainly would have been killed had they not used a gun, and apply this figure to [DGU estimates reported by persons in the past year], it yields national annual estimates of 340,000 to 400,000 DGUs of any kind, and 240,000 to 300,000 uses of handguns, where defenders stated, if asked, that they believed they almost certainly had saved a life by using the gun. Just how many of these were truly life-saving gun uses is impossible to know. As a point of comparison, the largest number of deaths involving guns, including homicides, suicides, and accidental deaths, in any one year in U.S. history was 38,323 in 1991. . . .

Conclusion

If one were committed to rejecting the seemingly overwhelming survey evidence on the frequency of DGU, one could speculate, albeit without any empirical foundation whatsoever, that nearly all of the people reporting such experiences are simply making them up. We feel this is implausible. . . . [L]ying with a false "yes" answer [would require] a good deal [of] imagination and energy. Since we asked as many as nineteen questions on the topic, this would entail spontaneously inventing as many as nineteen plausible and internally consistent bits of false information and doing so in a way that gave no hint to experienced interviewers that they were being deceived. . . .

By this time there seems little legitimate scholarly reason to doubt that defensive gun use is very common in the U.S., and that it probably is substantially more common than criminal gun use. . . .

The policy implications of these results are straightforward. These findings do not imply anything about whether moderate regulatory measures such as background checks or purchase permits would be desirable. Regulatory measures which do not disarm large shares of the general population would not significantly reduce beneficial defensive uses of firearms by noncriminals. On the other hand, prohibitionist measures, whether aimed at all guns or just at handguns, are aimed at disarming criminals and noncriminals alike. They would therefore discourage and presumably decrease the frequency of DGU among noncriminal crime victims because even minimally effective gun bans would disarm at least some noncriminals. The same would be true of laws which ban gun carrying. In sum, measures that effectively reduce gun availability among the noncriminal majority also would reduce DGUs that otherwise would have saved lives, prevented injuries, thwarted rape attempts, driven off burglars, and helped victims retain their property. . . .

DISCUSSION NOTES

1. Does the Kleck-Gertz study strike you as sound in its methodology? Kleck and Gertz are not alone in offering substantially higher DGU estimates than those offered by the U.S. government in the NCVS. Set forth in Table 2 below is a summary of the results of thirteen different DGU surveys, taken from Gary Kleck's book, Targeting Guns: Firearms and Their Control, at 187–89 (with minor modifications). As Kleck candidly admits, many of these surveys contained major flaws, including the failure to ask detailed DGU questions and the use of small samples. Some of the surveys also lump DGUs against criminals with DGUs against animals (e.g., wild dogs) and occupational uses (e.g., by police or security guards).

2. Note that the DGU estimates in the various telephone surveys range from 764,036 to 3,609,682. The U.S. Census Bureau's National Crime Victimization Survey (NCVS), on which many gun control proponents rely, estimates that DGUs occur at a rate of from 65,000 to 82,000 annually. If the NCVS figures were accurate, would it not be reasonable to expect that at least some of the DGU telephone survey results would more closely parallel them? Kleck and Gertz dismiss the NCVS results, stating: "The strongest evidence that a measurement is inaccurate is that it is inconsistent with many other independent measurements of observations of the same phenomenon." Is that a persuasive point?

3. A potentially important finding of the Kleck-Gertz study is that, while 99 percent of the gun-owning population experienced no DGUs at all in the last five years, nearly one-third of households (29.5 percent) that did report a DGU were involved in multiple DGUs within the previous five years. What does this say about the characters, personalities, or lifestyles of those who use guns in self-defense? That they tend to be concentrated among people in high-crime

TABLE 2 Summary of Defensive Gun Use Surveys

	Field	Bordua	DMI one	DMI two	Hart	Ohio	Mauser	Gallup	Gallup	Kleck and Gertz	L.A. Times	Tarrance	Police Information
Area	California	Illinois	U.S.	U.S.	U.S.	Ohio	U.S.	U.S.	U.S.	U.S.	U.S.	U.S.	U.S.
Year of Interviews	1976	1977	1978	1978	1981	1982	1990	1991	1993	1993	1994	1994	1994
Gun type covered	Handguns	All guns	All guns	All guns	Handguns	Handguns	All guns	All guns	All guns	All guns	All guns	All guns	All guns
Recall period	Ever/1, 2 years	Ever	Ever	Ever	5 years	Ever	5 years	Ever	Ever	1 year	Ever	5 years	1 year
Excluded uses against animals?	No	No	No	Yes	Yes	No	Yes	No	No	Yes	No	Yes	Yes
Excluded military, police uses?	Yes	No	Yes	Yes	Yes	No	Yes	No	Yes	Yes	Yes	Yes	Yes
DGU question refers to	Respondent	Respondent	Household	Household	Household	Respondent	Household	Respondent	Respondent	Respondent	Respondent	Respondent/ household	Respondent
% who used gun	1.4/3/8.6[a]	5.0	15	7	4	6.5	3.79	8	11	1.326	8[c]	1/2[d]	1.44
% who fired gun	2.9	n/a	6	n/a	n/a	2.6	n/a	n/a	n/a	0.63	n/a	n/a	0.7
Implied number of defensive gun uses[b]	3,052,717	1,414,544	2,141,512	1,098,409	1,797,461	771,043	1,487,342	777,153	1,621,377	2,549,862	3,609,682	764,036	2,730,000

[a] Breaks down as 1.4 percent in past year, 3 percent in past two years, 8.6 percent ever.

[b] Estimated annual number of DGUs of guns of all types against humans, excluding uses connected with military or police duties, after any necessary adjustments were made; for United States, 1993.

[c] Covered only uses outside the home.

[d] One percent of respondents, 2 percent of households.

Source: Gary Kleck, *Targeting Guns: Firearms and Their Control* (Hawthorne, NY: Aldine de Gruyter, 1997).

neighborhoods? Among people who do not take appropriate steps to avoid trouble? Something else?

4. Kleck takes the position that most DGUs involve illegal behavior on the part of the respondents. He emphasizes this point as an explanation for why he believes DGUs are more likely to be underreported than overreported. The DGU may be illegal in a variety of ways, some serious and some relatively benign. A lawful gun owner may not be sure whether his use of the gun was legal under the circumstances; the ownership of the gun may be illegal (e.g., the user did not comply with the state licensing system for the handgun he bought from his brother-in-law or is legally prohibited from owning a gun because of a past criminal conviction, dishonorable discharge from the military, or other reason); the gun, although legally owned, may have been illegally carried in public or in a car (either because the state does not issue gun carry permits or because the user did not or could not obtain one); or what the user reported as a DGU may not have been lawful self-defense but rather a criminal assault or brawl in which the gun user was the aggressor. Do you believe any or all of these circumstances renders the DGU illegitimate?

The 1994 National Survey of Private Ownership of Firearms asked respondents whether they had ever been arrested for a nontraffic offense. Twenty percent of gun owners who reported being involved in a DGU in the previous five years answered affirmatively, compared to 7.8 percent of gun owners who had never been involved in a DGU. (See Otis Dudley Duncan, *Gun Use Surveys: In Numbers We Trust?* 25 Criminologist 1, 2–3 [2000]). Whether a gun is being used offensively or defensively is often ambiguous, especially where the reported crime is an assault. If an altercation breaks out between two people and one of them pulls a gun, is that a DGU? Does it depend on the particular facts of the altercation? The gun user might report it as self-defense. The other party might report it as an assault. Kleck and Gertz report that 30 percent of the crimes being defended against in their studies involved assault, which is by far the most common type of major violent crime. Just how many of these were cases of "mutual combat" is unknown.

A point frequently made by Kleck, but rarely by others, is that criminals (or ex-criminals) tend to be at much higher risk of being criminally attacked than the rest of the population. This may be partly because people with criminal records tend to live in high-crime neighborhoods and to associate with other people who have criminal records.

5. One questionable implication of the Kleck-Gertz study is the number of lives saved annually due to defensive gun use. In the Kleck-Gertz study, 15.7 percent of the respondents who claimed to have been involved in a DGU stated that they or someone else "almost certainly would have been killed" had they not used a gun defensively. This yields national estimates of 340,000 to 400,000 DGU situations annually where defenders were almost certain they saved a life. Do these numbers sound plausible? Fewer than thirty thousand homicides occur annually in the United States. Do you think that defensive gun use is saving hundreds of thousands of lives each year?

Kleck-Gertz declined to vouch for the accuracy of the respondents' beliefs, stating: "Just how many of these were truly life-saving gun uses is impossible to know." But if the respondents in the Kleck-Gertz survey were wrong on this point, does it call into question the credibility of their other responses? If we cannot have confidence in the "almost certain" beliefs of the respondents regarding the number of lives they saved, should we be confident about their other answers?

6. One rough measure of the risk-utility calculus involving defensive gun use is to compare how often guns are used defensively with how often they are used in crime. Kleck and Gertz cite NCVS data that 847,652 violent gun crimes occurred in 1992, the highest number for any year, compared to their estimate that guns are used defensively 2.5 million times per year. Assume for the sake of argument that the NCVS estimate of the number of violent gun crimes in 1992 (847,652) is accurate. What number of DGUs would you personally require for that year before you believed the benefits of guns for self-defense outweighed the costs of gun crimes? Can society take steps to reduce gun crime, while simultaneously encouraging (or at least not reducing) genuine DGUs? Or is the issue all or nothing: one cannot reduce gun crime without eliminating DGUs as well?

THE GUN DEBATE'S NEW MYTHICAL NUMBER:
HOW MANY DEFENSIVE USES PER YEAR?

(16 Journal of Policy Analysis and Management 463 [1997])

Philip J. Cook, Jens Ludwig, and David Hemenway

In 1986, Peter Reuter suggested that the Association for Public Policy Analysis and Management (APPAM) consider offering an annual award for the "most outrageous number mentioned in a policy discussion by an elected official or agency head," with one of the criteria being that the number have "no reasonable basis."

In this article, we discuss the candidacy of one of the more surprising numbers to surface in the course of America's gun debate: that 2.5 million Americans use a gun defensively against a criminal attacker each year. News items, editorial writers, even the Congressional Research Service have mentioned the 2.5 million defensive gun uses (DGUs) as established fact. This number is considerably higher than our best estimates of the number of crimes committed each year with a firearm (1.3 million [in 1996]), and has been used as an argument against regulations that would restrict widespread firearms ownership. The implicit notion seems to be that if there are more legitimate uses than criminal uses of guns against people, then widespread gun ownership is a net plus for public safety.

For reasons documented in this article, we believe that the 2.5 million figure is an example of what Max Singer has termed a "mythical number." Singer notes, "[E]ven responsible officials, responsible newspapers, and responsible research groups pick up and pass on as gospel numbers that have no real basis in fact. . . . [B]ecause an estimate has been used widely by a variety of people who should know what they are talking about, one cannot assume that the estimate is even approximately correct."

Estimates for the number of defensive gun uses are likely to be substantially overstated because of the problem of "false positives." This source of bias is a common problem in survey estimates of rare events, but largely unrecognized or ignored. We recount the evidence which indicates that the 2.5 million DGU estimates is far too high, and suggest that [it has] implications for both the policy debate over gun regulation, and for survey research.

Survey Results on Self-Defense

What distinguished this remarkable statistic is the entirely respectable source and estimation method. We usually think of mythical numbers as coming from obviously flawed procedures, generated by advocates seeking attention for the problem of homelessness or heroin addiction or youthful predators or some other cause.

In contrast, the DGU estimate was calculated by researchers affiliated with a major research university . . . using widely accepted methods and published in a topflight, peer-reviewed criminology journal. . . . Although many mythical numbers may be debunked by simply probing beneath the press reports to identify the source, such is not the case with the DGU figure. . . .

[The Kleck-Gertz] survey appears to have been conducted according to current standards, and the results have been reproduced in several subsequent surveys. In 1994, for example, the National Institute of Justice sponsored a telephone survey of 2600 American adults examining gun ownership and uses, including defensive gun uses. This National Survey of Private Ownership of Firearms (NSPOF) incorporated a sequence of DGU questions very similar to that used by Kleck and Gertz. Each respondent was asked, "Within the past 12 months, have you yourself used a gun, even if it was not fired, to protect yourself or someone else, or for the protection of property at home, work, or elsewhere?" Respondents who reported experiencing a defensive gun use were then asked 30 additional questions concerning their most recent DGU. Two of us (Cook and Ludwig) have analyzed these data, and report on them here.

When we follow the example of Kleck and Gertz and exclude all respondents whose most recent DGU was part of military or law-enforcement work, who did not report a specific crime or use of the gun as part of the incident, or who did not actually see a perpetrator, we estimate 1.5 million defensive gun users. (Because many of the relevant respondents said that they experienced more than one, we estimate a total of 4.7 million defensive gun uses per annum.) Thus, our estimate, based on the NSPOF, is in the same ballpark as that propounded by Kleck and Gertz. . . .

Some Troubling Implications

One check on the credibility of these DGU estimates is made possible by the detailed follow-up questions included in both these surveys. In the NSPOF, respondents were asked whether they fired their guns, and if so, whether they managed to hit the mark. The responses to this item from our 19 "genuine" defensive gun users, multiplied by our sampling weights, imply that approximately 132,000 perpetrators were either wounded or killed at the hands of armed civilians in 1994. That number, it turns out, is just about the same as the total of all people who were shot and killed or received treatment for nonfatal gunshot wounds in an emergency room that year—yet we know that almost all of those are there as a result of criminal assault, suicide attempt, or accident. There is no trace in these official statistics of the wounded assailants.

Respondents are also asked to report the circumstances under which they were provoked into using their gun. From the NSPOF, we estimate that 322,000 used a gun to defend against a would-be rapist. But that is more than the total number of rapes and attempted rapes estimated from the best available source, the National Crime Victimization Survey (NCVS)!

Similar puzzles are found in Kleck and Gertz's findings. Our closer examination of the DGU reports in the NSPOF suggests that almost half of the incidents appear to contain some internal inconsistency, or otherwise do not make sense. We are persuaded that surveys of this sort generate estimates that grossly exaggerate the true number of DGUs. The most likely explanation provides an important insight about the limitations of the survey methods.

Why Surveys Overestimate Defensive Gun Use

Surveys which include questions about DGUs are trying to estimate a rare event, in which even a small false-positive rate will lead to a relatively large overestimate. . . .

Of course, in any survey there is a possibility of false negatives as well as false positives. Kleck and Gertz emphasize this possibility, arguing that because many respondents may worry that their defensive actions were somehow illegal, they will not admit to them during the survey interview. Kleck and Gertz argue that this effect should outweigh any other misreporting effects and lead to, if anything, an underestimate of the annual number of defensive uses.

Yet by any measure, including the Kleck-Gertz estimate, defensive gun use is a relatively rare event. If 0.5 percent of adults experience a DGU each year, in a survey of 1000 adults only about five would logically have the opportunity to provide a false negative. On the other hand, for 995 of the 1000 respondents, the only logically possible misclassification error is a false positive—and there are good reasons why some might falsely claim to have used a gun in self-defense. For one, using a gun defensively against a criminal may be a genuinely heroic act, and is often portrayed as such in movies and occasionally so in the nightly news. . . .

The falsehood may stem from real events, given that survey respondents typically wish to present themselves favorably to interviewers. The falsehood may also stem from confusion on the part of the respondent: memories fade, and they also distort. "Telescoping," for example, is a common problem in survey research, where respondents who are asked to report about events occurring during the previous year will report an event that in fact happened 13 months or more earlier. Actual experience may be revised in the telling, or may even elide with fiction. Given the prevalence of relevant mental disorders, a nationally representative sample would include a number who were delusional, senile, or intoxicated—people unlikely to be reliable reporters in social science surveys.

An additional possible source of false DGU reports is strategic responses by gun owners. With around 3 million National Rifle Association (NRA) members, it would not be surprising to have as much as 1 percent of respondents who are both aware of the ongoing empirical debate on this topic and feel a vested interest in the perpetuation of high DGU estimates.

Is More Better?

About 40 percent of American households currently own a gun, and 14 million people routinely carry one when they go out. Would we be better off if these figures were, say, 80 percent and 28 million carriers? No doubt that would increase the number of DGUs, however defined or measured. But what would be the net benefit?

The difficulty in answering this question arises in part because of the ambiguous nature of many gun uses that are reported as "defensive" by respondents. Among the incidents in the NSPOF that meet the Kleck and Gertz–type criteria for "genuine" defensive gun uses, in almost one third the most serious crime reported by the respondent is a fight or attack. Assigning fault in a violent encounter can be a daunting problem even to a detective who has a chance to interview everyone involved, let alone a survey interviewer who is asking a few questions of just one of the combatants. In a recent telephone survey of 1905 adults, 13 respondents reported a defensive gun use against a criminal attacker. In contrast, 38 respondents indicated that a gun had been displayed against them in a hostile manner during an argument or some other circumstance. We suspect that many of the 38 gun users involved in these hostile brandishings would have claimed self-defense if they had been contacted by telephone.

Moreover, it is difficult in many cases to determine whether the gun use leads to an outcome that is better in some sense than what *would have* happened had a gun not been available. For the DGU reports in the NSPOF, a theft or trespass is the most serious crime reported in one out of every five cases. In such instances, is society necessarily made better off when someone uses a gun rather than dials 911? . . .

Some Concluding Thoughts

The survey is a well-developed measurement tool which performs satisfactorily for a variety of purposes. But something goes wrong in the effort to use surveys to estimate defensive gun uses. False positives are always a problem, and if the event is rare enough, then they may swamp the truth. What is to be done?

One possibility has long been incorporated in the National Crime Victimization Survey (NCVS), conducted for the U.S. Department of Justice by the Census Bureau. In this survey the false-positive problem is minimized by the design of the questionnaire. The only respondents who are asked whether they attempted to defend themselves in a crime are those who indicated that they had been the victim of a crime in which they had direct contact with the perpetrator. Limiting the DGU question to this small group changes the false-positive arithmetic dramatically. The resulting estimate for the annual number of DGUs (1992–1994) is about 108,000, a small fraction of the Kleck-Gertz estimate.

Another approach is suggested by ordinary practice in medical screening: when an initial test comes out positive, a follow-up test is usually applied to distinguish "true" from "false" positives. If knowing the true prevalence is sufficiently important, then it is worthwhile devising systems for distinguishing true from false positives after the initial screen.

Determining the social value of reported gun uses will be at least as difficult as overcoming the false-positive problem. More detailed information about the entire sequence of events, including the respondent's actions prior to using a gun, is necessary. Another interesting exercise would start with a sample of gun uses that are reported to the police, and interview[ing] each of the participants. Comparisons between these responses and the results of the police investigations may provide some sense of the ways in which survey reports are "shaded."

Meanwhile, the myth that there are millions of legitimate DGUs each year influences public opinion and helps fuel the bandwagon to liberalize regulations on gun possession and carrying. With respect to gun regulations, 2.5 million is the wrong answer to the wrong question.

DISCUSSION NOTES

1. Note that Cook, Ludwig, and Hemenway do not take issue with the manner in which Kleck and Gertz carried out their telephone survey, describing the methods as "widely accepted." Instead, the primary point is that telephone surveys are an unreliable way to measure DGUs because even a small false-positive rate will greatly distort the results when trying to measure rare events. Kleck has accused pro-control researchers of shifting their basis for questioning high DGU estimates as the survey evidence mounted. According to Kleck, pro-control scholars uncritically accepted the low NCVS survey estimates prior to 1995. He points out that only after the Kleck-Gertz study and the Cook–Ludwig National Survey of Private Ownership of Firearms (NSPOF), which also yielded

high DGU estimates, did the pro-control researchers alter their position to the view that surveys are a flawed method for estimating DGUs. (Gary Kleck, *Degrading Scientific Standards to Get the Defensive Gun Use Estimate Down*, 11 Journal on Firearms and Public Policy 77, 87 [1999].)

Are telephone surveys a reliable way to estimate DGUs? Note that the total estimates are derived from very small numbers of actual persons reporting DGUs. In the Kleck-Gertz survey, the widely quoted 2.5 million estimate was derived from sixty-six persons (out of roughly five thousand total participants) who reported an "A"-type (most reliable) DGU within the previous year. In the NSPOF, the sample was even smaller: the DGU estimates were derived from a sample of nineteen persons (out of twenty-six hundred total participants) who reported an "A"-type DGU within the previous year.

2. Respondents in the Kleck-Gertz study reported wounding an adversary in 8.3 percent of encounters. Applied to the Kleck-Gertz national estimate of 2.5 million annual DGUs, this comes out to 207,000 criminals allegedly being wounded in defensive gun incidents each year. (See David Hemenway, *Survey Research and Self-Defense Gun Use: An Explanation of Extreme Overestimates*, 87 Journal of Criminal Law and Criminology 1430, 1442 [1997].) Cook and Ludwig's NSPOF also yielded high annual estimates (134,000) of DGU-inflicted gunshot wounds. During the survey years, roughly one hundred thousand nonfatal gunshot wounds were being treated annually in emergency rooms. Almost all of these were classified as victims of assaults, suicide attempts, or accidental shootings—not wounded criminals.

In their original study, Kleck and Gertz stated their belief that the reported 8.3 percent wounding rate is probably too high. However, Kleck also defends the high DGU-linked gunshot-wound estimates derived from his study as plausible, based on the argument that wounded criminals would be reluctant to seek medical treatment. He points out that many gunshot wounds, such as superficial wounds to a limb, are survivable without medical treatment. (See Gary Kleck, *Degrading Scientific Standards to Get the Defensive Gun Use Estimate Down, supra*, at 88–89, 113–114.) Do you think it is plausible that as many as two hundred thousand criminals each year receive gunshot wounds from DGUs for which they do not seek medical treatment?

3. What is your own estimated number of DGUs that occur in the United States annually, now that you've read the expert literature on the subject? As few as the sixty-five thousand to eighty-two thousand estimated by the U.S. government in the NCVS? Fewer? As many as the 2.5 million estimated by Kleck and Gertz? More? Write your own figure on a piece of paper. Examine it. Is your estimation of DGUs based on the material you just read? Your intuition? Common sense? Your prejudgment of the issue?

4. Statistics dominate the firearms policy debate. Should they? Do you think people make up their minds about gun-related issues based on statistics, or do you think people use statistics to bolster their preexisting beliefs? (For a parody of the use of statistics in the gun control debate, see Andrew J. McClurg, *Hold Your Fire*, A.B.A. Journal [Feb. 1999] at 14.) As an interesting classroom test of the persuasiveness of statistical construction and deconstruction, collect everyone's DGU figures from note 3 and write the numbers on the board. Do they appear random or is there a trend in the figures? Do they lean more toward the low-end NCVS figures or the high-end Kleck-Gertz figures? Is there an association between low-end estimates and pro-control students? Between high-end numbers and pro-rights students? If so, what does this say? Did any students change their opinions about gun control based on the reading material?

5. In addition to the utility for actual use in self-defense, firearms have the undoubted utility of giving their owners psychological security. Though intangible, "peace of mind" is an important benefit. Regardless of where you come down on the "number of DGUs" argument, should people have a right to possess firearms for the psychological security guns provide? How much should the psychological insecurity caused by gun ownership to many non-gun owners weigh in the equation?

B. Gun Ownership and Carrying as a Deterrent to Crime

In addition to the personal self-defense benefit of owning or carrying a firearm is a broader societal benefit. Some criminals are deterred from committing crimes by fear that the victim will be armed. In the early 1980s, James D. Wright and Peter H. Rossi surveyed nearly two thousand convicted felons serving time in state prisons regarding their acquisition, carrying, and use of firearms. A portion of the survey addressed felons' attitudes toward committing crimes against armed or potentially armed victims. Before looking at the Wright-Rossi survey results, consider the authors' general observations concerning the efficacy of an armed citizenry as a crime control measure.

ARMED AND CONSIDERED DANGEROUS: A SURVEY OF FELONS AND THEIR FIREARMS
(142–44 [1986])

James D. Wright and Peter H. Rossi

Generally speaking, a criminal poised at the edge of a decision to commit a crime faces a range of possible risks and benefits. The benefits consist of the potential economic or other gains, however conceived, from the contemplated crime; the costs include the possibility of being caught and imprisoned, of being shot at in the course of the crime, either by the police or by the victim, the likelihood of social disapproval, etc. . . . In standard utility theory, one commits the act in question if and only if the expected benefits exceed the expected costs. . . . Whether "the Armed Citizen" functions to deter, prevent, or thwart crime therefore appears to turn on two questions: First, what is the probability that a felon will encounter an armed victim in the course of his criminal affairs? Second, what are the potential costs of these encounters?

The probability of encountering a victim who possesses a firearm is by no means trivial, as it happens. National surveys conducted periodically since 1959 have routinely found that one-half the households in the United States possess at least one firearm. All else equal, then, a burglar would expect to find at least one gun in every second home. This, of course, is not to say that one-half of all households are fully prepared to thwart a crime with a gun: The weapons may be inaccessible, no ammunition may be present, there may be no one home to use the gun, etc.

Still, with one-half of all households possessing at least one gun, the prospect of encountering an armed victim who is at the time prepared to use his or her weapon is clearly greater than zero. We also emphasize again that criminals often prey upon each other: Those who would venture, say, to rob their own drug dealers can expect that the dealers would be armed and have their weapons ready to hand. . . .

The potential costs of encountering an armed victim vary all the way from being forced to abandon the intended crime and running away through being captured and turned over to the criminal justice system to being shot and physically harmed or killed. It is conceivable that would-be victims might be even more likely to fire their weapons than the police would be (when discovering a crime in progress), and if so, then the potential cost of encountering an armed victim may exceed the potential cost of, say, running into the police.

The possibility of greater damage from armed victims is offset by the possibility that victims might not have their guns handy, might not want to use their guns if they had them at hand, or for some other reasons might not want to risk escalating an encounter into a full scale shootout.

Whatever the true probabilities and costs, the prospects of an armed-victim encounter no doubt contribute to the general uncertainty of a life of crime. In the usual run of things, a criminal would seldom know for sure whether the intended victim were armed or what kinds of behaviors to expect even if the victim were armed. All he would know for sure is that there is some possibility the victim is carrying (or possesses) a gun and some possibility that the gun will be used against him. How large these probabilities are is unknown, but they are clearly larger than zero, and in the case of some classes of would-be victims, especially other criminals, store owners, banks, currency exchanges, etc., are likely to be quite high.

There is, in short, good reason to expect that felons would be made nervous by the possibility of running into an armed victim: Since there are so many armed potential victims "out there," the probability of such an encounter is relatively high and the possible consequences, potentially dreadful. On this basis, one may assume that criminals are no more anxious to encounter armed victims than victims are to encounter armed criminals.

DISCUSSION NOTES

1. Assume you are a criminal intent on burglarizing a dwelling. Applying the "utility theory" described by Wright and Rossi, which of the following factors would you consider most important and which factors least important in selecting your target (realizing that some of the factors overlap)?

    1. Fear of apprehension by police;
    2. Fear of getting shot by police;
    3. Fear of incarceration or other potential penalties if caught;
    4. Fear that the dwelling might be occupied;
    5. Fear of apprehension by occupants of the dwelling;
    6. Fear of getting shot by occupants of the dwelling;
    7. Perceived value of property inside the dwelling;
    8. Presence of barking dogs of any size;
    9. Presence of a large, aggressive dog;
    10. Presence of an alarm system;
    11. Presence of an alarm system linked to a security service;
    12. Other factors.

   Do you think that different types of risk might deter or not deter different types of burglars? Why?

2. Wright and Rossi asked their sampling of incarcerated felons a series of agree/disagree questions concerning their attitudes toward confronting armed victims. Below are the questions and the percentage of felons who stated they "strongly agree" or "agree" with the statements (*id.* at 146, table 6):

    1. A criminal is not going to mess around with a victim he knows is armed with a gun. (56 percent)
    2. One reason burglars avoid houses when people are at home is that they fear being shot. (74 percent)
    3. Most criminals are more worried about meeting an armed victim than they are about running into the police. (57 percent)
    4. A smart criminal always tries to find out if his potential victim is armed. (81 percent)
    5. A store-owner who is known to keep a gun on the premises is not going to get robbed very often. (58 percent)

6. Committing crime against an armed victim is an exciting challenge. (24 percent)

Only 24 percent of the Wright-Rossi respondents stated they were worried about being caught by the police. (*Id.* at 144–45.) Do these data results persuade you that an armed citizenry plays a role in deterring crime? Since 100 percent of the survey respondents were incarcerated, yet only 24 percent feared being caught by the police, does this suggest that some felons do not accurately perceive the costs and probabilities of committing crime?

3. Do you think all criminals act as rationally in real life as the responses to the Wright-Rossi survey appear to indicate? Are some criminals more rational than others? Note that 24 percent of the felons surveyed find excitement in committing crimes against armed victims. Is that a rational cost-benefit analysis? Do you think the responding felons were telling the truth or trying to appear tough? Could defensive gun ownership deter some types of crime or criminals, while encouraging others?

4. Given the Wright-Rossi survey, should non–gun owners feel safer in their homes at night knowing that criminals are unaware which households contain firearms and which do not? Would you feel more safe or less safe living in a neighborhood where all the households were known to be gun-free?

Gun Carrying

In 1997, John R. Lott Jr. published *More Guns, Less Crime: Understanding Crime and Gun Control Laws,* a massive nationwide statistical analysis that claims to prove that laws allowing licensed adults to carry concealed handguns reduce violent crime. Specifically, Lott focuses on what are known as nondiscretionary right-to-carry (RTC) laws (also known as "shall-issue" laws). Nondiscretionary RTC laws require state officials to issue a concealed handgun permit to any person who meets the state-prescribed criteria. The criteria generally include passing a background check and a firearms safety course.

The alternative to nondiscretionary RTC laws are discretionary laws, which allow state or local officials to make case-by-case determinations about whether or not to grant concealed weapons permits. (A few states have no provision at all for licensing.) In the discretionary states, local sheriffs or police chiefs have nearly unlimited freedom to issue or not issue permits. Some sheriffs or chiefs issue permits to friends or cronies; some issue very liberally; some set and abide by standard criteria; some issue only when the sheriff or chief believes there is a "compelling need"; and some refuse to issue to anyone.

Vermont and Idaho (outside incorporated cities, where shall-issue permits are needed) do not require any permit. Many states, especially in the west, ban only concealed guns and have no restrictions on open, unconcealed weapon carrying (although unconcealed carrying may still provoke a police response in the form of arrest for disorderly conduct, menacing, or some other offense).

Thirty-three states (counting both Idaho and Vermont) now have nondiscretionary RTC laws, a dramatic increase since 1985, when only eight states had such laws. Twenty-one states have adopted nondiscretionary RTC laws since 1995. Lott's book has received much attention in the gun debate and has provided potent ammunition for those who favor nondiscretionary RTC laws. Reading Lott's book is a good way for a layperson to learn about multivariate statistical analysis, but the book (the most complex and data-intensive study of any criminological topic ever) is far too complex to set forth in detail. Consider some excerpts:

More Guns, Less Crime: Understanding Crime and Gun-Control Laws
(5–6, 10–12, 19–23, 43–47, 51–54 [1st ed. 1998])

John R. Lott Jr.

Criminals are motivated by self-preservation, and handguns can therefore be a deterrent. The potential defensive nature of guns is further evidenced by the different rates of so-called "hot burglaries," where a resident is at home when a criminal strikes. In Canada and Britain, both with tough gun-control laws, almost half of all burglaries are "hot burglaries." In contrast, the United States, with fewer restrictions, has a "hot burglary" rate of only 13 percent. Criminals are not just behaving differently by accident. Convicted American felons reveal in surveys that they are much more worried about armed victims than about running into the police. The fear of potentially armed victims causes American burglars to spend more time than their foreign counterparts "casing" a house to ensure that nobody is home. Felons frequently comment in these interviews that they avoid late-night burglaries because "that's the way to get shot."

To an economist such as myself, the notion of deterrence—which causes criminals to avoid cab drivers, "dope boys," or homes where the residents are in—is not too surprising. We see the same basic relationships in all other areas of life: when the price of apples rises relative to that of oranges, people buy fewer apples and more oranges. To the noneconomist, it may appear cold to make this comparison, but just as grocery shoppers switch to cheaper types of produce, criminals switch to attacking more vulnerable prey. Economists call this, appropriately enough, "the substitution effect."

Deterrence matters not only to those who actively take defensive actions. People who defend themselves may indirectly benefit other citizens. . . . [C]ab drivers and drug dealers who carry guns produce a benefit for cab drivers and drug dealers without guns. In the example involving "hot burglaries," homeowners who defend themselves make burglars generally wary of breaking into homes. These spillover effects are frequently referred to as "third-party effects" or "external benefits." In both cases criminals cannot know in advance who is armed.

The case for allowing concealed handguns—as opposed to openly carried handguns—relies on this argument. . . .

Our primary questions are the following: Will allowing citizens to carry concealed handguns mean that otherwise law-abiding people will harm each other? Will the threat of self-defense by citizens armed with guns primarily deter criminals? Without a doubt, both "bad" and "good" uses of guns occur. The question isn't really whether both occur; it is, rather, Which is more important? In general, do concealed handguns save or cost lives? Even a devoted believer in deterrence cannot answer this question without examining the data, because these two different effects clearly exist, and they work in opposite directions. . . .

Some evidence on whether concealed-handgun laws will lead to increased crimes is readily available. Between October 1, 1987, when Florida's "concealed-carry" law took effect, and the end of 1996, over

380,000 licenses had been issued, and only 72 had been revoked because of crimes committed by license holders (most of which did not involve the permitted gun). . . .

In Virginia, "Not a single Virginia permit-holder has been involved in violent crime." In the first year following the enactment of concealed-carry legislation in Texas, more than 114,000 licenses were issued, and only 17 have so far been revoked by the Department of Public Safety (reasons not specified). After Nevada's first year, "Law enforcement officials throughout the state could not document one case of a fatality that resulted from irresponsible gun use by someone who obtained a permit under the new law." Speaking for the Kentucky Chiefs of Police Association, Lt. Col. Bill Dorsey, Covington assistant police chief, concluded that after the law had been in effect for nine months, "We haven't seen any cases where a [concealed-carry] permit holder has committed an offense with a firearm." In North Carolina, "Permit-holding gun owners have not had a single permit revoked as a result of use of a gun in a crime." Similarly, for South Carolina, "Only one person who has received a pistol permit since 1989 has been indicted on a felony charge, a comparison of permit and circuit court records shows. . . ."

During state legislative hearings on concealed-handgun laws, the most commonly raised concerns involved fears that armed citizens would attack each other in the heat of the moment following car accidents or accidentally shoot a police officer. The evidence shows that such fears are unfounded. . . .

Does gun ownership save or cost lives, and how do the various gun laws affect this outcome?

To answer these questions I use a wide array of data. For instance, I have employed polls that allow us to track how gun ownership has changed over time in different states, as well as the massive FBI yearly crime rate data for all 3,054 U.S. counties from 1977 to 1992. I use additional, more recently available data for 1993 and 1994 later to check my results. Over the last decade, gun ownership has been growing for virtually all demographic groups, though the fastest growing group of gun owners is Republican women, thirty to forty-four years of age, who live in rural areas. National crime rates have been falling at the same time as gun ownership has been rising. Likewise, states experiencing the greatest reductions in crime are also the ones with the fastest growing percentages of gun ownership.

Overall, my conclusion is that criminals as a group tend to behave rationally—when crime becomes more difficult, less crime is committed. Higher arrest and conviction rates dramatically reduce crime. Criminals also move out of jurisdictions in which criminal deterrence increases. Yet criminals respond to more than just the actions taken by the police and the courts. Citizens can take private actions that also deter crime. Allowing citizens to carry concealed handguns reduces violent crimes, and the reductions coincide very closely with the number of concealed-handgun permits issued. Mass shootings in public places are reduced when law-abiding citizens are allowed to carry concealed handguns.

Not all crime categories showed reductions, however. Allowing concealed handguns might cause small increases in larceny and auto theft. When potential victims are able to arm themselves, some criminals turn away from crimes like robbery that require direct attacks and turn instead to such crimes as auto theft, where the probability of direct contact with victims is small.

There were other surprises as well. While the support for the strictest gun-control laws is usually strongest in large cities, the largest drops in violent crime from legalized concealed handguns occurred in the most urban counties with the greatest populations and the highest crime rates. . . . Of all the methods studied so far by economists, the carrying of concealed handguns appears to be the most cost-effective method for reducing crime. Accident and suicide rates were unaltered by the presence of concealed handguns.

Guns also appear to be the great equalizer among the sexes. Murder rates decline when either more women or more men carry concealed handguns, but the effect is especially pronounced for women. One additional woman carrying a concealed handgun reduces the murder rate for women by about 3–4 times more than one additional man carrying a concealed handgun reduces the murder rate for men. This occurs because allowing a woman to defend herself with a concealed handgun produces a much larger change in her ability to defend herself than the change created by providing a man with a handgun. . . .

Despite intense feelings on both sides of the gun debate, I believe everyone is at heart motivated by the same concerns: Will gun control increase or decrease the number of lives lost? Will these laws improve or degrade the quality of life when it comes to violent crime? The common fears we all share with regard to murders, rapes, robberies, and aggravated assaults motivate this discussion.

To study these issues more effectively, academics have turned to statistics on crime. Depending on what one counts as academic research, there are at least two hundred studies on gun control. The existing work falls into two categories, using either "time-series" or "cross-sectional" data. Time-series data deal with one particular area (a city, county, or state) over many years; cross-sectional data look across many different geographic areas within the same year. The vast majority of gun-control studies that examine time-series data present a comparison of the average murder rates before and after the change in laws; those that examine cross-sectional data compare murder rates across places with and without certain laws. Unfortunately, these studies make no attempt to relate fluctuations in crime rates to changing law-enforcement factors like arrest or conviction rates, prison-sentence lengths, or other obvious variables.

Both time-series and cross-sectional analyses have their limitations. Let us first examine the cross-sectional studies. Suppose, as happens to be true, that areas with the highest crime rates are the ones that most frequently adopt the most stringent gun-control laws. Even if restrictions on guns were to lower the crime rates, it might appear otherwise. Suppose crime rates were lowered, but not by enough to reach the level of rates in low-crime areas that did not adopt the laws. In that case, looking across areas would make it appear that stricter gun control produced higher crime. Would this be proof that stricter gun control caused higher crime? Hardly. Ideally, one should examine how the high-crime areas that adopted the controls changed over time—not only relative to their past levels but also relative to areas without the controls. Economists refer to this as an "endogeneity" problem. The adoption of the policy is a reaction (that is "endogenous") to other events, in this case crime. To correctly estimate the impact of a law on crime, one must be able to distinguish and isolate the influence of crime on the adoption of the law.

For time-series data, other problems arise. For example, while the ideal study accounts for other factors that may help explain changing crime rates, a pure time-series study complicates such a task. Many potential causes of crime might fluctuate in any one jurisdiction over time, and it is very difficult to know which one of those changes might be responsible for the shifting crime rate. If two or more events occur at the same time in a particular jurisdiction, examining only that jurisdiction will not help us distinguish which event was responsible for the change in crime. Evidence is usually much stronger if a law changes in many different places at different times, and one can see whether similar crime patterns exist before and after such changes.

The solution to these problems is to combine both time-series and cross-sectional evidence and then allow separate variables, so that each year the national or regional changes in crime rates can be separated out and distinguished from any local deviations. For example, crime may have fallen nationally between 1991 and 1992, but what this study is able to examine is whether there is an additional decline over and above that national drop in states that have adopted concealed-handgun laws. I also use a set of measures that control for the average differences in crime rates across places even after demographic, income, and other factors have been accounted for. No previous gun-control studies have taken this approach. . . .

Keeping in mind all the endogeneity problems discussed earlier, I have provided in [a table that is not reproduced here] a first and very superficial look at the data for the most recent available year (1992) by showing how crime rates varied with the type of concealed-handgun law. According to the data presented in the table, violent-crime rates were highest in states with the most restrictive rules, next highest in the states that allowed local authorities discretion in granting permits, and lowest in states with nondiscretionary rules.

The difference is quite striking; violent crimes are 81 percent higher in states without nondiscretionary laws. For murder, states that ban the concealed carrying of guns have murder rates 127 percent higher than states with the most liberal concealed-carry laws. For property crimes, the difference is much smaller: 24 percent. States with nondiscretionary laws have less crime, but the primary difference appears in terms of violent crimes. . . .

While I am primarily interested in the impact of nondiscretionary laws, the estimates also account for many other variables: the arrest rate for each type of crime; population density and the number of people living in a county; measures of income, unemployment, and poverty; the percentage of the population that is a certain sex and race by ten-year age groupings (10 to 19 years of age, 20 to 29 years of age); and the set of variables described in the previous section to control for other county and year differences. The results clearly imply that nondiscretionary laws coincide with fewer murders, aggravated assaults, and rapes. On the other hand, auto theft and larceny rates rise. Both changes are consistent with my discussion of the direct and substitution effects produced by concealed weapons.

The results are also large, indicating how important the laws can be. When state concealed-handgun laws went into effect in a county, murders fell by about 8 percent, rapes fell by 5 percent, and aggravated assaults fell by 7 percent. In 1992, the following numbers were reported: 18,469 murders; 79,272 rapes; 538,368 robberies; and 861,103 aggravated assaults in counties without nondiscretionary laws. The estimated coefficients suggest that if these counties had been subject to state concealed-handgun laws and had thus been forced to issue handgun permits, murders in the United States would have declined by about 1,400.

Given the concern raised about increased accidental deaths from concealed weapons, it is interesting to note that the entire number of accidental handgun deaths in the United States in 1988 was only 200 (the last year for which these data are available for the entire United States). Of this total, 22 accidental deaths were in states with concealed-handgun laws, while 178 occurred in states without these laws. The reduction in murders is as much as eight times greater than the total number of accidental deaths in concealed-handgun states. . . . [I]f these initial results are accurate, the net effect of allowing concealed handguns is clearly to save lives, even in the implausible case that concealed handguns were somehow responsible for all accidental handgun deaths.

As with murders, the results indicate that the number of rapes in states without nondiscretionary laws would have declined by 4,200, aggravated assaults by 60,000, and robberies by 12,000.

On the other hand, property-crime rates increased after nondiscretionary laws were implemented. If states without concealed-handgun laws had passed such laws, there would have been 247,000 more property crimes in 1992 (a 2.7 percent increase). . . . Criminals respond to the threat of being shot while committing such crimes as robbery by choosing to commit less risky crimes that involve minimal contact with the victim. . . .

DISCUSSION NOTES

1. Do you accept or reject Lott's basic claim that allowing people to carry concealed weapons directly caused an overall 8 percent drop in murder rates, a 7 percent drop in aggravated assaults, and a 5 percent drop in rape?

2. Does the exactitude of Lott's claims support or detract from their credibility? For example, he states: "One additional woman carrying a concealed handgun reduces the murder rate for women by about 3–4 times more than one additional man carrying a concealed handgun reduces the murder rate for men." Do you think statistical analysis can reliably support such specific determinations?

3. Are you surprised by Lott's information regarding the lack of crimes committed by persons holding concealed-weapons permits?

4. The Lott and Wright-Rossi data suggest that non–gun owners enjoy almost all the deterrent benefits from gun ownership (since criminals do not know which homes have a gun or which persons on the street may be carrying a concealed handgun) but bear none of the expenses of gun ownership—such as the costs of buying a gun, licensing fees, training classes, practice time. Economists state that when the benefits of a product are shared by those who do not use the product, so that the purchaser receives only part of the product's total benefits, the product will be undersupplied.

   Consider a recent study of a device called LoJack, designed to prevent auto thefts. LoJack is a radio transponder, hidden in a car. When the car's owner reports that the car is stolen, law enforcement can activate the transponder via a radio signal. The LoJack transponder then begins emitting a radio signal, making it easy for police to locate the stolen car. Like guns in the home, LoJack is unobservable to a criminal considering potential targets. Thus, the deterrent effect of LoJack (like guns in the home) benefits the entire community equally, rather than conferring a benefit mainly on the owner. Two researchers did a study that they contend shows LoJack can be quite effective. They found that a 1 percent increase in LoJack installation in an area correlated with a 20 percent decline in car thefts in big cities and a 5 percent decline statewide. They assert that the total benefits of LoJack were fifteen times greater than the costs, but that only 10 percent of the total social benefits went to LoJack owners; the other 90 percent went to persons who did not install LoJack. As a result, the authors concluded that the LoJack was "dramatically undersupplied." The small insurance subsidies for LoJack installation were not sufficient to correct this problem. (Ian Ayres and Steven Levitt, *Measuring Positive Externalities from Unobservable Victim Precaution: An Empirical Analysis of LoJack,* 113 Quarterly Journal of Economics 43 [1998].) Do you think the LoJack was responsible for the declines in auto theft described in the study? Are guns undersupplied? If so, what could be done about the problem?

So-called free riders are one type of "externality" problem, in which costs and benefits are not fully internalized. A different form of externality is uncontrolled pollution. A factory owner may reap all the economic benefits of the factory, but the factory's air pollution drifts off-site and affects the health of people who derive no economic benefits from the factory. Does gun ownership have similar problems, in which people who do not own guns are forced to bear costs that should properly be allocated to gun owners? (See chapter 6 for more on this argument.)

5. In the second edition of his book, Lott details data that he claims show that mass public shooting incidents fall dramatically after RTC laws are passed. (John R. Lott Jr., *More Guns, Less Crime,* 2d ed. [Chicago: University of Chicago Press, 2000], at 100–103.) He focuses on states that adopted RTC laws between 1977 and 1992, noting that although a slight rise in mass shooting deaths immediately followed the passage of the laws, the mass shooting death rate "quickly falls after that, with the rate

reaching zero five years after the law is enacted." (*Id.* at 102.) As an explanation for why mass shooting deaths increased immediately after passage of RTC laws, he states: "Perhaps those planning such shootings do them sooner than they otherwise would have, before too many citizens acquire concealed-handgun permits." Lott argues that even though mass killers often expect to die at the end of their killing sprees, they can be deterred by the prospect that they might be killed before they get to kill others. He points to a bigot who wounded two adults and three children at a Jewish preschool in Granada Hills, California, in August 1999 and then murdered a Filipino postal worker. Before attacking the unguarded school, the man went to several other Jewish centers, found security guards there, and left.

What percentage of mass murderers do you think make decisions about whether to carry out their crimes based on the fear that they might be thwarted by a concealed-handgun carrier? Among the most notorious mass killers in recent times, several committed suicide during the attack; others were killed by police; and some received the death penalty and were executed. The rest are in prison. Do you think the reason mass shootings declined in the ten states that Lott studied is the ability of persons in those states to carry concealed weapons? Some people respond to Lott's argument by pointing out that mass public murders, while heavily publicized, are rare and should therefore not be a basis for setting public policy. Do you agree?

6. Regarding mass school shootings, Lott advocates that teachers be permitted and encouraged to carry concealed handguns at school to thwart mass shootings in progress. He notes that two school shootings (Edinboro, Pennsylvania, and Pearl, Mississippi) were halted by the intervention of armed adult civilians. He also points to the dramatic and immediate decline in Palestine Liberation Organization (PLO) attacks against schoolchildren that followed adoption of an Israeli policy of arming schoolteachers. (See John R. Lott Jr., *The Real Lesson of the School Shootings*, Wall Street Journal, Mar. 27, 1998, at A14.) Do you think it would be a good policy to arm some schoolteachers? If so, should there be special regulations about teachers possessing arms on school property? What would they say? Who should set the regulations?

"LOTTS" MORE GUNS AND OTHER FALLACIES INFECTING THE GUN CONTROL DEBATE
(11 Journal on Firearms and Public Policy 139 [1999])

Andrew J. McClurg

By any measure, *More Guns, Less Crime* is an important work, but is Lott's conclusion that right-to-carry laws deter and reduce violent crime valid? . . . Dependent as Lott's book is on reams of data and "cross-sectional," "time-series" and "regression" analyses, his statistical methodologies are impenetrable to most readers and, therefore, insulated from critical scrutiny to a large extent. . . .

What do other experts say of Lott's study? In the first published critique of Lott's work, Dan Black and Daniel Nagin reanalyzed the data and concluded it provides no basis for drawing confident conclusions about the impact of right-to-carry laws on violent crime. Among their findings:

> The estimates [of the impact of right-to-carry laws on violent crime] are disparate. Murders decline in Florida but increase in West Virginia. Assaults fall in Maine but increase in Pennsylvania. Nor are the estimates consistent within states. Murders increase, but rapes decrease in West Virginia. Moreover, the magnitudes of the estimates are often implausibly large. The parameter estimates that RTC laws increased murders by 105 percent in West Virginia but reduced aggravated assaults by 67 percent in Maine. While one could ascribe the effects to the RTC laws themselves, we doubt that any model of criminal behavior could account for the variation we observe in the signs and magnitudes of these parameters. [See Dan A. Black and Daniel S. Nagin, *Do Right-to-Carry Laws Deter Violent Crime?* 27 Journal of Legal Studies 209 (1998).]

Black and Nagin concluded that the large variations in state-specific estimates raised the concern that Lott's results could be dictated by a single state for which Lott's model poorly fitted the data. They decided that state was Florida, due to its volatile crime rates influenced by a flourishing drug trade and the Mariel boat lift of 1980 and the fact that Florida passed several gun control restrictions during the relevant period. Reanalyzing the data without Florida, Black and Nagin found:

While the estimated impact of RTC laws on assault is relatively unaffected, without Florida there is no evidence of any impact on homicides and rapes. Thus, for these two crimes—the two crimes that account for 80 percent of the total social benefit of the RTC laws . . . —the evidence of a deterrent effect vanishes with the removal of a single state from the analysis. . . .

"Who is right?" is not the relevant question for purposes of this essay. I note these critiques not to try to prove Lott wrong, but because they confirm my basic belief that it is impossible for any statistical study to reliably isolate one causal factor out of hundreds or thousands or millions and say this factor caused violent crime to decline by this amount. Lott boasts that his study contains "54,000 observations and hundreds of variables available over the 1977 to 1994 period" and that it contains "by far the largest data set that has ever been put together for any study of crime, let alone for the study of gun control." This may be a plus, but the more calculations involved, the more potential there is for bias and error to creep into the analysis. Even Lott makes statements such as:

Many potential causes of crime might fluctuate in any one jurisdiction over time, and it is very difficult to know which one of these changes might be responsible for the shifting crime rate.

While I make use of the arrest-rate information, I include a separate variable for each county to account for the different average crime rates each county faces, which admittedly constitutes a rather imperfect way to control for cross-country differences such as expected penalties.

This aggregation of crime categories makes it difficult to isolate crimes that might be deterred by increased handgun ownership and crimes that might be increasing as a result of a substitution effect.

Although Lott offers detailed solutions to the concerns he raises, the more he turns to alternative analyses and variables to compensate for possible shortcomings, the greater my perception of the study as one gigantic statistical bootstrap undertaking.

Interestingly, in refuting criticisms of his study, Lott's weakest defense is to the simplest complaint: that he is guilty of fallacious post hoc reasoning. He concedes in response that "[a]n obvious danger arises in inferring causality because two events may coincide simply by chance, or some unknown factor may be the cause of both events." He defends against the criticism by noting that "this study uses the most comprehensive set of control variables yet used in a study of crime." "For a critic to attack the paper," he opines, "the correct approach would have been to state what variables were not included in the analysis."

A multitude of causes contribute to either higher or lower violent crime rates. The deterrent effect of carrying concealed weapons is one of these factors. Other gun-related factors include the numbers of guns, gun distribution, gun marketing practices, types of guns, safe storage of guns, gun control laws, post-sale access to guns and firearm education. The list of non gun-related factors influencing the violent crime rate is almost endless: unemployment, poverty, illicit drug use, media violence, racial and ethnic demographics, police resources, mental illness, immaturity, alcohol abuse, arrest and conviction rates, lengths of prison sentences, the "broken window" effect, opportunity, the rise and decline of gangsta rap music, diet, climate, family status, cultural homogeneity, sexual disorders, bad tempers, road rage, private security guards, hopelessness, abuse as a child, despair, desperation, protective canines, crowded living conditions, home security systems, greed, educational levels, machismo, increased awareness of crime, gang membership and more.

Lott's study attempted to account for some of these causes, but not nearly all of them. There is no way it could. The bottom line is that any attempt to isolate the impact of one causal factor in a situation involving an extremely large number of other possible explanations seems doomed to be fallacious.

In discussing statistical cause and effect fallacies on the pro–gun control side, I mentioned the *Tale of Two Cities* study that attributed Vancouver's lower homicide rate in comparison to neighboring Seattle to the fact that Vancouver has stricter gun laws. [See John Henry Sloan et al., *Handgun Regulations, Crime, Assaults, and Homicide: A Tale of Two Cities*, 319 New England Journal of Medicine 1256 (1988).] Recall the blistering critique of that study by pro-gun criminologist Gary Kleck, who said "[t]here are literally thousands of differences across cities that could account for violence rates, and these authors just arbitrarily seized on gun levels and gun control levels as being what caused the difference." If there are "literally thousands of differences" between Vancouver and Seattle that contribute to gun violence rates, there must be literally millions of differences between the 3,054 counties in the United States studied by Lott.

My intuitive belief about the study is that—regardless of how carefully and thoroughly it was conducted—there are simply too many variables contributing to violent crime to isolate concealed weapons laws as a major cause in deterring or reducing it. It simply is not something that is capable of being proved by a statistical study. While Lott's study is obviously far more sophisticated than simple post hoc reasoning, in the end, I believe it amounts to basically a post hoc argument that: States passed nondiscretionary concealed weapons laws; violent crime went down in some categories in some states; therefore, nondiscretionary concealed weapons laws cause violent crime to go down. . . .

DISCUSSION NOTES

1. McClurg attacks the reasoning fallacy known as *post hoc, ergo propter hoc*, which translates to "after this, therefore because of this." *Post hoc* logic involves reasoning that because one event followed another, the latter was caused by the former. For example, one might reason: the rooster crowed; the sun rose; therefore the crowing caused the sun to rise. Or, more pertinent to this book, one might reason that the Brady Act was passed in 1994; afterward, crime, which had been declining, declined further; therefore the Brady Act caused the further decline. Reaching reliable conclusions regarding cause and effect is difficult, and may be impossible where many variables are involved. Numerous variables affect crime rates. Lott attempted to control for many variables in his massive study, including arrest rates, population, and changes in per capita income. Do you think he succeeded in isolating the passage of concealed-handgun laws as a cause of substantial reductions in violent crime?

2. Is it McClurg's view that cause-and-effect relationships in situations involving many variables are just too complex to be measured by statistical analysis? Do you agree? If cause-and-effect studies can ever be done

successfully, does Lott's study succeed because he used more data and more variables than anyone has ever used in such a study?

3. Like much gun policy research, Lott's conclusions are frequently cited on talk shows, in newspaper editorials, and in letters to the editor, usually with little or no explanation or background about the study itself. Is there danger in deciding important, complex issues based on truncated reporting of controversial, complex statistical analyses?

4. Handgun Control, Inc. (HCI) conducted an analysis that, the organization claims, shows violent crime has dropped precipitously in states without nondiscretionary RTC laws:

> From 1992 to 1998 (the last six years for which data exists), the violent crime rate in the strict and no-issue states fell 30% while the violent crime rate for the 11 states that had liberal CCW [concealed carrying of weapons] laws (where law enforcement must issue CCW to almost all applicants) during this entire period dropped only 15%. Nationally, the violent crime rate fell 25%. The decline in the crime rate of strict licensing and no-carry states was twice that of states with lax CCW systems, indicating that there are more effective ways to fight crime than to encourage more people to carry guns. New York and California— the two most populous states and ones with strict CCW licensing laws—experienced dramatic decreases in violent crime over the six-year period. New York experienced a 43% decline and California experienced a 37% decline, both without putting more concealed handguns on the streets. [See Handgun Control, Inc., *Concealed Weapons Laws and Trends in Violent Crime in the United States.*

Critics of this study point out that it does not control for any variables. They also point out that the start and end dates do not fit many of the states studied. In particular, many states changed their RTC laws during the 1992–98 period, but the HCI study does not account for this change. Does the HCI analysis influence your views on Lott's study? Can statistics be manipulated to support any position? Assuming statistics can be manipulated, can honest researchers produce studies that are reliable descriptions of the real world? (For various studies, of varying reliability, produced by the leading lobbies in the gun control debate, visit the Web sites for HCI [www.bradycenter.org] and the NRA [www.nra.org]).

5. Major crime has dropped significantly in recent years, both in states with and without nondiscretionary RTC laws. If Lott's conclusions are valid, concealed-weapons laws play a role in declining crime, but, as Lott concedes, there are many factors at work. Some scholars point to low unemployment and a robust economy, the end of the crack-cocaine epidemic, longer prison sentences, more police officers, and stronger gun control laws as major factors contributing to the decline. What do you think are the major reasons for the crime drop? Do you think that social science can tell us anything about the causes, or should people just rely on their intuition about the causes? As an exercise, make a list of the ten factors you think have had the greatest impact on declining crime, beginning with the most important factor.

C. Recreational Gun Use

Most gun owners purchase their firearms for recreational purposes: hunting, sport shooting, and collecting. Kleck has gathered data that allows us roughly to quantify the recreational uses of firearms (see Gary Kleck, *Targeting Guns: Firearms and Their Control*, at 86):

- In 1991, 14 million Americans hunted, each for an average of 17 days per year, 5 hours per day, for a total of 236 million hunting days.
- In 1992, 16 million persons held hunting licenses.
- In 1975, 10.4 million participants engaged in 149 million days of target shooting, while 5.7 million people engaged in 84 million days of "plinking" (non-formal target shooting of cans and other inanimate objects).
- Based on ammunition production reported by manufacturers to the Sporting Arms and Ammunition Manufacturers Institute, 3.8 billion shots were fired in 1992, almost all of which were associated with recreational gun use.

While misuse of guns in crime, defensive gun use, and (to a lesser extent) hunting receive the lion's share of public attention about guns, the overwhelming number of shots fired in any given year come from target shooters. (A typical hunting trip includes only a few shots fired or often none at all.)

Sport Shooting

Target shooting includes a vast number of competitions, including the Olympics, informal "plinking" at tin cans, and shooting at public or private ranges. The number of target-shooting disciplines is vast. They include: trap and skeet shooting (shooting at flying clay disks with shotguns); sporting clays (a newer discipline in which clay disks travel in more difficult paths—such as bouncing along the ground after being released from a hidden spring behind a bush); shooting at bulls-eye targets, with subcategories of high-powered rifle (calibers larger than .22), small-bore rifle (.22 caliber), high-power pistol (calibers larger than .22), and small-bore pistol (.22 caliber). Some competitions require very specific firearms, such as Glock pistols.

Other target shooters use airguns. Airguns are powered by compressed air or carbon dioxide rather than by a gunpowder explosion. (Thus airguns are "guns" but they are not "firearms." Nevertheless, this book uses "guns" only to refer to firearms, following common usage.) The best-known airguns, such as the Daisy Red Ryder, are inexpensive BB guns that shoot small round copper balls (BBs), but airguns can also fire specially shaped metal pellets. Expensive airguns are extremely accurate at long ranges; advanced shooters can put five shots into a space the size of nickel from two hundred yards away.

The target disciplines all have subcategories based on how the gun is held. For example, bench-rest shooters sit in a chair and rest the gun on a table (enhancing accuracy), while other shooters lie prone on the ground or stand.

The handgun sport of practical shooting (organized by the International Practical Shooting Confederation) has gained great popularity in the last two decades. Instead of firing at a fixed paper target from a fixed position, practical shooters move around a course that is set up to simulate defensive shooting scenarios. The shooter might enter a building (built out of plywood walls) in which the shooter is told that a hostage is being held in one of the rooms. (The hostage taker and the hostage are both life-sized card-board cutouts.) The practical shooter must move through the building without accidentally putting himself in the firing line of one of the bad guys and then must shoot the bad guy targets. Points are awarded for accuracy and speed, with large point deductions for shooting the wrong person.

The biathlon combines cross-country skiing with .22 caliber rifle shooting. At various stages along a 5K or 10K ski course, the skier must stop to shoot at a fixed bulls-eye target. One of this sport's greatest challenges is to control one's heart rate and breathing; both must be rapid for fast skiing but almost instantly reduced to achieve the stillness that is required for precise long-distance shooting.

Most forms of recreational gun use (except biathlon) that use modern guns have analogues in black-powder shooting. "Black powder" refers to the type of gunpowder that was used in the nineteenth century and before, as opposed to modern smokeless powder. Black-powder shooters use muzzle loaders and other old-fashioned firearms for hunting or target shooting. These guns can be exact replicas of older guns or modern "in-line" muzzle loaders that use an improved ignition system. Most states have special hunting periods for muzzle loaders only.

Many people manufacture their own ammunition at home, using special presses and dies. This is called "reloading." Typically, reloaders buy bullets, primers, and gunpowder and load them into recycled brass (rifle and pistol) or plastic (shotgun) shell casings. Some reloaders are frequent target shooters who save money on the thousands of rounds of ammunition they use each year. Others are hunters or other shooters who simply prefer to customize their ammunition, choosing the precise bullet shape and the type and exact quantity of gunpowder that best suit their needs.

Collecting

Gun collectors tend not to collect "guns in general" but to specialize in one or more discrete areas, such as "9 mm pistols from the 1930s" or "double-barreled shotguns" or "nineteenth-century Colt revolvers." Other people collect ammunition. As with any collecting hobby, the most-sought items tend to be rare and historical.

Hunting

The number-one purpose people give as a reason for purchasing guns is hunting. American game include turkeys, quail, deer, snow geese, cougars, elk, sheep, mountain lions, foxes, ducks, bears, raccoons, moose, pheasants, chukars, caribou, doves, squirrels, grouse, and more. Hunters use shotguns for birds, large-caliber rifles for big game, and .22 rifles for small game. Handgun hunting is legal in every state, although it is not nearly as popular as hunting with long guns. Hunting makes a large contribution to the local economy in popular hunting destinations.

In a 1999 survey conducted by the National Sporting Goods Association, hunting with firearms ranked as the seventeenth most popular sporting activity, as measured by the number of people over age seven who engaged in the activity more than one time a year (16.6 million participants, down from 17.7 million in 1989). The top five sporting activities were exercise walking, swimming, camping vacations, exercising with equipment, and fishing. Hunting trailed activities such as bowling, billiards, and dart throwing but ranked ahead of baseball, softball, soccer, and tennis. Hunting is, however, one of the few sports with a long-term negative growth rate.

The topic of hunting can generate emotional opinions, much like the gun control debate. Some people view hunting with guns as cruel and unsporting. They cannot understand how people could get enjoyment from "shooting Bambi." Hunters respond that hunting is no more cruel to animals than harvesting them for hamburgers, belts, shoes, and handbags. Hunters extol their sport hunting as an avenue to adventure, a way to commune with nature, and a bonding experience between parents and children. They also point out that the special taxes they pay subsidize conservation of wilderness areas that benefit all species, and that state fish and game commissions carefully regulate the number of hunting licenses so that hunting does not endanger the survival of any species.

DISCUSSION NOTES

1. Do you think hunting is cruel? Do you think hunters are cruel people? Do you know any hunters? Do you consider hunting to be a fair "sport-

ing" activity given that hunters are armed and the animals are unarmed? Is hunting for food better, worse, or the same as slaughtering domestic animals for food? What are the similarities and what are the differences between the two activities? When you think about hunting, what feelings does it evoke for you? Excitement? Exhilaration? Revulsion? Grief? Something else?

2. Do your feelings about hunting depend on the purpose of the hunting? One veteran hunter identified three categories of hunters: "1) those who hunt exclusively for meat; 2) those who want meat but first hold out for an impressive animal; and 3) the pure trophy hunter" (Jim Zumbo, *Meat Hunting Is Okay! For Many Hunters, Game Meat Is the Best Trophy of All*, Outdoor Life, Nov. 1998, at 30). Zumbo cites a Yale study by Dr. Stephen Kellert which found that 80 percent of Americans approve of hunting for meat, while 60 percent do not approve of hunting for recreation or sport. For some hunters, particularly the rural poor, the success of a fall hunting trip makes a big difference in how much meat the family eats during the winter. Some states have laws designed to prohibit trophy hunters (those seeking antlers or pelts) from wasting the edible meat of their prey. For example, a Montana law makes it a crime for a hunter to abandon any portion of a game animal, bird, or fish that is suitable for food. (See *Mont. Code Ann.* § 87-3-102.) Each year, hunters kill 50 million doves, 25 million rabbits and squirrels, 25 million quail, 20 million pheasants, 10 million ducks, 2 million geese, and 4 million deer. If you were a legislator, would you support or oppose a bill to outlaw hunting in your state? All hunting? Trophy hunting? Meat hunting? Hunting of specific types of animals?

3. For hunting opponents: Do you eat meat? Wear leather goods? Use other products made from animal by-products? Is it inconsistent to eat meat and wear leather goods while opposing hunting, or are you able to articulate reasons harmonizing these activities and beliefs? Do you oppose fishing as well as hunting? If not, why not?

4. Do your views on hunting depend on the type of animal involved? Do you think, for example, it is acceptable to shoot ducks but not deer? Why? Do your views depend on the method of hunting? Does it make a difference to you whether the hunter is using a firearm or bow and arrow? Ethical hunters are trained to take only shots calculated to produce a

quick kill (as opposed to a shot at a leg). A bow and arrow, though, is harder to shoot precisely than is a firearm and is therefore much less likely than a firearm to produce a quick kill. The result may be that the animal escapes, only to die later of lingering wounds.

5. Hunting is a recreational activity engaged in mostly by white males, although many women have taken up hunting in recent years. While blacks comprise 12 percent of the population, they comprise only 2 percent of hunters. Why do think this is so? (See Carolee Boyles-Sprenkel, *Minorities: How Do You Reach This Untapped Market?* Shooting Industry, Jan. 1997, at 32.) See chapter 5 for data regarding lower black gun ownership rates in general.

6. Mary Zeiss Stange, who teaches at Skidmore College, has orthodox feminist positions on most issues, but is a strong advocate of women engaging in hunting. Can a woman be a feminist and a hunter? Is hunting (and all use of animals for human purposes) part of a larger scheme of patriarchal oppression of the less powerful, as some feminists suggest? Are females who hunt helping to deconstruct traditional gender stereotypes and empowering themselves? Should feminism have only one answer to the issue of female hunters? For more on gun ownership by women, see chapter 5.

7. Make a list of five personality traits you most strongly associate with hunters. Are they positive traits? Negative? A combination of both? Are these traits based on your personal knowledge of hunters or on conjecture? How do you think people who do not personally know or associate with law students might describe the personality traits of such students? Of undergraduate students? Would they be right?

8. Do you object to target shooting as a recreational activity? If so, why? Is it qualitatively different as a hobby from, say, golf or tennis? If so, how? Does it make a difference to you whether the participants are shooting at clay disks, bulls-eye targets, or silhouettes of human beings? If so, why?

9. Do you object to gun collecting as a hobby? If so, why? Is it qualitatively different from collecting stamps, model trains, or other collectible items?

10. Do the activities of target shooting and gun collecting, even if benign, create collateral risks, such as the risk that guns will be stolen and mis-

used by criminals? Do these risks outweigh the benefits of the activities? Should people who engage in these activities be legally required to take steps to reduce such risks?

Many gun laws have different impacts on various types of gun owners. For example, a law that all guns must be stored in one safe and the ammunition stored in a separate safe might have a large impact on people who want to use guns defensively in the home, a minimal impact on wealthy trophy hunters who use their guns only a few times a year, and a medium impact on rural people who hunt for food (since the cost of a safe might be very large in relation to the family's income). Which, if any, types of gun ownership (defensive, collecting, various kinds of target shooting, various kinds of hunting) should lawmakers be especially careful about not harming?

11. Do you have a hobby or activity from which you get tremendous enjoyment that other people might not understand or appreciate because they do not engage in that hobby or activity? For example, are you a "fanatical football fan"? Would you want people or the government telling you that you should give up that activity because watching football is a waste of time and brainpower? Are you an avid skier? Would you want people or the government telling you not to ski because of the high risk of knee or other injuries? Are these apt analogies to hunting, target shooting, or gun collecting or inapt because football and skiing don't present risks of physical harm to non–participants?

CHAPTER 2

THE COSTS OF FIREARMS

Having considered the benefits of firearms in chapter 1, it is now time to look at the costs of firearms. This chapter examines the following costs of guns to U.S. society: homicides and other crime, suicides, accidental shootings, financial costs, and fear.

The direct costs of firearms to society are fairly easy to identify and quantify. Firearms are the second leading cause of nonnatural death in the United States, surpassed only by automobiles. In 1997, 32,436 firearm fatalities occurred, including homicides (criminal and lawful), suicides, and accidental shootings. This total is a substantial decline from the record 39,595 deaths in 1993. Hospital emergency departments treated an estimated 64,000 nonfatal firearm injuries in 1997 (down from 104,000 in 1993).

In addition to these direct human costs, firearms carry other, less obvious costs. These include substantial financial costs for the medical treatment of gunshot victims, police and emergency services, funerals, lost wages and productivity of victims and the family members who care for them, and pain and suffering. Finally, there is the intangible cost of fear and psychological insecurity from gun-related crime.

It should be noted that firearms deaths and injuries have declined significantly in recent years, part of an overall drop in crime nationwide. Serious crimes in the United States dropped for a record eighth consecutive year in 1999. In New York City, murders declined to rates not seen since the 1960s: in 1990 there were 2,290 homicides in New York City, compared to 630 in 1998. This chapter concentrates on the most recent available statistics in assessing the costs of guns. If the chapter had been written ten years earlier, the costs would be much higher. Thus, in thinking about the costs of firearms, remember that these costs are variable depending on fluctuations in the crime rate; benefits, of course, are variable too, since increased crime may necessitate more frequent armed defense, or decreased crime may be partly a result of armed deterrence.

A. Homicides and Other Intentional Shootings

Homicides and intentional criminal shootings receive most of the attention when people consider the costs of guns to society, in part because intentional gun violence generates so much media attention. What is the connection between firearms and homicide? The statistics below set forth some of the key facts; Discussion Notes on these are followed by an excerpt addressing the firearms-violence connection.

Homicides by Weapon Type, 1999: handgun—7,950; other gun—2,168; knife —2,049; blunt object—903; other weapon—2,460. (Source: Bureau of Justice Statistics, *Weapons Used in Homicide Trends in the U.S.* [2001].) The numbers include lawful homicides.

U.S. Stock of Guns, 1998: 254,199,406 total guns, including 92,767,049 handguns. (Source: Gary Kleck, communication with editors.)

TABLE 3 Historrical Rates of Gun Ownership, Crime, and Gun Crime

Year	Guns per 100,000 pop.	Handguns per 100,000 pop.	Homicides per 100,000 pop.	Gun homicides per 100,000 pop.	Handgun homicides per 100,000 pop.	Robberies per 100,000 pop.	Gun robberies per 100,000 pop.
1946	34,430	9,120	6	3.5			
1947	35,080	9,130	5.7	3.4			
1948	36,260	9,270	5.6	3.3			
1949	37,110	9,290	5.1	2.8			
1950	38,130	9,350	5	2.7			
1951	38,960	9,410	4.7	2.5			
1952	39,610	9,560	4.9	2.7			
1953	40,230	9,670	4.6	2.5			
1954	40,500	9,730	4.6	2.5			
1955	40,820	9,800	4.3	2.3			
1956	41,310	9,950	4.4	2.4			
1957	41,720	10,080	4.3	2.3			
1958	42,010	10,210	4.3	2.4			
1959	42,530	10,390	4.5	2.5			
1960	43,060	10,540	4.5	2.6			

(continued)

TABLE 3 *(continued)*

Year	Guns per 100,000 pop.	Handguns per 100,000 pop.	Homicides per 100,000 pop.	Gun homicides per 100,000 pop.	Handgun homicides per 100,000 pop.	Robberies per 100,000 pop.	Gun robberies per 100,000 pop.
1961	43,460	10,660	4.5	2.6			
1962	43,930	10,830	4.7	2.7			
1963	44,880	11,030	4.7	2.7			
1964	45,180	11,260	5	2.9			
1965	46,240	11,650	5.4	3.2			
1966	47,550	12,150	5.8	3.5	2.5	80.8	
1967	49,170	12,880	6.6	4.2	3.2	102.8	
1968	51,310	13,970	7.2	4.7	3.6	131.8	
1969	53,200	14,680	7.5	5.1	3.8	148.4	
1970	54,870	15,320	8.1	5.5	4.2	172.1	
1971	56,730	16,010	8.9	6	4.5	188	
1972	58,770	16,870	9.2	6.4	5	180.7	
1973	61,030	17,590	9.5	6.5	5	183.1	
1974	62,700	18,490	9.9	6.9	5.3	209.3	93.6
1975	65,710	19,280	9.7	6.6	5	218.2	97.8
1976	67,850	20,080	8.9	5.9	4.4	195.8	83.6
1977	69,670	20,810	9	5.9	4.3	187.1	77.8
1978	71,560	21,530	9.1	6	4.5	194.3	78.1
1979	72,090	21,920	9.9	6.5	4.9	212.1	84.2
1980	73,790	22,750	10.5	6.8	5.2	243.5	98.1
1981	75,510	23,720	10.2	6.6	5	258.7	103.7
1982	76,930	24,560	9.5	6	4.5	238.9	95.3
1983	77,960	25,160	8.5	5.1	4	216.5	79.5
1984	79,160	25,750	8.3	5	3.9	205.4	73.5
1985	80,130	26,240	8.2	5	3.9	208.5	73.6
1986	80,860	26,630	8.9	5.4	4.3	225.1	77.2
1987	81,940	27,160	8.6	5.2	4.2	212.7	70.2
1988	83,150	27,830	8.9	5.6	4.5	220.9	73.8
1989	84,470	28,520	9.1	5.9	4.7	233	77.4
1990	85,330	29,070	9.9	6.5	5.4	257	94.1
1991	85,940	29,520	10.4	7	6	272.7	108.8
1992	87,070	30,290	9.9	6.9	5.9	263.6	106.2
1993	88,700	31,390	9.9	7.1	6.1	255.8	108.5
1994	90,500	32,520	9.5	6.7	5.9	237.7	98.9
1995	91,630	33,100	8.6	6	5.2	220.9	90.6
1996	92,500	33,600	7.4	5	4	202.4	82.4
1997	93,200	34,000	6.8	4.6	3.6	186.1	73.9
1998	94,000	34,300	6.3	4.1	3.3	165.4	63.2
1999	95,000	35,000	5.7	3.7	2.9	150.2	59.9

Sources: Gary Kleck, *Targeting Guns: Firearms and Their Control* (Hawthorne, NY: Aldine de Gruyter, 1997) tables 1.2, 3.1, 7.3; Federal Bureau of Investigation, *Uniform Crime Report*; personal communication with Gary Kleck, Jan. 2001 (gun ownership rates 1996–98); editors' calculations. Homicide figures include lawful defensive killings (as classified by FBI crime statistics); excluding lawful homicides reduces the total homicide rate by about 0.5 in a typical year. For an argument that the FBI data substantially undercount lawful homicides (and therefore overstate the number of unlawful homicides), see Gary Kleck, *Point Blank* 112–13 (1991).

DISCUSSION NOTES

1. Study the table above. What patterns or trends can you discern from the crime and gun-density data? What kinds of relationships do you find between gun ownership (or handgun ownership) and homicide or robbery? How do gun homicide, handgun homicide, or gun robbery relate to gun ownership and other data? What do you think explains these relationships?

2. Are you surprised by how much gun ownership has increased since 1946? What are some reasons that might explain the increase? When was the rate of increase the fastest? What might explain these especially rapid increases? How has the proportion of handguns as a percentage of the total gun stock changed over the last five decades? What might explain this trend?

FIREARMS AND VIOLENCE: INTERPRETING THE CONNECTION
(65 Popular Government 3 [2000])

Stevens H. Clarke

The annual homicide rate in the United States reached its highest point ever in the twentieth century—10.7 homicides per 100,000 residents in 1980. The rate declined afterward, to 8.4 in 1984, but subsequently increased again, to 10.5 in 1991. Since then it has declined, reaching 7.8 in 1996, the latest year for which mortality data are available from the U.S. Centers for Disease Control and Prevention. . . .

Despite the recent drop, the United States has a much higher level of homicide than comparable nations. A comparison of homicide rates during the 1990s in the twenty-six nations that the World Bank considers highly industrialized reveals that the United States has the highest rate. In fact, the U.S. rate is more than twice that of every other highly industrialized nation except Northern Ireland (treated in these statistics as a separate country), whose rate of 6.1 is a close second.

A comparison of rates of homicide committed with firearms reveals an even more striking difference: the U.S. rate of 5.29 in 1996 was more than

five times that of every other highly industrialized country except Northern Ireland with 5.24 and Italy with 1.66.

The United States also leads the highly industrialized nations in fatal
violence involving children and youth. On the basis of annual rates measured during 1990–95, the United States had 2.57 homicides per 100,000
children under age fifteen, compared with 0.51 for the twenty-five other
highly industrialized countries combined (that is, for the total population of the twenty-five countries). For homicide with firearms, the U.S.
rate was 0.94, compared with 0.06 for the other twenty-five countries, a
ratio of nearly 16 to 1. Suicides and accidental deaths by firearm also were
much higher for the United States. Among teenagers and young adults
as well as among young children, in the late 1980s the United States had
a rate of 8.6 homicides per 100,000 people aged five to twenty-four, more
than six times that of Canada (1.3), which had the second-highest rate
among the G-7 countries (the Group of Seven Industrial Nations).

Homicides with firearms account for most of the difference in homicide rates between the United States and other nations. For this reason,
people seeking to explain the high level of fatal violence in the United
States tend to look first at firearms as a possible cause. . . .

Defensive Gun Use versus Criminal Gun Use

Some studies that address the crime-inducing effect of guns measure how
often guns are used to kill in self-protection, compared with how often
they are used in criminal homicides, suicides, and accidental deaths. For
example, looking at all 743 gunshot deaths in King County, Washington,
from 1978 and from 1983, physicians Arthur Kellermann and Donald
Reay found that 398 (54 percent) had occurred in the home where the
firearm was kept. Only 11 of the gun killings in the home were justifiable
in that they involved either the killing of a felon during the commission
of a crime or legitimate self-defense as determined by police. For every
instance in which a gun in the home was used in justifiable killing, the
authors reported 4.6 criminal homicides, 37.0 firearm suicides, and 1.3
unintentional deaths. The inference from such studies is that guns in the
home are far more likely to be used in illegal or undesirable killings than
in legitimate ones. [See Arthur L. Kellermann and Donald T. Reay, *Pro-*

tection or Peril? An Analysis of Firearm-Related Deaths in the Home, 314
New England Journal of Medicine 1557 (1986).]

[Gary] Kleck contemptuously rejects the Kellermann-Reay study and
others like it, contending that they enormously undercount uses of guns
to defend people against crime. Very few defensive gun uses involve
killing a criminal, Kleck asserts. To assess the true defensive benefits of
guns in the home, one must count not only defensive killings but also instances in which people or property are protected without killing—for
example, the number of burglars captured, frightened off, deterred from
attempting burglaries, or displaced to unoccupied premises [by deterrence through the fear of armed householders] where they could not injure any victims.

Kleck makes a good point that nonfatal defensive uses should be
counted. On the other hand, one must consider as well the nonfatal undesirable or criminal uses of guns, which also are not counted in the studies of deaths by gunshot. For example, a gun could be used unjustifiably
to threaten or to shoot other members of a household, with no one dying
as a result. Undesirable nonfatal use, like defensive nonfatal use, probably is more common than fatal use.

Other studies have examined nonfatal as well as fatal uses of firearms.
These studies help answer some of Kleck's criticisms and also raise
doubts about his position on the relative frequency of justifiable defensive use compared with criminal use. For example, a study by Arthur
Kellermann and others of fatal and nonfatal gunshot injuries in three
cities in the United States suggests that defensive use is almost insignificant. Fewer than one percent of the injurious shootings in the three cities
were justifiably defensive actions by private citizens. More than three-
quarters involved criminal assault or homicide, and most of the rest were
accidental injuries, suicides, or attempted suicides. [See Arthur L.
Kellermann et al., *Injuries due to Firearms in Three Cities,* 335 New England Journal of Medicine 1438 (1996).]

Kleck does not dispute that when fatal use of guns in the home is involved, undesirable or illegal killings far outnumber desirable or justifiable killings. Even if in some instances private citizens use firearms to
prevent crime, the much larger number of criminal shootings may be a
high price to pay for the crime prevention.

The Contribution of High Gun Availability to Homicide

"Guns don't kill people—people kill people" was once a popular bumper-sticker statement. [Franklin] Zimring and [Gordon] Hawkins analyze its meaning. The statement is true in the sense that guns are harmless without people firing them—and most people who own guns do not attack other people with them. The statement is true in another sense: people can and do kill one another without guns (according to FBI data, 32 percent of homicides in 1996 were committed without firearms). However, the statement also suggests a more doubtful proposition: that the same number of people would be killed regardless of guns. Zimring and Hawkins reject this proposition:

> The most accurate label for the role of firearms in those cases of death and injury from intentional attacks in which they are used is *contributing cause*. Even where the availability of a gun plays no important role in the decision to commit an assault, the use of a gun can be an important contributing cause in the death and injury that results [from] gun attacks. When guns are used in a high proportion of such attacks, the death rate from violent attack will be high. Current evidence suggests that a combination of the ready availability of guns and the willingness to use maximum force in interpersonal conflict is the most important single contribution to the high U.S. death rate from violence. Our rate of assault is not exceptional; our death rate from assault is exceptional. [Franklin Zimring and Gordon Hawkins, *Crime Is Not the Problem: Lethal Violence in America*, 122–23 (New York: Oxford University Press, 1997)]

Our death rate from assault—that is, the homicide rate in the United States—is far greater than the homicide rates of other highly industrialized countries, as explained earlier. For robbery and assault, the most common serious nonfatal violent crimes, international comparison tells a different story: U.S. rates, though on the high side, do not greatly differ from those of comparable nations. Zimring and Hawkins discuss crime victimization surveys carried out by United Nations–sponsored researchers in twenty nations in the late 1980s and early 1990s, using an identical telephone survey instrument in each country. According to

these surveys, five countries had robbery rates per 100 residents aged sixteen or older within 30 percent of the U.S. rates, and seven had assault
rates within 30 percent of the U.S. rate. This comparison is quite different from the homicide rate comparison, in which the United States far
exceeds the other countries.

These data suggest that, although Americans do not commit more
robberies and assaults than the residents of comparable countries do,
they commit far more murders. If Americans decide to commit a robbery
or an assault, so Zimring and Hawkins's thinking goes, the greater availability of guns in this country means that the crime is more likely to result in the victim's death. The perpetrator may not necessarily intend to
kill the victim, but the instrumentality of the firearm makes killing much
more likely. "People kill people" is a true statement, but armed attackers
are more likely than unarmed attackers to kill their victims.

Kleck has different views on this issue, expressed in his latest book,
Targeting Guns. He concedes that the United States has high levels of
both violence and gun ownership. Nevertheless, he says, high levels of
gun ownership are not necessarily the cause of high levels of violence; the
same amount of violence might occur without the guns. Kleck rejects
analysis based on international comparisons because, he says, it all rests
on just one special case, the United States, with uniquely high rates of
both homicide and gun ownership. Also, Kleck says, there may be a
causal connection between gun ownership and violence, but the causation may work the other way: a high level of violence may cause people
to acquire guns.

The reasoning in *Targeting Guns* can be summarized as follows: According to NCVS [National Crime Victimization Survey] data, about
half of assaults are threats without any physical attack. When physical attacks occur, about half result in injury. Only 1.4 percent of these injuries
result in death. What is the possible contribution of gun possession at
each of the points in this "hierarchy of violence"? With regard to initiat-
ing assaults, research is inconclusive on whether gun possession encourages this behavior—for example, whether having a gun makes attacking
a stronger adversary easier or stimulates people to behave more aggressively than they otherwise would. With regard to causing injury, NCVS
data show that attacks with guns resulted in wounding the victim only 18

percent of the time while attacks with knives resulted in injuries 45 percent of the time. Kleck implies that if assailants de-escalated from guns to knives, injuries would not lessen. However, Kleck offers no evidence that if guns were harder to get, people would use knives rather than other less dangerous weapons or no weapons. With regard to causing death, research by Zimring and others suggests that firearms use makes some assault injuries fatal that otherwise would not be fatal. Killers frequently do not intend to kill, or are just "average Joes" (not hardened felons) who lose their temper and happen to have a gun handy. But Kleck rejects these studies, asserting that the average killer has a long criminal history, even the perpetrator of a "crime of passion" in a domestic dispute. Thus one cannot assume that a killer did not intend to kill or would not have killed if he or she had not had a gun.

Kleck cites research by himself and Gary Patterson on the association between gun ownership levels and violent crime rates in 170 cities in the United States. He and Patterson concluded that, although the level of gun ownership had no effect on the total rate of violent crime, the rates of homicide, gun assault, and rape all tended to increase the level of gun ownership.

Kleck concludes as follows:

> When aggressors possess guns, this has many effects on the outcome of violent incidents, some tending to make harmful outcomes more likely, some making them less likely. . . . On the other hand, aggressor possession of guns has the overall effect of reducing the likelihood of attack, probably because it often makes attack unnecessary, and of reducing the probability of an injury being inflicted, while [defensive] gun use by victims reduces the likelihood of injury or crime completion. . . . *Consequently, the hypothesis that general gun availability causes increases in rates of homicide and other violent crimes is not supported. The policy implication is that nothing appears to be gained from reducing the general gun ownership level.* [Gary Kleck, *Targeting Guns: Firearms and Their Control*, 258 (Hawthorne, NY: Aldine de Gruyter, 1997) (emphasis added by Clarke)]

Kleck's analyses and conclusions differ in a number of respects from those of other distinguished criminologists who have studied this issue.

Perhaps the most important difference is in the degree to which they consider the crime-preventing effects of gun possession to outweigh the crime-causing effects. Other criminologists concede that having firearms prevents or disrupts some crime, but they think that such prevention is far too little to outweigh the role that guns play as a contributing cause of violent crime. Their position is based on (1) their conclusion . . . that Kleck enormously overestimates the frequency of justifiable defensive gun use and (2) the lack of solid evidence that defensive gun ownership deters crime. . . .

Involvement of Children and Youth with Firearms

As explained at the beginning of this article, the United States leads the industrialized world in homicides of children and youth, especially homicides committed with firearms. Many homicides of young people are committed by young people. For example, in North Carolina in 1992, of murders of white males aged fifteen to twenty-four, according to police data, 27 percent of the suspected killers were in the same age range, and another 39 percent were twenty-five to thirty-four years of age. Of murders of black males aged fifteen to twenty-four, 67 percent of the suspected killers were in the same age group. Most of these murders were committed with firearms, primarily handguns.

Young people sometimes kill older people as well. The [North Carolina] State Bureau of Investigation reports that in 1997, of murders of victims of all ages in which police believed they knew the age of the killer (these constituted 77 percent of all murders), youth aged fifteen to nineteen were responsible for 24 percent, and those aged eleven to fourteen were responsible for just under 1 percent. Again, many of these murders were committed with firearms. . . .

Other studies have found that gun-owning youth are disproportionately represented among those in serious trouble with the law. For example, Joseph Sheley and James Wright surveyed 835 male inmates in juvenile correctional facilities in California, Illinois, Louisiana, and New Jersey in 1991, as well as 758 male students in ten inner-city public high schools near these correctional institutions. Twenty-two percent of the students said that they owned some kind of firearm at the time of the survey; in contrast, 83 percent of the inmates said that they had owned one just before confinement. Ninety percent of the inmates had friends or associates who owned and carried guns routinely. Sheley and Wright comment as follows:

> Thus, in the street environment inhabited by these juvenile offenders, owning and carrying guns were virtually universal behaviors. Further, in this same environment, the inmate respondents regularly experienced threats of violence and violence itself. A total of 84 percent reported that they had been threatened with a gun or shot at during their lives. . . . [Joseph F. Sheley & James D. Wright, *Gun Acquisition and Possession in Selected Juvenile Samples*, 4 (Office of Juvenile Justice and Delinquency Prevention, U.S. Department of Justice, 1993)]

DISCUSSION NOTES

1. Do you think a causal connection exists between firearms availability and homicide rates? Between firearms and other violent crimes? What inferences can you draw from the data in Clarke's article? The Centers for Disease Control (CDC) reported 13,522 firearm homicides in 1997, as compared with 14,327 in 1996, 15,835 in 1995, and 17,866 in 1994. Nonfatal firearm injuries reached a high of 104,200 in 1993 but declined to 64,200 in 1997. Sixty-two percent of these injuries resulted from criminal assaults. Following the overall decline in violent crime, nonfatal firearm injuries from crime declined 39 percent during the 1993–97 period, from 64,100 in 1993 to 39,400 in 1997. (Marianne W. Zawitz and Kevin J. Strom, Bureau of Justice Statistics, U.S. Department of Justice, *Firearm Injury and Death from Crime, 1993–97*, NCJ-182993, at 2 (2000), at http://www.ojp.usdoj.gov/bjs/abstract/fidc9397.htm.)

2. Gun control proponents frequently draw comparisons between homicide rates in the United States and in countries such as England, Canada, and Japan, which impose very tight restrictions on guns. Are these valid comparisons? The homicide rate differential is dramatic, but is it attributable to guns or to broader cultural differences? Gun rights supporters point to countries such as Israel and Switzerland, which, like

the United States, have high gun-density rates but which have relatively low homicide rates.

For more on other countries, see David B. Kopel, *The Samurai, the Mountie, and the Cowboy: Should America Adopt the Gun Controls of Other Democracies?* (Amherst, NY: Prometheus Books, 1992)(comparative study of gun policy in Japan, England, Canada, Australia, New Zealand, Jamaica, Switzerland, and the United States); David B. Kopel and Linda Gorman, *Self Defense: The Equalizer*, 15 Forum for Applied Research and Public Policy 92 (no. 4, Winter 2000); Joseph E. Olson and David B. Kopel, *All the Way Down the Slippery Slope: Gun Prohibition in England and Some Lessons for Civil Liberties in America*, 22 Hamline Law Review 399 (1999); David B. Kopel, *Gun Control in Great Britain: Saving Lives or Constricting Liberty?* (Chicago: University of Illinois at Chicago, Office of International Criminal Justice 1992); David B. Kopel, *Japanese Gun Control*, 2 Asia Pacific Law Review 26 (1993); David B. Kopel, *Canadian Gun Control: Should America Look North for a Solution to Its Firearms Problem?* 5 Temple International and Comparative Law Journal 1 (1991).

3. There are important technical difficulties in comparing international crime rates. For example, American homicide rates are based on arrests, while British rates are based on convictions. Thus, in the United States, if a person is arrested for a shooting but the prosecutor decides not to prosecute because she determines the shooting was lawful self-defense, the shooting is still recorded as an unjustifiable homicide in FBI statistics. In Great Britain, if a jury acquits a person of homicide—for example, because the jury believes it is a case of mistaken identity—the acquittal will remove the homicide from British statistics. Nor are "political" killings counted in the homicide rate, meaning that deaths from "the troubles" in Northern Ireland are not reflected in statistics. Also, U.S. homicide rates, but not British ones, include lawful homicides by police (of which there are hundreds per year in the United States and many fewer in Britain). Finally, an American homicide arrest for which the accused is acquitted on grounds of self-defense still counts as an unjustifiable homicide in the (arrest-based) American data but would not appear in the British statistics. (Kleck argues that there are fifteen hundred to

three thousand such homicides annually in the United States. See Gary Kleck, *Point Blank* 112–13 [1991].) How large of a role do you think differences in crime reporting procedures between the United States and Britain play in explaining the vast disparity in firearm homicide rates between the two countries? In 1996, there were 9,390 handgun homicides in the United States and thirty in Britain. California alone had 1,866 handgun homicides in 1996, more than 62 times as many as Britain. (*Pulling the Trigger*, Washington Post, Apr. 4, 1998, at A18) Here are some other international handgun homicide figures for 1996: Australia, 13; Canada, 106; Germany, 213; Japan, 15; Sweden, 36. (*Id.*)

What do you think explains the large disparities in firearm homicides between the United States and other countries? Different crime reporting procedures? Easier access to guns? A culture of violence fueled by media portrayals of violence? The violent nature of Americans? Make a list of the top five factors that you think contribute to higher firearm homicide rates in the United States as compared to the other countries listed above.

4. To get a sense of the challenges posed by comparative criminology, go the Web site for the FBI's Uniform Crime Reports and other criminal data (http://www.fbi.gov/ucr/ucr.htm). Then go to the Web site of the British Home Office (http://www.homeoffice.gov.uk), whose responsibilities include compiling criminal statistics. Contrast the enormously detailed data about violent crime that the FBI provides with the much vaguer figures from the equivalent British documents. For example, the FBI documents provide official U.S. homicide rates and rape rates. The British documents do not; instead, homicide and rape are combined with various other crimes for an overall "violent crime" rate. Now contrast the American and British crime reporting styles with the Japanese government's annual "White Paper on Crime" (http://www.moj.go.jp/ENGLISH/).

What do you think accounts for the different crime reporting policies of the American, British, and Japanese governments? Why does Japan publish an English version of its crime report, but the British and American governments publish only in their native languages? What do the different reports suggest about what is considered important about crime in each culture?

5. Firearms were used in 69 percent of all murders occurring in the United States from 1993 to 1997 (Zawitz and Strom, *supra*). What is the answer to the "chicken-and-egg" dispute discussed by Clarke? Does gun ownership cause violence, or does violence cause gun ownership? Both? Do you think that higher gun prevalence increases the risk of violent crime, reduces the risk, has no effect, or has different effects depending on the circumstances?

6. If firearms were not readily available, do you think fewer homicides would occur, or would people simply resort to other weapons such as knives and blunt instruments? Do you think that if guns did not exist, many criminals who use guns would switch to knives? Note Clarke's data that, while the U.S. assault rate is proportionate to the assault rate of some other industrialized nations, our death rate from assault is much higher. In 1998, 10,976 homicides by firearm occurred in the United States, compared to 2,252 by knife, 892 by blunt object, and 2,791 by other weapons (Bureau of Justice Statistics, U.S. Department of Justice, at http://www.ojp.usdoj.gov/bjs/homicide/weapons.txt).

7. Can you think of reasons why some murders occur only because of the ready availability of a firearm? Do firearms lend themselves to crimes of anger or passion more than other weapons? Have you ever felt "mad enough to kill someone"? Did you then try to kill the person? Is it easier to kill someone with a gun than with a knife or blunt object? More convenient? Quicker? Cleaner? Safer? A large portion of firearm homicides result from altercations—fights in bars, disputes between drug dealers, and the like. In 1998, 5,822 homicides resulted from arguments, with 62 percent of these being committed with a firearm (Bureau of Justice Statistics, U.S. Department of Justice, at http://www.ojp.usdoj.gov/bjs/homicide/circumgun.txt).

8. Clarke quotes Gary Kleck's argument that gun possession by a criminal may actually reduce the likelihood of injury because it obviates the need for a physical attack. Would you rather face a criminal armed with a gun, a criminal with a knife or blunt weapon? Would it depend on what the criminal did with the weapon?

9. One important subset of firearm violence is youth violence. Teen and young adult homicides are more likely to be committed with a gun than homicides of adults (Bureau of Justice Statistics, U.S. Department of

Justice). What do you think explains this statistic? Why are youths in this country so much more murderous than in other industrialized countries? Is it because of gangs? Violent video games? Other media violence? Bad parenting? Bad schools? Drugs? Guns? (For more on the issue, see David B. Kopel, *Guns, Gangs, and Preschools: Moving beyond Conventional Solutions to Confront Juvenile Violence*, 1 Barry University Law Review 63 [2000].) As an exercise, list five reasons, in descending order, that you think best explain the youth homicide rate in America.

10. The public school shootings in Littleton, Colorado; Conyers, Georgia; Springfield, Oregon; Jonesboro, Arkansas; Paducah, Kentucky; Edinboro, Pennsylvania; and Pearl, Mississippi, in 1997–99 fueled the call for greater gun control. Do you think guns were a contributing cause of the shootings? The shootings in Mississippi and Pennsylvania were both halted by the appearance of an adult with a firearm who told the shooters to stop. (See David B. Kopel, *What If We Had Taken Columbine Seriously?* Weekly Standard, April 24, 2000.) Do you think that teachers or other adults have an obligation to protect students? Kopel argues that only two firearms policies could have made a difference at Columbine: a complete and effective ban on all guns or allowing teachers or other approved adults to possess firearms on school property, subject to appropriate regulation. Do you agree?

11. Firearms violence has dramatically disproportionate effects on persons of different races. (See chapter 5 for detailed information.)

12. Another subset of firearm homicide cases is domestic violence. Guns are used in 61 percent of domestic homicides. Approximately eighteen hundred murders annually (9 percent of total homicides) arise from domestic violence situations. In the past two decades, 33,500 persons have been killed with firearms by their intimate partners. Although the rate of domestic homicides committed with guns has declined, firearms remain the most common method for killing intimate partners. (See Arthur Kellermann and Sheryl Heron, *Firearms and Family Violence*, 17 Emergency Medicine Clinics of North America 699, 702–3 [1999].) A study of 215,000 murders over a twelve-year period showed that women were more than twice as likely to be killed by their inti-

mate partner using a firearm than to be killed by a stranger using any method. (See *id.* at 703.) Do these statistics bolster the argument for disarming men or support the argument for arming women? (See chapter 5 for commentary regarding the value of firearms to women for self-defense purposes.)

There has been an overall decline in domestic violence homicides in recent years, with the most dramatic drop occurring in the number of men murdered by intimates. The number of men murdered by their partners dropped 60 percent between 1976 and 1998. The number of women killed by their partners remained steady for two decades but has declined somewhat since 1993 (Bureau of Justice Statistics, U.S. Department of Justice, at http://www.ojp.usdoj.gov/bjs/homicide/intimates.htm). If a woman uses a firearm to shoot an abusive partner, do you think the shooting is a tragedy or a better outcome than continuing abuse? Does your answer depend on particular facts of the situation?

13. Clarke cites two studies by Dr. Arthur Kellermann and colleagues that purport to show that guns kept in the home are far more likely to be used to kill or injure in a homicide, suicide attempt, or accidental shooting than to be used to kill or injure in self-defense. Gun rights advocates argue that these studies are misleading because most episodes of defensive gun use do not result in death or injury. In most cases, they argue, simply brandishing a weapon is enough to frighten off a criminal, incidents that are not counted in these studies. (See chapter 1 for thorough discussion of defensive gun use.) Clarke responds that the same can be said of firearm misuse; that is, most incidents of misuse of a gun do not result in death or injury and therefore are not counted in the Kellermann studies. Do you think guns in the home make homes safer or more dangerous? Does it depend on the home? Do you think academic or scientific studies can capture an accurate picture of domestic violence?

14. Kopel offers a different critique of the Kellermann data: that it fails to consider the type of home in which the gun is kept. Among people with violent criminal records, violent mental illness, or substance abuse problems, guns in the home may present a very large risk, while a gun

in the home of a law-abiding, responsible family may pose very little risk. Kopel concludes:

> To study these high-risk homes and to jump to conclusions about the general population is illogical. We know that possession of an automobile by an alcoholic who is prone to drunk driving may pose a serious health risk. But proof that autos in the hands of alcoholics may be risky doesn't prove that autos in the hands of non-alcoholics are risky.
>
> Yet the famous Seattle "43 to 1" figure is based on lumping the homes of violent felons, alcoholics, and other disturbed people in with the population as a whole. The study fails to distinguish between the large risks of guns in the hands of dangerous people, with the tiny risks (and large benefits) of guns in the hands of ordinary people. (David E. Kopel, *The 43:1 Fallacy*, National Review Online, Jan. 31, 2001, at http://www.nationalreview.com/kopel/kopel013101.shtml.)

Can gun laws effectively distinguish between the at-risk population and the general population? Or does allowing any ownership of guns make it impossible, in practical terms, to keep guns out of the wrong hands? Among the laws that attempt, in various ways, to distinguish dangerous from nondangerous gun owners are the Gun Control Act of 1968 (banning gun possession by certain categories of people); the National Instant Check System (requiring an FBI or state criminal records check for all retail gun purchases); laws requiring that all firearms sales among private individuals be routed through a licensed firearms dealer for background checks (a state law in California and some other states); gun registration; limits on how many guns can be bought in a period of time; and gun storage and gun design laws intended to reduce gun thefts. Some of these laws are discussed in chapter 6 as well as later in this chapter.

Which of the above listed laws do you think are most effective in keeping guns out of the hands of dangerous users? Can you think of other laws that might have that effect without denying guns to safe, legitimate users? Would an overall reduction in the national gun supply help to keep guns from illegitimate users or only legitimate users? Both?

15. The Kellermann studies relied on by Clarke are just two examples of what are referred to as "public health" studies of guns. In considering the costs of firearms to victims and society, you should be aware of a contentious dispute regarding these studies. In the early 1980s, the U.S. Centers for Disease Control decided to study injuries as a public health problem. In 1988, two CDC investigators published a commentary in the *New England Journal of Medicine* advocating that firearm injuries be studied using epidemiological methods, which traditionally have been used to study diseases. Over the years, the CDC has sponsored dozens of studies regarding firearms and firearm casualties. Virtually all the public health studies reach conclusions advocating greater gun control or a reduction of guns in homes. The studies are often cited by the media and gun control organizations in making the case against guns. Gun rights supporters have vigorously attacked both the methodologies and the conclusions reached by many of the public health studies. (See Don B. Kates et al., *Guns and Public Health: Epidemic of Violence or Pandemic of Propaganda?* 62 Tennessee Law Review 513, 522 [1995].) Kates characterizes many of the public health gun studies as "sagecraft" literature, in which partisan academic "sages" prostitute scholarship, systematically inventing, misinterpreting, selecting, or otherwise manipulating data to validate preordained political conclusions. He offers examples to support this charge. The Kates article includes an extended critique of a famous study that claimed to find that owning a gun in the home triples the risk that a person will be murdered (Arthur L. Kellermann et al., *Gun Ownership as a Risk Factor for Homicide in the Home,* 329 New England Journal of Medicine 1084 [1993]; see also Gary Kleck, *Can Owning a Gun Really Triple the Owner's Chance of Being Murdered?* 5 Homicide Studies 64 [2001]).

In 1996, in response to NRA lobbying, congressional critics of the CDC's firearms research eliminated funding. Subsequently, the National Institute of Justice (part of the Department of Justice) began funding many of the same gun control researchers whose CDC funding had been cut. The editor of the *New England Journal of Medicine,* publisher of many of the CDC-funded studies, called the attempt to withdraw funding for CDC firearms research "an attack that strikes at the very heart of scientific research" (Jerome P. Kassirer, *A Partisan Assault on Science: The Threat to the CDC,* 333 New England Journal of Medicine 793 [1995]).

Although the CDC disavows the agency is pursuing an anti-gun agenda, virtually every study funded by the CDC reaches "anti-gun" conclusions. Moreover, some persons associated with the CDC and its studies have taken public stands against firearms. Do you oppose or support using tax dollars to fund research into firearm injuries? Does it depend on whether the research is actually of high scientific quality or (as Kates charges in his long article criticizing particular studies) is shoddy, dishonest, and grossly manipulated to achieve particular results? Do you think that firearm injuries qualify as a "public health" problem? Does the fact that researchers hold personal opinions on an issue call into question the credibility of their scientific research of that issue? Is it possible for anyone on either side of the gun debate to approach research into such a controversial and emotional issue without harboring some preconceived notions about it? Healthy skepticism is probably appropriate when considering research and statistical claims on both sides of the aisle.

B. Suicide

Many persons are unaware that suicides comprise the majority of firearm deaths in America each year. For cultural and religious reasons, suicide is a highly stigmatized topic that gets little attention in the popular press, despite that fact that forty-six people commit suicide with firearms in the United States every day. How much of a role should suicides play in determining national firearms policy? Relevant statistics are presented below; the Discussion Notes for these statistics are followed by an article focusing on adolescent firearm suicides.

TABLE 4 Historical Suicide and Gun Suicide Rates
(per 100,000 residents)

Year	Suicide rate	Gun suicide rate
1949	11.4	4.8
1950	11.3	4.9
1951	10.3	4.5
1952	10	4.5
1953	10	4.6
1954	10.1	4.7
1955	10.2	4.7
1956	10	4.7
1957	9.7	4.6
1958	10.6	5.1
1959	10.5	5
1960	10.6	5
1961	10.4	4.9
1962	10.9	5.1
1963	11	5.1
1964	10.8	5.1
1965	11.1	5.1
1966	10.9	5.3
1967	10.8	5.3
1968	10.7	5.5
1969	11.1	5.6
1970	11.5	5.8
1971	11.6	5.9
1972	11.9	6.4
1973	11.9	6.3
1974	12	6.7
1975	12.6	6.9
1976	12.3	6.8
1977	13	7.3
1978	12.3	6.9
1979	12.2	7
1980	11.8	6.8
1981	12	7
1982	12.2	7.2
1983	12.1	7.1
1984	12.4	7.2
1985	12.3	7.3
1986	12.8	7.5
1987	12.7	7.5
1988	12.3	7.4
1989	12.2	7.4
1990	12.4	7.6
1991	12.2	7.4
1992	12	7.1
1993	12.1	7.6
1994	12	7.2
1995	11.9	7

Source: Gary Kleck, *Targeting Guns: Firearms and Their Control*
(Hawthorne, NY: Aldine de Gruyter 1997)

TABLE 5 U.S. Firearm and Nonfirearm Suicide Death Rates by Age Group, 1994–97
(per 100,000 Residents)

Age Group	1997 Firearm Suicide Death Rate	1997 Nonfirearm Suicide Death Rate	1996 Firearm Suicide Death Rate	1996 Nonfirearm Suicide Death Rate	1995 Firearm Suicide Death Rate	1995 Nonfirearm Suicide Death Rate	1994 Firearm Suicide Death Rate	1994 Nonfirearm Suicide Death Rate
00–04	0.00	0.00	0.00	0.00	0.00	0.00	0.00	0.00
05–09	0.01	0.02	0.01	0.02	0.01	0.03	0.01	0.02
10–14	0.66	0.93	0.85	0.72	0.97	0.78	1.00	0.70
15–19	5.95	3.50	6.15	3.59	6.97	3.43	7.77	3.22
20–24	8.29	5.32	8.98	5.49	9.98	6.05	10.66	5.64
25–29	7.83	6.53	8.31	6.50	8.58	6.60	9.14	6.66
30–34	7.39	6.89	7.21	7.05	8.09	7.52	8.04	6.98
35–39	7.54	7.52	7.84	7.56	7.61	7.32	7.88	7.57
40–44	7.56	7.99	7.91	7.77	7.80	7.68	7.77	7.34
45–49	7.83	7.34	8.14	6.96	7.75	6.91	8.10	6.33
50–54	7.92	6.24	8.66	6.07	8.43	6.02	8.27	6.04
55–59	9.03	5.44	8.68	5.54	8.13	4.81	8.25	5.12
60–64	7.93	4.45	8.56	4.54	9.04	4.59	8.88	4.51
65–69	9.36	3.86	10.20	4.14	9.98	4.50	9.62	4.28
70–74	11.36	4.35	11.68	4.12	12.41	4.86	12.05	4.91
75–79	13.18	5.27	13.50	5.12	14.48	5.07	15.07	5.48
80–84	14.58	6.03	15.84	6.32	15.86	6.63	15.93	6.62
85+	12.76	8.03	13.29	6.89	13.61	7.89	14.03	8.87
Total	6.56	4.85	6.85	4.80	7.04	4.86	7.21	4.75

Source: Data from Centers for Disease Control and Prevention, National Center for Injury Prevention and Control.

TABLE 6 U.S. Firearm Suicide Death Rates by Sex and Age Group, 1994–97
(per 100,000 Residents)

Age Group	1997 Male	1997 Female	1996 Male	1996 Female	1995 Male	1995 Female	1994 Male	1994 Female
00–04	0.00	0.00	0.00	0.00	0.00	0.00	0.00	0.00
05–09	0.01	0.00	0.01	0.00	0.01	0.00	0.01	0.00
10–14	1.00	0.30	1.32	0.36	1.41	0.51	1.45	0.53
15–19	9.92	1.73	10.31	1.71	11.96	1.66	13.19	2.01
20–24	14.58	1.68	15.91	1.69	17.42	2.19	18.93	2.03
25–29	13.53	2.09	14.37	2.21	15.07	2.03	15.93	2.30
30–34	12.54	2.27	12.43	2.02	13.80	2.40	13.62	2.49
35–39	12.56	2.54	13.17	2.54	12.88	2.38	13.01	2.80
40–44	12.47	2.73	13.30	2.63	13.10	2.60	13.08	2.57
45–49	13.24	2.61	14.08	2.40	13.14	2.56	13.72	2.67
50–54	13.60	2.53	14.48	3.14	14.40	2.77	13.93	2.92
55–59	16.19	2.42	15.80	2.10	14.54	2.22	15.14	1.90
60–64	14.84	1.75	15.67	2.23	16.33	2.56	16.38	2.23
65–69	18.11	2.00	19.81	2.15	19.25	2.27	18.69	2.14
70–74	23.27	2.15	24.57	1.75	25.98	1.98	25.08	2.06
75–79	29.74	1.54	30.77	1.48	32.69	1.97	34.61	1.81
80–84	36.88	1.54	39.86	2.01	40.69	1.82	41.77	1.57
85+	42.45	0.80	44.59	0.85	45.12	1.22	47.25	1.10
Total	11.60	1.74	12.18	1.74	12.49	1.82	12.80	1.86

Source: Data from Centers for Disease Control and Prevention, National Center for Injury Prevention and Control.

TABLE 7 U.S. Firearm Suicide Death Rates by Race and Age Group (Both Sexes), 1996–97 (per 100,000 Residents)

Age Group	1997 White	1997 Black	1997 Other	1996 White	1996 Black	1996 Other
00–04	0.00	0.00	0.00	0.00	0.00	0.00
05–09	0.01	0.00	0.00	0.01	0.00	0.00
10–14	0.70	0.65	0.20	0.88	0.76	0.60
15–19	6.24	5.00	4.40	6.38	5.17	5.54
20–24	8.41	8.24	6.67	9.23	9.03	5.22
25–29	8.24	6.65	4.95	8.70	7.15	5.63
30–34	7.97	5.43	3.35	7.88	4.66	2.98
35–39	8.40	3.46	3.40	8.56	4.87	2.96
40–44	8.50	3.06	2.34	8.71	4.35	2.52
45–49	8.73	3.23	2.41	9.01	3.56	2.51
50–54	8.84	2.40	1.79	9.55	4.03	1.41
55–59	9.93	3.39	4.15	9.61	3.35	2.06
60–64	8.65	3.58	2.72	9.26	4.82	1.99
65–69	10.03	5.35	2.97	11.06	5.16	0.68
70–74	12.13	5.75	2.94	12.47	5.54	3.49
75–79	14.17	4.27	3.77	14.50	4.56	3.37
80–84	15.55	5.23	3.27	16.96	5.00	2.30
85+	13.67	4.44	2.68	14.30	4.19	1.45
Total	7.24	3.56	2.78	7.52	3.95	2.64

Source: Data from Centers for Disease Control and Prevention, National Center for Injury Prevention and Control.

DISCUSSION NOTES

1. Study the above charts. What patterns or trends can you discern from the suicide data? Identify and come to class prepared to discuss at least one suicide trend or pattern for each of the four major categories covered by the data: age, sex, race, and firearm-versus-nonfirearm use.

2. Study the age-based table. Note that the highest firearm suicide rates by far are for persons age sixty-five and older but that nonfirearm suicide rates for this age group are less than or roughly equivalent to that for adults in lower age brackets. What factors might explain this phenomenon? Note also, in Table 5, that the highest firearm suicide rates for persons below age sixty-five are for the age groups of twenty to twenty-four and twenty-five to twenty-nine. Can you think of reasons why persons in their twenties commit suicide by firearm at higher rates than those in bordering age groups?

3. Whites commit suicide at higher rates than nonwhites. Why do you think this is so? (Suicide rates for blacks have been increasing in recent

years. Table 7 shows that in 1996 and 1997 the firearm suicide rates for blacks and whites in the age group of twenty to twenty-four were roughly equivalent.)

4. Men commit suicide at higher rates than women. Note in Table 6 the tremendous disparity in firearm suicide rates between men and women. Females attempt suicide three times as often as males, but males complete suicide four times as often as females. The difference in success rate is attributable largely to the choice of method, especially firearms. (See Ann F. Garland and Edward Zigler, *Adolescent Suicide Prevention: Current Research and Social Policy Implications,* 48 American Psychologist 169, 170 [1993].) Why do you think men use firearms and other lethal suicide methods at much higher rates than women? Are they more determined to die? Are they more likely to have access to firearms? To know how to use them? Is using a firearm a more "macho" way to die than, for example, taking an overdose of pills? Do women prefer to die in a "clean" manner?

The Public Health Case for the Safe Storage of Firearms: Adolescent Suicides Add One More "Smoking Gun"
(51 Hastings Law Journal 953 [2000])

Andrew J. McClurg

. . . Suicide is the second leading cause of death among youths between the ages of 15 and 19 and the third leading cause of death for youths aged 15–24. In 1994, 2,270 persons under age 20 committed suicide. While the overall suicide rate in the United States has remained relatively stable since 1950, the rate of suicide for adolescents has more than tripled.

Firearms account for 60 percent of all suicides in this country, including youth suicides, even though they are used in only a small percentage of suicide attempts. The firearm suicide rate in the United States for children under age 15 is eleven times higher than that of any industrialized nation in the world. The dramatic escalation in adolescent suicide rates is accounted for almost entirely by an increase in the use of firearms as the method of suicide attempt, with little rise in suicides by other means.

Between 1980 and 1992, guns accounted for 81 percent of the increase in the suicide rate for persons aged 15–19. . . .

Suicide is the forgotten statistic in the popular gun control debate. Most people are surprised to learn that annual firearm suicides routinely outpace firearm homicides. In 1996, the most recent year for which figures are available, 18,166 Americans committed suicide with a firearm, substantially more than the 14,327 victims of homicide by firearm the same year. Firearm suicides have exceeded firearm homicides in forty of the sixty years between 1933 and 1992. For all our fear of being victims of a violent criminal attack, "[i]f a randomly chosen person adds up the probabilities that each of the 5.2 billion other people in the world will kill her, the sum . . . is still less than the probability she'll kill herself. . . ."

Suicidal ideation and suicide attempts are far more common than most people are aware. "Anyone can become suicidal when the situation producing the emotional pain is believed to be inescapable, never ending, and unbearable" [quoting Dr. Jorg J. Pahl]. An estimated 20 percent of Americans contemplate suicide at some point in their lives.

The problem is more acute for youths. A 1997 survey of 16,262 high school students found that one in five students had seriously considered suicide in the previous year. A survey of 5,000 rural teenagers revealed 40 percent had entertained suicidal thoughts at some point in their lives. Another study found that 62 percent of high school students sampled had experienced suicidal ideation or exhibited suicidal behavior. Between 6 percent and 13 percent of adolescents report having attempted suicide at least once in their lives.

Adolescents see suicide as a quick and easy way to escape pain. They lack the experience to understand that most pain is transitory or even that death is permanent. Consider this sentiment expressed by a suicidal fifteen-year-old girl: "I want to kill myself, but I don't want to be dead. I mean, I want to be dead, but I don't want to be dead forever. I only want to be dead until my eighteenth birthday." Relatively minor tribulations of everyday life—a breakup, bad grade, an argument or the death of a pet—can be the triggering event for a suicide attempt. A fourteen-year-old boy shot himself because he was upset about getting braces. A young girl killed herself minutes after her father refused to let her watch a television show. "For adolescents, the moment is everything," said psychiatrist Samuel Klagsbrun. "They think, 'I've got pain, and the pain is lasting for more than two minutes—that means the pain will last forever.'" In America, where more than 220 million privately-owned firearms are kept in 40 percent of all households, two minutes may be too long. . . .

Guns are the most lethal method of suicide, succeeding in eight or nine out of every ten attempts. Firearms are responsible for 60 percent of successful adolescent suicides, despite the fact that they are used in only a small percentage of attempts. An Oregon study of youth suicide rates found that firearms were successful in 78.2 percent of attempts, although they accounted for only 0.6 percent of total attempts. In stark comparison, drug overdose was the chosen suicide method in 75.5 percent of attempts, but was successful only 0.4 percent of the time. Perhaps most significantly, the study found that while firearms were used in only 0.6 percent of all attempts, they were responsible for 63.7 percent of all fatal attempts. Firearms are used in more successful suicides in the United States than all other methods combined.

The Firearms-Suicide Studies

. . . A large and growing body of public health evidence confirms that easy access to firearms significantly increases the risk of suicide.

Arthur Kellermann and colleagues conducted the largest and most well-publicized study of the nexus between firearms and suicide, which concluded that keeping guns in the home is associated with an almost fivefold increase in the risk of suicide. [See Arthur L. Kellermann et al., *Suicide in the Home in Relation to Gun Ownership*, 327 New England Journal of Medicine 467 (1992).] Kellermann studied all suicides occurring in Shelby County, Tennessee (Memphis area) and King County, Washington (Seattle area) during a thirty-two month period between 1987 and 1990. Data was collected for each suicide from the police, medical examiner and by interviewing proxies for the victim concerning risk factors for suicide such as alcohol and drug use, history of depression or mental illness and gun ownership. Answers to the interview questions were compared to a set of control subjects from the same neighborhood, matched with the victim by sex, race and approximate age. The result was 438 matched pairs of suicide victims and controls. The study included these findings:

- Guns were kept in 65 percent of the suicide victims' homes compared to only 41 percent of the control subjects' homes.
- Handguns were kept in 49.5 percent of the victims' homes, but only 23.4 percent of the controls' homes. Handguns were used in 72 percent of the suicides involving a firearm.
- In homes with guns, a firearm was the method of suicide in 86 percent of the cases.
- In homes where guns were not normally kept, only 6 percent of the victims committed suicide with a firearm.

The most startling conclusion of the study was that keeping one or more firearms was strongly associated with an increased risk of suicide in the home by a ratio of 4.8 to 1 [nearly 5 to 1]. . . .

Although the pro-gun forces have been quick to attack the public health research regarding guns, they cannot point to any evidence refuting the conclusion that firearms in the home increase the risk of suicide. However, even without the strong evidentiary support provided by the multiple public health studies, we could draw the same conclusion the old-fashioned way. Simple logic informs us that an easily accessible hand-held instrumentality that can instantly end life is a potent risk to persons with suicidal ideation.

The Myth of Method Substitution

The overall suicide rate in the United States ranks lower than the suicide rate in some other countries with stricter gun laws. From this, gun advocates assert that, despite the fact that the United States has by far the highest firearms suicide rate in the world, firearms availability and gun laws have little or no connection to the suicide rate. They assert that if guns were not available for use in suicide, attempters would simply substitute a different method.

It is true that the overall suicide rate in this country falls only about midway on the list of suicide rates among industrialized countries. Countries such as Hungary, Denmark, Finland, Switzerland and Japan have higher overall suicide rates than the United States, while countries such as Ireland, Italy, Spain and Greece have lower rates. It is also true that some countries with higher suicide rates than the United States have much lower gun density.

However, international comparisons are of questionable validity in this area due to the many cultural differences between nations. World suicide rates have remained remarkably stable over time, suggesting that cultural factors best explain the differences in national suicide rates. Gun proponents are fond of drawing comparisons to Japan, a virtually gun-free society with a significantly higher suicide rate than the United States, in arguing that firearms availability does not play a role in suicide rates. But unlike the United States, where suicide is considered an anti-religious and cowardly act, Japanese culture traditionally glorified suicides committed in the name of honor.

Even if there were some merit to the method substitution argument based on worldwide comparison of suicide rates, the argument falls apart when one isolates adolescent suicides. While the United States falls only midway on the worldwide list for overall suicide rates, our adolescent suicide rate leads the world. A study of suicides in twenty-six industrialized countries during a one year period showed that 54 percent of the total worldwide suicides for children under age 15 occurred in the United States. The suicide rate for children under 15 in the United States was two times higher than that in the other twenty-five countries combined. . . . [Centers for Disease Control and Prevention, U.S. Department of Health and Human Services, Rep. No. 5, *Rates of Homicide and Firearm-Related Deaths Among Children—26 Industrialized Countries*, 46 Morbidity & Mortality Weekly Report 101 (Feb. 7, 1997)]

Assuming *arguendo* that method substitution has validity, society and potential victims of suicide would still benefit by having fewer guns available. Because guns are the most lethal method for attempting suicide, resort to other methods would result in fewer lives lost. . . . The weapons-choice theory holds that where the resolve to kill is weak or short-lived, death rates will be influenced by the availability of particular weapons. Because firearms are more likely to cause death than other instrumentalities, reducing access to firearms will result in lower death rates, even if the number of suicide attempts remains the same. While some people select guns because they are determined to kill or die, others do so only because a gun is readily available.

This appears to true with regard to many adolescent suicides. In one of his several studies in the area, David Brent asserted that method substitution may be less likely to occur in adolescents and young adults due to the prominent role impulsiveness and substance abuse play in youthful suicide. In other words, firearms access probably plays a greater role in lethal suicide attempts among youths than in older adults who are more committed to the idea of suicide. . . .

DISCUSSION NOTES

1. What are your feelings toward persons who attempt suicide? Do you condemn them? Feel compassion for them? Do you view suicide as a cowardly act? An insane act? An immoral act? Do negative views about suicide victims help explain why they get so little attention in the gun debate? Is the fact that suicide is an intentional, self-regarding act (as opposed to the killing of someone who does not want to be killed or an unintended, accidental killing) a factor? In the Founding Era, some sermons condemned suicide and the failure to defend oneself from deadly attack on precisely the same grounds: the squandering of the God-given gift of life. Do you agree?

2. Some people argue that American suicide is increased by a "culture of death," which includes the use of the death penalty in the United States, abortion, and firearms. What do you think of this argument?

3. Firearms figure prominently as a method of "successful" suicide. In 1991, firearms and explosives accounted for 65 percent of male suicide deaths and 40 percent of female suicide deaths. Poisoning was the second most common method of completed suicide for women (37 percent), while hanging ranked second for men (15.1 percent). Hanging ranked third for women (13.4 percent) and poisoning ranked third for men (13 percent). Jumping ranked fourth for both sexes (2 percent for men and 3.5 percent for women). (See Frederic Seltzer, *Trend in Mortality from Violent Deaths: Suicide and Homicide, United States, 1960–1991,* 75 Statistical Bulletin 10, 14 [1994].) Have you ever felt suicidal? Did you ever experience suicidal ideation as an adolescent? If so, did these feelings pass? Do

you think that reducing guns in homes or mandating the safe storage of guns in homes would be effective ways to reduce the teenage suicide rate? The adult suicide rate?

4. Suicide attempts far outnumber completions. The most widely accepted estimated ratio is eight attempts for every completed suicide. (See Judith M. Stillion and Eugene E. Mcdowell, *Suicide across the Life Span* 103 [1996].) The success rate for suicides varies, however, by age group. Adolescents have a much higher ratio of unsuccessful suicide attempts to completions. In one study, only 12 percent of a group of 1,103 adolescent suicide attempters stated in emergency room interviews that they wished to die as a result of their act. (See David K. Curran, *Adolescent Suicidal Behavior* 45 [1987].) Why do you think there are so many unsuccessful suicide attempts?

5. How does one explain that the United States has by far the highest firearm suicide rate in the world but ranks only midway among industrialized nations in terms of overall suicide rates? Consider Japan, a virtually gun-free society: although the Japanese firearm suicide rate is one-fiftieth of the U.S. rate, the overall suicide rate is nearly twice that of the United States. Kopel raises the possibility that the prohibition of firearms in Japan may actually contribute to higher suicide rates:

> Of the many reasons suggested by researchers for the high Japanese suicide rate, one of the most startling is weapons control. Japanese scholars like Mamon Iga and Kichinosuke Tatai argue that one reason Japan has a suicide problem is that people have little sympathy for suicide victims. Iga and Tatai suggest that the lack of sympathy (and hence the lack of social will to deal with a high suicide rate) is based on the Japanese feelings of insecurity and consequent lack of empathy. They trace the lack of empathy to a "dread of power." That dread is caused in part by the awareness that a person cannot count on others for help against violence or against authority. In addition, say Iga and Tatai, the dread of power stems from the people being forbidden to possess swords and firearms for self-defense. (David B. Kopel, *The Samurai, the Mountie, and the Cowboy* 44 [Amherst, NY: Prometheus Books, 1992].)

What do you think of this argument?

6. What do you think about the method-substitution argument? If guns

were not available to commit suicide, would people simply resort to other means? If you were truly committed to the idea of suicide, which method would you choose? If a gun were not available, would you jump off a building? Hang yourself? Note that drug overdose, while by far the most common method of suicide attempt, is also the least likely method to be successful, in part because it is relatively easy to control the dose and consume a nonfatal amount. The preference for drug overdose as a method of suicide probably is a reflection, at least in part, of the fact that many suicide attempters do not really wish to die.

7. Kleck critiques the gun/suicide studies as follows:

> [S]elf-inflicted shootings are not significantly more likely to lead to the victim's death than suicide attempts by hanging, CO poisoning, or drowning. Given no significantly greater lethality than other easily available methods of suicide, what extraordinary suicide-facilitating attributes could guns possess that enable them to increase the risks of suicide by a factor of . . . even two?
>
> An hour is sufficient time to hang oneself, fill the interior of a car with CO and inhale a lethal dose, or drive to a body of water large and deep enough for drowning. Thus, the only impulsive suicide attempts where the quick availability of a gun would be crucial in leading to death would be attempts that (1) were serious enough to induce the attempter to shoot himself, if a gun were available, yet (2) were so impulsive that the suicidal motive persisted for less than an hour. . . . Advocates of the "impulsive adolescent" thesis have presented no evidence that suicide attempts of this description occur at all, never mind often enough for gun ownership to elevate the suicide rate among adolescents. . . . (Gary Kleck, Targeting Guns 283–84 [1997])

Kleck notes that at least three effective suicide methods (hanging, carbon monoxide poisoning, and drowning) can be carried out within one hour, implying that impulsive suicide attempters have means other than guns at their disposal. Considering that an unsecured, loaded gun can be removed from a cabinet and discharged in less than one minute, is an hour a relatively long time by comparison to actively engage in a suicide attempt? If hanging, carbon monoxide poisoning, and drowning are effective and easy suicide methods, why do relatively few suicide completers choose them as compared to guns? (See note 3, above, for relative percentages of the most "successful" methods of suicide.) Do guns present advantages or disadvantages over these other methods to suicide attempters? If so, what are they? If you were determined to commit suicide, which of the following four methods would you choose: a gun, hanging, carbon monoxide poisoning, or drowning? Why? Do you think some people would be able to point a gun at themselves and pull the trigger but would not be able to carry out a hanging, carbon monoxide poisoning, or drowning? If so, why?

8. Data cited by McClurg indicate that, for adolescents, the United States has both the highest firearm suicide rate and the highest overall suicide rate in the world. Do these data suggest that the method-substitution argument has less force with respect to adolescents? Can you think of reasons why this might be so?

9. Like many of the public health studies, the Kellermann suicide study has been critiqued by other scholars. Don Kates writes:

> Another popular factoid—having a gun in the home increases the risk of suicide by almost five times—is also based on a Kellermann study. . . .
>
> Although press reports about gun research commonly treat correlation and causation as one and the same, this association does not prove that having a gun in the house raises the risk of suicide. We can imagine alternative explanations: Perhaps gun ownership in this sample was associated with personality traits that were, in turn, related to suicide, or perhaps people who had contemplated suicide bought a gun for that reason. To put the association in perspective, it's worth noting that living alone and using illicit drugs were both better predictors of suicide than gun ownership was. That does not necessarily mean that living alone or using illegal drugs leads to suicide.
>
> Furthermore, Kellermann and his colleagues selected their sample with an eye toward increasing the apparent role of gun ownership in suicide. They started by looking at all suicides that occurred during a 32-month period in King County, Washington, and Shelby County, Tennessee, but they excluded cases that occurred outside the home—nearly a third of the original sample. "Our study was restricted to suicides occurring in the victim's home," they explained with admirable

frankness, "because a previous study has indicated that most suicides committed with guns occur there." (Don B. Kates, *Public Health Pot Shots: How the CDC Succumbed to the Gun "Epidemic,"* Reason, April 1997, at 24, 27–28.)

Are these valid criticisms? Do they undermine the findings of the study? Kates emphasizes a possible alternative explanation for the association between guns in the home and firearm suicides—that gun ownership may be associated with personality traits related to suicide. The study authors noted this same possibility, however, stating: "[W]e cannot exclude the possibility that gun owners (and people who live in homes with guns) may be psychologically predisposed to commit suicide." Kates also accuses the authors of biasing the study by excluding suicides outside the home. Is there bias in limiting the study to guns in the home if the expressly stated purpose of the study is to examine the relationship between suicide and guns kept in homes? (Kellerman's article is titled *Suicide in the Home in Relation to Gun Ownership.*) Was it legitimate to study home suicides exclusively, or should the study have looked at total suicides, since nonhome suicides are more likely to include nonfirearms methods such as jumping or drowning in a large body of water?

C. Accidental Shootings

Although accidental shootings comprise by far the smallest statistical category of firearm death and injury, they garner a lot of attention in the gun debate because they sometimes involve children. Gary Kleck sheds light on fatal gun accidents in chapter 9 of his book *Targeting Guns.*

Targeting Guns: Firearms and Their Control
(293, 296–302, 308–9, 310–11, 321–22 [1997])

Gary Kleck

The 1225 fatal gun accidents that were reported in 1995 claimed about 3% of the total gun deaths that year. The significance of gun accidents therefore is not due to their dominance in the firearms death statistics. Rather, this category of gun misuse is important because of the pivotal role it plays in the debate over whether keeping a gun in the home for protection entails more risk than benefit for the average household. . . .

Most defensive gun owners do not perceive themselves or members of their immediate family as prone to crime or suicide, so it is difficult to persuade them that such risks apply to them. On the other hand, many people regard accidents as events that can happen to anyone. It is plausible that even the most responsible and law-abiding family can experience a gun accident if they keep a firearm in the home, particularly if it is kept loaded for self-defense. . . .

[Data regarding fatal gun accidents (FGAs)] for the United States from 1933 to 1995 [combined with data regarding gun ownership] seem to present an anomaly: as the size of the private gun stock increased sharply from 1967 to 1994, the number and rate of FGAs sharply declined. To some degree this trend is undoubtedly attributable to the same causes driving down rates of accidental death in general, since the latter have been declining since the 1930s. However, whereas the general rate declined by only 18% from 1977 to 1987, the FGA rate dropped by 33%. . . .

The peak in the FGA rate, within the last thirty years, occurred in 1967 and the sharpest increases occurred in the 1965–1967 period. . . .

The decreases in FGAs from 1967 to 1986 may be partly attributable to improvements in medical treatment of gunshot wounds. Certainly, over a long period of the past, there have been dramatic improvements in survival rates of gunshot victims. The mortality rate for abdominal gunshot wounds treated at a midwestern urban hospital was 60% in the 1930–1938 period, 36% in 1938–1946, 16% in 1955–1962, and 12.7% in 1962–1970.

Post-1967 declines may . . . be due to shifts in the types of guns owned and, more importantly, the types routinely kept loaded. FGAs occur only with loaded guns, and most of the guns routinely kept loaded are handguns owned for self-defense. The fraction of the civilian gun stock claimed by handguns increased in the past several decades and it is possible that an increasing fraction of these handguns were the cheap, small-caliber, low-power handguns known as Saturday night specials (SNSs). Since these are less lethal than other guns and are probably mainly owned for self-defense, an increased share of loaded guns being either handguns in general or specifically SNSs would lower the mortality rate among accidental woundings.

Children and Gun Accidents

The image of a small child finding his parents' gun and killing himself or a playmate is an emotionally powerful one. Advocates of stricter gun control often lay special stress on the risks of gun accidents to children. Accidents of this sort can more easily be blamed on the mere availability of guns per se, rather than to correctable problems with how they are handled, since all small children are assumed to be irresponsible by adult standards and therefore cannot be taught safety precautions with the same assurance of effectiveness as would be the case with adolescents or adults. It can be argued, then, that this sort of risk applies to all households with guns and children, not just those with unusually irresponsible older persons.

Perhaps the most widespread myth about gun accidents is that gun accidents primarily involve children. This is a dangerous misdiagnosis of the problem, which can misdirect control efforts into ineffective or irrelevant paths.

In reality, FGAs rarely involve children, if one defines "child" as a person who has not reached adolescence. Instead, the victims of FGAs, like victims of intentional homicides, are concentrated most heavily among adolescents and young adults. In 1993, 119 children under the age of 13, including 30 under the age of 5 were killed in accidents officially classified as FGAs.

The frequency of FGAs involving children is often inflated by the inclusion of adolescent FGAs in the "child" total. In some extreme cases, authors have even included 18–24-year-old adults in the "children" total.

Grouping children with adolescents seems to serve no purpose other than the propagandistic one of misleading people into believing that accidental gun deaths are common among children. Among the 800 FGAs among young people aged 0–24 in 1993, only 15% involved preadolescent children (under age 13), and less than 4% involved small children under 5. This practice is especially common among pro-control propagandists and among physicians and public health authors. For example, in a propaganda sheet compiled by the Center to Prevent Handgun Violence, a claim was made about the number of "children" killed with guns each year, but the statistic pertained to deaths among persons aged 19 and under, almost all of which in fact involved adolescents.

The practice is misleading and unhelpful because it mixes a population of preadolescent children who have a near-zero rate of involvement in gun accidents together with a very high-rate population, adolescents and young adults.

The lumping together of children and adolescents, two radically different populations, obscures differences between the groups in the accident-prevention potential of various measures. For example, various mechanical devices for child-proofing guns, such as pressure-sensitive grips, might prevent some of the few dozen fatal gun accidents involving very small children, but would rarely prevent accidents among older children or adolescents. The repeated citation of statistics that actually pertain predominantly to adolescents as if they pertained to children encourages an exaggerated notion of the accident-preventing potential of such devices.

More generally, the focus on the accident-reducing importance of how guns are stored, i.e., whether they are stored loaded and/or unlocked is partly a product of an unduly narrow focus on the tiny share (almost certainly less than 7%) of FGAs that have child shooters. In particular, a narrow focus on accidents among urban children who gained unauthorized access to guns ignores the fact that most gun accidents neither occur in urban areas nor involve children. Instead, 60% occur in small towns and rural areas and probably more than 93% of shooters involved in the FGAs are adolescents or adults. In rural areas, it is common for adolescents to personally own guns, as hunting is the most common reason for owning guns in such areas, and hunting is more common among adolescents than in any other age group. Therefore, the fact that nearly all shooters in FGAs are adults or adolescents means that nearly all of them are old enough to personally own their own guns, and strongly suggests that the vast majority had authorized access to the guns. Thus, even if guns and/or ammunition were kept locked, accidental shooters ordinarily would have the requisite keys or lock combinations to gain access. Consequently, while "safe storage" of guns is a prudent practice, and may well be partly responsible for gun accidents being as rare as they are, it has only limited relevance to producing further reductions in gun accidents.

A study of newspaper accounts of handgun accidents among children age sixteen or younger found that the accidents disproportionately occurred during summer months and afternoon hours, with 66% occurring when no adult was present. Analysis of a subset of these cases indicated that 50% occurred in the victim's home and 30% in a friend's home. In 45% of the two hundred cases where the location was known, the child found the gun in the bedroom, presumably his parents' bedroom. This corresponds closely to the 42% of all guns that are kept in the owner's bedroom. In 47% of the cases, the gun was owned by the victim's parents and in 28% of the cases by parents of a friend of the victim. A study of eighty-eight California FGAs with victims under age fifteen found that in at least 48% of the residential deaths, the gun was kept loaded and unlocked. Thus a typical handgun accident with a child shooter or victim involved the child finding his parents' loaded and unlocked gun in their bedroom during the early afternoon in the summer school vacation period, while without adult supervision. . . .

Gun accidents may be conveniently divided into two categories: those occurring in the home, which claimed 67.5% in FGAs in 1993 where location was known, and those occurring outside the home, as many as half of which are hunting accidents.

Hunting Accidents

Hunting accidents seem to be a different sort of event from home gun accidents, involving much less clear evidence of reckless behavior. It is known that over 96% of fatal hunting accidents with guns involve long guns. Further, all hunting is done in outdoor locations. Therefore, almost the only FGAs that could plausibly be hunting accidents are those that involved shotguns or rifles and that occurred in an outdoor locale suitable for hunting. For the United States in 1991, of 454 FGAs where gun type and place of the accident were specified, only 75, or 16.5%, involved shotguns or rifles and occurred on a farm, in a place for recreation and sport, or in other specified places that theoretically could have been places suitable for hunting.

Hunting accidents are more genuinely accidental, as opposed to the unsurprising result of reckless conduct, than home gun accidents. At worst, the bulk of hunting accidents may involve poor judgment or momentary lapses in concentration rather than gross negligence. The most common circumstance was a hunter who was obscured by brush and possibly his own camouflage clothing.

Target or sport shooting at gun ranges and other formal shooting facilities seems virtually free of FGAs. In 1991, in the entire United States there were only sixteen FGAs, involving any type of gun, that occurred in a place for recreation and sport, about 1% of the FGA total.

Conclusions

Fatal gun accidents commonly involve unusually reckless behavior. The typical accident involves a shooter intentionally pulling the trigger, but hitting someone he did not intend to hit. About half of accidental gun deaths are self-inflicted. Most gun accidents occur in the home, many (perhaps most) of them involving guns kept for defense. However, very few accidents occur in connection with actual defensive uses of guns. Gun accidents are generally committed by unusually reckless people with records of heavy drinking, repeated involvement in automobile crashes, many traffic citations, and prior arrests for assault. Gun accidents, then, involve a rare and atypical subset of the population, as both shooters and victims. They rarely involve children, and most commonly involve adolescents and young adults. Accident rates are also higher among males, blacks, lower-income persons, single people, rural people, and southerners, i.e., the same segments of the population that show higher rates of intentional violence.

The risk of gun accident is extremely low, even among defensive gun owners, except among a very small, identifiably high-risk subset of the population. Consequently, it is doubtful whether, for the average gun owner, the risk of a gun accident could counterbalance the benefits of keeping a gun in the home for protection: the risk of an accident is quite low overall, and is virtually nonexistent for most gun owners.

DISCUSSION NOTES

1. Are you surprised by Kleck's data regarding accidental shootings? Were you under the impression that most accidental shootings involve small children, rather than adolescents? Were you aware that deaths from accidental shootings have declined for almost three decades? Where did you derive your impressions regarding this issue? Both sides in the gun control debate are frequently guilty of using emotional, inflammatory rhetoric to influence public opinion. (See Andrew J. McClurg, *The Rhetoric of Gun Control*, 42 American University Law Review 53, 65–79 [1992], analyzing emotional fallacies employed in the gun debate.) Politicians and gun control organizations, aware that injury to children generates strong emotions, often invoke the specter of accidental child deaths in arguing for greater gun control.

2. Suicides account for many more firearms deaths than accidents. Why do you think that accidents (especially child accidents) receive so much more media and political attention? Twice as many children ages five to fourteen die in bike accidents as in gun accidents (Centers for Disease Control and Prevention, at http://webapp.cdc.gov/sasweb/ncipc/mortrate.html). Why are there no newspaper editorials calling for "bike control"? Why are there no groups dedicated to reducing the proliferation of bikes or to keeping bikes away from children, or arguing that all bikes should be locked up when not in use so as to prevent unauthorized access by children? Do bikes have social utility to children? Do guns? Is an analogy between bikes and children apt? Or inapt because the intended purposes of bikes are non-deadly transportation and recreation? Is the product's intended purpose as important as (or even more important than) the raw number of accidents associated with the product? What are the intended uses of guns?

   In much of rural America, and in previous generations in some parts of urban America, many children owned or had easy access to guns and used them frequently for recreation. Do the public policy issues about gun safety that center on children involve cultural conflicts? Could one reason that bike accidental deaths are more frequent than accidental gun deaths be that bikes are more frequently used, and used by a significantly larger fraction of young people, than firearms?

3. Do you accept as valid Kleck's criticism that in tabulating child accidental-shooting deaths, "[g]rouping children with adolescents seems to serve no purpose other than the propagandistic one of misleading people into believing that accidental gun deaths are common among children"? Are the characteristics of adolescents more like those of children or those of adults with respect to the factors that influence accidental shootings? What qualities of childhood do you associate with accidental shootings? Do adolescents share these qualities? Do some adults? Does Kleck overstate his case when he refers to the "near-zero rate" of children involved in fatal gun accidents? (Kleck cites 119 fatal gun accidents in 1993 that involved children under the age of 13.)

4. Accidental shooting deaths in the United States have declined even as the number of guns owned has climbed. The highest number of accidental shooting deaths registered in one year occurred in 1933, when 3,014 fatal gun accidents occurred. The second highest year was 1967, with 2,896 fatalities. Since 1973, when 2,618 fatalities occurred, fatal gun accidents have declined each year. According to the National Safety Council, in 1998 there were nine hundred accidental firearms deaths. The age breakouts were: up to age four, 30 accidental deaths; ages five to fourteen, 80 deaths; ages fifteen to twenty-four, 310 deaths; ages twenty-five to forty-four, 260 deaths; ages forty-five to sixty-four, 130 deaths; ages sixty-five to seventy-four, 40 deaths; age seventy-five and older, 50 deaths (National Safety Council, *Injury Facts*, 1999 ed., at 9 [2000]).

The decline occurred despite the number of guns owned by Americans doubling between 1973 and 1998 (from an estimated 128 million to about 254 million). What do you think are the primary reasons for the decline? Kleck cited one important reason: improvements in emergency medical care, which have contributed to a decline in the death rate for all types of accidents. Can you think of other reasons? One factor may be that coroners in previous decades may have been more likely to classify suicides as accidents, out of respect for the surviving family's concern for the deceased's reputation. Do you think gun owners are more aware of the dangers of unsafe storage today? More likely to fear sanctions, such as social stigma and civil and criminal liability?

5. Fourteen states (California, Connecticut, Delaware, Florida, Hawaii, Iowa, Maryland, Minnesota, New Jersey, North Carolina, Rhode Island,

Texas, Virginia, and Wisconsin) have what are known as Child Access Prevention (CAP) laws. These laws impose criminal penalties on gun owners who negligently store firearms, if a child gains access to a gun and uses it to cause harm. Bills for a federal CAP law have been introduced in Congress without success. Depending on the state, gun owners may not be subject to penalty if the gun was stored with a trigger lock or in a lockbox, if the child gained access to the gun by illegal entry, or if the gun was kept in "close proximity" to the owner. (See Andrew J. Mc-Clurg, *Child Access Prevention Laws: A Common Sense Approach to Gun Control*, 18 St. Louis University Public Law Review 47 [1999], analyzing all state CAP laws.) Should gun owners be required to keep their guns locked up? Should they be subject to criminal penalties if they fail to do so and if children gain access to the guns and use them to cause harm? Should gun owners be subject to civil liability in these cases? The NRA Web site admonishes gun owners, "Store guns so that they are inaccessible to children and other unauthorized users," adding that "[g]un shops sell a wide variety of safes, cases, and other security devices" for accomplishing this goal (*A Parent's Guide to Gun Safety*, National Rifle Association.

A study by two physicians of the effects of CAP laws in twelve states claimed to find that unintentional firearm-related deaths among children younger than fifteen were 23 percent lower than expected. (Peter Cummings and Frederick P. Rivara, *State Gun Safe Storage Laws and Child Mortality due to Firearms*, 278 Journal of the American Medical Association 1084 [1997].) The authors attributed the lower death rate to the CAP laws. Critics of the study said that almost all the decline was attributable to Florida, and that the study did not control for the possible influence of the NRA's "Eddie Eagle" gun safety program (which was introduced at about the same time as the Florida CAP law).

Two other researchers conducted a statistical study that reached an opposite conclusion. They said they found "no consistent evidence that safe storage laws reduce accidental gun deaths. . . . [O]ne possible reason for these laws not having an effect is that accidental deaths primarily occur among the not so law-abiding segments of society, and these groups do not appear to care very much whether a law exists regarding the storage of guns. . . . [F]or 15 to 19 year olds, there is some weak evidence that gun suicides are reduced by safe storage laws, but whatever benefit is produced is offset by these teenagers switching to other methods to kill themselves." The study also claimed rapes, robberies, and burglaries rise by 9, 11, and 6 percent, respectively, as a result of safe storage laws and that states with safe storage laws could be expected to experience 168 more murders in the first full year that the law is in effect. (John R. Lott Jr. and John E. Whitley, *Safe Storage Gun Laws: Accidental Deaths, Suicides, and Crime,* Yale Law School, Program for Studies in Law, Economics, and Public Policy, Working Paper no. 237 [2000].)

Do you think that CAP laws (or publicity about CAP laws) can produce effects—either beneficial or harmful—as large as the two different studies suggest? Do you favor CAP laws or oppose them?

6. Would you support a federal law requiring that all guns be stored in a particular way? In Canada, all firearms must be stored unloaded, and no firearm may be stored with ammunition unless the ammunition is kept in a separate, locked container. Moreover, all firearms must be stored in a manner that renders them inoperable. For most firearms, this requires that they be stored with an attached locking device and kept in a securely locked container or room that cannot be easily broken open or in a locked vault or room that has been specifically constructed for the purpose of securely storing firearms. (See *Storage, Display, Transportation and Handling of Firearms by Individuals, Regulations under the Firearms Act,* Consolidated Regulations of Canada SOR/98-209: 5(a), 6(a) [1998].) In England, gun owners are required to keep their guns in high-quality safes, and the police may conduct home inspections before issuing or renewing a gun license, and less frequently, during the period the license is in effect. (Joseph E. Olson and David B. Kopel, *All the Way Down the Slippery Slope: Gun Prohibition in England and Some Lessons for Civil Liberties in America,* 22 Hamline Law Review 399, 423–24 [1999].) In Canada, the police have the authority to enter homes with "reasonable" notice based on either a warrant or the consent of the owner in order to inspect storage conditions. ([Canadian] Firearms Act, Consolidated Statutes of Canada §§ 102–104.) Do these laws violate privacy, protect criminals, or increase safety? All three?

7. Can you spot the risk-utility trade-off quandary in requiring safe gun

storage? Gun rights proponents argue that requiring safe storage decreases the usefulness of guns for self-defense by interfering with their accessibility when needed. For example, John Lott has argued against requiring locks on guns, stating: "[L]ocked, unloaded guns offer far less protection from intruders and so requiring locks would likely greatly increase deaths resulting from crimes." (See John R. Lott Jr., *Childproof Gun Locks: Bound to Misfire*, Wall Street Journal, July 16, 1997, at A22.) McClurg responds to this argument as follows:

> There are at least four reasons why the "interference with self-defense" argument in the context of safe storage lacks merit. First, most gun owners lack the ability to effectively use even their negligently stored guns in self-defense. As gun experts know, simply "having" a gun does not make it useful for self-defense. Effective self-defense using a firearm requires, like every other skill in life, an organized plan and practice to implement it. In an article on the use of firearms for home defense, a leading expert summed up his advice as follows, "Train yourself or, better yet, get yourself trained." However, too many gun owners simply buy a gun, load it and store it, with no thought about what to do with it if they need it. "Somewhere in the closet," one friend said, when asked where her handgun was kept stored. Rehearsing self-defense drills with a safely stored gun would result in much quicker response times than most gun owners could presently muster with their unsecured guns.
>
> Second, manufacturers are developing a variety of safe storage devices made with quick access in mind. These devices are designed to be opened or released in a matter of seconds, even in total darkness.
>
> Third, gun experts, including those writing for pro-gun audiences in pro-gun magazines, agree that guns must be stored in a manner to prevent them from being accessed by unauthorized users. These experts presumably know of what they speak.
>
> Fourth, and perhaps most telling, despite John Lott's dramatic claim of a "greatly increase[d]" death rate from crime resulting from safely stored guns, there is not a single recorded incident of a person suffering injury from a criminal due to an inability to gain access to a secured

firearm. This is true even though fourteen states (including three of the nation's four most populous states in California, Florida and Texas) have Child Access Prevention laws. . . . If safe gun storage really interfered with self-defense, is it not reasonable to expect that there would be at least some evidence to support that claim? (Andrew J. McClurg, *Armed and Dangerous: Tort Liability for the Negligent Storage of Firearms*, 32 Connecticut Law Review 1189, 1212–13 [2000].)

8. In Merced, California, in August 2000, a pitchfork-wielding man attacked and murdered Jessica Carpenter's seven-year-old brother and nine-year-old sister while their parents were not home. Jessica's father kept a gun in the home that was, in accordance with the California CAP law, locked up. According to the family, Jessica, age fourteen, is a very good shot, and had the gun not been securely stored, Jessica might have been able to retrieve it and use it to fend off the murderer. Do you think it would be a good or bad idea for parents to leave firearms accessible to their minor children when the parents are away from home, so that the children could use the guns to defend themselves from possible criminal attack?

9. McClurg argues that safe gun storage would help reduce accidental shootings, suicides, and criminal misuse of stolen guns. Do you think mandating safe firearms storage is "worth the candle" in terms of the trade-off between safety and reduced utility of guns for self-protection? Numerous studies have been conducted of firearm storage practices. One study of all fifty states estimates that 6.8 million U.S. households contain at least one loaded and unlocked gun, including 1.8 million households with children. (Gail Stennies et al., *Firearm Storage Practices and Children in the Home, United States, 1994*, 153 Archives of Pediatrics and Adolescent Medicine 586, 588 [1999].) Other studies have found that more than 50 percent of handguns are stored unlocked. (Yvonne Senturia et al., *Children's Household Exposure to Guns: A Pediatric Practice-based Survey*, 93 Pediatrics 469 (1994). See McClurg, *Armed and Dangerous: Tort Liability for the Negligent Storage of Firearms, supra*, at 1190–1200, summarizing ten gun storage studies.) Is it responsible for a gun owner to store a gun that is loaded and unlocked? That is unloaded but unlocked? Does it depend on whether children are present in the

household? Whether the gun owner lives in a high-crime neighbor-hood? Other factors?

10. Gun rights advocates argue that mechanical locking devices, even those that manufacturers claim can be removed in a few seconds by the owner, are not always reliable. They point to a well-publicized incident in which Maryland governor Parris Glendening, a gun control advo-cate, conducted an unsuccessful public demonstration of a gun lock-ing device in which he fumbled with the lock for nearly two minutes and was able to remove it only with assistance. Removal of the device required pushing a button of which the governor was unaware. (There was no indication the device malfunctioned.) How reliable do locking devices have to be in order not to interfere unacceptably with defensive firearm use? Always readily removable by any authorized user, even in the dark and under stress? Removable 99 percent of the time? A lower percentage, and if so, what? If one views civilian defensive gun use as categorically unwise or immoral, does this change the calculation? Does your percentage change if, rather than viewing the reliability and ease of removal of the gun-locking device in isolation, you balance those factors against the reduction in access to guns by unauthorized users such as children, criminals and potential adolescent suicide at-tempters that can result from safe storage?

D. The Financial Costs of Firearms Crime

Firearms deaths and injuries impose substantial financial costs on victims and society. These include not only the direct medical costs of treating gun-shot injuries but the financial value of other tangibles and intangibles such as property loss, mental health care for crime victims and their survivors, police and emergency services, lost wages and productivity, and lost qual-ity of life.

Several studies have attempted to estimate the direct costs of treating gunshot injuries. In 2000, Philip Cook and Jens Ludwig authored *Gun Vi-olence: The Real Costs* (New York: Oxford University Press), an elaboration of an article by Philip J. Cook et al., *The Medical Costs of Gunshot Injuries in the United States*, 282 Journal of the American Medical Association 447

(1999). Although previous researchers have attempted to estimate gunshot costs, the Cook study appears to be more reliable than previous attempts because it employed the most up-to-date sources available and larger samples of patients.

Intentional self-inflicted gunshot wounds resulted in average medical costs of $5,400 per gunshot victim who sought medical care (because most such injuries are instantly effective suicides and thus cause few medical costs); gun assault injuries averaged $18,400 in medical costs; accidental shootings averaged $22,400. Cook and Ludwig estimated that there were 113,000 gunshot wounds in 1997, with a total of $1.9 billion in treatment costs over the victims' lives. Sixty percent of these costs were attributable to the 2 percent of gunshot wounds that cause spinal cord injury (Cook and Ludwig, *Gun Violence*, at 65).

Because some gunshot victims (like smokers) die prematurely, they do not consume medical services that would otherwise have been spent on them over the course of their lives. Accounting for this unfortunate form of cost savings is estimated to reduce the net medical cost of gun injuries by about half (see *id.* at 71). The study also sought to determine the source of payment for gunshot-related medical costs. It estimated that government (i.e., taxpayers) pays 49 percent of the total cost; private insurance pays for 18 percent; and 33 percent comes from other sources, such as self-pay (see *id.* at 68). Because many victims of gun injuries are indigent, the government share of medical costs is much higher than for medical costs in general.

Because a person who is killed is eliminated from the labor force (either in a paying job or in the home), the lifetime estimated earnings and household-production losses per person from fatal gunshot injuries is between $460,000 and $580,000 (*id.* at 77). The Cook and Ludwig estimate accounts for the fact that gunshot victims tend to be poorer and less educated than the overall population. While the earning loss may be catastrophic to the victim's family, there may be no net economic effect on society. Cook and Ludwig explain that a person's economic benefit to society is the excess of his production over his consumption. Given the lower socioeconomic status of many firearms victims, the aggregate impact on society of lost economic productivity appears to be small. Depending on assumptions about worker replacement via immigration, there may be no net impact at all (*id.* at 81–83). Do these findings trouble you? Why?

Besides the obvious financial issues of medical care and lost years of work, there are other financial costs of guns that are more difficult to quantify. These include the expense of security measures (including airline-passenger screening); activities that are avoided because, for example, a person is afraid to go out at night; and emotional suffering (difficult to quantify in dollars). Of course, to whatever extent guns prevent or reduce crime (see chapter 1), there are corresponding benefits, such as avoided medical costs to those who might otherwise be victims of gun or other crime.

DISCUSSION NOTES

1. Although the costs of firearm injuries are difficult to pin down, they are substantial by any measure. Who should pay these costs? Should firearms makers, who profit from the sale of guns, be required to share some of the costs? Or would this be like making automobile manufacturers pay for the costs of drunk driving and other automobile crimes? (Chapter 6 examines the potential civil liability of gun manufacturers.) Should gun owners, who directly benefit from firearms, pay a portion of the costs?

2. Are gun owners already saving money for everyone, by improving personal and community defense (as discussed in chapter 1)? Or are they costing everyone money by increasing the risks of accidental shootings, lethal domestic violence, suicides, and the criminal misuse of stolen guns? (From 1985 to 1994, an annual average of 274,000 firearms were reported stolen, from all sources. See Marianne W. Zawitz, U.S. Department of Justice, *Guns Used in Crime* 3 [1995].)

3. Would you favor a special tax on firearms and/or ammunition sales to help defray the costs of firearms injuries? Would such a tax violate the Second Amendment or similar provisions in state constitutions? Regarding the First Amendment, the Supreme Court has held that it is constitutional to apply general taxes to the press (e.g., sales taxes) but not to apply special taxes aimed at suppressing newspapers. (See *Grosjean v. American Press Co.*, 297 U.S. 233 [1936], finding that a 2 percent gross receipts tax on large circulation newspapers violated the First Amendment; *Follett v. McCormick*, 321 U.S. 573 [1944], striking a "flat license" tax on evangelists and preachers.) Would you view special taxes on firearms as aimed at suppressing Second Amendment rights or as a

legitimate means to offset some of the societal costs of firearms? Do you place First Amendment rights and Second Amendment rights on the same plane of importance? If not, which right do you consider more important? Are they inter-connected?

E. FEAR

Fear is another intangible cost of firearms in our society. Surveys consistently show crime to be a top concern of the American public. Although some recent surveys show that fear of crime has declined concomitant with the nationwide decline in violent crime during the 1990s, it remains on the minds of most Americans. For example, a March 2000 Minnesota poll of 1,021 adults found that fear of crime had dropped to its lowest level in seventeen years. Nevertheless, the respondents still ranked "crime, drugs and violence" as the second most important problem facing the country. (These surveys were conducted before the terror attacks on the United States.) The essay excerpted below discusses some of the consequences to society of fearing crime. Although the essay addresses fear of crime in general, there can be little doubt that guns play a major role in the public's fear of crime.

FEAR OF CRIME IN THE UNITED STATES: AVENUES FOR RESEARCH AND POLICY

(4 Measurement and Analysis of Crime and Justice 452 [National Institute of Justice 2000], at http://www.ojp.usdoj.gov/nij/ criminal_justice2000/vol4_2000.html)

Mark Warr

Criminal events, at their most elemental level, are frightening events. They are reminders to all that the world is not a safe place, that danger can strike at any time or location, and that life, in the end, is tenuous and precious.

Some three decades ago . . . the President's Commission on Law Enforcement and Administration of Justice offered this brief but trenchant observation: "The most damaging of the effects of violent crime is fear,

and that fear must not be belittled." That statement prefigured a fundamental shift in the way that criminologists think about the consequences
of crime, one that was to heavily influence the course of criminological research in years to come. To fully understand the social consequences of
crime, criminologists came to realize, investigators cannot focus merely on
those who become direct victims of crime. Important as these individuals
surely are, researchers must also concentrate on those who suffer forms of
indirect victimization, the most egregious of which is fear of crime.

In the final analysis, what makes fear of crime so important as a social
problem is the depth and breadth of its consequences for our society.
Over the years, investigators have identified many behavioral precautions
associated with fear of crime. These range from relatively trivial and
nearly universal behaviors (e.g., turning on lights and locking doors
when leaving home) to more personally and socially consequential actions (not leaving the house at night or going out alone).

What is often missing in research on fear of crime, however, are studies of the large-scale social consequences of fear. To illustrate, it appears
that the ecology of American cities is regulated to a considerable degree
by fear of crime. According to survey data, the single most common reaction to fear of crime in the United States is spatial avoidance; that is,
staying away from places that are perceived to be dangerous. In surveys
of Seattle and Dallas, for example, 63 percent and 77 percent of respondents, respectively, reported that they "avoided certain places in the city,"
and when Dallas residents were asked to identify the most dangerous
areas of their city, more than four of five reported that they did not go
near or through those areas regularly. Along with spatial avoidance per
se, fear of crime also seems to affect the routes that people take when they
travel, the form of transportation they employ, and the times they choose
to leave their residence.

Such habits of avoidance must inevitably affect commerce, road use,
leisure activities, and social interaction. Retail businesses that are located
in putatively dangerous areas are likely to suffer a shortage of customers,
and reputedly dangerous neighborhoods are likely to find themselves socially isolated. Remarkably, however, there is no systematic evidence on
the financial impact of fear of crime on retail business, nor evidence on
the degree to which fear isolates neighborhoods from ordinary social

intercourse. The same is true when it comes to leisure activities. The impact of fear on interstate and intercity tourism is an obvious topic for research, but aside from occasional journalistic accounts (as in the infamous murders of tourists in Florida in the early 1990s), there is little research on the economic consequences of fear on tourism. Additionally, public use of facilities such as parks, beaches, campsites, and other recreational areas is surely affected by fear, but the nature and magnitude of this effect remains unknown.

There is another potential consequence of fear. Some commentators have remarked on the apparent tendency of Americans to spend increasing amounts of time, including their own leisure time, in their own homes, in what amounts to a general withdrawal from the outside world. The trend is sometimes described in humorous terms (like "couch potato") and supported by reference to sale of items such as big-screen TVs, home theaters, and hot tubs. Assuming that this trend is indeed under way, what are its causes? One cause, of course, may be public fear of crime and the avoidance behavior it engenders. Although survey data show little change in the prevalence of fear in recent decades, a significant national increase in fear did occur in the late 1960s. Even a constant crude prevalence rate of fear can produce changes in behavior if those changes stem from cumulative exposure to fear. If this process is in fact under way, its scale and depth are sobering: "free" society increasingly retreats to its dwellings in a form of asylum from an ostensibly dangerous world.

The asylum argument touches on a major longstanding controversy concerning fear of crime. Is fear ultimately a disintegrative force in a society? Does it disrupt normal social intercourse, making citizens afraid to greet or talk to one another, and undermine the civility and trust that makes civic life possible? When substantial portions of the American public are in fact afraid to leave their house at night, when they are afraid to travel on foot or traverse certain sections of their city, it is difficult to deny the power of fear to tear the social fabric asunder.

DISCUSSION NOTES

1. Do you or have you altered your daily life because of fear of being a victim of crime? In what ways?

2. Do firearms play a role in your fear? Suppose you avoid visiting or traveling through a particular part of town because it is known to be a high-crime area. Would you act differently if you knew to a certainty that no firearms were present? Would you be more fearful or less fearful to know that only the military and the police had guns? Only the military, the police, and determined criminals?

3. Do your main fears about crime involve crimes in which guns are used frequently? Gun are used in about 67 percent of homicides, 40 percent of robberies, and 7 percent of rapes. Or are your crime fears more tied to nonconfrontational crimes, such as auto theft?

4. Does gun ownership reduce fear by making gun owners feel more secure? If gun ownership reduces crime (particularly home-invasion burglaries), as is claimed by gun rights proponents (see discussion in chapter 1), does or should gun ownership reduce fear among non–gun owners?

5. Does the knowledge that many citizens, both criminals and law-abiding people, are armed affect your social interaction? In response to criminologist Gary Kleck's argument that widespread gun ownership serves as a check on criminals, Richard Alba and Steven Messner raised questions about the quality of life in a massively armed society. They expressed concern that in a society where most people are armed, citizens will be afraid to assert themselves in encounters with strangers, for instance, by honking their horns when cut off in traffic. They posit that fear is the primary emotion imposed by pervasive gun ownership and characterize the gains from guns as a check from criminals as "a hellish bargain" (Richard D. Alba and Steven F. Messner, *"Point Blank" against Itself: Evidence and Inference about Guns, Crime and Gun Control*, 11 Journal of Quantitative Criminology 391 [1995]). Do guns do more to increase or alleviate fear of crime? Does it depend on who owns the guns? On other factors? There are few communities in the United States in which there are not a substantial number of gun owners, although in some of those communities (e.g., parts of Manhattan), gun owners may not disclose their gun-owning status to their neighbors out of concern about being stigmatized. Should people fear their neighbors who own guns? Hypothesize that the availability of firearms in a society has the following effects: (a) it makes it too dangerous to honk at rude drivers

or similarly confront rude strangers; (b) it makes the violent-crime rate 10 percent lower than it would otherwise be. Is this "a hellish bargain" or a good deal? What if the violent-crime reduction were 1 percent? Fifty percent?

6. Is our fear of crime properly calibrated with the actual risk? Warr suggests that fear of criminal victimization is exaggerated, due largely to distorted reporting of crime by the news media:

> What is the image of crime presented in the mass media? A number of forms of distortion in news coverage of crime have been identified and documented, distortions that tend to exaggerate the frequency and the seriousness of crime. In the real world, for example, crimes occur in inverse proportion to this seriousness; the more serious the crime, the more rarely it occurs. Thus, in the United States, burglaries occur by the millions, robberies by the hundreds of thousands, and homicides by the thousands. In news coverage of crime, however, the emphasis is on "newsworthiness," and a key element of newsworthiness is seriousness; the more serious a crime, the more likely it is to be reported. By using seriousness as a criterion, however, the media are most likely to report precisely those crimes that are least likely to occur.
>
> Among other things, this "mirror image" depiction of crime means that the media place extraordinary emphasis on violent crime. Skogan and Maxfield reported that homicides and attempted homicides constituted one-half of all newspaper crime stories in the cities they examined, even though homicides are but a minute fraction of all offenses. (Warr, *Fear of Crime in the United States, supra,* at 467.)

Take a barometer reading of your own fear of being a victim of crime. Do you think it is an exaggerated fear, an accurate fear in which your perceived risk more or less correlates with actual risk, or do you think you underestimate the risk to yourself? The chance of being murdered at a public school is less than the chance of being killed by lightning. Why do you think the media report school murders so thoroughly, and lightning deaths hardly at all?

7. In *The Rhetoric of Gun Control,* McClurg criticized participants on both sides of the gun control debate for exploiting public fear to bolster support for their respective positions. On the pro-rights side, he cited ad-

vertisements by the NRA. After the 1992 Los Angeles riots that followed in the wake of a jury's decision to acquit most of the police officers charged with using excessive force against motorist Rodney King, the NRA ran a four-page advertisement featuring color pictures of looters and burning buildings and asking: "Must your glass be shattered? Must your flesh and blood be maimed? Must your livelihood be looted? Must all you've built be torn down? . . . What will it take before you stand up with the one group that will stand for no more?" In 1988 the NRA bought full-page newspaper advertisements suggesting that unarmed women are more likely to be victims of violent crime. One ad depicted a mangled locket under the headline "Your mother just surprised two burglars who don't like surprises." Another showed a high-heeled shoe with the heel broken off and read: "He's followed you for two weeks. He'll rape you in two minutes."

On the pro-control side, McClurg cited a speech by Senator Edward Kennedy (D-Mass.) urging passage of gun control legislation. In just the first four paragraphs of the speech, Kennedy used emotionally loaded words and phrases such as "fusillade of bullets," "carnage," "assassin," "fears and . . . tears," "haunted," "end the arms race in our neighborhoods," "relentless toll climbs higher," "epidemic," and "plagues the Nation." (See Andrew J. McClurg, *The Rhetoric of Gun Control*, 42 American University Law Review 53, 65–70 [1992].)

Gun manufacturers have been accused of exploiting women's fear of violent crime as a way to boost product sales. (See Joy Horowitz, *Arms and the Woman*, Harper's Bazaar, Feb. 1994, at 166, calling gun manufacturer advertisements designed to market guns to women "a classic study in the exploitation of fear." See chapter 5 for more discussion of this issue.) Do you see problems for society in using fear as a rhetorical tool? Warr argues that reducing fear is not necessarily an unqualified social good, because some fear may be warranted. Artificial fear reduction may induce people to fail to take necessary safety precautions against real risks of crime. In contrast, if we "turn the [fear] dial too far to the right, people would engage in needless precautions and unnecessarily constrain their own lives. At the extreme is a 'fortress society' in which citizens withdraw from public life altogether and everyday social intercourse is sharply curtailed" (Warr, *Fear of Crime in the United States, supra*, at 461).

8. In 1998, 670,500 victims of violent crimes (robbery, aggravated assault, and sexual assault) faced attackers who were armed with a firearm. (See *Firearms and Crime Statistics,* Bureau of Justice Statistics, U.S. Department of Justice, at http://www.ojp.usdoj.gov/bjs/guns.htm.) From 1993 to 1997, an estimated 19.2 million incidents of nonfatal violent crime occurred. Twenty-eight percent of these crimes were committed with a firearm. Four percent of violent-crime victims suffered injury. Fewer than 1 percent suffered gunshot wounds. (See Marianne W. Zawitz and Kevin J. Strom, *Firearm Injury and Death from Crime, 1993–97, NCJ-182993,* Bureau of Justice Statistics, U.S. Department of Justice, at 2 [2000].) Do these data increase or decrease your fear of being the victim of a gun crime? Of being shot during such a crime?

9. Thirty-three states now have laws permitting persons to carry concealed handguns. Do you think people who carry concealed weapons have a greater or lesser fear of crime than those who do not carry concealed weapons? Or does it depend on the person?

10. A variety of studies show that people tend to exaggerate rare but catastrophic events (e.g., the chance of dying in a commercial jet crash) and to underestimate more mundane risks (e.g., the risks of heart disease). (See generally, W. Kip Viscusi, *Fatal Tradeoffs: Public and Private Responsibilities for Risk* [1995].) As an exercise, ask three people you know to estimate: the number of gun homicides in the United States each year; the number of gun suicides; the number of fatal gun accidents; the number of fatal gun accidents involving children fourteen years or younger; the number of guns in the United States (not counting guns owned by the military). Record their answers and bring them to class for purposes of comparison. How accurate are their answers? What implications does public misinformation about the risks of firearms have for the possibility of public participation in the creation of rational gun policy?

PHILOSOPHICAL ROOTS OF THE RIGHT TO ARMS AND OF OPPOSITION TO THAT RIGHT

This chapter examines the philosophical roots in support of and in opposition to a right to arms. The chapter does not address legal materials, which are covered in chapter 4. Necessarily, the chapter is weighted toward advocates of a right to arms, since they are the ones who have discussed the importance of such a right. It also includes writings by political philosophers who have discussed the potential dangers of widespread arms possession. In addition, the chapter looks at the right (or duty) of self-defense. As we shall see below, the existence of a right of self-defense is one of the key issues in the modern gun control and gun rights debate. (Self-defense is also discussed extensively in chapter 1, which analyzes the benefits of guns to society.)

As you read these entries, consider the different rationales offered by the various philosophers in favor of arms rights: maintenance of political order and prevention of tyranny, community protection against outside invasion, and personal defense. Note also the continuing dialogue between those who believe a country should be defended by a professional standing army and those who favor a citizen militia.

A. Self-Defense as a Natural Right

Among the most studied of the classical authors was the great Roman orator Cicero (106–43 B.C.). One of his most famous speeches grew out of the infamous trial of T. Annius Milo in 52 B.C. Milo and Clodius were rival demagogues and gang leaders in the decaying Roman Republic. When Milo and his gang ran into Clodius and his gang on the Appian Way (the main intercity road), Clodius ended up dead. Milo was put on trial, with Cicero serving as his defense attorney. While Cicero wrote a brilliant argument in Milo's defense, he was intimidated into not delivering it after Milo's enemy Pompey surrounded the courtroom with troops. Although Milo was deprived of the benefits of Cicero's eloquence, history was not. The written version of the speech survived, to be studied by many high school and grammar school students in colonial America and the early Republic.

In Defence of Titus Annius Milo
(in *Selected Political Speeches of Cicero*, ed. and
trans. Michael Grant, 222, 234 [1969])

Cicero

[T]here exists a law, not written down anywhere but inborn in our hearts; a law which comes to us not by training or custom or reading but by derivation and absorption and adoption from nature itself; a law which has come to us not from theory but from practice, not by instruction but by natural intuition. I refer to the law which lays it down that, if our lives are endangered by plots or violence or armed robbers or enemies, any and every method of protecting ourselves is morally right. When weapons reduce them to silence, the laws no longer expect one to await their pronouncements. For people who decide to wait for these will have to wait for justice, too, and meanwhile they must suffer injustice first. Indeed, even the wisdom of a law itself, by sort of tacit implication, permits self-defense, because it does not actually forbid men to kill; what it does, instead, is to forbid the bearing of a weapon with the intention to kill. When, therefore, inquiry passes beyond the mere question of the weapon and starts to consider the motive, a man who has used arms in self-defense is not regard is having carried with a homicidal aim. . . . [M]y defence is that [Milo] was justified in acting to save his life. Civilized people are taught by logic, barbarians by necessity, communities by tradition; and the lesson is inculcated even in wild beasts by nature itself. They learn that they have to defend their own bodies and persons and lives from violence of any and every kind by all the means within their power.

Hugo Grotius (1583–1645) is generally considered the father of international law. In 1625 he published *De Jure Belli ac Pacis* (The law of war and peace), which was one of the first attempts to synthesize what was then known as the law of nations. The work is divided into three books: the first considers whether any war is just; the second concerns the causes of wars, property and personal rights affected by war, the rights secured by compacts, and the interpretations of treaties, among other topics; the third asks what is lawful war and addresses issues of military conventions and of the resolution of war.

THE RIGHTS OF WAR AND PEACE
(ed. A. C. Campbell, 76–77, 83 [1901])

Hugo Grotius

[W]hen our lives are threatened with immediate danger, it is lawful to kill the aggressor, if the danger cannot otherwise be avoided. . . . [T]his kind of defence derives its origin from the principle of self-preservation, which nature has given to every living creature. . . . For I am not bound to submit to the danger or mischief intended, any more than to expose myself to the attacks of a wild beast. [Though the danger must be immediate,] [i]t must be confessed, that when an assailant seizes any weapon with an apparent intention to kill me I have a right to anticipate and prevent the danger. What has been already said of the right of defending our persons and property . . . may nevertheless be applied to public hostilities. . . . [S]overeign powers have a right not only to avert, but to punish wrongs. From whence they are authorised to prevent a remote as well as an immediate aggression. . . .

Thomas Hobbes (1588–1679) was an English philosopher and political theorist, best known for his work *Leviathan*. In it Hobbes noted that in the state of nature "the life of man [is] solitary, poore, nasty, brutish, and short," and that "during the time men live without a common Power to keep them all in awe, they are in that condition which is called Warre; and such a warre, as is of every man, against every man." It was, therefore, the first order of government to provide security for persons and property. Failure to do so was the only instance in which overthrow of the government was permissible, according to Hobbes.

LEVIATHAN
(ed. Richard Tuck, 98 [1991])

Thomas Hobbes

A Covenant not to defend my selfe from force, by force, is alwayes voyd. For . . . no man can transferre, or lay down his Right to save himselfe from Death, Wounds, and Imprisonment . . . and therefore the promise of not resisting force, in no Covenant transferreth any right; nor is obliging.

John Locke's (1632–1704) *Second Treatise on Government* is the classic statement of government predicated on the "consent of the governed" and constituted to secure "life, liberty, and property." Locke's *Second Treatise* and its philosophy informed the drafting of the Declaration of Independence, as well as other aspects of revolutionary and constitutional thought in first the colonies, then the United States of America.

SECOND TREATISE ON GOVERNMENT
(in *Two Treatises on Government*, ed. Peter Laslett, 278–81, 284, 411, 417 [1988])

John Locke

The *State of War* is a State of Enmity and Destruction; And therefore declaring by Word or Action . . . a sedate setled Design, upon another Mans Life, *puts him in a State of War* with him against whom he has declared such an Intention, and so has exposed his Life to the others Power to be taken away by him, or any one that joyns with him in his Defence, and espouses his Quarrel: it being reasonable and just I should have a Right to destroy that which threatens me with Destruction. For *by the Funda-*

mental Law of Nature . . . one may destroy a Man who makes War upon him . . . for the same Reason, that he may kill a *Wolf* or a *Lyon*; because such Men are not under the ties of the Common Law of Reason, have no other Rule, but that of Force and Violence, and so may be treated as Beasts of Prey. . . .

And hence it is, that he who attempts to get another Man into his Absolute Power, does thereby *put himself into a State of War* with him; It being . . . a Declaration of a Design upon his Life. For . . . he who would get me into his Power without my consent, would use me as he pleased, when he had got me there, and destroy me too when he had fancy to it: for no body can desire to *have me in his Absolute Power*, unless it be to compel me by force to that, which is against the Right of my Freedom, *i.e.* make me a Slave. To be free from such force is the only security of my Preservation. . . . He that in the State of Nature, *would take away the Freedom*, that belongs to any one in that State, must necessarily be supposed to have a design to take away every thing else, that *Freedom* being the Foundation of all the rest: As he that in the State of Society would take away the *Freedom* belonging to those of that Society or Commonwealth, must be supposed to design to take away from them every thing else, and so to be looked on as *in a State of War.*

This makes it Lawful for a Man to *kill a Thief*, who has not in the least hurt him, nor declared any design upon his Life, any farther then by the use of Force, so to get him in his Power, as to take away his Money, or what he pleases from him: because using force, where he has no Right, to get me in his Power, let his pretence be what it will, I have no reason to suppose, that he, who would *take away my Liberty*, would not when he had me in his Power, take away everything else. And therefore it is Lawful for me to treat him, as one who has put *himself into a State of War* with me, *i.e.* kill him if I can; for to that hazard does he justly expose himself, whoever introduces a State of War, and is *aggressor* in it. . . .

[While persons in civil society were obliged to seek redress for wrongs under the law, Locke argued that where law] cannot interpose to secure my Life from present force, which if lost, is capable of no reparation, [natural law] permits me to kill the aggressor, because the aggressor allows not time to appeal to our common Judge, nor the decision of the law, for remedy in a Case, where the mischief may be irreparable. [Or, as

Locke colorfully put it later in the book: "The Law could not restore Life to my dead Carcass."] . . .

[Equating slavery with a sort of civil death to be resisted according to the natural law of self-preservation, Locke noted that compacts where one enslaved one's self by submission to absolute authority were akin to civil suicide and were likewise contrary to the law of nature.] For a Man, not having the Power of his own Life, *cannot,* by Compact, or his own Consent, *enslave himself* to any one, nor put himself under the Absolute, Arbitrary Power of another, to take away his Life, when he pleases. . . .

[Locke, in a response to Hobbes, argued that a people may dissolve a government that attempts to exercise absolute power over its citizens to the point where the citizens become no better than slaves.] To tell *People* they may *provide for themselves,* by erecting a new Legislature, when by Oppression, Artifice, or being delivered over to a Foreign Power, their old one is gone, is only to tell them they may expect Relief, when it is too late, and the evil is past Cure. This is in effect no more than to bid them first to be Slaves, and then to take care of their Liberty; and when their Chains are on, tell them, they may act like Freemen. . . . Men can never be secure from Tyranny, if there be no means to escape it, till they are perfectly under it: And therefore it is, that they have not only a Right to get out of it, but to prevent it. . . .

If the innocent honest Man must quietly quit all he has for Peace sake, to him who will lay violent hands upon it, I desire it may be consider'd, what a kind of Peace there will be in the World, which consists only in Violence and Rapine; and which is to be maintain'd only for the benefit of the Robbers and Oppressors. Who would not think it an admirable Peace betwixt the Mighty and the Mean, when the Lamb, without resistance, yielded his Throat to be torn by the imperious Wolf?

At the age of twenty-six, the Italian Cesare Beccaria (1738–1794) found himself an international celebrity following the publication of his masterwork *On Crime and Punishment (Delitti e delle pene)*. Beccaria's book created both the modern social science of criminology and the first systematic theory of criminal behavior and public policy control of crime. He denounced torture, secret trial, corrupt judges, and degrading punishments. Thomas Jefferson liked *On Crime and Punishment* so much that he carefully copied many lengthy passages, including the one excerpted here, into his "Commonplace Book," containing Jefferson's favorite sayings.

ON CRIME AND PUNISHMENT

(in *On Crime and Punishment and Other Essays,* trans. Richard Davies, Virginia Cox, and Richard Bellamy, ed. Richard Bellamy, 101 [1995])

Cesare Beccaria

It is a false idea of utility that sacrifices a thousand real advantages for a single chimerical or unimportant disadvantage, that would deprive men of fire because it burns or water because it drowns, and only remedy evils by destruction.

The laws which forbid men to bear arms are of this sort. They only disarm those who are neither inclined nor determined to commit crimes. Can it be supposed that those who have the courage to violate the most sacred laws of humanity and the most important in the civil code will respect the lesser and more arbitrary laws, which are easier and less risky to break, and which, if enforced, would take away the personal freedom— so dear to man and to the enlightened lawgiver—and subject the innocent man to all the annoyances which the guilty deserve? These laws make the victims of attack worse off and improve the position of the assailant. They do not reduce the murder rate but increase it, because an unarmed man can be attacked with more confidence than an armed man. These laws are not preventative but fearful of crime, they originate from the disturbing impression arising out of a few particular cases rather than from a reasonable consideration of the advantages and disadvantages of a universal law.

DISCUSSION NOTES

1. Consider the quotation from Cicero. Is the state morally or legally required to permit individuals to kill in self-defense? If self-defense is

permitted, is there an argument that individuals must also be afforded the means by which self-defense can be secured, for example, the right to own firearms? (See Victoria Dorfman and Michael Koltonyuk, *When the Ends Justify the Means: Self Defense and the Right to Counsel*, 3 Texas Review of Law and Politics 381 [1999]); Samuel C. Wheeler III, *Self-Defense: Rights and Coerced Risk-Acceptance*, 11 Public Affairs Quarterly 431 [Oct. 1997].)

2. Is the perceived need to own guns for purposes of self-defense tied to the fact that we are a nation where about a quarter of a billion firearms are owned by private citizens? In other words, does the very risk presented by gun proliferation in the United States support the utility of guns for self-defense purposes? Which of the following countries would you feel safer living in: Country A, in which citizens are free to own guns for self-defense but large numbers of criminals also own guns, or Country B, in which citizens are prohibited from owning guns for self-defense but few criminals own guns? Would your answer depend on the government's ability to ensure that the ability of criminals to obtain guns is negligible?

3. Does the right of self-defense require that all means must be made available, or may the state impose limitations? May it ban the most effective means, if inferior ones remain available? Does it depend on whether the practical effect would be that aggressors would also be less (significantly less?) likely to acquire the most effective means for causing harm?

4. If self-defense is a right, do laws that make gun ownership less affordable for some poor people violate that right? What about laws that make it illegal for all felons to possess firearms, even after completing their prison, parole, or probation sentence? Since 1968, federal law has imposed on all convicted felons a lifetime ban on gun possession (18 *U.S. Code* § 922[g]). Do you agree with this ban, or do you think it deprives convicted felons of their most effective means for exercising their right to self-defense? Should it apply only to some felons (e.g., those who have committed recent violent or all violent armed felonies) and not to others (e.g., those who committed nonviolent tax- or drug-law violations)? Historically, hardly any states imposed lifetime gun possession bans for all felonies. Since 1996, persons convicted of domestic-violence misde-

meanors (violence against any person in one's family or household) have also been banned for life from possessing guns. This ban applies retroactively, so that a 1964 conviction now operates as a lifetime ban. Do you agree with this law? What about for other misdemeanors, such as possession of drug paraphernalia? Should all persons convicted of any misdemeanor be prohibited from possessing a gun?

5. The above writings all precede the development of professional police forces. Since modern American communities have full-time, professional police forces, could it be said that all self-defense needs are taken care of by the government? Most such needs? If so, could a state ban all homicides, even those undertaken in self-defense? Even if police protection is imperfect, could a state ban all defensive killings on the grounds that they are disorderly, as England did in the early years of the second millennium? Should states approve defensive killings where justified but impose additional restrictions on the availability of guns?

6. Note Locke's statement that it is "Lawful for a Man to *kill a Thief,* who has not in the least hurt him, nor declared any design upon his Life." Do you agree? Should citizens have a lawful right to shoot persons who try to steal, for example, their wallet or car stereo? Do you view Locke's perspective on killing thieves as extremist or sound? If the former, does this call into question his other views on the issues of self-defense?

7. Thomas Jefferson liked Beccaria's quotation so much that Jefferson copied it into his personal "Commonplace Book" of favorite quotations. To what extent does the philosophical basis for the right to arms depend on whether Beccaria and Jefferson were empirically correct in their criticism of gun prohibition? To what extent does their philosophical basis for the right to arms depend on the time in which they lived, a time when communities were regularly subject to attack by invading states and native tribes? Or is the right to arms, like the right to freedom of speech or religion, a fundamental human right that does not depend on particular social circumstances? In *United States v. Cruikshank* (92 U.S. 542 [1875]), the U.S. Supreme Court appeared to suggest that the First Amendment right of assembly and the Second Amendment right to arms were both "found wherever civilization exists." (See chapter 4 for more on Supreme Court cases.)

8. Is self-defense "taking the law into one's hands"? Or is it merely performing a lawful act, in accordance with legal rules?

B. Arms Bearing as an Incident of Citizenship

Aristotle (384–322 B.C.) was a student of Plato and studied at Plato's Academy outside Athens. In *The Politics*, he criticized the theory of another philosopher (Hippodamus) who wanted a strict division of roles between skilled labor, agriculture, and defense.

The Politics
(in 2 *The Complete Works of Aristotle*, trans. Benjamin Jowett,
ed. Jonathan Barnes, 2108, 2109 [1984])

Aristotle

Let us then enumerate the functions of a state, and we shall easily elicit what we want. . . . [T]hirdly, there must be arms, for the members of a community have need of them, and in their own hands, too, in order to maintain authority both against disobedient subjects and against external assailants. . . . [S]ince it is an impossible thing that those who are able to use or to resist force should be willing to remain always in subjection . . . those who carry arms can always determine the fate of the constitution. . . . [The government should be confined to those who carry arms.]

DISCUSSION NOTES

1. In classical Greece, why was there such a strong connection between one's status as a free citizen and the ownership of arms? What about in our time?
2. Should persons wishing to own weapons be required, as a condition of ownership, to undergo training in their use? Or should all free adults (or free males?) be required to participate in training for community or national defense?

3. Throughout history, including in our own country during colonial times, only men were thought fit to carry arms. Has arms carrying by men, purportedly for the purpose, at least in part, of avoiding subjugation by tyrants, helped perpetuate the subjugation of women? (See chapter 5 for more discussion.) Does it trouble you that so many early statements on the right to bear arms portray the right as a necessary condition of liberty yet implicitly, and sometimes explicitly through law (such as Congress's 1792 Militia Act that required all males between the ages of eighteen and forty-five to enroll in the militia and supply their own arms), do not impose this obligation of citizenship on adult women?

Niccolo Machiavelli (1469–1527) was a Florentine statesman and political theorist. Although his most famous book, *The Prince*, has been mistaken as an apology for despotism, much of Machiavelli's writing is devoted to the maintenance and preservation of republics, exemplified for him by the glory of the ancient Roman Republic, before it was destroyed by the moral and political corruption of the citizens and emperors.

Machiavelli's political writings stress the need for a well-ordered republic to rely on armed citizen-soldiers organized in a militia for its defense, rather than relying on a professional or mercenary army, as many continental European nations did. Machiavelli greatly influenced English political theorist James Harrington, who in turn influenced the Founding Fathers. (On the connections between Machiavelli and later English "republican" theorists, for whom "standing armies" were anathema, see J. G. A. Pocock, *The Machiavellian Moment* [Princeton University Press, 1975].)

THE ART OF WAR
(in 2 *Machiavelli: The Chief Works and Others*,
trans. Allan Gilbert, 576 [1989])

Niccolo Machiavelli

A well-ordered city will . . . decree that [the] practice of warfare shall be used in times of peace for exercise and in times of war for necessity and for glory, and will allow the public alone to practice it as a profession, as did Rome. Any citizen who in such activity has another purpose is not a good citizen, and any city that conducts itself otherwise is not well governed.

DISCUSSION NOTES

1. The connection between full citizenship and the ability to bear arms, and conversely, the equation of being disarmed to being enslaved, recurs throughout Machiavelli's writings. Compare the following statement made in 1819 by a member of Britain's Parliament: "I hold that the distinctive difference between a free man and a slave is the right to possess arms, not so much, as has been stated, for the purpose of defending his property, as his liberty" (41 *The Parliamentary Debates from the Year 1803 to the Present Time*, ed. T. C. Hansard, 1130–31 [1819], statement of George Bennet, M.P., speaking in opposition to the Seizure of Arms Act in the House of Commons. See also *Dred Scott v. Sanford*, 60 U.S. 393, 417 [1856]: to recognize free blacks as citizens "would give them the full liberty . . . to keep and carry arms wherever they went.") Was this perceived connection between the deprivation of arms and deprivation of freedom ever historically valid? Explain in what circumstances this connection is or is not valid today.

2. Under federal law, the persons not permitted to possess firearms are convicted felons, fugitives from justice, unlawful users of controlled substances, adjudicated mental defectives, illegal aliens, persons who have been dishonorably discharged from the armed forces, U.S. citizens who have renounced their citizenship, persons subject to domestic-violence restraining orders, and persons who have been convicted of a misdemeanor crime for domestic violence (18 *U.S. Code* § 922[g]). Do you consider people in these categories to have been deprived of their freedom? Properly or improperly so? If you were a lawmaker, would you remove any of the above categories from the gun prohibition list? Would you add any categories of prohibited gun possessors? Minors, for example? No federal law prohibits long-gun possession by minors, although federal law does restrict handgun possession by people under eighteen, and allows sales from federally licensed dealers only to persons eighteen

and older (for long guns) or twenty-one and older (for handguns). Some states impose additional restrictions on gun purchases or possession (especially for handguns) by young people. If it were up to you, what age would you set as the minimum age to *possess* a long gun? A handgun? What age would you set as the minimum age to *purchase* a long gun? A handgun?

3. Is a person who will not take up arms to defend his country a bad person? A coward? Does it depend on the reason?

Thomas Jefferson (1743–1826) never lost his faith in the republican vision of the United States as an agrarian nation peopled with independent yeoman farmers. Jefferson fervently believed that the best defense for the nation was to be found in those sturdy yeoman, who would defend home and hearth with arms. In the letter below, Jefferson argues against restricting voting to people who have enough wealth to pay taxes. People who serve in the militia should also vote, even if they have little property, he suggests.

LETTER TO SAMUEL KERCHEVAL (JULY 12, 1816)
(in 10 *The Writings of Thomas Jefferson*, ed. Paul Leicester Ford, 39 [1898])

Thomas Jefferson

The true foundation of republican government is the equal right of every citizen, in his person and property, and in their management. . . . Let every man who fights or pays, exercise his just and equal right in their election.

Joel Barlow (1754–1812) was an American author and diplomat who, along with fellow Yale graduates John Trumbull and Timothy Dwight, sought to carve out a distinctively "American" identity in literature and the arts. While in England, Barlow wrote *Advice to the Privileged Orders*, in which he contrasted the form of government established in the United States with those then extant in Europe. *Advice* was considered so radical for its time that the British government sought to ban it.

ADVICE TO THE PRIVILEGED ORDERS

(in 1 *The Works of Joel Barlow,* ed. William K. Bottorff and Arthur L. Ford,
115, 116–17, 119, 160, 161–62 [1970])

Joel Barlow

In the United States of America, the science of liberty is universally understood, felt and practiced, as much by the simple as the wise, the weak as the strong. Their deep-rooted and inveterate habit of thinking is, that *all men are equal in their rights,* [and] that *it is impossible to make them otherwise.* . . . Many operations, which in Europe have been considered as incredible tales or dangerous experiments, are but the infalible consequences of this great principle. . . .

[One] of these operations is making every citizen a soldier, and every soldier a citizen; not only *permitting* every man to arm, but *obliging* him to arm. This fact told in Europe previous to the French Revolution, woul[d] have gained little credit; or at least it would have been regarded as a mark of an uncivilized people, extremely dangerous to a well-ordered society. . . . It is *because the people are civilized, that they are with safety armed.* It is an effect of their conscious dignity, as citizens enjoying equal rights that they wish not to invade the rights of others. The danger (where there is any) from armed citizens, is only to the *government,* not to the *society*; and as long as they have nothing to revenge in the government (which they cannot have while it is in their own hands) there are many advantages in their being accustomed to the use of arms, and no possible disadvantage. . . .

But it is said, These things will do very well for America . . . but they will not apply to Europe. This objection deserves a reply, not because it is solid, but because it is fashionable. . . . Let the people have time to become thoroughly and soberly grounded in the doctrine of *equality,* and there is no danger of oppression either from government or from anarchy. . . .

[To keep up] the military spirit of the noblesse [it is necessary to grant] titles and pensions, and to keep in pay a vast number of troops who know no other God but their king; who lose all ideas of themselves, in contemplating their officers; and who forget the duties of a man, to practice those of a soldier—this is but half the operation: an essential part of the military system is to disarm the people, to hold all the functions of war, as well the arm that executes, as the will that declares it, equally above their reach. This part of the system has a double effect, it palsies the hand and brutalizes the mind; an habitual disuse of physical forces totally destroys the moral; and men lose at once the power of protecting themselves, and of discerning the cause of their oppressions. . . .

Only admit the original, unalterable truth, *that all men are equal in their rights,* and the foundation of every thing is laid; to build the superstructure requires no effort but that of natural deduction. . . . Another deduction follows, That the people will be universally armed: they will assume those weapons for security, which the art of war has invented for destruction. You will then have removed the *necessity* of a standing army by the organization of the legislature, and the *possibility* of it by the arrangement of the militia; for it is as impossible for an armed soldiery to exist in an armed nation, as for a nobility to exist under an equal government. . . .

DISCUSSION NOTES

1. Are Americans today as morally fit to possess arms as were the Americans of Barlow's day? Would Barlow believe that today's American character degenerated because some people do not possess and practice with arms, because the people do not really govern themselves, or for other reasons?

2. For an argument that the Second Amendment and the right to bear arms depended on the existence of a virtuous and unified citizenry, and that once that precondition disappeared, the amendment ceased to have meaning, see David C. Williams, *Civic Republicanism and the Citizen Militia: The Terrifying Second Amendment,* 101 Yale Law Journal 551 (1991). Should other American rights be reevaluated in light of the (alleged) degeneration of American moral character?

   Barlow states that "[t]he danger . . . from armed citizens, is only to the government, not to the society," and that as long as armed citizens have no grievance against the government, "there are many advantages in their being accustomed to the use of arms, and no possible disadvantage." Do you agree? Is American society more advantaged or disadvantaged by the widespread availability of firearms? Would your views be different if you were living in Barlow's time?

3. A group of academics led by George Washington University professor Amitai Etzioni attempted to fashion an "ideology for the 1990s" that emphasized the duties and obligations citizens of a civil society owed to one another, as opposed to what they perceived as an excessive focus on individuals' rights against government and society. They used the term *communitarian* to describe their movement and promulgated a statement of their beliefs. In one part of their platform, they call the Second Amendment "a Communitarian clause" that "call[ed] for community militias, not individual gunslingers" (Brannon P. Denning and Glenn Harlan Reynolds, *It Takes a Militia: A Communitarian Case for Compulsory Arms Bearing*, 5 William and Mary Bill of Rights Journal 185, 186 [1996]). Yet, in the same section is a recommendation for "domestic disarmament" (*id.* at 194 and n. 66). Do you think that public safety would be enhanced by widespread, direct civil participation in law enforcement and national defense? Why or why not? Would your answer depend on whether citizens received training? Would you feel safer living in a neighborhood that had a neighborhood-watch program in which participants were armed? Might sensitivity to the civil rights of those being policed be enhanced if members of law enforcement came from the community they were policing and had to live there? Consider this passage from Denning and Reynolds's article:

> [T]he existence of a citizen militia responsible in some way for the security of a given community also might reintroduce responsibility into the administration of law enforcement. Although law enforcement officials formerly were liable . . . in trespass for improperly serving a search warrant or for breaking into the wrong house to make an arrest [certain legal concepts] now present almost insuperable barriers for citizens wishing to hold law enforcement officers accountable for mistakes or abuses. Further, the recent phenomenon of the "militarization" of law enforcement at all levels of government evokes sinister analogies to authoritarian regimes. . . . Professional law enforcement officers clad in Nomex coveralls and face shields, after all, hardly seem to represent the community even in their own minds, much less in the minds of

many onlookers. Encouraging communities to take responsibility for their security might also have the effect of making those charged with law enforcement duties *morally* responsible to their friends and neighbors, and thus help them exercise greater care and restraint in carrying out their law enforcement duties. Though many might raise the specter of vigilantism and argue for respecting the domain of law enforcement professionals, the recent behavior of some law enforcement agencies implies that a "professional" record is not always something to which communities should aspire. Likewise, charging members of a community with its security will sensitize them to the link between rights and responsibilities. Moreover, requiring that community members police the "rights-responsibilities" boundary will highlight the social cost that accompanies the exercise of rights in a diverse and plural community. (*Id.* at 208.)

Do you agree? Have the authors adequately addressed potential problems?

Does your neighborhood have a neighborhood-watch program? Do you participate? Why or why not? Would you be willing to serve as a member of an armed "citizen militia" to safeguard your neighborhood? Whose law enforcement views should prevail in a dispute between an armed citizen group and professional police officers? How would such disputes be resolved? Do you think armed citizen groups would lessen the tension between the police and communities? Aggravate it? How do you think police officers would view such groups?

Why do you think communitarians such as Professor Etzioni do not discuss the possibility of recreating community institutions that link gun ownership with community responsibility? Consider this possibility, suggested by Denning and Reynolds:

It is impossible to read the Communitarian literature without suspecting that the "community" envisioned by most Communitarians looks much like Ann Arbor, Michigan; Charlottesville, Virginia; or Cambridge, Massachusetts: communities with a disproportionate number of Volvos and Montessori schools. There is nothing wrong with such communities; they are nice places to live. It is a mistake, however, to think that the community values of Ann Arbor, for example, are the only ones that matter, or should matter. America possesses many communities where pickup trucks are more common than Volvos and where community members believe in values that Communitarians find unimportant, such as independence and the responsible use of arms. (*Id.* at 211.)

Would you trust your neighbors to police your community? Do you think they would do as good a job as professional law enforcement officers? For more on Communitarians, see David B. Kopel and Christopher C. Little, *Communitarians, Neorepublicans, and Guns: Assessing the Case for Firearms Prohibition*, 56 Maryland Law Review 438 [1997].)

C. THE PROPENSITY OF ABSOLUTE RULERS TO DISARM THEIR SUBJECTS

THE POLITICS
(in 2 *The Complete Works of Aristotle*, trans. Benjamin Jowett, ed. Jonathan Barnes, 2059, 2081 [1984])

Aristotle

The devices by which oligarchies deceive the people are five in number; they relate to . . . [4] the use of arms; [5] gymnastic exercises. . . . Concerning [4] the possession of arms, and [5] gymnastic exercises, [oligarchies] legislate in a similar spirit [trying to keep the poor from participating]. For the poor are not obliged to have arms, but the rich are fined for not having them; and in like manner no penalty is inflicted on the poor for non-attendance at the gymnasium, and consequently, having nothing to fear, they do not attend, whereas the rich are liable to a fine, and therefore they take care to attend. . . .

As of oligarchy so of tyranny. . . . Both mistrust the people, and therefore deprive them of their arms.

Plato's greatest work of political philosophy is *The Republic*, written in the first part of the fourth century B.C. In *The Republic*, Plato explains his theory for why societies always progress from oligarchy (rule by a small group of elite rich) to democracy (rule by the people) to despotism (rule by a single man). At each step, the control of arms is crucial.

THE REPUBLIC
(trans. Benjamin Jowett, 302, 303, 310–11, 328–29 [1941])

Plato

[In an oligarchy,] [t]hey next proceed to make a law which fixes a sum of money as the qualification of citizenship; the sum is higher in one place and lower in another, as the oligarchy is more or less exclusive; and they allow no one whose property falls below the amount fixed to have any share in the government. These changes in the constitution they effect by force of arms, if intimidation has not already done their work. . . .

[Plato points out one of the disadvantages of oligarchy:] Another discreditable feature is, that, for a like reason, they are incapable of carrying on any war. Either they arm the multitude, and then they are more afraid of them than of the enemy; or, if they do not call them out in the hour of battle, they are oligarchs indeed, few to fight as they are few to rule. . . .

[Eventually, the oligarchy is supplanted by democracy,] whether the revolution has been effected by arms, or whether fear [of the possibility of armed revolution] has caused the opposite party to withdraw. . . .

[But after a while, the people succumb to demagogy, and a tyrant arises. The tyrant does not begin his worst abuses until after he has disarmed his victims, as is explained in the following teacher-student dialogue.]

> Teacher: Then the parent (the people) will discover what a monster he has been fostering in his bosom; and, when he wants to drive him out, he will find that he is weak and his son (the tyrant) strong.
> Student: Why, you do not mean to say that the tyrant will use violence? What! Beat his father if he opposes him?
> Teacher: Yes, he will, having first disarmed him.

In Plato's ideal state, the one-man rule of a tyrant is replaced by the one-man rule of a philosopher-king. The king uses a professional military/police class—the Guardians—to keep everyone else in line. The common people of Plato's ideal state would be trained once a month in use of arms but would have no right to arms, and arms would be centrally stored in state armories.

THE LAWS
(ed. A. E. Taylor, 335 [1966])

Plato

[N]o man, and no woman, be ever suffered to live without an officer set over them, and no soul of man to learn the trick of doing one single thing of its own sole motion, in play or in earnest, but, in peace as in war, ever to live with the commander in sight, to follow his leading, and take its motions from him to the least detail. . . .

THE ART OF WAR
(in 2 *Machiavelli: The Chief Works and Others,* trans. Allan Gilbert, 578 [1989])

Niccolo Machiavelli

[The Roman emperors] thinking more about their own power than about the public advantage, began to disarm the Roman people in order to command them more easily and to keep those same armies continually on the frontiers of the Empire. And because they still did not judge that they would be enough to hold in check the Roman people and the Senate, they set up an army called Praetorian, which remained near the walls of Rome and was like a castle over that city. Because they then freely began to allow men chosen for those armies to practice soldiering as their profession, these men . . . were dangerous to the Senate and harmful to the Emperor. The result was that many emperors were killed through the arrogance of the soldiers, who gave the Empire to whom they chose, and took it away. . . . From these things resulted, first the division of the Empire, and finally its ruin.

Perhaps no French political philosopher was more important to the development of absolutism than Jean Bodin (1530–1596). Bodin's major work was *Six livres de la republique* (Six books of a commonweal), published in 1576. France in the sixteenth century had suffered terrible religious wars between French Catholics and French Protestants (Huguenots). Bodin's solution to the strife was to make the subject's obedience to the king the central fact of life. One's duty to God was subordinate to one's duty to the king. At the same time, the king had no obligation to obey the laws he made.

THE SIX BOOKES OF A COMMONWEALE
(ed. Kenneth Douglas McRae, 542, 543, 615 [1962])

Jean Bodin

[T]he most useful way to prevent sedition, is to take away the subjects armes. . . . For so *Aristotle*, speaking of the Barbarians, accounteth it for a strange thing, that a man should in a quiet and peaceable citie weare a sword or a dagger in time of peace: which by our lawes, as also by the manners and customes of the Germaines and Englishmen is not onely lawfull; but by the lawes and decrees of the Swissers even necessarily commanded: the cause of an infinite number of murders, hee which weareth a sword, a dagger, or a pistoll, being more fierce and insolent to offer unto others injury, as also to commit murder if any injurie be offered him: whereas if he were disarmed, he should doe neither the one nor the other; neither should he incurre the infamy and disgrace which followeth them, who when they are wronged, dare not to draw their weapons. The Turkes herein go yet farther, not onely in punishing with all severity the seditious and mutinous people, but also forbidding them to beare armes, yea even in time of warre, except it bee when they are to give battle. . . .

Amongst many the lawdable manners and customes of the policy of

Paris, there is . . . a very good one . . . which is, That no car-man or porter shall weare a sword, dagger, knife, or any other offensive weapon. . . . For it is not the part of a wise politician, neither of a good governour, to expect untill the murder be committed, or that the sedition be raysed, before he forbid the bearing of armes, but as a good [physician] preventeth diseases: and if chaunce be that the parties be [suddenly] attainted with any violent griefe, he first [assuages] the present paine, and that done applyeth convenient remedies unto the causes of the diseases. . . .

It was an antient custome among the Romans towards those with those whom they had not joyned in league, nor contracted friendship upon equall tearmes, never to govern them peaceably, untill they had [yielded] up all, delivered hostages, disarmed them, and put garrisons in their townes. For we may not think ever to keepe that people in subjection which hath alwayes lived in libertie, if they not be disarmed. . . .

English émigré Thomas Paine (1737–1809) did much more than any other person to convince Americans that independence was the only solution to the problems with English rule. Six months after the January 1776 publication of his best-selling *Common Sense*, the Continental Congress declared independence. Later, in 1776–77, Paine published a series of pamphlets titled *The American Crisis*, which were intended to boost morale as the patriot cause suffered a series of military reversals. In one, Paine warned his adopted countrymen to guard as well against the "cunning of the fox" as "the violence of the wolfe."

The American Crisis
(vol. 1, in *Thomas Paine: Collected Writings*, ed. Eric Foner, 97–98 [1995])

Thomas Paine

[General Sir William] Howe's first object is partly by threats and partly by promises, to terrify or seduce the people to deliver up their arms, and receive mercy. The ministry recommended the same plan to [General Thomas] Gage, and this is what the Tories call making their peace. . . . A peace which would be the immediate forerunner of a worse ruin than any we have yet thought of. . . . Were the back counties to give up their arms, they would fall an easy prey to the Indians, who are all armed: This is perhaps what some Tories would not be sorry for. Were the home counties to deliver up their arms, they would be exposed to the resentment of the back counties, who would then have it in their power to chastise their defection at pleasure. And were any one State to give up its arms, THAT State must be garrisoned by all Howe's army of Britons and Hessians to preserve it from the anger of the rest. . . . Howe is mercifully inviting you to barbarous destruction, and men must be either rogues or fools that will not see it.

DISCUSSION NOTES

1. Bodin's death penalty for carrying weapons was not adopted by France; but today, Malaysia does impose the death penalty for possession or carrying of firearms or ammunition (except by authorized government employees). Would such a policy help reduce crime? Reduce changes in government?

2. Why does Bodin link the ability to exercise free speech with the right to bear arms? (For a recent exploration of the connection between the right of free speech and the right to keep and bear arms, see L. A. Powe Jr., *Guns, Words, and Constitutional Interpretation,* 38 William and Mary Law Review 1311 [1997].)

3. Is it necessarily true that tyrannical governments must disarm their subjects? Even if the tyranny is generally popular?

4. The American founders looked to Rome's degeneration from republic to empire as the epitome of everything they wanted America to avoid. Does modern America more resemble a virtuous republic or a decadent empire? Would Rome have been better off if the people had been as well armed and well trained as the Praetorian Guard? (The Praetorian Guard was an elite military unit, almost always stationed in Rome, under the direct control of the emperor. Usually, the guard enforced the emperor's power, but emperors who were unpopular with the guard were sometimes deposed by the guard. Other times, after an emperor died, the guard would choose the new emperor, and the Senate would ratify the choice in a rubber-stamp vote.)

5. Many gun control advocates argue that only members of the police forces and the military ought to have access to firearms. Do the examples from history suggest possible dangers of allowing the government to have a monopoly on instruments of violence? Do we now have political safeguards and long-term governmental stability sufficient to prevent the government, were it able to secure such a monopoly, from abusing its power once widespread disarmament was effected? (For modern viewpoints of the ownership of arms as a precaution against tyranny, see Samuel C. Wheeler III, *Arms as Insurance*, 13 Public Affairs Quarterly 111 [April 1999]; David B. Kopel, book review of Aaron Zelman et al., *Lethal Laws*, 15 New York Law School Journal of International and Comparative Law 355 [1995], discussing twentieth-century genocide and the propensity of genocidal governments to disarm their victims first.)

6. Aristotle maintains that tyrants use disarmament as a way to consolidate and maintain their power over their subjects. It is estimated that Americans own about a quarter of a billion firearms and that firearms are kept in approximately 40 percent of all households. Is disarmament of the American populace by federal or state governments a realistic threat?

7. If laws were passed requiring U.S. citizens to surrender their firearms to government officials, would you obey or disobey such laws? What fraction of gun owners do you think would comply? Do you think such laws would ever have a realistic chance of being passed by the Congress? The Brady bill imposed a background check and five government working-day waiting period for handgun purchasers starting in 1994. In 1998, the waiting period was replaced by an "instant check" on all retail gun purchases. The Brady Act consumed years of contentious debate before its passage. (See Andrew J. McClurg, *The Rhetoric of Gun Control*, 42 American University Law Review 53, 54 n. 3 [1992], tracing the history of the Brady bill's passage.) Do you consider the Brady bill restrictions to be reasonable or unreasonable? Does the fact that it took several years of heated debate to pass a bill requiring background checks for gun purchases suggest that the fears of many gun owners—that the government will someday confiscate all guns—are unwarranted? Or does the fact that the Brady bill passed suggest that we have moved one step closer to gun confiscation?

D. The Citizen Militia as Dual Safeguard against Tyranny and Foreign Invasion

Discourses on Livy
(trans. Harvey C. Mansfield and Nathan Tarcov 54, 200–201 [1996])

Niccolo Machiavelli

Present princes and modern republics that lack their own soldiers for defense and offense ought to be ashamed of themselves and to think . . . that such a defect is not through a lack of men apt for the military but through their own fault, that they have not known how to make their men military. . . .

Beginning with [our republic] of Florence, in times past, when its reputation was greater, there was no lordling in the Romagna who did not have a stipend from it. . . . [I]f that city had been armed and vigorous, all would have gone to the contrary: to have protection from it, many would have given money to it, and sought not to sell it their friendship but to buy its. Nor have the Florentines alone lived in cowardice, but also the Venetians, and the king of France, who with so great a kingdom lives as a tributary of the Swiss and of the king of England. All of which arises from his having disarmed his people and from that king and the others named before having wished rather to enjoy the present utility of being able to plunder their peoples, and to escape an imagined rather than a true danger, than to do things that might secure them and make their states perpetually happy. . . . The Romans observed this generosity and this mode of life while they lived freely; but later, when they entered under the emperors, and the emperors began to be bad and to love the shade more than the sun, they also began to buy themselves off [from foreign threats], which was the beginning of the ruin of so great an empire.

Similar inconveniences proceed . . . from having disarmed your people, from which results another greater one: that the nearer the enemy draws to you, the weaker he finds you. . . . [T]he heart and the vital parts of a body have to be kept armed and not its extremities, since without the latter it lives, but if the former are hurt it dies; and these states keep the heart unarmed and the hands and feet armed.

DISCUSSION NOTES

1. Why does Machiavelli argue that the militia, that is, a band of citizen-soldiers, is superior to professional soldiers or mercenaries?

2. What is the relevance to our time of the connection between one's status as a citizen and the ability to bear arms in defense of the state? Is there any?

3. Beginning in the 1990s, groups of citizens fearful of perceived governmental efforts to curtail civil liberties generally and private gun ownership in particular began forming armed bands around the country, which they called "militias," and prepared for possible armed conflict with the government or with hostile foreign powers. Are these groups different from the militias of which Machiavelli wrote approvingly? The ideology of many of today's militias includes the belief that most federal governmental actions in the United States are illegitimate. Many of their strongest beliefs center on the right to bear and stockpile arms. Some of them adhere to extreme racist views. (See generally *The Militia Movement*, At Issue Series, ed. Charles P. Cozic [San Diego: Greenhaven Press, 1997]; David B. Kopel and Joseph Olson, *Preventing a Reign of Terror: Civil Liberties Implications of Terrorism Legislation*, 21 Oklahoma City University Law Review 247 [1996].) Do you fear modern militias or take comfort in their existence as a bulwark against tyranny?

4. Does Machiavelli's linkage between arms bearing and military service have implications for the private ownership of weapons for self-defense? Can it be argued that citizens' bearing arms in collective defense of the state is merely the right of the individual to defend herself and her family writ large? Or is membership in a formal, military organization a precondition for exercise of the right? (Compare Don B. Kates Jr., *The Second Amendment and the Ideology of Self-Protection*, 9 Constitutional Commentary 87 [1992] with Dennis A. Henigan, *Arms, Anarchy and the Second Amendment*, 26 Valparaiso Law Review 107 [1991].)

5. Does Machiavelli's approval of warfare as a legitimate instrument of territorial expansion make his brand of republicanism less relevant to us today? Repugnant? Dangerous? Does the need for a militia sometimes exist for defensive purposes?

Andrew Fletcher of Saltoun (1653–1716) was a Scottish nobleman, professor of divinity, and member of the Scottish parliament. A vocal proponent of liberty, Fletcher was exiled after an unsuccessful Scottish rebellion in 1685; he returned to Scotland after William and Mary were offered the crowns of England and Scotland in 1689. In the late 1690s, Fletcher published an essay arguing against the maintenance of a peacetime standing army and in favor of the traditional militia. In it Fletcher not only made the historical and philosophical case for the superiority of the militia but also made concrete proposals for establishing camps within Scotland and England for the universal military training of all young men in both countries.

A DISCOURSE OF GOVERNMENT WITH
RELATION TO MILITIAS
(in *Andrew Fletcher of Saltoun: Selected Political Writings and Speeches,*
ed. David Daiches, 18–19 [1979])

Andrew Fletcher

A good militia is of such importance to a nation, that it is the chief part of the constitution of any free government. For though as to other things, the constitution be never so slight, a good militia will always preserve the public liberty. But in the best constitution that ever was, as to all other parts of government, if the militia be not upon a right foot, the liberty of the people must perish. The militia of ancient Rome, the best that ever was in any government, made her mistress of the world: but standing armies enslaved that great people, and their excellent militia and freedom perished together. The [Spartans] continued eight hundred years free, and in great honour, because they had a good militia. The Swisses at this day are the freest, happiest, and the people of all Europe who can best defend themselves, because they have the best militia. . . .

[T]he whole free people of any nation ought to be exercised to arms. . . . I cannot see why arms should be denied to any man who is not a slave, since they are the only true badges of liberty . . . neither can I understand why any man that has arms should not be taught the use of them.

By the constitution of the present militia in both nations [England and Scotland], there is but a small number of the men able to bear arms exercised; and men of quality and estate are allowed to send any wretched servant in their place: so that they themselves are become mean, by being disused to handle arms; and will not learn the use of them, because they are ashamed of their ignorance: by which means the militias being composed only of servants, these nations seem altogether unfit to defend themselves, and standing forces to be necessary. Now can it be supposed that a few servants will fight for the defence of their masters' estates, if their masters only look on? . . . No bodies of military men can be of any force or value, unless many persons of quality or education be among them; and such men should blush to think of excusing themselves from serving their country, at least for some years, in a military capacity. . . . Is it not a shame that any man who possesses an estate, and is at the same time healthful and young, should not fit himself by all means for the defence of that, and his country, rather than to pay taxes to maintain a mercenary, who . . . will be sure to insult and enslave him in time of peace?

DISCUSSION NOTES

1. Compare Fletcher's views on the utility and indispensability of the militia with the later views of Adam Smith, who argued, contra Fletcher and the other pro-militia writers, that militia were never as good as professional armies, and that professional armies were necessary to protect a country that was beginning to develop industry.

2. To reinvigorate the militia, Fletcher proposed a series of camps in both England and Scotland where the youth of each country would be sent to experience discipline and deprivation, all to prevent the decay and corruption that, of necessity, according to Fletcher, accompany the employment of a "mercenary" army (*id.* at 20–26). What would you think of the adoption of such a system in the United States? Switzerland requires several weeks of militia training for most able-bodied adult males. (See David B. Kopel, *The Samurai, the Mountie, and the Cowboy: Should America Adopt the Gun Controls of Other Democracies?* [Amherst, NY: Prometheus Books, 1992], chap. 7.)

3. Whatever value militias may have once had in the United States, are they now an anachronism? Would you prefer to rest the defense of the United States on a militia or on a standing army? Or on a combination of both? Would you have answered any of these questions differently before September 11, 2001, when terrorists commandeered airliners and deliberately crashed them into the World Trade Center towers in New York City and the Pentagon in Washington, D.C.?

4. Note that Fletcher's call for universal armament of the people expressly excludes slaves. Is this consistent with his view that arms possession is "the only true badge of liberty"?

Future president James Madison argued against the anti-federalist claim that the federal government created by the proposed U.S. Constitution could become tyrannical.

THE FEDERALIST NO. 46

(in *The Federalist Papers*, ed. Clinton Rossiter, 298, 299–300 [1961])

James Madison

The only refuge left for those who prophesy the downfall of the State governments is the visionary supposition that the federal government may previously accumulate a military force for the projects of ambition. . . . Let a regular army, fully equal to the resources of the country, be formed; and let it be entirely at the devotion of the federal government: still it would not be going too far to say that the State governments with the people on their side would be able to repel the danger. The highest number to which, according to the best computation, a standing army can be carried in any country does not exceed one hundredth part of the whole number of souls; or one twenty-fifth part of the number able to bear arms. This proportion would not yield, in the United States, an army of more than twenty-five or thirty thousand men. To these would be opposed a militia amounting to near half a million of citizens with arms in their hands [approximately the entire adult free male population], officered by men chosen from among themselves, fighting for their common liberties, and united and conducted by governments possessing their affections and confidence. It may well be doubted, whether a militia thus circumstanced could ever be conquered by such a proportion of regular troops. Those who are best acquainted with the last successful resistance of this country against the British arms, will be most inclined to deny the possibility of it. Besides the advantage of being armed, which the Americans possess over the people of almost every other nation, the existence of subordinate governments, to which the people are attached and by which the militia officers are appointed, forms a barrier against the enterprises of ambition, more insurmountable than any which a simple government of any form can admit of. Notwithstanding the military establishments in the several kingdoms of Europe, which are carried as far as the public resources will bear, the governments are afraid to trust the people with arms. And it is not certain that with this aid alone they would not be able to shake off their yokes. But were the people to possess the additional advantages of local governments chosen by themselves, who could collect the national will and direct the national force, and of officers appointed out of the militia by these governments and attached both to them and to the militia, it may be affirmed with the greatest assurance, that the throne of every tyranny in Europe would be speedily overturned in spite of the legions which surround it. Let us not insult the free and gallant citizens of America with the suspicion that they would be less able to defend the rights of which they would be in actual possession than the debased subjects of arbitrary power would be to rescue theirs from the hands of their oppressors. . . .

DISCUSSION NOTES

1. Do you fear the United States government? Do you think that any Americans have ever had a legitimate reason to fear their government? Do (some) Americans have a legitimate reason to fear the government today, to the extent of requiring arms as a defense against tyranny? Could it ever be necessary in the future?

2. The framers of the Declaration of Independence and the Constitution also understood the dangers inherent in exercising the right of resist-

ance. In the Declaration of Independence, after affirming "the Right of the People to alter or abolish" governments that no longer operate with the consent of the governed, Jefferson wrote: "Prudence, indeed, will dictate that Governments long established should not be changed for light and transient causes; and accordingly all experience hath shown, that mankind are more likely to suffer, while evils are sufferable, than to right themselves by abolishing the forms to which they are accustomed." What kind of rights violations would you accept, rather than work to overthrow a tyrannical government? The Declaration of Independence lists a long string of abuses by the British government and the government's consistent refusal to redress those grievances, despite many peaceful requests. What would it take for you to believe that there was no peaceful prospect of redressing a major government abuse of fundamental rights? Are there any circumstances under which it would be legitimate to violently resist a government? Is a tyrannical government really a government or (as the Founders argued) merely a usurper of powers it was never granted?

3. Some writers react strongly against the notion that the Constitution could sanction armed revolt against tyrannical government. (See, e.g., Dennis A. Henigan, *Arms, Anarchy and the Second Amendment*, 26 Valparaiso Law Review 107 [1991].) Henigan calls this the "insurrectionist theory" of the Second Amendment. Do you believe that any attempt to overthrow a government is necessarily treasonous? What if the intent is to restore constitutional order from a government that is violating its constitution? How can one tell when, if ever, resistance becomes legitimate? (For an excellent discussion of the "right of resistance" and of the careful constraints that developed to guard against excesses, see Pauline Maier, *From Resistance to Revolution* [1972; reprint, New York: Vintage Books, 1974] chap. 2.) Can you think of an act of the U.S. government in our past that would have justified armed revolution? Armed resistance? Can you hypothesize a future act that would justify armed revolution or resistance?

4. Suppose the federal government passed laws banning the possession of all firearms. Which of the following would be your preferred response to such an action by the citizenry: (a) accept it; (b) fight the measure in the courts; (c) fight the measure in the streets. Assuming the courts

upheld the ban, would you prefer that the citizenry abide by it or engage in armed revolt against it?

5. A number of state constitutions written in the late eighteenth and early nineteenth centuries contained explicit "alter or abolish" clauses that authorize, even require, resistance to tyranny. (See, e.g., Tennessee Constitution, art. 1, §§ 1–2; Massachusetts Constitution, art. 7; Pennsylvania Constitution, art. 1, § 2; Virginia Constitution, art. 1, § 3.) Do constitutional provisions encouraging armed resistance to tyranny convert the U.S. Constitution into "a suicide pact"? Or do they prevent murder by government and other harms? Is an armed population such a deterrent to tyranny that the actual need to revolt may never occur, as long as the people are armed?

6. For an argument that the right to resist tyranny is simply the right of personal self-defense writ large, see Don B. Kates Jr., *The Second Amendment and the Ideology of Self-Protection*, 9 Constitution Commentary 87 (1992). Do you agree with Thomas Paine, William Blackstone, and other authors in the Kates article that resisting a pair of criminals is not fundamentally different from resisting a criminal such as Hitler, Stalin or bin Laden who has a large number of armed helpers? (One reason Paine, Blackstone, and others saw no fundamental difference was that standing armies often tended to act like large criminal gangs in the towns they occupied, even in friendly territory.)

7. Many of the early writings in support of a right to bear arms are concerned with ensuring the ability of a nation-state to protect itself from external invasion. Assuming the concern was a legitimate one at the time the writings were penned, does it have any relevance in the modern gun control debate?

8. Following the September 11, 2001 terrorist attacks on New York City and Washington, D.C., gun dealers nationwide experienced an upsurge in sales of firearms. Do you think this is a reflexive expression of national security? An overreaction? Can armed civilians help prevent terrorist attacks like those that occurred on September 11? If you think that they can, explain how. Kopel has suggested that airline pilots be armed, so that they might be effectively able to resist would-be hijackers. (See *Arms in the Air*, available at http://www.nationalreview.com/kopel/kopel092601.shtml.) The pilots' union, the Air Line Pilots Association,

also supports this proposal. Do you think it is a good idea? What might be some of the problems related to arming airline pilots?

One of the editors spoke to a Continental Airlines pilot about the issue, who expressed three reasons for his opposition to gun-carrying by pilots: 1. "We're busy flying the plane." 2. "We're not trained as gunfighters." 3. "If we already have guns on the plane, the terrorists won't have to worry about bringing their own. They'll just have to figure out a way to get to ours." Possible responses to the pilot's concerns include: 1. Pilots, like the captain of a ship, have a duty to maintain order on the plane; 2. Many pilots are ex-military personnel who have received arms training, and various firearms academies have offered free training to any pilot who wants it; and 3. Guns carried by pilots, stewards, or passengers could be concealed, rather than worn in open holsters where they could be easily grabbed. Because pilots do have responsibilities for flying the plane, is that an argument for arming other members of airline flight crews? Should the government regularly place armed personnel ("sky marshals") on airplanes as a way to reduce the likelihood that the acts of September 11 will be repeated?

9. More than fifty years have passed since foreign soldiers last set foot on U.S. soil in a hostile capacity, when the Japanese seized some Alaskan islands during World War II. Does the personal possession of firearms by citizens play any role in keeping the United States secure against foreign invasion? Could possession be of any significance in the future? In the nuclear age, do you think the defense of the United States will ever reach the point of activating citizens for home defense against potential invaders, as occurred in Maryland, Virginia, and Hawaii during the Second World War?

10. Do the terrorist attacks of September 11, 2001 highlight the need for active participation of United States citizens in the protection of the country from terrorist attacks? If so, what form should that participation take? Should we attempt to revive the classical idea of a militia composed of citizens ready to take up arms at a moment's notice? Should the focus be on other, noncombatant roles that civilians could play in home defense, such as disaster relief workers, or emergency medical technicians? Following the September 11, 2001 attacks, Professor Randy Barnett argued that armed civilians ought to comprise an

"anti-terrorist militia," on the theory that the army and police cannot be everywhere at once, but citizens can be. (See *Saved by the Militia*, available at http://www.nationalreview.com/comment/comment-bar-nett091801.shtml). Would you feel safer if large numbers of civilians were organized into anti-terrorist patrols? Less safe? Would you worry about vigilantism? What if you are or were of Arab descent?

Who should regulate such militias? Should they be regulated by the government? In what ways? Would government regulation run contrary to the concept of a citizen militia? Should we rely on self-regulation? Some existing self-styled citizen militia groups favor the violent overthrow of the U.S. government. A month after the terror attacks, August Kries, the webmaster for the neo-Nazi Sheriff's Posse Comitatus, in Ulysses, Pennsylvania, wrote: "May the WAR be started. DEATH to His (God's) enemies, may the World Trade Center BURN TO THE GROUND! . . . We can blame no others than ourselves for our problems due to the fact that we allow . . . Satan's children, called jews today, to have domain over our lives." (Jim Nesbitt, Newhouse News, Sept. 25, 2001, available at *America's Racist-Right Fringe Groups Laud Terror Attack*, Plain Dealer, Sept. 26, 2001, at A4) Do you think it is wise or unwise to rely on unregulated citizen groups for homeland defense? Does your answer apply to all citizen groups or just some? How would we decide and enforce which groups are appropriate for homeland defense? What about encouraging individual citizens to carry arms, in accordance with their state's laws, so that they could resist a terrorist at a shopping mall, business office, or other public place?

11. Many early commentators on the right to bear arms (e.g., James Harrington and Andrew Fletcher) argued for militias and against standing armies as an essential means to preserve liberty. Would the United States exist today if not for our standing army? If not for the militias in the American Revolution? (For more on the militias in the Revolution, see Mark W. Kwasny, *Washington's Partisan War: 1775–1783* [Kent, OH: Kent State University Press, 1996].)

12. Since the War of 1812, the militia has not played a major role in defending the United States from foreign invasion. Would the militia be able to do so successfully today? Is the concept of a militia outdated in light of the armaments, ships, submarines, aircraft, satellites, commu-

nications equipment, and so forth required to wage modern warfare? If these writers were wrong about the undesirability of standing armies, could they also be wrong about the desirability of maintaining unorganized militias?

E. Doubts about the Efficacy of Militias

In 1776 an obscure Scottish professor of moral philosophy named Adam Smith (1723–1790) published what is commonly regarded as the most famous work in the modern science of economics, titled *An Inquiry into the Nature and Causes of the Wealth of Nations*. But to call Smith's epic merely a treatise on economics does not begin to do justice to its scope, which includes excursions in history and philosophy as well as discussions of trade, commerce, and taxation. When discussing the "expenses of the sovereign," Smith argued forcefully that the most economical mode of providing for a country's defense was to employ a well-trained, professional army. He vigorously disputed the received wisdom that a militia was a match for an army and that a standing army in peacetime endangered the liberties of a free people.

AN INQUIRY INTO THE NATURE AND CAUSES OF THE WEALTH OF NATIONS
(ed. R. H. Campbell, A. S. Skinner, and W. B. Todd, 698, 699–700, 706–708 [1976])

Adam Smith

[T]here seem to be but two methods, by which the state can make any tolerable provision for the publick defence.

It may either, first, by means of a very rigorous police, and in spite of the whole bent of the interest, genius and inclinations of the people, enforce the practice of military exercises, and oblige either all the citizens of the military age, or a certain number of them, to join in some measure the trade of a soldier to whatever other trade or profession they may happen to carry on.

Or, secondly, by maintaining and employing a certain number of citizens in the constant practice of military exercises, it may render the trade of a soldier a particular trade, separate and distinct from all others.

If the state has recourse to the first of those two expedients, its military force is said to consist in a militia; if to the second, it is said to consist in a standing army. . . . In a militia, the character of the labourer, artificer, or tradesman, predominates over that of the soldier: in a standing army, that of the soldier predominates over every other character; and in this distinction seems to consist the essential difference between those two different species of military force. . . .

Before the invention of fire-arms, that army was superior in which the soldiers had, each individually, the greatest skill and dexterity in the use of their arms. Strength and agility of body were of the highest consequence, and commonly determined the fate of battles. . . . Since the invention of fire-arms, strength and agility of body, or even extraordinary dexterity and skill in the use of arms, though they are far from being of no consequence, are, however, of less consequence. . . .

Regularity, order, and prompt obedience to command, are qualities which, in modern armies, are of more importance towards determining the fate of battles, than the dexterity and skill of the soldiers in the use of their arms. But the noise of fire-arms, the smoke, and the invisible death to which every man feels himself every moment exposed, as soon as he comes within cannon-shot, and frequently a long time before the battle can be well said to be engaged, must render it very difficult to maintain any considerable degree of this regularity, order, and prompt obedience, even in the beginning of a modern battle. . . .

A militia, however, in whatever manner it may be either disciplined or exercised, must always be much inferior to a well disciplined and well exercised standing army.

The soldiers, who are exercised only once a week, or once a month, can never be so expert in the use of their arms, as those who are exercised every day, or every other day; and though this circumstance may not be of so much consequence in modern, as it was in antient times, yet the acknowledged superiority of the Prussian troops, owing, it is said, very much to their superior expertness in their exercise, may satisfy us that it is, even at this day, of very considerable consequence.

The soldiers, who are bound to obey their officer only once a week or once a month, and who are at all other times at liberty to manage their own affairs their own way, without being in any respect accountable to him, can never be under the same awe in his presence, can never have the same disposition to ready obedience, with those whose whole life and conduct are every day directed by him, and who every day even rise and go to bed, or at least retire to their quarters, according to his orders. In what is called discipline, or in the habit of ready obedience, a militia must always be still more inferior to a standing army, than it may sometimes be in what is called the manual exercise, or in the management and use of its arms. But in modern war the habit of ready and instant obedience is of much greater consequence than a considerable superiority in the management of arms. . . .

Men of republican principles have been jealous of a standing army as dangerous to liberty. It certainly is so, wherever the interest of the general and that of the principal officers are not necessarily connected with the support of the constitution of the state. . . . But where the sovereign is himself the general, and the principal nobility and gentry of the country the chief officers of the army; where the military force is placed under the command of those who have the greatest interest in the support of the civil authority, because they have themselves the greatest share of that authority, a standing army can never be dangerous to liberty. On the contrary, it may in some cases be favourable to liberty. The security which it gives to the sovereign renders unnecessary that troublesome jealousy, which, in some modern republicks, seems to watch over the minutest actions, and to be at all times ready to disturb the peace of every citizen. Where the security of the magistrate, though supported by the principal people of the country, is endangered by every popular discontent; where a small tumult is capable of bringing about in a few hours a great revolution, the whole authority of government must be employed to suppress and punish every murmur and complaint against it. To a sovereign, on the contrary, who feels himself supported, not only by the natural aristocracy of the country, but by a well-regulated standing army, the rudest, the most groundless, and the most licentious remonstrances can give little disturbance. He can safely pardon or neglect them, and his consciousness of his own superiority naturally disposes him to do so. That degree of liberty which approaches to licentiousness can be tolerated only in countries where the sovereign is secured by a well-regulated standing army. It is in such countries only, that the publick safety does not require, that the sovereign should be trusted with any discretionary power, for suppressing even the impertinent wantonness of the licentious liberty. . . .

The great change introduced into the art of war by the invention of firearms, has enhanced still further both the expence of exercising and disciplining any particular number of soldiers in time of peace, and that of employing them in time of war. Both their arms and their ammunition are become more expensive. . . . In modern times many different causes contribute to render the defence of the society more expensive. The unavoidable effects of the natural progress of improvement have, in this respect, been a good deal enhanced by a great revolution in the art of war, to which a mere accident, the invention of gun-powder, seems to have given occasion.

In modern war the great expence of fire-arms gives an evident advantage to the nation which can best afford that expence; and consequently, to an opulent and civilized, over a poor and barbarous nation. In antient times the opulent and civilized found it difficult to defend themselves against the poor and barbarous nations. In modern times the poor and barbarous find it difficult to defend themselves against the opulent and civilized. The invention of fire-arms, an invention which at first sight appears to be so pernicious, is certainly favourable both to the permanency and to the extension of civilization.

DISCUSSION NOTES

1. Is it realistic to expect that large numbers of amateur "citizen-soldiers" would ever be as effective as a professional army? Effective enough to deter or limit abuses by a standing army? Adam Smith and Alexander Hamilton (below) suggest that such a vision was fanciful even in the late eighteenth century. (See also Edmund S. Morgan, *Inventing the People* 153–73 [New York: Norton, 1988], arguing that the "cherished tenet of the yeomanry in arms, embodied in militias, as the best and only safe form of military protection for a republic" was "at odds with the facts.")

2. Have advances in military technology and tactics rendered the notion of relying on militias for national defense entirely implausible? (See Col. Charles J. Dunlap Jr., *Revolt of the Masses: Armed Civilians and the Insurrectionary Theory of the Second Amendment*, 62 Tennessee Law Review 643 [1995], arguing that armed citizens would be no match for a professional military. But see Gary Hart, *The Minuteman: Restoring an Army of the People* [New York: Free Press, 1998] arguing for greater public participation in the armed forces through the use of militia-type units or reserve forces. See also John A. McPhee, *La Place de la Concorde Suisse* [New York: Farrar, Straus & Giroux, 1984], describing the Swiss militia.) Even assuming that a citizen militia would not be as effective as a standing army in direct combat against professional troops, might it be effective against "irregular" forces, like terrorists? In light of the September 11, 2001 attacks on the World Trade Center and the Pentagon, some have argued for a creation of a citizen militia to serve as a defense against terrorism. What do you think of such a proposal? Could a citizen militia have prevented the September 11 attacks? In what ways could a militia function to combat terrorism? Any? (See Discussion Note 10, page 145, for additional questions regarding this issue.)

3. Consider Smith's view that a large standing army may actually increase liberty because it allows the sovereign to tolerate a degree of criticism and licentiousness among the citizenry without the fear of being overthrown. Do you agree? If not for a strong standing army and stable political system, would the U.S. government feel the need to violently crush dissidents, including modern militia groups?

THE FEDERALIST NO. 29
(in *The Federalist Papers*, ed. Clinton Rossiter, 183, 184–85 [1961])

Alexander Hamilton

If a well-regulated militia be the most natural defense of a free country, it ought certainly to be under the regulation and at the disposal of that body which is constituted the guardian of the national security. If standing armies are dangerous to liberty, an efficacious power over the militia, in the body to whose care the protection of the State is committed, ought, as far as possible, to take away the inducement and the pretext to such unfriendly institutions. If the federal government can command the aid of the militia in those emergencies which call for the military arm in support of the civil magistrate, it can the better dispense with the employment of a different kind of force. If it cannot avail itself of the former, it will be obliged to recur to the latter. To render an army unnecessary, will be a more certain method of preventing its existence than a thousand prohibitions upon paper. . . .

By a curious refinement upon the spirit of republican jealousy, we are even taught to apprehend danger from the militia itself in the hands of the federal government. It is observed that select corps may be formed, composed of the young and ardent, who may be rendered subservient to the views of arbitrary power. What plan for the regulation of the militia may be pursued by the national government, is impossible to be foreseen. But so far from viewing the matter in the same light with those who object to select corps as dangerous, were the Constitution ratified and were I to deliver my sentiments to a member of the federal legislature from this State on the subject of a militia establishment, I should hold to him, in substance, the following discourse:

> The project of disciplining all the militia of the United States is as futile as it would be injurious, if it were capable of being carried into execution. A tolerable expertness in military movements is a business that requires time and practice. It is not a day, or even a week, that will suffice for the attainment of it. To oblige the great body of the yeomanry and of the other classes of the citizens, to be under arms for the purpose of going through military exercises and evolutions, as often as might be necessary to acquire the degree of perfection which would entitle them to the character of a well-regulated militia, would be a real grievance to the people and a serious public inconvenience and loss. It would form an annual deduction from the productive labor of the country, to an amount which, calculating upon the present numbers of the people, would not fall far short of the whole expense of the civil establishments of all the States. To attempt a thing which would abridge the mass of labor and industry to so considerable an extent would be unwise: and the experiment, if made, could not succeed, because it would not long

be endured. Little more can reasonably be aimed at with respect to the people at large than to have them properly armed and equipped; and in order to see that this be not neglected, it will be necessary to assemble them once or twice in the course of a year.

But though the scheme of disciplining the whole nation must be abandoned as mischievous or impracticable; yet it is a matter of the utmost importance that a well-digested plan should, as soon as possible, be adopted for the proper establishment of the militia. The attention of the government ought particularly to be directed to the formation of a select corps of moderate extent, upon such principles as will really fit them for service in case of need. By thus circumscribing the plan, it will be possible to have an excellent body of well-trained militia ready to take the field whenever the defense of the State shall require it. This will not only lessen the call for military establishments, but if circumstances should at any time oblige the government to form an army of any magnitude that army can never be formidable to the liberties of the people while there is a large body of citizens, little if at all inferior to them in discipline and the use of arms, who stand ready to defend their own rights and those of their fellow-citizens. This appears to me the only substitute that can be devised for a standing army, and the best possible security against it, if it should exist. . . .

DISCUSSION NOTES

1. Hamilton's preferences for what was then termed a "select militia" prefigures the rise of the National Guard. (On the history of the National Guard's formation, see Brannon P. Denning, *Palladium of Liberty? The Causes and Consequences of the Federalization of State Militia in the Twentieth Century*, 21 Oklahoma City University Law Review 191, 217–227 [1996]; see also Alan Hirsch, *The Militia Clauses of the Constitution and the National Guard*, 56 University of Cincinnati Law Review 919 [1988].) While states have some control over National Guard operations, the federal government supplies it with modern weaponry, regulates it for quality standards, and can send the National Guard overseas, even over the objection of a state's governor (who is the nominal commander of the state National Guard). (See *Perpich v. Department of Defense*, 496

U.S. 334 [1990].) Does the National Guard, by blending a state citizen army with modern equipment and training, represent the "best of both worlds" with respect to the militia? Does it obviate the need for other state militia? As detailed in chapter 4, many gun control advocates adhere to a "collectivist" view of the Second Amendment under which only formally organized, state-sponsored defense organizations such as the National Guard would qualify as protected "militias" with regard to the right to bear arms.

THE RIGHT TO ARMS IN THE SECOND
AMENDMENT AND STATE CONSTITUTIONS

Cases and Commentary

Any discussion of gun control or gun rights inevitably raises questions as to the meaning of the Second Amendment to the United States Constitution, which provides: "A well regulated Militia, being necessary to the security of a free State, the right of the people to keep and bear Arms, shall not be infringed." What does the Second Amendment mean? Did it guarantee an individual right to possess firearms? Or only a collective, state right to maintain organized militias? This is the essence of the Second Amendment debate. It is an important debate because the constitutionality of many gun control measures that affect individuals might depend on which position ultimately prevails.

One might think such a fundamental debate concerning the meaning of a constitutional right would be settled at this late date, but the Second Amendment is unusual in this regard. Unlike the First or Fourth Amendment, for example, both of which the U.S. Supreme Court has interpreted in scores of cases, the meaning of the Second Amendment has been squarely tackled by the Court only once in history: sixty years ago in a case called *United States v. Miller*, 307 U.S. 174 (1939). Both sides of the gun control debate draw support from this ambiguous decision.

In this chapter we present representative cases, including *Miller*, from federal and state courts interpreting the Second Amendment, and also analogous state guarantees of a right to keep and bear arms. In addition, we include articles outlining the current academic debate on the meaning of the Second Amendment.

When reading the materials in this chapter, consider—in addition to the central question regarding the "collectivist" versus "individualist" meaning of the Second Amendment—the following questions: Which of the themes invoked to justify either securing or restricting a right of private arms ownership, discussed in chapter 3, appear in court opinions concerning the Second Amendment or its state counterparts? Are there any themes not present in chapter 3 that appear in these decisions?

Consider the somewhat divergent views on the right to bear arms expressed by lower federal courts and state courts. Almost all lower federal courts that have addressed the issue have endorsed the collectivist interpretation of the Second Amendment. Many state courts, by contrast, have given a broader reading of state guarantees of the right to keep and bear arms. What might explain the different attitudes of federal and state courts? Which of the accounts of the Second Amendment presented in the scholarly debate seems most persuasive to you? Even if history supports a reading of the Second Amendment that secures an individual right to gun ownership, should that be binding on us in the twenty-first century? Should it preclude all gun regulations or only some? Which ones?

A. The Second Amendment in the Supreme Court

The earliest Supreme Court cases concerning the Second Amendment dealt not with the substantive meaning of the amendment but with the issue of whether or not the amendment applied to actions taken by the states. The Bill of Rights (the first ten amendments to the U.S. Constitution, including the Second Amendment) was adopted four years after the Constitution to alleviate the fears of some states concerning the powers of the newly created federal government. In 1833, in *Barron v. Baltimore*, 32 U.S. 243 (1833), the U.S. Supreme Court held that the rights contained in the Bill of Rights operated only as restrictions on federal action and did not apply to actions taken by the states. It is difficult to overstate the importance of this issue: to rule that the Bill of Rights did not apply to the states meant that states were not prohibited from abridging freedom of speech or religion, the right to jury trial, freedom from self-incrimination, the right to bear arms, and any other federal constitutional liberties. Most scholars, although not all, agree that the Court correctly interpreted the intent of the Founding Fathers in deciding that the Bill of Rights did not limit state action. (See Michael Kent Curtis, *No State Shall Abridge: The Fourteenth Amendment and the Bill of Rights* 1 [Durham: Duke University Press, 1986].)

In 1868, however, the Fourteenth Amendment was ratified. It provides, in pertinent part: "No State shall make or enforce any law which shall abridge the privileges or immunities of citizens in the United States; nor shall any State deprive any person of life, liberty, or property, without due process of law." Questions arose as to whether the Fourteenth Amendment was intended to make the Bill of Rights applicable to state action, through either the "privileges or immunities clause" or the "due process clause."

The Supreme Court never accepted that the privileges or immunities clause was intended to prevent states from violating the Bill of Rights (although Curtis, *supra*, makes a compelling argument to the contrary in his excellent book). In the hundred years following ratification of the Fourteenth Amendment, however, the Court did hold that most liberties contained in the Bill of Rights apply to state action through the due process clause. The fragmented and often-torturous process by which this was accomplished is too complicated to explain in detail here. The approach finally settled on by the Court is known as "selective incorporation," a process by which the Court held, on a case-by-case basis (that is, selectively), that various freedoms in the Bill of Rights either were or were not sufficiently "fundamental" that they constituted part of due process of law. Once the Court made a determination that a particular liberty was part of due process of law under the Fourteenth Amendment, it absorbed or "incorporated" that right into the due process clause and made it binding on the states. Although the Court applied some rights to the states prior to the 1960s, the vast majority of Supreme Court decisions making liberties in the Bill of Rights binding on the states occurred from 1961 to 1968, under the auspices of Chief Justice Earl Warren's Court.

In the late 1800s, long before the Court settled on the jurisprudence of selective incorporation, the Court considered whether the Second Amendment operated to restrict state action.

PRESSER V. ILLINOIS
116 U.S. 252 (1886)

[Presser was indicted and convicted for violating a state statute that prohibited any body of men whatever, other than the regular organized volunteer militia of this state and the troops of the United States, to associate themselves together as a military company or organization or to drill or parade with arms in any city or town of the state of Illinois, without the license of the governor thereof. Justice Woods delivered the opinion of the Court.]

Presser . . . belonged to a society called the "Lehr und Wehr Verein," a corporation organized . . . "for the purpose," as expressed by its certificate of association, "of improving the mental and bodily condition of its members so as to qualify them for the duties of citizens of a republic. Its members shall, therefore, obtain, in the meetings of the association, a knowledge of our laws and political economy, and shall also be instructed in military and gymnastic exercises. . . . [In] December, 1879, [Presser] marched at the head of said company, about 400 in number, in the streets of the city of Chicago, he riding on horseback and in command; . . . the company was armed with rifles, and Presser with a cavalry sword; . . . the company had no license from the governor of Illinois to drill or parade as a part of the militia of the state, and was not a part of the regular organized militia of the state, nor a part of troops of the United States, and had no organization under the militia law of the United States. . . . The case was taken to the supreme court of Illinois, where the judgment was affirmed. Thereupon Presser brought the present writ of error for a review of the judgment of affirmance. . . .

[Presser argued] that the entire statute under which he was convicted was invalid and void because its enactment was the exercise of a power by the legislature of Illinois forbidden to the states by [article 1, § 8 of the U.S. Constitution, which grants Congress the power to raise and support armies and to organize, arm, and discipline the militia; article 1, § 10, which prohibits states from keeping standing armies in times of peace; and the Second Amendment, among others.]

We are next to inquire whether the fifth and sixth sections of article II of the Military Code are in violation of the other provisions of the constitution of the United States relied on by the plaintiff in error. The first of these is the second amendment, which declares: "A well regulated militia being necessary to the security of a free State, the right of the people to keep and bear arms shall not be infringed."

We think it clear that the sections under consideration, which only forbid bodies of men to associate together as military organizations, or to drill or parade with arms in cities and towns unless authorized by law, do not infringe the right of the people to keep and bear arms. But a conclusive answer to the contention that this amendment prohibits the legislation in question lies in the fact that the amendment is a limitation only upon the power of congress and the national government, and not upon that of the state. It was so held by this court in the case of *U. S. v. Cruikshank* in which the chief justice, in delivering the judgment of the court, said that the right of the people to keep and bear arms is not a right granted by the constitution. Neither is it in any manner dependent upon that instrument for its existence. The second amendment declares that it shall not be infringed, but this, as has been seen, means no more than that it shall not be infringed by congress. This is one of the amendments that has no other effect than to restrict the powers of the national government, leaving the people to look for their protection against any violation by their fellow-citizens of the rights it recognizes to . . . the "'powers which relate to merely municipal legislation, or what was perhaps more properly called internal police,' 'not surrendered or restrained' by the constitution of the United States. . . ."

It is undoubtedly true that all citizens capable of bearing arms constitute the reserved military force or reserve militia of the United States as well as of the states, and, in view of this prerogative of the general government, as well as of its general powers, the states cannot, even laying the constitutional provision in question out of view, prohibit the people from keeping and bearing arms, so as to deprive the United States of their rightful resource for maintaining the public security, and disable the people from performing their duty to the general government. But, as already stated, we think it clear that the sections under consideration do not have this effect. . . .

DISCUSSION NOTES

1. The group of which Presser was a member, Lehr und Wehr Verein, was a German socialist group founded to urge workingmen to arm themselves against private guards employed by companies against labor unions. (See generally Stephen P. Halbrook, *The Right of Workers to Assemble and to Bear Arms: Presser v. Illinois, One of the Last Holdouts against Application of the Bill of Rights to the States*, 76 University of Detroit Mercy Law Review 943, 946–52 [1999].) The events in *Presser* were intertwined with the 1886 Chicago Haymarket Riot, in which, during a confrontation between striking workers and police, a bomb was thrown, killing one policeman and injuring seventy others. Angry police then set upon the crowd of workers with guns and clubs. (For more on the Haymarket Riot, see Paul Avrich, *The Haymarket Tragedy* [Princeton: Princeton University Press, 1984].) To what extent should courts consider the social context, as opposed to purely legal issues, in deciding constitutional cases?

2. Although the Supreme Court did so in *dicta* (statements made by a court that are not necessary to its holding and thus not of binding precedential value), the Court distinguished between the right to keep and bear arms and the authority of a state to pass laws banning the drilling or parading of nongovernmental military organizations. Implicit in the distinction, however, seems to be recognition that the right to keep and bear arms is something amenable to exercise by *individuals*. Should the right to arms be considered solely in an individual context, or should the right also protect organized assemblies of armed people?

3. While holding that the Second Amendment did not apply directly to the states, the Court did remark that the state could not "prohibit the people from keeping and bearing arms, so as to deprive the United States of their rightful resource for maintaining the public security, and disable the people from performing their duty to the general government." What implications might this have, if any, for state gun control efforts? Should modern courts care if a state gun law interferes with the federal militia, which is still recognized by statute (10 *U.S. Code* § 311) but which is not currently used for national defense or other purposes?

4. In the 1990s, a great deal of attention was paid to self-styled "militias" which met for firearms and survival training and political discussion. Some states have outlawed various sorts of group paramilitary training. (For an analysis of the constitutionality of such statutes, see Joelle E. Polesky, Comment, *The Rise of Private Militia: A First and Second Amendment Analysis of the Right to Organize and the Right to Train,* 144 University of Pennsylvania Law Review 1593 [1996].) Should meetings and training sessions by such groups be banned? Would bans drive the training underground? Should people be afraid of assemblies of armed people who have unconventional views of politics, which for modern militias often includes the belief that almost all acts of the U.S. government are illegitimate and have no binding effect on them?

5. The Second Amendment remains one of only three individual liberties contained in the Bill of Rights (the other two being the Fifth Amendment right to indictment by a grand jury and the Seventh Amendment guarantee of a jury trial in a civil case) that have not been made binding on the states by the U.S. Supreme Court. The Supreme Court could choose to revisit *Presser* and overrule it, or the Supreme Court could incorporate the Second Amendment under the "due process" theory, without having to overrule *Presser* (since *Presser* did not address the as-yet-uncreated due process theory). Should the Court do so?

   In determining whether a right is part of due process of law so as to make it binding on the states, the essential question that must be answered affirmatively under the Court's incorporation jurisprudence is whether the right is "fundamental." The Court has used varying language to describe the level to which the right must rise in order to meet this standard. It has been said the right must be "implicit in the concept of ordered liberty," (*Palko v. Connecticut,* 302 U.S. 319, 325 [1937]) "so rooted in the traditions and conscience of our people as to be ranked fundamental," (*id.*) or "lie at the base of all our civil and political institutions." (*Id.* at 328.) Is the Second Amendment right to keep and bear arms fundamental under these standards?

6. Do you see the implications of the *Presser* holding? In *Quillici v. Village of Morton Grove,* 695 F. 2d 261 (7th Cir. 1983), several citizens challenged the constitutionality of an ordinance passed by the village of Morton Grove, Illinois that prohibited the possession of handguns within the

village's borders. The plaintiffs argued that the Second Amendment applies to state and local governments. The federal court of appeals rejected the argument, stating:

> While reluctantly conceding that Presser v. Illinois . . . held that the second amendment applied only to action by the federal government, [plaintiffs] nevertheless assert that Presser also held that the right to keep and bear arms is an attribute of national citizenship which is not subject to state restriction. Finally, apparently responding to the district court's comments that "[p]laintiffs . . . have not suggested that the Morton Grove Ordinance in any way interferes with the ability of the United States to maintain public security" . . . [plaintiffs] argue in this court that the Morton Grove Ordinance interferes with the federal government's ability to maintain public security by preventing individuals from defending themselves and the community from "external or internal armed threats."

As we have noted, the parties agree that Presser is controlling, but disagree as to what Presser held. It is difficult to understand how appellants can assert that Presser supports the theory that the second amendment right to keep and bear arms is a fundamental right which the state cannot regulate when the Presser decision plainly states that "[t]he Second Amendment declares that it shall not be infringed, but this . . . means no more than that it shall not be infringed by Congress. This is one of the amendments that has no other effect than to restrict the powers of the National government. . . ." As the district court explained in detail, appellants' claim that Presser supports the proposition that the second amendment guarantee of the right to keep and bear arms is not subject to state restriction is based on dicta quoted out of context. This argument borders on the frivolous and does not warrant any further consideration.

Apparently recognizing the inherent weakness of their reliance on Presser, appellants urge three additional arguments to buttress their claim that the second amendment applies to the states. They contend that: (1) Presser is no longer good law because later Supreme Court cases incorporating other amendments into the fourteenth amendment have effectively overruled Presser; (2) Presser is illogical; and (3) the entire Bill of Rights has been implicitly incorporated into the fourteenth amendment to apply to the states.

None of these arguments has merit. First, appellants offer no authority, other than their own opinions, to support their arguments that Presser is no longer good law or would have been decided differently today. Indeed, the fact that the Supreme Court continues to cite Presser [court cites a 1964 Supreme Court case] leads to the opposite conclusion. Second, regardless of whether appellants agree with the Presser analysis, it is the law of the land and we are bound by it. Their assertion that Presser is illogical is a policy matter for the Supreme Court to address. Finally, their theory of implicit incorporation is wholly unsupported. The Supreme Court has specifically rejected the proposition that the entire Bill of Rights applies to the states through the fourteenth amendment. (*Id.* at 269–70.)

Were you aware that the Second Amendment does not apply to the actions of state or local governments? Does this fact change your view about gun control restrictions at the state or local level? Would you favor or oppose an ordinance in your city or town banning the possession of handguns? All guns?

UNITED STATES V. MILLER
307 U.S. 174 (1939)

[The National Firearms Act (NFA) of 1934 required that people who wished to possess or sell machine guns, short shotguns, and short rifles pay a federal tax and register the gun pursuant to the tax payment. (See 26 *U.S. Code* § 5801 et seq., modern codification of NFA.) Near the Arkansas-Oklahoma border, a pair of bootleggers named Jack Miller and Frank Layton were caught in possession of a short shotgun. The original indictment was quashed by an Arkansas district court, which ruled that the NFA violated the Second Amendment. (*United States v. Miller*, 26 F. Supp. 1002 [W.D. Ark. 1939].) The federal government subsequently appealed the case, while Miller and Layton disappeared. Accordingly, in the Supreme Court case, only the government presented arguments. Justice McReynolds delivered the opinion of the Court.]

An indictment in the District Court Western District Arkansas, charged that Jack Miller and Frank Layton did unlawfully, knowingly, willfully, and feloniously transport in interstate commerce from the town of Claremore in the State of Oklahoma to the town of Siloam Springs in the State of Arkansas . . . a double barrel 12-gauge Stevens shotgun having a barrel less than 18 inches in length . . . [without] having registered said firearm . . . and not having in their possession a stamp-affixed written order for said firearm as [required by the National Firearms Act of 1934].

[The defendants] alleged: The National Firearms Act is not a revenue measure but an attempt to usurp police power reserved to the States, and is therefore unconstitutional. Also, it offends the inhibition of the Second Amendment to the Constitution, U.S.C.A.—"A well regulated Militia, being necessary to the security of a free State, the right of the people to keep and bear Arms, shall not be infringed."

The District Court held that section 11 of the Act violates the Second Amendment. It accordingly sustained the demurrer and quashed the indictment.

The cause is here by direct appeal. . . .

[The Court first held that the tax on firearms was valid and did not usurp the reserved powers of the state under the Tenth Amendment.]

In the absence of any evidence tending to show that possession or use of a "shotgun having a barrel of less than eighteen inches in length" at this time has some reasonable relationship to the preservation or efficiency of a well regulated militia, we cannot say that the Second Amendment guarantees the right to keep and bear such an instrument. Certainly it is not within judicial notice that this weapon is any part of the ordinary military equipment or that its use could contribute to the common defense.

The Constitution as originally adopted granted to the Congress power—"To provide for calling forth the Militia to execute the Laws of the Union, suppress Insurrections and repel Invasions; To provide for organizing, arming, and disciplining, the Militia, and for governing such Part of them as may be employed in the Service of the United States, reserving to the States respectively, the Appointment of the Officers, and the Authority of training the Militia according to the discipline prescribed by Congress." U.S.C.A. Constitution, Article 1, s 8. With obvious purpose to assure the continuation and render possible the effectiveness of such forces the declaration and guarantee of the Second Amendment were made. It must be interpreted and applied with that end in view.

The Militia which the States were expected to maintain and train is set in contrast with Troops which they were forbidden to keep without the consent of Congress. The sentiment of the time strongly disfavored standing armies; the common view was that adequate defense of country and laws could be secured through the Militia—civilians primarily, soldiers on occasion.

The signification attributed to the term Militia appears from the debates in the Convention, the history and legislation of Colonies and States, and the writings of approved commentators. These show plainly enough that the Militia comprised all males physically capable of acting in concert for the common defense. "A body of citizens enrolled for military discipline." And further, that ordinarily when called for service these men were expected to appear bearing arms supplied by themselves and of the kind in common use at the time.

Blackstone's Commentaries, Vol. 2, Ch. 13, p. 409 points out "that king Alfred first settled a national militia in this kingdom" and traces the subsequent development and use of such forces.

Adam Smith's *Wealth of Nations,* Book V, Ch. 1, contains an extended account of the Militia. It is there said: "Men of republican principles have been jealous of a standing army as dangerous to liberty. In a militia, the character of the labourer, artificer, or tradesman, predominates over that of the soldier: in a standing army, that of the soldier predominates over every other character; and in this distinction seems to consist the essential difference between those two different species of military force."

The American Colonies In The 17th Century, Osgood, Vol. 1, ch. XIII, affirms in reference to the early system of defense in New England:

In all the colonies, as in England, the militia system was based on the principle of the assize of arms. This implied the general obligation of all adult male inhabitants to possess arms, and, with certain exceptions, to cooperate in the work of defence.

The possession of arms also implied the possession of ammunition, and the authorities paid quite as much attention to the latter as to the former. A year later (1632) it was ordered that any single man who had not furnished himself with arms might be put out to service, and this became a permanent part of the legislation of the colony (Massachusetts).

Most if not all of the States have adopted provisions touching the right to keep and bear arms. Differences in the language employed in these have naturally led to somewhat variant conclusions concerning the scope of the right guaranteed. But none of them seem to afford any material support for the challenged ruling of the court below. . . .

We are unable to accept the conclusion of the court below and the challenged judgment must be reversed. The cause will be remanded for further proceedings. Reversed and remanded.

DISCUSSION NOTES

1. What is the holding in *Miller*?
2. Those who argue that the Second Amendment does not protect an individual right to keep and bear arms point to the *Miller* decision in support of their position. Does the *Miller* decision actually say, as several lower federal courts have interpreted it, that individuals have no right to keep and bear arms? (For a critical survey of lower courts' characterization of Miller, see Brannon P. Denning, *Can the Simple Cite Be Trusted? Lower Court Interpretation of United States v. Miller and the Second Amendment,* 26 Cumberland Law Review 961 [1996].)
3. Gun control advocates argue that the Second Amendment protects only a state's right to have an armed militia and that this "collective right" is all that *Miller* found guaranteed in the amendment. However, note that the *Miller* Court used "militia" in the sense of a body of universal (male) membership: "The militia," the Court wrote, "comprised all males physically capable of acting in concert for the common defense" and were "civilians primarily, soldiers on occasion." Does the definition of militia suggest that, even if the right to bear arms is limited to the militia, it is still a broad right?
4. Note that the militia included only males. Does this mean that women do not enjoy the right to bear arms because they were never part of the militia to which the right was tied? Does it make a difference to your an-

swer that women can now serve in the federal armed forces (some in combat roles), and that many states have rewritten their militia statutes to include women?

5. Michigan Supreme Court judge (and also University of Michigan law professor) Thomas Cooley was a leading constitutional scholar in the latter part of the nineteenth century. Regarding the Second Amendment, Cooley wrote:

> *The Right is General.*—It may be supposed from the phraseology of this provision that the right to keep and bear arms was only guaranteed to the militia; but this would be an interpretation not warranted by the intent. The militia, as has been elsewhere explained, consists of those persons who, under the law, are liable to the performance of military duty, and are officered and enrolled for service when called upon. But the law may make provision for the enrolment of all who are fit to perform military duty, or of a small number only, or it may wholly omit to make any provision at all; and if the right were limited to those enrolled, the purpose of this guaranty might be defeated altogether by the action or neglect to act of the government it was meant to hold in check. The meaning of the provision undoubtedly is, that the people, from whom the militia must be taken, shall have the right to keep and bear arms, and they need no permission or regulation of law for the purpose. But this enables the government to have a well regulated militia; for to bear arms implies something more than the mere keeping; it implies the learning to handle and use them in a way that makes those who keep them ready for their efficient use; in other words, it implies the right to meet for voluntary discipline in arms, observing in doing so the laws of public order. (Thomas M. Cooley, *The General Principles of Constitutional Law in the United States of America* 271–72 [Boston: Little, Brown & Co., 1880].)

Is Cooley right that allowing the government to define militia membership narrowly would eviscerate the Second Amendment as a check on abusive government? Are Cooley's views consistent with the *Presser* and *Miller* decisions?

6. In the brief filed in *Miller*, the U.S. Department of Justice argued that "the very language of the Second Amendment discloses that this right

has reference only to the keep and bearing of arms by the people as members of the state militia or other similar military organization provided for by law." (Brief of the United States, *United States v. Miller*, 307 U.S. 174 [1939] [No. 696], at 4–5.) It further argued that the Second Amendment "gave sanction only to the arming of the people as a body to defend their rights against tyrannical and unprincipled rulers" and "did not permit the keeping of arms for private defense" (*id.* at 12). The Second Amendment's prefatory language about a well-regulated militia, argued the government, "indicates that the right [to keep and bear arms] is not one which may be utilized for private purposes but only one which exists where the arms are borne in the militia or some other military organization provided for by law and intended for the protection of the state" (*id.* at 15). Did the Court adopt the government's position, or did it implicitly reject it by relying on one of the government's fall-back positions, namely, that the types of weapons Miller and his accomplice were convicted of possessing are not the type of weapons useful to the militia? Is it surprising that the federal government argued that the main purpose of the Second Amendment is to enable the maintenance of an institution that could effectuate armed revolt against "tyrannical and unprincipled rulers"?

7. Why did the Supreme Court send the case back to the trial court for further proceedings? Recall that the Court said only that it had no evidence supporting a sawed-off shotgun's military utility and could not take judicial notice (i.e., acknowledge without supporting evidence presented by the parties) thereof. Suppose that Miller and Layton had not disappeared during their appeal and had appeared for the remanded case in federal district court. Could they have proven that short shotguns (sometimes used for home defense, and for trench combat in World War I) had militia utility? Do you think Miller and Layton would have won the case if their gun had proven militia utility, even though they were not enrolled in any militia?

8. What would a "state's rights" Second Amendment mean? Would a state legislature be free to declare that its militia consisted of the entire adult population? If so, would that create a de facto individual right for each citizen to bear arms? Do you think your own state legislature would consider taking such action to enhance the right to bear arms? Could a

state government arm its militia with weapons that the federal government wanted to ban, such as new "assault weapons," which Congress banned in 1994? Could the state direct the state militia to arm itself with machine guns? Surface-to-air missiles? If the Second Amendment does protect state militias (rather than individual people), what kind of laws restricting arms ownership would the federal government be prohibited from enacting? Any? Could the federal government pass any laws it wished to under such an interpretation, or would there still be restrictions? (For an interesting exploration of these questions, see Glenn Harlan Reynolds and Don B. Kates Jr., *The Second Amendment and States Rights: A Thought Experiment*, 36 William and Mary Law Review 1737 [1995].)

9. Following *Miller* to its logical conclusions, suggested by Justice McReynolds's opinion, does the Second Amendment offer more protection for individuals seeking to possess military weapons, such as machine guns, and less protection for inexpensive handguns, which likely do not meet military specifications? Does it protect edged weapons, such as swords and knives? State court opinions from the nineteenth century tended to rule that the Second Amendment protected swords but not some kinds of knives (such as bowie knives) that were thought to be useful only for brawling or crime. (See David B. Kopel, *The Second Amendment in the Nineteenth Century*, 1998 Brigham Young University Law Review 1359, 1432–33 [1998], summarizing the case law.) What about cannon, mortars, artillery, or rockets?

10. As the only Supreme Court decision squarely addressing the meaning of the Second Amendment, *Miller* has assumed large importance in the gun control debate. But what does it really mean? Consider McClurg's evaluation of the case:

> Did *Miller* endorse the collective right view or the individual right view of the Second Amendment? . . .
>
> Pro-gun control commentators interpret Miller as clearly establishing a collective right "organized militia" view of the Second Amendment, stating:
>
> • The Supreme Court in *Miller* "ruled . . . that the Second Amendment has nothing to do with individual rights to bear arms but

rather the right of the states to an armed militia." (Amitai Etzioni, *Gun Control: A Vanilla Agenda*, 1 Responsive Community 6, 9 [1991]).

- The Supreme Court has "ruled at least three times that the Second Amendment has not the slightest thing to do with an individual's right to bear arms," citing *Miller* as "the most trenchant of these decisions." (Wayne King, *Sarah and James Brady; Target: The Gun Lobby*, N.Y. Times Magazine, Dec. 9, 1990, at 80).

- "These words alone [two sentences from the Court's opinion] undercut any individual right interpretation of the Second Amendment." (Roy G. Weatherup, *Standing Armies and Armed Citizens: An Historical Analysis of the Second Amendment*, 2 Hastings Constitutional Law Quarterly 961, 999 [1975]).

- "It is firmly settled that there is no constitutional right to bear arms," citing *Miller*. (Eric A. Pullen, *Guns, Domestic Violence, Interstate Commerce, and the Lautenberg Amendment: "Simply Because Congress May Conclude That A Particular Activity Substantially Affects Interstate Commerce Does Not Necessarily Make It So,"* 39 South Texas Law Review 1029, 1070 n.308 [1998]).

In stark contrast to these collective right interpretations, pro–gun rights commentators have asserted about Miller:

- "[I]t is clear that *Miller*, even with its limitations, supports the view that the second amendment guarantees an individual right to keep and bear guns, including handguns." (Richard E. Gardiner, *To Preserve Liberty—A Look at the Right to Keep and Bear Arms*, 10 Northern Kentucky Law Review 63, 92 [1982]).

- "[D]espite the shortcomings of the *Miller* opinion, the Supreme Court correctly concluded that the Second Amendment protects an individual's right to keep and bear arms and thus rejected the untenable collective right theory." (Nelson Lund, *The Second Amendment, Political Liberty, and the Right to Self-Preservation*, 39 Alabama Law Review 103, 110 [1987]).

- "*Miller* remains an affirmation of the constitutional protection of the popular right to keep and bear military weapons." (Ronald Docal, Comment, *The Second, Fifth and Ninth Amendments—The*

> *Precarious Protectors of the American Gun Collector*, 23 Florida State
> University Law Review 1101, 1120 [1996]).

Are all these excerpts referring to the same case? *Miller* could not have
established *both* a collective right interpretation and an individual
right interpretation of the Second Amendment. . . . The truth is,
Miller offered a little something for everyone. It is an ambiguous decision that failed to unequivocally adopt either a collective right or an
individual right interpretation of the Second Amendment. . . .

[W]hen all is said and done, the only certainty about *Miller* is that
it failed to give either side a clear-cut victory. Most modern scholars
recognize this fact. For example, Professor Eugene Volokh describes
Miller as "deliciously and usefully ambiguous" in an article about
using the Second Amendment as a teaching tool in constitutional law.
That is probably the most accurate statement that can be made about
the case. (Andrew J. McClurg, *"Lotts" More Guns and Other Fallacies
Infecting the Gun Control Debate*, 11 Journal on Firearms and Public
Policy 139, 147–150 [1999].)

Does the confusion regarding the meaning of such an important case
make it curious that the Supreme Court has declined to revisit the issue
since *Miller*? (There have been about two dozen Supreme Court references to the Second Amendment since *Miller* [as dicta in other cases].
Most of these are consistent with an individual rights view, but some
are more supportive of a militia-only view. (See David B. Kopel, *The
Supreme Court's Thirty-five Other Gun Cases: What the Supreme Court
Has Said about the Second Amendment*, 18 St. Louis University Public
Law Review 99 [1999].)

11. Why do you think the Court has not agreed to hear a Second Amendment case since 1939? Do you agree with some gun control advocates
who argue that the Supreme Court has not taken more cases because
the *Miller* decision is so clear? Could the Court be conserving its political capital by avoiding a contentious social issue? Could the justices
simply be less interested in guns than in topics such as free speech or
anti-trust law? Is it possible the justices do not want to disturb existing
law (interpreting, for the most part, *Miller* as standing for only a collectivist right) even if it is wrong, because of the social implications

such a decision would have? It is often difficult to know what weight to give a Supreme Court decision *not* to take up an issue when assessing the merits of a case. (For an illuminating discussion of the factors that influence members of the Supreme Court in selecting cases to hear, see H. W. Perry Jr., *Deciding to Decide: Agenda Setting in the United States Supreme Court* [Cambridge, MA: Harvard University Press, 1991].)

12. Many Second Amendment claims are raised by convicted felons who have been found guilty of possessing firearms in violation of federal law. Might the Court be reluctant to address the Second Amendment in a case with such unfavorable or unsavory appellants? Do you think that the Supreme Court would continue to hold Second Amendment questions at arm's length if sweeping gun control legislation that significantly limited the ability of otherwise law-abiding persons to possess certain types of common firearms was enacted by Congress? If law-abiding gun rights supporters are confident that the Second Amendment stands for a strong individual right, why do you think they have not filed more lawsuits challenging gun control restrictions on Second Amendment grounds? A few cities (e.g., Chicago and the District of Columbia) have essentially banned handguns. Why do you think lawsuits have not been filed challenging such stringent restrictions? Because *Presser* forecloses challenges to nonfederal gun laws? Because gun owners and gun lobbying organizations are worried about establishing an adverse precedent? The National Association for the Advancement of Colored People (NAACP) long thought that public school segregation was unconstitutional but waited until the 1950s to bring such a controversial issue to the Supreme Court; in the 1930s and 1940s, the NAACP focused on winning victories on smaller issues about segregation, hoping to set the stage for bigger victories in the future. Are Second Amendment lawyers behaving the same way—postponing their most controversial claims until they believe the courts are ready?

13. From time to time, individual justices have expressed opinions about the Second Amendment. What light, if any, do the following excerpts shed on the meaning of *Miller* or on the Supreme Court's assessment of the Second Amendment's scope?

   • The defendant in *Adams v. Williams*, 407 U.S. 143 (1972), was convicted in a Connecticut state court of illegal possession of a handgun found during a "stop and frisk." The Supreme Court upheld his conviction, reversing a lower court decision that held the stop-and-frisk search constituted a violation of Williams's Fourth Amendment right against unreasonable searches and seizures. In a dissenting opinion, Justice Douglas wrote:

> Connecticut allows its citizens to carry weapons, concealed or otherwise, at will, provided they have a permit. . . . Connecticut law gives its police no authority to frisk a person for a permit. Yet the arrest was for illegal possession of a gun. The only basis for that arrest was the informer's tip on the narcotics. Can it be said that a man in possession of narcotics will not have a permit for his gun? Is that why the arrest for possession of a gun in the free-and-easy State of Connecticut becomes constitutional?
>
> The police problem is an acute one not because of the Fourth Amendment, but because of the ease with which anyone can acquire a pistol. A powerful lobby dins into the ears of our citizenry that these gun purchases are constitutional rights protected by the Second Amendment, which reads, "A well regulated Militia, being necessary to the security of a free State, the right of the people to keep and bear Arms, shall not be infringed."
>
> There is under our decisions no reason why stiff state laws governing the purchase and possession of pistols may not be enacted. There is no reason why pistols may not be barred from anyone with a police record. There is no reason why a State may not require a purchaser of a pistol to pass a psychiatric test. There is no reason why all pistols should not be barred to everyone except the police.
>
> The leading case is United States v. Miller, upholding a federal law making criminal the shipment in interstate commerce of a sawed-off shotgun. The law was upheld, there being no evidence that a sawed-off shotgun had "some reasonable relationship to the preservation or efficiency of a well regulated militia." . . . The Second Amendment, it was held, "must be interpreted and applied" with the view of maintaining a "militia. . . ."
>
> Critics say that proposals like this water down the Second Amendment. Our decisions belie that argument, for the Second Amend-

ment, as noted, was designed to keep alive the militia. But if water-ing-down is the mood of the day, I would prefer to water down the Second rather than the Fourth Amendment. . . . (*Id.* at 149–51.)

• In *Lewis v. United States*, 445 U.S. 55 (1980), a defendant challenged his conviction for violation of a federal law that prohibited convicted felons from possessing firearms. The Court upheld the statute even in cases where the underlying felony conviction was constitutionally invalid (because the convict had been denied his right to counsel during the trial). After ruling that the ban did not violate the Sixth Amendment right to counsel, Justice Blackmun wrote:

> The firearm regulatory scheme at issue here is consonant with the concept of equal protection embodied in the Due Process Clause of the Fifth Amendment if there is "some rational basis" for the statutory distinctions made . . . or . . . they "have some relevance to the purpose for which the classification is made. . . ."
>
> Section 1202(a)(1) clearly meets that test. Congress, as its expressed purpose in enacting [the statute] reveals . . . was concerned that the receipt and possession of a firearm by a felon constitutes a threat, among other things, to the continued and effective operation of the Government of the United States. The legislative history of the gun control laws discloses Congress' worry about the easy availability of firearms, especially to those persons who pose a threat to community peace. And Congress focused on the nexus between violent crime and the possession of a firearm by any person with a criminal record. . . . Congress could rationally conclude that any felony conviction, even an allegedly invalid one, is a sufficient basis on which to prohibit the possession of a firearm. . . . This Court has recognized repeatedly that a legislature constitutionally may prohibit a convicted felon from engaging in activities far more fundamental than the possession of a firearm. See [cases involving voting, office holding, and the practice of medicine]. (*Id.* at 65–66.)

In a footnote, Justice Blackmun explained:

> These legislative restrictions on the use of firearms are neither based upon constitutionally suspect criteria, nor do they trench upon any

constitutionally protected liberties. See United States v. Miller . . . (the Second Amendment guarantees no right to keep and bear a firearm that does not have "some reasonable relationship to the preservation or efficiency of a well regulated militia"). (*Id.* at 65 n.8.)

• Most recently, in *Printz v. United States*, 521 U.S. 898 (1995), the Supreme Court struck down provisions of the Brady Handgun Violence Protection Act that required local law enforcement personnel to participate in the administration of a federal program by conducting background checks on prospective purchasers of handguns and related tasks. The Court found that the act violated principles of federalism that prohibited the federal government from "commandeering" state and local officials to carry out provisions of federal law. The Second Amendment was not raised as an issue in the case. In a concurring opinion, however, Justice Clarence Thomas offered a few thoughts on the Second Amendment implications of the Brady Act:

> Even if we construe Congress' authority to regulate interstate commerce to encompass those intrastate transactions that "substantially affect" interstate commerce, I question whether Congress can regulate the particular transactions at issue here. The Constitution, in addition to delegating certain enumerated powers to Congress, places whole areas outside the reach of Congress' regulatory authority. The First Amendment, for example, is fittingly celebrated for preventing Congress from "prohibiting the free exercise" of religion or "abridging the freedom of speech." The Second Amendment similarly appears to contain an express limitation on the government's authority. That Amendment provides: "[a] well regulated Militia, being necessary to the security of a free State, the right of the people to keep and bear arms, shall not be infringed." This Court has not had recent occasion to consider the nature of the substantive right safeguarded by the Second Amendment.[1] If, however, the Second Amendment is read to confer a personal right to "keep and bear arms," a colorable argument exists that the Federal Government's regulatory scheme, at least as it pertains to the purely intrastate sale or possession of firearms, runs afoul of that Amendment's protections.[2] As the parties did not raise this argument, however, we need not consider it here. Perhaps, at some

future date, this Court will have the opportunity to determine whether Justice Story was correct when he wrote that the right to bear arms "has justly been considered, as the palladium of the liberties of a republic." 3 J. Story, Commentaries § 1890, p. 746 (1833). (*Id.* at 937–39.)

Justice Thomas's footnotes read as follows:

1. Our most recent treatment of the Second Amendment occurred in United States v. Miller, 307 U.S. 174, 59 S.Ct. 816, 83 L.Ed. 1206 (1939), in which we reversed the District Court's invalidation of the National Firearms Act, enacted in 1934. In Miller, we determined that the Second Amendment did not guarantee a citizen's right to possess a sawed-off shotgun because that weapon had not been shown to be "ordinary military equipment" that could "contribute to the common defense." Id., at 178, 59 S. Ct., at 818. The Court did not, however, attempt to define, or otherwise construe, the substantive right protected by the Second Amendment.

2. Marshaling an array of historical evidence, a growing body of scholarly commentary indicates that the "right to keep and bear arms" is, as the Amendment's text suggests, a personal right. See, e.g., J. Malcolm, *To Keep and Bear Arms: The Origins of an Anglo-American Right* 162 (1994); S. Halbrook, *That Every Man Be Armed, The Evolution of a Constitutional Right* (1984); Van Alstyne, *The Second Amendment and the Personal Right to Arms*, 43 Duke Law Journal 1236 (1994); Amar, *The Bill of Rights and the Fourteenth Amendment*, 101 Yale Law Journal 1193 (1992); Cottrol and Diamond, *The Second Amendment: Toward an Afro-Americanist Reconsideration*, 80 Georgetown Law Journal 309 (1991); Levinson, *The Embarrassing Second Amendment*, 99 Yale Law Journal 637 (1989); Kates, *Handgun Prohibition and the Original Meaning of the Second Amendment*, 82 Michigan Law Review 204 (1983). Other scholars, however, argue that the Second Amendment does not secure a personal right to keep or to bear arms. See, e.g., Bogus, *Race, Riots, and Guns*, 66 Southern California Law Review 1365 (1993); Williams, *Civic Republicanism and the Citizen Militia: The Terrifying Second Amendment*, 101 Yale Law Journal 551 (1991); Brown, *Guns, Cowboys, Philadelphia Mayors, and Civic Republicanism: On Sanford Levinson's The Embarrassing Second Amendment*, 99

Yale Law Journal 661 (1989); Cress, *An Armed Community: The Origins and Meaning of the Right to Bear Arms*, 71 Journal of American History 22 (1984). Although somewhat overlooked in our jurisprudence, the Amendment has certainly engendered considerable academic, as well as public, debate.

14. Note that Justice Douglas, in *Adams, supra*, expresses the opinion that *Miller* stands only for a collective state right to bear arms, while Justice Thomas, in *Printz*, suggests it may stand for an individual right. Does the fact that even Supreme Court justices disagree on the meaning of *Miller* make it all the more strange that the Court has not revisited the issue in more than sixty years? Based on the above quotations and other cases, Kopel suggests that the Rehnquist Supreme Court in the 1990s became more consistently friendly to the individual rights view of the Second Amendment than the Warren Court had been in the 1960s (Kopel, *The Supreme Court's Thirty-five Other Gun Cases, supra*).

B. The Second Amendment in Lower Federal Courts

The final group of federal cases comes from the lower federal courts and includes the 1999 case of *United States v. Emerson*, in which a federal district court—for the first time since the district court in *Miller* struck down the National Firearms Act of 1934—invalidated a federal gun control measure on Second Amendment grounds.

Hickman v. Block
81 F. 3d 98 (9th Cir. 1996)

[Hickman, a California security alarm company operator and federally licensed firearms dealer, sought a concealed weapons permit so that he could become a bodyguard. His applications were denied, and he sued municipal authorities for violating his constitutional rights, including his rights under the Second Amendment. Judge Hall delivered the opinion of the court.]

. . . Hickman argues that the Second Amendment requires the states to regulate gun ownership and use in a "reasonable" manner. The question presented at the threshold of Hickman's appeal is whether the Second Amendment confers upon individual citizens standing to enforce the right to keep and bear arms. We follow our sister circuits in holding that the Second Amendment is a right held by the states, and does not protect the possession of a weapon by a private citizen. We conclude that Hickman can show no legal injury, and therefore lacks standing to bring this action.

Article III of the Constitution restricts the federal courts to adjudicating actual "cases" or "controversies." . . . Among the cluster of doctrines that ensure our adherence to the case-or-controversy requirement, the "doctrine that requires a litigant to have 'standing' to invoke the power of a federal court is perhaps the most important." . . . Article III standing is a jurisdictional prerequisite. . . .

[To satisfy constitutional standing requirements] . . . the plaintiff must have suffered injury to a legally protected interest. . . . This injury must be both concrete and particularized, . . . and "actual or imminent" rather than "conjectural or hypothetical." . . .

This case turns on . . . whether Hickman has shown injury to an interest protected by the Second Amendment. We note at the outset that no individual has ever succeeded in demonstrating such injury in federal court. The seminal authority in this area continues to be *United States v. Miller* . . . in which the Supreme Court upheld a conviction under the National Firearms Act . . . for transporting a sawed-off shotgun in interstate commerce. The Court rejected the appellant's hypothesis that the Second Amendment protected his possession of that weapon. Consulting the text and history of the amendment, the Court found that the right to keep and bear arms is meant solely to protect the right of the states to keep and maintain armed militia. In a famous passage, the Court held that:

> [i]n the absence of any evidence tending to show that the possession or use of a "shotgun having a barrel of less than eighteen inches in length" at this time has some reasonable relationship to the preservation or efficiency of a well-regulated militia, we cannot say that the Second Amendment guarantees the right to keep and bear such an instrument.
> 307 U.S. at 178, 59 S. Ct. at 818.

The Court's understanding follows a plain reading of the Amendment's text. The Amendment's second clause declares that the goal is to preserve the security of "a free state"; its first clause establishes the premise that a "well-regulated militia" is necessary to this end. Thus it is only in furtherance of state security that "the right of the people to keep and bear arms" is finally proclaimed. . . .

Following Miller, "[i]t is clear that the Second Amendment guarantees a collective rather than an individual right." . . . Because the Second Amendment guarantees the right of the states to maintain armed militia, the states alone stand in the position to show legal injury when this right is infringed.

Nevertheless, Hickman argues that under the Second Amendment, individuals have the right to complain about the manner in which a state arms its citizens. We fail to see the logic in this argument. The Second Amendment creates a right, not a duty. It does not oblige the states to keep armed militia, . . . or to arm their citizens generally, although some states do preserve, nominally at least, a broad individual right to bear arms as a foundation for their state militia. . . . Even in states which profess to maintain a citizen militia, an individual may not rely on this fact to manipulate the Constitution's legal injury requirement by arguing that a particular weapon of his admits some military use, or that he himself is a member of the armed citizenry from which the state draws its militia. . . .

Hickman's claim amounts to a "generalized grievance" regarding the organization and training of a state militia. . . . We do not involve ourselves in such matters. As the Supreme Court has observed, "decisions as to the composition, training, equipping, and control of a military force are essentially professional military judgments," and as such are nonjusticiable. . . . "[I]t is difficult to conceive of an area of governmental activity in which the courts have less competence." . . . For this reason, among others, we leave military matters to the elected branches of government. . . .

Because the right to keep an armed militia is a right held by the states alone, Hickman has failed to show "injury" as required by constitutional standing doctrine. Accordingly, we have no jurisdiction to hear his appeal.

DISCUSSION NOTES

1. Read Judge Hall's characterization of *Miller*'s holding, then read *Miller* again. Does she correctly state the holding? Does her description of the case reflect what went on? Recall that *Miller* was an appeal by the *government* from an adverse decision in a lower court regarding the constitutionality of the National Firearms Act. The defendant in the lower court was not represented at the Supreme Court because his indictment had been quashed. Moreover, the government was the only party that either filed a brief before the Court or participated in oral argument. (See Brannon P. Denning, *Gun Shy: The Second Amendment as an "Underenforced Constitutional Norm,"* 21 Harvard Journal of Law and Public Policy 719, 732–35 [1998], discussing *Miller*; Brannon P. Denning, *Can the Simple Cite Be Trusted? Lower Court Interpretations of United States v. Miller and the Second Amendment,* 26 Cumberland Law Review 961, 973–75, 997–98 [1996], discussing *Miller* and *Hickman.*)

2. Again, reflecting on the holding in *Miller*, does it support Judge Hall's unqualified statement that it is clear that the Second Amendment protects only a *state's* right to have an armed militia?

3. Consider Judge Hall's argument that Hickman did not have "standing" to bring the claim. Neither Miller nor his codefendant was a member of a state militia, nor did either man claim that possession of the sawed-off shotgun was in furtherance of such membership. If Judge Hall is correct, why do you think that the Supreme Court in *Miller* did not discuss the standing issue? Does the Court's failure to do so suggest that the Court might have assumed that *individuals* could invoke the amendment? Or only that the issue was not raised or considered important by the Court?

4. *Hickman* is one of more than thirty lower federal court opinions rejecting the view that the Second Amendment creates and protects an individual right to bear arms. Until 1999, no federal court holding took a contrary view, other than the district court in *Miller*, which was reversed by the U.S. Supreme Court (although a few federal courts offered dicta about an individual right). Does the sheer weight of judicial authority against an individual-right interpretation persuade you that the Second Amendment does not protect an individual right to keep and bear arms?

Or, if most of these opinions are based on *Miller*, are they called into question by the ambiguous nature of *Miller's* holding, as discussed above? Have lower court decisions, such as *Hickman*, cited *Miller* for propositions not fairly attributable to the opinion? (See, e.g., Denning, *Can the Simple Cite Be Trusted? supra*.)

UNITED STATES V. EMERSON
46 F. Supp. 2d 598 (N.D. Tex. 1999)

[Judge Cummings wrote the opinion.]

. . . On August 28, 1998, Emerson's wife, Sacha, filed a petition for divorce and application for a temporary restraining order in the 119th District Court of Tom Green County, Texas. The petition stated no factual basis for relief other than the necessary recitals required under the Texas Family Code regarding domicile, service of process, dates of marriage and separation, and the "insupportability" of the marriage. The application for a temporary restraining order—essentially a form order frequently used in Texas divorce procedure—sought to enjoin Emerson from engaging in various financial transactions to maintain the financial status quo and from making threatening communications or actual attacks upon his wife during the pendency of the divorce proceedings.

On September 4, 1998, the Honorable John E. Sutton held a hearing on Mrs. Emerson's application for a temporary restraining order. Mrs. Emerson was represented by an attorney at that hearing, and Mr. Emerson appeared pro se. Mrs. Emerson testified about her economic situation, her needs in the way of temporary spousal support and child support, and her desires regarding temporary conservatorship of their minor child.

During the hearing, Mrs. Emerson alleged that her husband threatened over the telephone to kill the man with whom Mrs. Emerson had been having an adulterous affair. However, no evidence was adduced concerning any acts of violence or threatened violence by Mr. Emerson against any member of his family, and the district court made no findings to that effect. Furthermore, the court did not admonish Mr. Emerson that if he granted the temporary restraining order, Mr. Emerson would be subject to federal criminal prosecution merely for possessing a firearm while being subject to the order.

[Judge Cummings then extensively discussed the text, history, structure, and Supreme Court treatment of the Second Amendment.]

It is difficult to interpret Miller as rendering the Second Amendment meaningless as a control on Congress. Ironically, one can read Miller as supporting some of the most extreme anti–gun control arguments; for example, that the individual citizen has a right to keep and bear bazookas, rocket launchers, and other armaments that are clearly used for modern warfare, including, of course, assault weapons. Under Miller, arguments about the constitutional legitimacy of a prohibition by Congress of private ownership of handguns or, what is much more likely, assault rifles, thus might turn on the usefulness of such guns in military settings. . . .

Miller did not answer the crucial question of whether the Second Amendment embodies an individual or collective right to bear arms. Although its holding has been used to justify many previous lower federal court rulings circumscribing Second Amendment rights, the Court in Miller simply chose a very narrow way to rule on the issue of gun possession under the Second Amendment, and left for another day further questions of Second Amendment construction [citing Justice Thomas's concurring opinion in *Printz*, excerpted *supra* pp. 175–77]. . . .

[Judge Cummings then addressed the argument that, assuming an individual right is protected by the Second Amendment, the social costs outweigh the benefits.]

As Professor Ronald Dworkin has argued, what it means to take rights seriously is that one will honor them even when there is significant social cost in doing so. Protecting freedom of speech, the rights of criminal defendants, or any other part of the Bill of Rights has significant costs—criminals going free, oppressed groups having to hear viciously racist speech and so on—consequences which we take for granted in defending the Bill of Rights. This mind-set changes, however, when the Second Amendment is concerned. "Cost-benefit" analysis, rightly or wrongly, has become viewed as a "conservative" weapon to attack liberal rights. Yet the tables are strikingly turned when the Second Amendment comes into play. Here "conservatives" argue in effect that social costs are irrelevant and "liberals" argue for a notion of the "living Constitution" and "changed circumstances" that would have the practical consequence of erasing the Second Amendment from the Constitution. . . .

[C]oncerns about the social costs of enforcing the Second Amendment must be outweighed by considering the lengths to which the federal courts have gone to uphold other rights in the Constitution. The rights of the Second Amendment should be as zealously guarded as the other individual liberties enshrined in the Bill of Rights. . . .

18 U.S.C. § 922(g)(8) is unconstitutional because it allows a state court divorce proceeding, without particularized findings of the threat of future violence, to automatically deprive a citizen of his Second Amendment rights. The statute allows, but does not require, that the restraining order include a finding that the person under the order represents a credible threat to the physical safety of the intimate partner or child. . . . If the statute only criminalized gun possession based upon court orders with particularized findings of the likelihood of violence, then the statute would not be so offensive, because there would be a reasonable nexus between gun possession and the threat of violence. However, the statute is infirm because it allows one to be subject to federal felony prosecution if the order merely "prohibits the use, attempted use, or threatened use of physical force against [an] intimate partner. . . ."

All that is required for prosecution under the Act is a boilerplate order with no particularized findings. Thus, the statute has no real safeguards against an arbitrary abridgement of Second Amendment rights. Therefore, by criminalizing protected Second Amendment activity based upon a civil state court order with no particularized findings, the statute is overbroad and in direct violation of an individual's Second Amendment rights.

By contrast, § 922(g)(8) is different from the felon-in-possession statute . . . because once an individual is convicted of a felony, he has by his criminal conduct taken himself outside the class of law-abiding citizens who enjoy full exercise of their civil rights. Furthermore, the convicted felon is admonished in state and federal courts that a felony conviction results in the loss of certain civil rights, including the right to bear arms. This is not so with § 922(g)(8). Under this statute, a person can lose his Second Amendment rights not because he has committed some wrong in the past, or because a judge finds he may commit some crime in the future, but merely because he is in a divorce proceeding. Although he may not be a criminal at all, he is stripped of his right to bear arms as much as a convicted felon. Second Amendment rights should not be so easily abridged.

It is absurd that a boilerplate state court divorce order can collaterally and automatically extinguish a law-abiding citizen's Second Amendment rights, particularly when neither the judge issuing the order, nor the parties nor their attorneys are aware of the federal criminal penalties arising from firearm possession after entry of the restraining order. That such a routine civil order has such extensive consequences totally attenuated from divorce proceedings makes the statute unconstitutional. There must be a limit to government regulation on lawful firearm possession. This statute exceeds that limit, and therefore it is unconstitutional.

[The court's discussion of the due process clause of the Fifth Amendment and the Tenth Amendment is omitted.]

Because 18 U.S.C. § 922(g)(8) violates the Second and Fifth Amendments to the United States Constitution, the Court GRANTS Emerson's Motion to Dismiss the Indictment. A judgment shall be entered in conformity with this opinion.

DISCUSSION NOTES

1. The United States appealed Judge Cumming's order in *Emerson*. On October 16, 2001, the U.S. Court of Appeals for the Fifth Circuit issued a lengthy opinion in *United States v. Emerson* that, although reversing Judge Cumming's order dismissing the indictment against Emerson, endorsed an individual rights reading of the Second Amendment. After extensively reviewing the text and history of the framing of the Second Amendment and the U.S. Supreme Court's decision in *United States v. Miller*, the court rejected the collective rights approach to the Second Amendment, stating:

> We hold, consistent with *Miller*, that it [the Second Amendment] protects the right of individuals, including those not then actually a member of any militia or engaged in active military service or training, to privately possess and bear their own firearms, such as the pistol involved here, that are suitable as personal, individual weapons.

. . . *United States v. Emerson,* 270 F.3d 203, 260 (5th Cir. 2001) (Garwood, J.).

The court recognized "that almost all of our sister courts have rejected any individual rights view of the Second Amendment," but opined that "all or almost all of these opinions seem to have done so either on the erroneous assumption that *Miller* resolved that issue or without sufficient articulated examination of the history and text of the Second Amendment." (*Id.* at 227.)

Despite the court's endorsement of the individual rights view, it nevertheless reversed the district court's decision to dismiss the indictment brought against Emerson.

> Although . . . the Second Amendment does protect individual rights, that does not mean that those rights may never be made subject to any limited, narrowly tailored specific exception or restrictions for particular cases that are reasonable and not inconsistent with the right of Americans generally to keep and bear their private arms as historically understood in this country. (*Id.* at 261.)

Emerson had argued that the federal statute under which he was convicted should have required a specific finding of a threat to his wife and child before subjecting him to the federal law criminalizing possession of weapons by those subject to certain restraining orders. The Court of Appeals disagreed:

> [W]e cannot say that [the statute's] lack of a requirement for an explicit, express credible threat finding by the court issuing the order . . . renders that section infirm under the Second Amendment. The presence of such an explicit finding would likely furnish *some* additional indication that the issuing court properly considered the matter, but such findings can be as much "boilerplate" or in error as any other part of such an order. (*Id.* at 263.)

The court concluded that the evidence presented in the original restraining order was sufficient to show that he presented a threat to his wife and children and thus was sufficient to bring him within the scope of the federal statute barring his possession of firearms. In other words, the court concluded that while the Second Amendment guarantees an individual right, the statute at issue does not unreasonably or unduly infringe on that right by limiting it with respect to certain people adjudged to be a danger to others.

Judge Robert M. Parker filed a special concurrence refusing to join in that part of the majority's opinion regarding the Second Amendment. Parker argued that the court's discussion on that point is "dicta [statements by judges in cases that are not necessary to resolve the legal matters at issue and thus not binding as statements of law] and is therefore not binding on us or on any other court." (*Id.* at 272.)

He also argued that the debate regarding whether the Second Amendment creates an individual or collective right is misplaced, stating:

> In the final analysis, whether the right to keep and bear arms is collective or individual is of no legal consequence. It is, as duly noted by the majority opinion, a right subject to reasonable regulation. If determining that Emerson had an individual Second Amendment right that could have been successfully asserted as a defense against the charge of violating [the statute], then the issue would be cloaked with legal significance. As it stands it makes no difference. [The statute] is simply another example of a reasonable restriction on whatever right is contained in the Second Amendment. (*Id.* at 273 [Justice Parker specially concurring].)

In a footnote, the majority responded to Parker's criticism that it unnecessarily addressed the issue of whether the right to keep and bear arms was an individual or a collective one, stating:

> That precise issue was decided by the district court and was briefed and argued by both parties in this court and in the district court. Moreover, in reaching that issue we have only done what the vast majority of other courts faced with similar contentions have done (albeit our resolution of that question is different). The vast majority [of courts] have not . . . simply said that it makes no difference whether or not the Second Amendment right to keep and bear arms is an individual right because even if it were an individual right the conviction (or the challenged

statute) would be valid. In this case, unless we were to determine the issue of the proper construction of [the statute] in Emerson's favor (which the special concurrence does *not* suggest), resolution of this appeal *requires* us to determine the *constitutionality* of [the statute] . . . under the Second Amendment. (*Id.* at 264 n.66.)

The appeal in *Emerson* attracted a great deal of attention from those involved in the gun debate, as evidenced by the fact that all three editors of this book either prepared or signed on to *amicus curiae* ("friend of the court") briefs in the case. With its opinion in *Emerson,* the divided Fifth Circuit appellate panel produced the most extensive analysis of the Second Amendment ever to come from a federal court. As noted by both the majority opinion and the special concurrence, most U.S. Circuit Courts of Appeal have reached the opposite conclusion, ruling or stating in dicta that the Second Amendment protects only a collective state right to keep and bear firearms. Do you think (hope) *Emerson* marks a crucial turning point in judicial interpretation of the Second Amendment? Or do you think (hope) it is an aberration?

2. As indicated in note 1, in the appeal of Emerson's Second Amendment case, many organizations filed *amicus* briefs for or against Emerson's Second Amendment argument. Even the *amici* who sided with the district court's decision agreed that if Emerson had been issued a restraining order based on specific evidence that he might be a threat, it would not violate the Second Amendment to ban him from possessing guns. Do you agree that it is permissible to prohibit a person from exercising a constitutional right based on evidence that he might abuse the right in the future?

3. What do you think of Judge Cummings's contention that, unless the Second Amendment is repealed, we must enforce the Second Amendment regardless of the social costs of allowing widespread private gun ownership? What about the counterargument that the framers of the Constitution could not have imagined the sorts and volume of violence of which modern weaponry has rendered individuals capable? If you agree with the latter argument, how does this compare to the unforeseen social costs imposed on society by other constitutional rights, such as

the First Amendment (which protects much offensive or abusive speech on television and the Internet from governmental regulation) or the criminal procedure amendments (which can pose "technical" obstacles to the prosecution of dangerous criminals such as terrorists)? (For more on the costs of guns, see chapter 2.)

4. Consider Judge Cummings's interesting point about the curious role reversal between "liberals" and "conservatives" when it comes to the Second Amendment. With regard to individual liberties such as free speech or procedural protections for suspects of crimes, liberals often argue in favor of expansive readings of such rights, even when they entail substantial costs to the community. Conservatives often argue for the opposite with respect to such rights, emphasizing the need to protect communitarian interests at the expense of individual liberty. But everything becomes topsy-turvy when the issue is the Second Amendment, with liberals emphasizing the communitarian need for greater restrictions on the right to bear arms and conservatives arguing for expansive protections for individual liberties. What do you think explains this unusual role reversal?

5. Are we "missing the boat" in focusing so much attention on whether the Second Amendment protects an individual right or only a collective state right? How important is it which view of the amendment is ultimately adopted? Note in *Emerson* that the Fifth Circuit Court of Appeals, while endorsing an individual right approach to the Second Amendment, upheld the statutory bar on firearm possession by persons subject to domestic restraining orders and indicated that reasonable restrictions on firearms are valid. Was Judge Parker correct or incorrect in arguing in his special concurrences in the *Emerson* appeal that "[I]n the final analysis, whether the right to keep and bear arms is collective or individual is of no legal consequence"?

No right is absolute. The First Amendment is clear in its proscription that "Congress shall make no law" abridging freedom of speech or of the press or of religion; yet most people accept that one is not permitted falsely to shout "Fire!" in a crowded theater; that child pornography should be illegal; and that persons who are libeled have a right to sue for damages. As an exercise, assume that the Second Amendment protects an individual right to bear arms. Which of the following restrictions on guns, if any, would you personally find to be an uncon-stitutional infringement of the right to keep and bear arms: (a) waiting periods to purchase firearms; (b) mandatory background checks to pur-chase firearms; (c) laws requiring that all guns be kept locked in secure safes when not in use; (d) laws limiting handgun purchases to one gun per month or one gun per year; (e) laws requiring that all gun owners pass a firearms safety course and be licensed; (f) laws requiring that all gun-purchase transactions be registered with the state or federal gov-ernment; (g) laws requiring that all guns incorporate individual lock-ing devices or personalized technology; (h) laws requiring that all guns be kept stored at secure armories, to be checked out as needed by own-ers; (i) laws banning handguns; (j) laws banning "assault weapons"? (For more on assault weapons, see David B. Kopel, *Rational Basis Analysis of "Assault Weapon" Prohibition*, 20 Journal of Contemporary Law 381 [1994].)

6. What about the specific facts of *Emerson*? Do you think it is reasonable or unreasonable to ban firearms possession by a person who has been ac-cused by his or her partner of threatening domestic violence? Should it matter that the alleged threat of violence in *Emerson* was against the spouse's adulterous paramour (which, legally speaking, is not "domes-tic" violence)? Should a threat be enough, or should proof of an actual violent act be required? (See chapter 5 for more about domestic violence and guns.)

C. Scholarly Commentary on the Second Amendment

As Glenn Harlan Reynolds pointed out in 1995, by the mid-1990s most law professors who wrote about the Second Amendment had arrived at a schol-arly consensus regarding the Second Amendment. Borrowing from the world of physics, Reynolds called this consensus the "Standard Model." His description of the Standard Model interpretation of the Second Amendment is presented below. After the Discussion Notes, an article by historian Saul Cornell questions the accuracy and historical verity of the Standard Model and argues that many more questions must be answered before the debate surrounding the proper interpretation of the Second Amendment can be considered settled.

A Critical Guide to the Second Amendment
(62 Tennessee Law Review 461 [1995])

Glenn Harlan Reynolds

I. Introduction

. . . [W]hat distinguishes the Second Amendment scholarship from that relating to other constitutional rights, such as privacy or free speech, is that there appears to be far more agreement on the general outlines of Second Amendment theory than exists in those other areas. Indeed, there is sufficient consensus on many issues that one can properly speak of a "Standard Model" in Second Amendment theory, much as physicists and cosmologists speak of a "Standard Model" in terms of the creation and evolution of the Universe. In both cases, the agreement is not complete: within both Standard Models are parts that are subject to disagreement. But the overall framework for analysis, the questions regarded as being clearly resolved, and those regarded as still open, are all generally agreed upon. This is certainly the case with regard to Second Amendment scholarship. Unfortunately, despite the existence of unusually broad areas of scholarly consensus, this literature has so far had less of a disciplinary effect on public debate than might otherwise be hoped. . . .

II. The Standard Model

A. The Individual Right to Keep and Bear Arms under the Standard Model

The Standard Model is rooted in two main sources: the text of the Second Amendment and its historical underpinnings. Both are interpreted to support an individual right to keep and bear arms. The text's support is seen as straightforward: the language used, after all, is "right of the people," a term that appears in other parts of the Bill of Rights that are universally interpreted as protecting individual rights. Thus, any argument that the right protected is not one enforceable by individuals is undermined by the text:

> To deny that the right protected is one enforceable by individuals the following set of propositions must be accepted: (1) when the first Congress drafted the Bill of Rights it used "right of the people" in the first amendment to denote a right of individuals (assembly); (2) then, some sixteen words later, it used the same phrase in the second amendment to denote a right belonging exclusively to the states; (3) but then, forty-six words later, the fourth amendment's "right of the people" had reverted to its normal individual right meaning; (4) "right of the people" was again used in the natural sense in the ninth amendment; and (5) finally, in the tenth amendment the first Congress specifically distinguished "the states" from "the people," although it had failed to do so in the second amendment. (Don B. Kates, Jr., *Handgun Prohibition and the Original Meaning of the Second Amendment*, 82 Mich. L. Rev. 204, 218 [1982].)

Thus, say Standard Model writers, the Second Amendment protects the same sort of individual right that other parts of the Bill of Rights provide. To hold otherwise, these writers argue, is to do violence to the Bill of Rights since, if one "right of the people" could be held not to apply to individuals, then so could others. . . .

This textual argument is also supported by reference to history. Standard Model scholars muster substantial evidence that the Framers intended the Second Amendment to protect an individual right to arms. The first piece of evidence for this proposition is that such a right was protected by the English Bill of Rights of 1689. As such, it became one of the "Rights of Englishmen" around which the American Revolutionaries initially rallied. Standard Model scholars also stress that the right to keep and bear arms was seen as serving two purposes. First, it allowed individuals to defend themselves from outlaws of all kinds—not only ordinary criminals, but also soldiers and government officials who exceeded their authority, for in the legal and philosophical framework of the time no distinction was made between the two. Just as importantly, the presence of an armed populace was seen as a check on government tyranny and on the power of a standing army. With the citizenry armed, imposing tyranny would be far more difficult than it would be with the citizenry defenseless.

. . . [T]he right to keep and bear arms . . . can [also] be understood as yet another of the forms of division of power that the Framers created to protect citizens' liberties. . . . [T]he Framers divided power within the federal government, by apportioning it among three branches, and that the Framers divided government power in general by splitting it between the federal government and the governments of the states. But under the Standard Model approach it is fair to say that the Framers divided power yet another way, by ensuring that the citizenry possessed sufficient military power to offset that of the Federal government. . . . If the federal and state governments are merely agents of the people, it is logical that the people would be reluctant to surrender a monopoly on military power to their servants, for fear that their servants might someday become their masters.

B. The Militia and the People

One modern critic of the Standard Model, Dennis Henigan of the Center to Prevent Handgun Violence, dismisses this basis for the Second Amendment. Henigan describes what I call the "Standard Model" as the "insurrectionist theory" of the Second Amendment. According to Henigan, it is absurd to believe that the Framers intended to include a right of revolution in the Constitution. Henigan's argument suffers from a number of problems, not least of which is that in fact the Framers did seem to believe in just such a right. . . . [T]he 1794 Tennessee Constitution . . . contains an explicit recognition of the right—and in fact the duty—of citizens to rebel against a tyrannical government. . . . [Article 1, section 1 of the Tennessee Constitution provides: "That all power is inherent in the people, and all free governments are founded on their authority, and instituted for their peace, safety, and happiness; for the advancement of those ends they have at all times, an unalienable and indefeasible right to alter, reform, or abolish the government in such manner as they may think proper." Article 1, section 2 provides: "That government being instituted for the common benefit, the doctrine of non-resistance against arbitrary power and oppression is absurd, slavish, and destructive of the good and happiness of mankind."]

. . . And, of course, the Declaration of Independence states the same theory. So the argument that a constitutional right of revolt was unthinkable or absurd to the Framers contradicts some rather obvious historical evidence to the contrary. . . .

Nonetheless, there is that troubling language about the "well regulated militia." The Second Amendment *does* contain a preamble of sorts, and . . . criticism of arguments in favor of a personal right to bear arms always seems to turn on that point. The argument is that because the Second Amendment opens with the words, "A well regulated Militia, being necessary to the security of a free State," it must therefore not protect a right that can be asserted by individuals. Standard Model scholars disagree. . . .

First, as William Van Alstyne points out, the "right of the people" described in the Second Amendment is "to keep and bear arms," not to belong to a militia. . . . In other words, the right to keep and bear arms is not subordinate to the purpose of having a militia—the notion of a "well regulated militia" is subordinate to the purpose of having an armed citizenry. Furthermore, Van Alstyne points out, the reference in the Second Amendment's opening clause is "an express reference to the security of a 'free state.' It is not a reference to the security of the state." Thus, the purpose of the Second Amendment is to ensure an armed citizenry, from which can be drawn the kind of militia that is necessary to the survival of a free state.

There is other textual support as well. Significantly, Madison's own proposal for integrating the Bill of Rights into the Constitution was not to add them at the end (as they have been) but to interlineate them into the portions of the original Constitution they affected or to which they related. If he had thought the Second Amendment would alter the military and/or militia provisions of the Constitution he would have interlineated it in Article I, Section 8, near or after clauses 15 and 16. Instead, he planned to insert the right to arms with freedom of religion, the press and other personal rights in Section 9 following the rights against bills of attainder and ex post facto laws. This too supports the notion that the Second Amendment isn't about making the state militarily strong (an odd function for one-tenth of the Bill of Rights), but about protecting the rights of people in the same fashion as those other provisions.

Standard Model scholars cite ample historical evidence to support this reading of the text. These range from statements of the Framers concerning the makeup of the militia, such as George Mason's "Who are the militia? They consist now of the whole people," to contemporaneous legal documents, such as the Virginia Constitution of 1776, which describes "a well-regulated militia, composed of the body of the people," to historical analysis of the colonial militia as it developed from English practice. As Standard Model writers report, arms-bearing began as a duty, and continued as a right. Citizens were required to possess arms suitable for militia service, and were liable to show up for inspection from time to time to prove that they possessed them and knew how to use them, and to receive training in militia tactics. A "well regulated militia" was thus one that was well-trained and equipped; not one that was "well-regulated" in the modern sense of being subjected to numerous government prohibitions and restrictions. . . .

C. The Standard Model: A Summary

The picture that emerges from this scholarship is a coherent one, consistent with both the text of the Constitution and what we know about the Framers' understanding. The purpose of the right to bear arms is twofold: to allow individuals to protect themselves and their families, and to ensure a body of armed citizenry from which a militia could be drawn, whether that militia's role was to protect the nation, or to protect the people from a tyrannical government. . . . The mainstream scholarly interpretation of the Second Amendment—what I have been calling the Standard Model—has thus succeeded in making clear the meaning of a text that many modern readers may find unclear. This is no small accomplishment. It also provides many useful answers to questions that may occur to some readers, answers that I will summarize here.

1. THE NATIONAL GUARD

One commonplace assertion of newspaper editorialists and others who discuss the Second Amendment in the popular press is that the National Guard is the "militia" protected by that Amendment. This is clearly wrong. As mentioned above, the "militia" referred to in the Second Amendment was to be composed of the entire populace, for only such a body could serve as a check on the government. . . .

Today's National Guard . . . might more properly be thought of as "troops" than "militia" anyhow . . . and can hardly be expected to substitute for the "whole body of the people."

Under the current system, National Guard officers have dual status: they are both members of the State Guard and members of the federal armed forces. They are armed, paid, and trained by the federal government. They can be called out at will by the federal government, and such call-outs cannot be resisted, in any meaningful fashion, by them or by their states. They are subject to federal military discipline on the same basis as members of the national government's armed forces. And they are required to swear an oath of loyalty to the United States government, as well as to their states. . . . It is thus difficult to argue that the "militia" referred to in the Second Amendment is merely today's National Guard, or, for that matter, any other select governmental body. . . . [O]ne need look no further than the statute books to see that such an assertion is incorrect: the National Guard and the militia are distinct entities. At both the federal and state levels, the "unorganized militia" is defined as essentially the entire population except for the old and the very young—with the difference that many states include women. . . .

2. WHAT WEAPONS ARE PROTECTED?

Discussion of the right to keep and bear arms seems to lead inevitably to questions of whether the existence of such a right necessitates the right to own, for instance, a howitzer or a nuclear weapon. . . .

The right to keep and bear arms is no more absolute than, say, the right to free speech. Just as the demand "your money or your life" is not protected by the First Amendment, so the right to arms is not without limits. But the right to arms is no more undone by this fact than freedom of speech is undone by the fact that that right is not absolute either.

Mainstream scholars of the Second Amendment draw limits from the text and from the purpose of the provision. Textually, the language "keep and bear arms" is interpreted as limiting the arms protected to those that an individual can "bear"—that is, carry. This fact, together with the fact that the right is seen as one pertaining to individuals, leaves out large crew-served weapons such as howitzers, machine guns, nuclear missiles, and so on. Presumably individuals (if wealthy and eccentric enough) could "keep" such weapons, but they could not "bear" them.

Because one purpose of the right is to allow individuals to form up into militia units at a moment's notice, the kinds of weapons protected are those in general military use, or those that, though designed for civilians, are substantially equivalent to those military weapons. Because another purpose is the defense of the home, Standard Model writers also import common-law limitations on the right to arms, as they existed at the time of the framing. Under the common law, individuals had a right to keep and bear arms, but not such arms as were inherently a menace to neighbors, or that had an unavoidable tendency to terrify the community. Thus, weapons such as machine guns, howitzers, or nuclear weapons would not be permitted. Note however that the much-vilified "assault rifle" would be protected under this interpretation—not in spite of its military character, but because of it. . . .

3. WHO HAS A RIGHT TO KEEP AND BEAR ARMS?

Despite the claims of some prominent gun-lobby spokespersons, and of a vast number of radio talk show callers, the Standard Model interpretation of the Second Amendment does not guarantee a right to keep and bear arms for everyone. The right to arms always extended beyond the core membership of the militia, encompassing those (like women, seamen, clergymen, and those beyond the upper age for militia service) who could not be called out for militia duty. . . . [But] felons, children, and the insane were excluded from the right to arms precisely as (and for the same reasons) they were excluded from the franchise—though some (women for example) who lacked the right to vote nonetheless possessed the right to arms. . . .

This means that the right to arms does not extend to minors. . . . Nor does the right extend to felons or the insane. Furthermore, licensing laws, background checks, and waiting periods—so long as all are reasonable and not simply covert efforts at restricting the availability of guns to those who qualify—do not violate the right, arguments of overzealous gun enthusiasts to the contrary notwithstanding. After all, the "well regulated militia" of which every citizen was presumed a part included the necessity of showing up occasionally in person to prove that one possessed the necessary weapons and knew how to use them. If that could be required, then it is hard to argue that citizens cannot be required to fill out a form or two. Similarly, laws regulating the wearing of arms are generally regarded as acceptable under the Standard Model . . . . [W]hatever the asserted benefits of laws that allow citizens to carry weapons freely, the Standard Model stresses that there is no Second Amendment right to do so—though there may, of course, be Fourteenth Amendment rights not to be discriminated against in the granting of any such licenses a state may choose to permit.

4. HAVE TIMES CHANGED?

Another argument frequently heard is that the Second Amendment is militarily obsolete. The argument is that lightly-armed civilians simply cannot defend themselves against a modern army, and that as a result an armed citizenry would not serve as a remedy for, or even a deterrent against, a tyrannical government. Thus, the Second Amendment should not be taken seriously, even if it is admitted that it was intended to protect an armed citizenry in precisely the fashion described in the Standard Model.

It is hard to know what to say about this argument. First, of course, it is something of an act of faith to believe that *any* constitutional right will ultimately protect against a tyrannical government. . . . [T]here is no guarantee that a free press will prevail over the long term either. . . . Yet we do not generally require proof of efficacy where other Constitutional rights are concerned, so it seems a bit unfair to demand it solely in the case of the Second Amendment.

At any rate, the argument that irregulars with light arms are ineffective against modern armies—though no doubt pleasing to the self-esteem of military professionals—is not especially compelling based on the facts. . . . In my lifetime, we have seen modern armies defeated or embarrassed by lightly armed irregulars from Vietnam, to Afghanistan, to Lebanon to Somalia. It thus seems rather believable that an armed citizenry could frustrate tyranny, or at least make would-be tyrants weigh the high costs against the dubious benefits of, say, a military coup.

5. IS THE RIGHT WORTH THE COST?

The final popular argument against a Second Amendment right to keep and bear arms is that, regardless of what the right is supposed to accomplish, it is simply too expensive. That is, with all of the violence in America, the cost of having guns readily available exceeds any benefit that an armed citizenry might provide.

My usual response to such arguments is that as a professor of constitutional law I am as sublimely indifferent to the question of whether the availability of guns leads to crime as I am to the question of whether pornography causes sexual offenses. In either case, the Constitution has spoken, and that is enough. Such consequential concerns may be relevant to, say, the question of whether to repeal the First or Second Amendments, but they should certainly have no role in how we interpret or apply them. . . .

[T]he Constitution, and particularly the Bill of Rights, is not a buffet line from which we can take those items that look appetizing while leaving behind those that do not appeal. It is a package deal. Thus, arguments that disfavored rights should be balanced away while favored rights should be retained should be recognized for what they are. On the other hand, arguments that *all* of the Bill of Rights should be jettisoned when inconvenient, though intellectually honest, should also be rejected. . . . The Bill of Rights does not exist to make it easy for us to do what we want. It exists to make it hard for us to do what we shouldn't. . . .

DISCUSSION NOTES

1. What does Reynolds mean by a "Standard Model" of the Second Amendment? Why might he have chosen that term?
2. Why does the Standard Model reject the position adhered to by many that the phrase "[a] well regulated Militia, being necessary to the secu-

rity of a free State"—often referred to as the Second Amendment's "preamble"—limits the right to keep and bear arms?

For examples from earlier, state constitutions of the same sort of prefatory language, which have not been held to limit those state rights, see Eugene Volokh, *The Commonplace Second Amendment*, 73 New York University Law Review 793 (1998). Volokh calls these introductory phrases "purpose clauses." He maintains they illuminate the purpose of the right but do not override the right protected in the main clause. Of course, another possibility is that the preamble, not included in any other amendment, was intended to limit the right of the people to keep and bear arms to that necessary to maintain the "well regulated" militia. If the Framers did not intend to limit the right to bear arms, why would they use a prefatory clause only for the Second Amendment? In contrast, why would the Framers have limited this one right, when they didn't limit any other right the same way? One scholar argues that in drafting the Second Amendment, Madison combined two distinct strands of political philosophy: the "republican" theory of the militia, with its emphasis on the balance of power in a free society (the prefatory clause of the Second Amendment), and the "human rights" theory of the personal right to arms. (David Hardy, *Armed Citizens, Citizen Armies: Toward a Jurisprudence of the Second Amendment*, 9 Harvard Journal of Law and Public Policy 559 [1986].)

3. What does the Standard Model hold the function(s) of the Second Amendment to be?

4. What is Reynolds's support for the argument that the Second Amendment protects a right to self-defense?

5. In *Perpich v. Dept. of Defense*, 496 U.S. 334 (1990), the Supreme Court held that the U.S. National Guard was the "militia" under article 1, § 8 of the Constitution, and that it was subject to congressional control. Does this decision suggest that the right to keep and bear arms is just guaranteed to the National Guard? Does such an argument mean that the class of persons to whom the right is guaranteed could be expanded by changing the definition or characterization of who comprises the "militia"? How might proponents of the Standard Model respond?

6. Is a "constitutional" right to revolt nonsensical? If it existed, how could the government ever successfully prosecute those engaged in treason or

put down an insurrection? (See U.S. Constitution, art. 1, § 8, cl. 15; art. 3, § 3.) Could one invoke the right to revolt as a defense against an indictment for treason? Or does the Second Amendment protect only possession and training with arms, in case of a need for revolution—the justice of which revolution would be left to the "appeal to heaven"? Do you accept that a legitimate function of the Second Amendment is to enable the people to take up arms against the federal government? (See Brief of the United States, *United States v. Miller*, 307 U.S. 174 [1939] [No. 696], at 12, stating that the Second Amendment "gave sanction . . . to the arming of the people as a body to defend their rights against tyrannical and unprincipled rulers.")

7. After Texas law professor Sanford Levinson wrote an influential essay titled *The Embarrassing Second Amendment* (99 Yale Law Journal 637 [1989]), in which he suggested that the Second Amendment probably protected an individual right and that the individual right was intended to give the people the means to resist a tyrannical government, Dennis A. Henigan responded by labeling Levinson's interpretation the "insurrectionist theory" of the Second Amendment (Dennis A. Henigan, *Arms, Anarchy and the Second Amendment*, 26 Valparaiso Law Review 107 [1991].) "By what standards," Henigan wrote,

> [a]re the courts to determine whether the government has become sufficiently "tyrannical" so that armed insurrection becomes constitutionally protected? If the right guaranteed by the Second Amendment is an "individual" right, must not the courts defer to the judgment of the individual asserting the right on the question of whether or not the government has become a tyranny? Surely the right would be an empty one if it permitted governmental authority, in the form of the courts, to substitute its judgment for that of the individual citizen on the issue of whether the government has abused its power.
>
> The logical extension of Levinson's position is that courts are powerless to punish armed insurrection against the government as long as the revolutionaries believe in good faith that the government had become a tyranny. Presumably, this would mean that the government could not constitutionally prosecute persons for shooting public officials, as long as the shooting was motivated by the belief that the offi-

cial was abusing his/her power. No one could deny that such a doctrine would be a prescription for anarchy. . . .

. . . [T]he existence of a constitutional right to use arms against tyranny would, itself, create the conditions for tyranny. As Dean Roscoe Pound wrote, "In the urban industrial society of today a general right to bear efficient arms so as to be enabled to resist oppression by the government would mean that gangs could exercise an extra-legal rule which would defeat the whole Bill of Rights." This is the insurrectionist vision of America. . . . (*Id.* at 123, 128–29.)

Do you agree with Henigan? Would an individual rights interpretation of the Second Amendment prohibit the government from prosecuting a future Timothy McVeigh for an act of domestic terrorism, if the individual believed in good faith that he or she was striking a blow for freedom? Even if the government could successfully prosecute domestic terrorists, do you think that advocating the view that the Second Amendment protects the right to armed revolt against a tyrannical government encourages or emboldens persons to commit violent acts against the government? What of Henigan's broad point: who is to decide when armed revolt is appropriate against the government? Individual citizens? Groups of citizens? What kind of groups? Militias? Gangs? Others? Does widespread private gun ownership, with the necessary consequence that the government does not have a monopoly on instruments of violence, effectively deter would-be governmental tyrants? Do you think the United States' political system includes enough checks and balances to preclude a tyrannical government? Would the onset of tyranny require a violent overthrow of our current system? Or could tyranny occur while all three branches of government continue functioning? Many members of modern militias believe the U.S. government is already tyrannical. Is tyranny in the eyes of the beholder? What are the implications of a "yes" answer with respect to the issue of using armed revolt to combat tyranny?

8. Does Henigan's view encourage or embolden governments to oppress subjects who are certain not to be able to resist? Is Henigan's theory consistent with the political theory of the Declaration of Independence and of the American Revolution that people have a right to revolution

against tyranny? (See chapter 3 for more on the connection between the right to arms and resistance to tyranny.) Can a constitutional government recognize a *right* to possess arms as a safeguard against tyranny, while still retaining the power to punish politically motivated *uses* of arms?

9. Is it "enough" to say, as Reynolds does, that "the Constitution has spoken" regarding guns, in dismissing arguments that the benefits of private gun ownership exceed the costs? Are such cost-benefit questions always irrelevant when interpreting a constitutional right? Is it clear from reading the text that the Second Amendment has, in fact, "spoken" one way or the other?

10. Note that Reynolds agrees that, even if interpreted as protecting an individual right, the Second Amendment is not absolute. He acknowledges that "licensing laws, background checks, and waiting periods—so long as all are reasonable and not simply covert efforts at restricting the availability of guns to those who qualify—do not violate the right." Yet many gun rights supporters and the National Rifle Association have vigorously opposed restrictions of the type listed by Reynolds. Why do you think that is so? Do you think it is because they believe restrictions such as licensing laws, waiting periods, or background checks at gun shows violate the Second Amendment? Or because they fear that these restrictions will be a step down the "slippery slope" toward more extensive regulations? (The slippery-slope argument is common in the law. It arises in many situations involving proposals to place restrictions on constitutional rights. See Frederick Schauer, *Slippery Slopes*, 99 Harvard Law Review 361, 361–62 [1985], defining "slippery slope" as an argument "that a particular act, seemingly innocuous when taken in isolation, may yet lead to a future host of similar but increasingly pernicious events." McClurg has suggested the slippery-slope argument may have more merit in the Second Amendment context than in the context of other rights because many people who seek restrictions on guns support policies that would prohibit all guns, or at least all handguns. To the contrary, people who support restrictions on, for example, speech do not generally favor banning speech. See Andrew J. McClurg, *The Rhetoric of Gun Control*, 42 American University Law Review 53, 84–89 [1992]. In this respect, opponents of restrictions

on abortions—e.g., waiting periods for persons seeking abortions and requirements that abortion providers keep extensive records—share something in common with gun control opponents: a mistrust of the motives of those doing the regulating. For an application of Schauer's theory to the actual destruction of the right to arms in England, see David B. Kopel and Joseph E. Olson, *All the Way Down the Slippery Slope: Gun Prohibition in England and Some Lessons for Civil Liberties in America*, 22 Hamline Law Review 399 [1999], tracing the British path from handgun licensing to handgun confiscation.)

11. Carried to its logical extreme, the argument that the Second Amendment protects a right to keep and bear arms necessary to the maintenance of a militia to defend against foreign invaders or the federal government could be extended to include powerful military weapons.

Even if one accepts Reynolds's textual construction that the arms protected by the Second Amendment are only those that a person can keep and "bear," such a reading could still include rocket-propelled grenade launchers, handheld surface-to-air missiles, and machine guns. Reynolds says the right does not include machine guns but does include semiautomatic "assault weapons." Why the latter but not the former? Are the restrictions Reynolds is willing to accept on the types of weapons that are protected by the amendment based on the text of the amendment itself? On reliable historical evidence regarding the type of weapons that individual members of a militia might use? On his own subjective opinion? In the absence of either plain text or clear historical support, is there any way to know what types of arms are protected by the Second Amendment? Are courts interpreting the Second Amendment in the same position as courts interpreting the First Amendment, which must determine what kinds of "freedom of speech" are protected? (For example, does the amendment protect only literally "speech" or also written communication, nonverbal symbols such as armbands, and expressive conduct such as picketing?) To what do courts look when interpreting other phrases of the Constitution, such as "commerce among the several states," "equal protection of the laws," and "unreasonable searches and seizures"?

12. Even accepting that the Standard Model of the Second Amendment is accurate, what is the significance of the words *well regulated* in the

amendment? Do they suggest that a greater amount of government regulation of the right to arms is permissible than in the case of other rights in the Bill of Rights, since no other amendment contains express, limiting language? Does "well-regulated" mean "government-regulated"? (See 2 Oxford English Dictionary 2473, compact ed. [Oxford: Oxford University Press, 1989] defining *regulated*, when used to describe troops, to mean "properly disciplined." In the eighteenth and nineteenth centuries it would be common to speak of "regulating" a clock by adjusting it so that it kept proper time; today, a gunsmith "regulates" the barrels of a double-barreled gun by adjusting them so that they shoot at the same point.) What kind of regulation and by whom do you think the framers had in mind in referring to a "well regulated militia"?

COMMONPLACE OR ANACHRONISM: THE STANDARD MODEL, THE SECOND AMENDMENT, AND THE PROBLEM OF HISTORY IN CONTEMPORARY CONSTITUTIONAL THEORY

(16 Constitutional Commentary 221–23, 227–31, 233–34, 237–38, 245–46 [1999])

Saul Cornell

A new consensus on the meaning of the Second Amendment appears to be crystallizing among constitutional scholars. This new model asserts that the Second Amendment protects both an individual and a collective right of the people to bear arms. Proponents of this interpretation also argue that Amendment is part of a checking function designed to enable the people to resist government tyranny, by arms if necessary. . . .

The growing chorus of support for the Standard Model among legal scholars contrasts with the cool reaction to the Standard Model among early American historians. While legal scholars have confidently asserted the emergence of a new orthodoxy, there is little sign that historians are likely to come to a similar agreement. . . .

The flaws in the Standard Model are emblematic of deeper problems in the way history has been used by constitutional scholars. Partisans of the Standard Model have not only read constitutional texts in an anachronistic fashion, but have also ignored important historical sources vital to understanding what Federalists and Anti-Federalists might have meant by the right to bear arms. The structure of legal scholarship has served to spread these errors rather than to contain them. Once published, these errors enter the canons of legal scholarship and are continuously recycled in article after article. . . .

A systematic survey of the full range of American ideas about rights in the Revolutionary era examining the broad range of relevant sources would be a monumental undertaking. Yet such an exhaustive inquiry is not necessary to raise profound questions about the accuracy of the Standard Model. Consider the case of Pennsylvania, one of the many constitutional examples cited by supporters of the Standard Model. . . . Pennsylvania is . . . a crucial test case for the Standard Model. In addition to the fact that the Standard Modelers rely on it, there are other reasons why Pennsylvania provides an excellent venue to contextualize the debate over the meaning of the Second Amendment. Ratification in this key state produced one of the most lively public debates over the meaning of the Constitution, and the writings of Federalists and Anti-Federalists in Pennsylvania were among the most influential and widely distributed of any essays published during ratification.

How did Pennsylvanians understand the right to bear arms? Rather than demonstrate consensus, the historical evidence suggests that there was considerable conflict over how to understand this right. Indeed, one need not even look beyond the ranks of Pennsylvania Anti-Federalists to see the contested nature of this seemingly commonplace idea. When the views of Pennsylvania Anti-Federalists are examined in historical context, they raise serious doubts about the historical validity of the Standard Model.

Rethinking the Meaning of Liberty and Rights: The Pennsylvania Constitution of 1776

[Cornell notes that although the Pennsylvania Constitution guaranteed citizens a right to "bear arms for the defense of themselves and the state," the state also adopted acts that required its citizens, on pain of loss of civil rights—including the right to arms—to swear loyalty to the state.]

The evidence of the Test Acts shows that . . . [g]un ownership in Pennsylvania was based on the idea that one agreed to support the state and to defend it against those who might use arms against it. Only citizens who were willing to swear an oath to the state could claim the right to bear arms. Gun ownership in Pennsylvania was thus predicated on a rejection of the very right of armed resistance posited by the Standard Model. . . .

Proponents of the Standard Model concede that the republican emphasis on virtue justified the exclusion of a small category of citizens [such as criminals, children, or the mentally ill] from gun ownership. . . . This generalization clearly needs to be re-examined. Pennsylvania Constitutionalists, the supporters of the state constitution of 1776, believed that a much wider group of citizens could be excluded from the right to bear arms.

Pennsylvania Anti-Federalists and the Right to Bear Arms

. . . Although assembled in some haste, the views expressed in the Dissent attained a semi-official status as the statement of the Anti-Federalist minority of Pennsylvania's ratification convention. The Dissent not only provided a concise statement of Anti-Federalist objections to the Constitution, but also offered one of the first proposals for amendments to the Constitution, including two provisions on the right to bear arms.

. . . The Dissent of the Minority recommended the following amendments to the Constitution:

> That the people have a right to bear arms for the defense of themselves and their own state, or the United States, or for the purpose of killing game; and no law shall be passed for disarming the people or any of them, unless for crimes committed, or real danger of public injury from individuals; and as standing armies in the time of peace are dangerous to liberty, they ought not to be kept up; and that the military shall be kept under strict subordination to and be governed by the civil powers. . . . The inhabitants of the several states shall have the liberty to fowl

and hunt in seasonable times, on the lands they hold, and on all other lands in the United States not enclosed, and in like manner to fish in all navigable waters, and others not private property, without being restrained therein by any laws to be passed by the legislature of the United States.

The key phrase in the first provision of the Dissent, which is generally overlooked, is the clause that allows individuals who pose a danger to the public to be disarmed. Anti-Federalists clearly read this clause in extremely broad terms. The second provision, it is worth noting, bars Congress *but not the states* from placing restrictions on hunting. Rather than revealing an expansive individual right to bear arms, the Dissent reflects the strong states rights conception of liberty defended by Pennsylvania Anti-Federalists. While Anti-Federalists in this state may have feared a distant government, they placed enormous faith in their state government.

Only by understanding the nature of Pennsylvania Anti-Federalism can the claim of John Smilie in the Pennsylvania ratifying Convention be properly contextualized. Smilie argued that "[w]hen a select militia is formed; the people in general may be disarmed." What did Smilie mean? If lifted out of context, Smilie's words would seem to provide strong proof of the claims of Standard Modelers. Yet, Smilie . . . a strong supporter of his state's Test Acts, clearly accepted that serious restraints could be placed on the right to bear arms without undermining the idea of a liberty. Although he feared that federal control of the militia might disarm citizens, he showed no similar concern about his own state government—which had done precisely that with its Test Act. Smilie shared with many Anti-Federalists considerable faith in the ability of state government to regulate gun ownership. The state would decide who among the people demonstrated sufficient virtue to be trusted with the important task of serving in the militia. . . .

The fact that so many Anti-Federalists believed that one could exclude large numbers of individuals from the right of gun ownership suggests that a significant portion of Americans in eighteenth-century America understood liberty in terms rather different than those of modern liberal rights-based constitutional theories. Indeed, it is important to recall that the right of gun ownership was connected with an obligation of militia service. Governments could not only compel attendance at militia musters, but the failure to comply could result in fines. In general, modern rights are not subject to these sorts of restrictions and seldom carry with them these types of obligations.

Natural or Constitutional Right: The Right to Bear Arms as a Check on Tyranny

For Standard Modelers, the checking function of the Second Amendment was intended by the framers to incorporate a right of revolution into the fabric of constitutionalism. In his provocative article, "The Embarrassing Second Amendment," Sanford Levinson argues that the entire body of the people in arms, "or at least all of those treated as full citizens of the community," provided the ultimate constitutional check on government tyranny. To the extent that Americans of the Revolutionary era were Lockeans, such a claim is a truism. Most Americans did accept a right of revolution. Such a right, however, was not a constitutional check, but a natural right that one could not exercise under a functional constitutional government. The people had a right to abolish their government and resort to armed resistance in defense of their liberties when the constitutional structures of government ceased to function. Even if some Anti-Federalists accepted the notion that certain natural rights might be judicially enforceable, few mainstream Anti-Federalists would have accepted that revolution was such a right.

[Professor Cornell argues that examples of civil unrest, and the Federalists' and Anti-Federalists' reaction to them, demonstrated that contemporary expressions of support for "a right to keep and bear arms" in Pennsylvania did not *ipso facto* translate into support for a right to armed revolt when a segment of the population was unhappy with the present regime.]

Rather than view the right to bear arms as an expression of a right of resistance, it would be far more accurate to see the language of both the Pennsylvania state constitution and the federal Constitution as part of an effort to provide the state with a means to crush such resistance. The examples of Shays's Rebellion and the Whiskey Rebellion both demonstrate that the militia was far more likely to be used to support the state than to provide a means to challenge the authority of the state.

History and the Second Amendment: An Open Question

The presence of such profound differences within the ranks of Anti-Federalists (even within a single state) raises serious questions about the assumption of the Standard Model that there was a broad consensus in post-Revolutionary America on how the right to bear arms ought to be interpreted. Efforts to discern a monolithic original intent on this issue seem historically naive. The case of Pennsylvania suggests that Americans may have been as deeply divided then as they are now over this question. . . . Even if the case of Pennsylvania Anti-Federalism proves to be exceptional, the claim that a single paradigm can explain all of American constitutional thought on an issue as complicated as the right to bear arms runs counter to dominant trends in recent historical scholarship on the character of early American constitutional and political thought. It would be nothing short of astonishing if there were no significant regional or class variations on an issue as complex as the right to bear arms. Without further historical research and analysis, the truth of the Standard Model appears to be anything but a commonplace.

DISCUSSION NOTES

1. Where, according to Professor Cornell, does the Standard Model err in its interpretation of the Second Amendment?
2. Despite the language of the First Amendment, the Federalist Congress in 1798 passed the Alien and Sedition Acts to muzzle opponents. Vigorous judicial enforcement of the First Amendment began only in the 1930s. (See David M. Rabban, *Free Speech in Its Forgotten Years* [Cambridge: Cambridge University Press, 1997].) Cornell points out that some people in Pennsylvania did not mean that the state's strongly worded constitutional right to arms would apply to everyone—as shown by the fact that various groups were barred from arms possession. To what extent should we rely on historical practices, as opposed to constitutional text, to decide the meaning of constitutional terms? Should

the First Amendment be reinterpreted to allow laws like the 1798 Sedition Act, which made it a crime to criticize the president?

3. If Cornell is correct and many Pennsylvanians did allow greater restrictions on arms bearing than the proponents of the Standard Model suppose, does this mean that the people of Pennsylvania thought of the right as any less of an *individual* one? Could it merely mean that, as now, there was diverse opinion as to the scope of the right and what constituted reasonable regulation of that right? If historians show that in the early Republic various large groups (e.g., women, people without a certain amount of property) were prohibited from voting, does this prove that the right to vote was not important or was not an individual right?

4. If, as many historians agree, the Reconstruction-era Congress sought, in passing the Fourteenth Amendment, to secure to freed blacks and others the right to keep and bear arms for self-defense, should this affect the interpretation of the Second Amendment? Does it undermine Cornell's arguments against the Standard Model? (See Akhil Reed Amar, *The Bill of Rights: Creation and Reconstruction* 257–68 [New Haven: Yale University Press, 1998]; Stephen P. Halbrook, *Freedmen, the Fourteenth Amendment, and the Right to Bear Arms, 1866–1876* [New York: Praeger, 1998].) Other historians argue that the Fourteenth Amendment was meant to protect only a very limited set of civil rights, such as the right to testify in court and to sign contracts. To what extent can the Fourteenth Amendment, enacted almost eight decades after the Second Amendment, affect or change the Second Amendment's meaning?

5. Should people today care about the intentions of those who signed the Constitution more than two hundred years ago? Why or why not?

6. Assuming the original intention of the constitutional framers to be important, is it possible to discern that intent? Consider Mark Tushnet's observations on this issue:

> The first problem is deciding whose intentions count, and in what ways. The Constitution was written by a group of men who were intensely aware of the political dimensions of their actions. . . . Some of the framers, like Benjamin Franklin, opposed specific provisions but thought that the Constitution overall should be adopted. Others op-

posed the entire Constitution. During the debates, some framers gave their views on many of its provisions; others spoke only a few times. . . . [When the Constitution was submitted to the states] [m]any people voted to oppose ratification. Whose views should we examine when we try to determine "original intention"?

. . . Once we know who to count, we somehow have to add up the views of men who disagreed about many important matters. . . .

[A third problem is that it's] not easy to figure out what *any* framer's intention was about the issues that we face today.

. . . The most that we know is what the framers thought about specific problems. And somehow we have to infer from that what their views were, or would have been, about a different set of problems.

. . . The social changes over the past two hundred years pose a final difficulty. . . . Today our governments deal with many problems that were unknown to the framers, or whose dimensions have changed so much that it is misleading to think of the problems as the same in any useful sense. (Mark Tushnet, *The U.S. Constitution and the Intent of the Framers*, 36 Buffalo Law Review 217, 219–23 [1988].)

Do Tushnet's observations cast doubt on the accuracy or wisdom of interpreting the Constitution by trying to divine the original intention of the framers? Since many people were involved in writing the Constitution—people with widely varying views on different issues—can we divine a unified intent regarding the Second Amendment? Other rights? Do you think the framers would have drafted the Second Amendment differently if they were writing it today? Is the answer to the challenges of discerning original intent to abandon adherence to original intent, even when it is easy to discern? Should we simply rely on the actual text of the Constitution, since that is what was actually proposed and ratified? Should we interpret the Constitution with a view toward keeping it "up to date" with respect to problems and issues that those who signed the document could not have anticipated? Should this approach be followed even if it results in deviations from original intent? From the actual constitutional text? Since many constitutional provisions are written in vague terms that are not self-defining, what sources should judges rely on in interpreting the Constitution once they abandon original intent as their guide? Their own values? Popular opinions? Something else?

7. Congratulations! You've just been appointed as a framer of the Constitution. Your job is to redraft the Second Amendment as you think it should have been originally written. Would you decide not to include any right to bear arms in the Constitution? Assume you must include such a right in some form. Take your time and think about this important assignment. Prepare a first draft. Study it and revise it as necessary. Be prepared to explain the choices you make to your class.

D. THE RIGHT TO KEEP AND BEAR ARMS UNDER STATE CONSTITUTIONS

Of the original thirteen states, four—Pennsylvania, North Carolina, Vermont, and Massachusetts—included specific rights to keep and bear arms in their constitutions. Four others—Virginia, Maryland, Delaware, and New Hampshire—included provisions endorsing a well-regulated militia. The Second Amendment may be a result of Madison combining these two ideas. Today, forty-four states have a specific guarantee of the right to keep and bear arms in their constitutions. The only states that do not are California, Iowa, Maryland, Minnesota, New Jersey, and New York. Since 1970, fourteen states—Alaska, Delaware, Idaho, Louisiana, Maine, Nebraska, Nevada, New Hampshire, New Mexico, North Dakota, Utah, Virginia, West Virginia, and Wisconsin—either have amended their constitutions to include the guarantee or have strengthened existing guarantees, stressing that the right is an individual one and encompasses the right to own guns for self-defense, hunting, and recreation.

Since most lower federal courts have (with the exception of *Emerson*, *supra*) rejected an individual-rights interpretation of the Second Amendment, and since the Supreme Court has not applied the Second Amendment against the states, some gun owners have tried to use *state* constitutional provisions to secure protection for individual gun ownership. Over the years, about two dozen gun control laws have been held unconstitutional under state constitutions, while many others have been upheld. (See David B. Kopel, Clayton E. Cramer and Scott G. Hattrup, *A Tale of*

Three Cities: The Right to Bear Arms in State Courts, 68 Temple Law Review 1177 [1995], listing cases; Clayton E. Cramer, *For the Defense of Themselves and the State* [New York: Praeger, 1994], a comprehensive analysis of all state cases.)

The state court opinions present the same issues discussed earlier in this chapter: Do individuals have a right to own guns? What kinds and for what purposes? What is the scope of the right? To what extent may the state regulate that right?

As you read these opinions, consider whether and to what extent the differences in wording between state right-to-keep-and-bear-arms provisions and the Second Amendment determine the outcome. Note, too, the state judges' interpretation of these provisions. Should the United States Supreme Court ever hear another Second Amendment case, could it make use of the arguments presented in the following cases? Should it? Note the emphasis on self-defense as a primary rationale for private ownership of arms both in the state court opinions and in many recent state constitutional provisions. Should this emphasis—as opposed to an emphasis on arms ownership as a bulwark against government tyranny—have any bearing on a contemporary interpretation of the Second Amendment?

For a complete list of state constitutional right-to-arms provisions, with helpful, side-by-side comparisons to earlier versions of the provision in each state, see Eugene Volokh, *State Constitutional Right to Keep and Bear Arms Provisions*, available at http://www.law.ucla.edu/faculty/volokh/beararms/statecon.htm. Start your study of state constitutional arms rights by looking up your own state's constitutional provision on Volokh's Web site.

Andrews v. State
50 Tenn. (3 Heisk.) 165 (1871)

[The case arose from appeals of convictions for violation of a Tennessee statute prohibiting the "public or private" carrying of "a dirk, swordcane, Spanish stiletto, belt or pocket pistol or revolver." The court first rejected a Second Amendment challenge, noting that the Bill of Rights was addressed to the federal government, not the states. Article 1, Section 26 of the Tennessee Constitution read: "That the citizens of this State have a right to keep and bear arms for their common defense. But the Legislature shall have power by law, to regulate the wearing of arms, with a view to prevent crime." Justice Freeman delivered the opinion of the court.]

The right to keep arms, necessarily involves the right to purchase them, to keep them in a state of efficiency for use, and to purchase and provide ammunition suitable for such arms, and to keep them in repair. And clearly for this purpose, a man would have the right to carry them to and from his home, and no one could claim that the Legislature had the right to punish him for it, without violating this clause of the Constitution.

But farther than this, it must be held, that the right to keep arms involves, necessarily, the right to use such arms for all the ordinary purposes, and in all the ordinary modes usual in the country, and to which arms are adapted, limited by the duties of a good citizen in times of peace; that in such use, he shall not use them for violation of the rights of others, or the paramount rights of the community of which he makes a part. . . .

What, then, is he protected in the right to keep and thus use? Not every thing that may be useful for offense or defense; but what . . . are found to make up the usual arms of the citizen of the country, and the use of which will properly train and render him efficient in defense of his own liberties, as well as of the State. . . . [W]e would hold, that the rifle of all descriptions, the shot gun, the musket, and repeater, are such arms; and that under the Constitution the right to keep such arms, can not be infringed or forbidden by the Legislature. Their use, however, to be subordinated to such regulations and limitations as are or may be authorized by the law of the land, passed to subserve the general good, so as not to infringe the right secured and the necessary incidents to the exercise of such right.

What limitations, then, may the Legislature impose on the use of such arms, under the second clause of the 26th section, providing: "But the Legislature shall have power, by law, to regulate the wearing of arms, with a view to prevent crime"?

. . . It is insisted by the Attorney General that this clause confers power on the Legislature to prohibit absolutely the wearing of all and every kind of arms, under all circumstances. To this we can not give our assent. The power to regulate, does not fairly mean the power to prohibit; on the contrary, to regulate, necessarily involves the existence of the thing or act to be regulated. . . . Adopt the view of the Attorney General, and the Legislature may, if it chooses, arbitrarily prohibit the carrying all manner of arms, and then, there would be no act of the citizen to regulate.

But the power is given to regulate, with a view to prevent crime. The enactment of the Legislature on this subject, must be guided by, and restrained to this end, and bear some well defined relation to the prevention of crime, or else it is unauthorized by this clause of the Constitution.

It is insisted, however, by the Attorney General, that, if we hold the Legislature has no power to prohibit the wearing of arms absolutely . . . then the citizen may carry them at all times and under all circumstances. This does not follow by any means, as we think. . . .

. . . [A] man may well be prohibited from carrying his arms to church, or other public assemblage, as the carrying them to such places is not an appropriate use of them, nor necessary in order to his familiarity with them, and his training and efficiency in their use. As to arms worn, or which are carried about the person, not being such arms as we have indicated as arms that may be kept and used, the wearing of such arms may be prohibited if the Legislature deems proper, absolutely, at all times, and under all circumstances. . . .

The principle on which all right to regulate the use in public of these articles of property, is, that no man can so use his own as to violate the rights of others, or of the community of which he is a member.

So we may say, with reference to such arms, as we have held, he may keep and use in the ordinary mode known to the country, no law can punish him for so doing, while he uses such arms at home or on his own premises. . . . Yet, when he carries his property abroad, goes among the people in public assemblages where others are to be affected by his conduct, then he brings himself within the pale of public regulation, and must submit to such restriction on the mode of using or carrying his property as the people through their Legislature, shall see fit to impose for the general good. . . .

In a word, as we have said, the statute amounts to a prohibition to keep and use such weapon for any and all purposes. It therefore, in this respect, violates the constitutional right to keep arms, and the incidental right to use them in the ordinary mode of using such arms and is inoperative.

If the Legislature think proper, they may by a proper law regulate the carrying of this weapon publicly, or abroad, in such a manner as may be deemed most conducive to the public peace, and the protection and safety of the community from lawless violence. We only hold that, as to this weapon, the prohibition is too broad to be sustained.

The question as to whether a man can defend himself against an indictment for carrying arms forbidden to be carried by law, by showing that he carried them in self-defense, or in anticipation of an attack of a dangerous character upon his person, is one of some little difficulty.

The real question in such case, however, is not the right of self-defense . . . but the right to use weapons, or select weapons for such defense, which the law forbids him to keep or carry about his person. If this plea could be allowed as to weapons thus forbidden, it would amount to a denial of the right of the Legislature to prohibit the keeping of such weapons; for, if he may lawfully use them in self-defense, he may certainly provide them, and keep them, for such purpose; and thus the plea of right of self-defense will draw with it, necessarily, the right to keep and use everything for such purpose, however pernicious to the general interest or peace or quiet of the community. Admitting the right of self-defense in its broadest sense, still on sound principle every good citizen is bound to yield his preference as to the means to be used, to the demands of the public good. . . .

For this error the cases will be reversed; the indictments quashed, and remanded to the Circuit Courts. . . .

DISCUSSION NOTES

1. The *Andrews* case is very typical of nineteenth-century state court cases on the right to arms. Like the *Andrews* court, most state courts held that there were some weapons outside the scope of the right to arms (some courts disagreed), that the right was an individual one (only one judge, in Arkansas, disagreed), and that some controls on the right—especially in public places—were permissible. (See David B. Kopel, *The Second Amendment in the Nineteenth Century*, 1998 Brigham Young Law Review 1359 [1998]. For more on Tennessee's right-to-keep-and-bear-arms provi-

sion, see Glenn Harlan Reynolds, *The Right to Keep and Bear Arms under the Tennessee Constitution: A Case Study in Civic Republican Thought*, 61 Tennessee Law Review 647 [1994].) What is the scope of Tennessee's constitutional right, according to the court? What are its limits?

2. Note that the concern of the court still focuses on the connection between the right to keep and bear arms and service (or at least potential service) in a state military organization. The right of self-defense is conceded; but did the defendant have the right to employ any sort of weapon that might be effective for self-defense? Recall that keying the level of constitutional protection to a weapon's military utility seemed to be a prominent theme in the U.S. Supreme Court's decision in *Miller*. Note also that the Tennessee opinion predates *Miller* by almost seventy years. (Compare the Oregon Supreme Court's approach in 1980, holding that a billy club was protected under that state's constitution: *State v. Kessler*, 614 P. 2d 94 [Ore. 1980]. For *Kessler*, see pp. 222–26.)

3. In contrast to the majority's approach in *Andrews*, Justice Nelson wrote separately, expressing the opinion that the legislature had no power to abrogate a man's ability to defend himself: "In accordance with this view, I hold that when a man is really and truly endangered by a lawless assault, and the fierceness of the attack is such as to require immediate resistance in order to save his own life, he may defend himself with any weapon whatever, whether seized in the heat of the conflict, or carried for the purpose of self-defense." Justice Nelson further stated that a man who fears for his safety "is not bound to humiliate or, perchance, to perjure himself, in the slow and often ineffectual process of 'swearing the peace,' or to encourage the onslaught of his adversary by an acknowledgment of timidity or cowardice." Does it surprise you to hear a judge express such views? Some sociologists suggest that the Southern concept of "honor" is responsible for the relatively higher rates of violence in the South, as compared to other parts of the country, and also for greater judicial leniency toward the use of deadly force in self-defense. Does the language of Justice Nelson's opinion tend to support such a thesis? Note that similar sentiments were also expressed by state supreme courts in Ohio, Indiana, and Wisconsin in the late nineteenth and early twentieth centuries. (See David B. Kopel, *The Self-Defense Cases*, 27 American

Journal of Criminal Law 293, 307 [2000]. For more on the connection between gun violence and region, see chapter 5.)

4. Did the court strike down the challenged statute *in toto*? If not, what part(s) did it uphold?

5. Note the court's approach to the question of whether one may claim necessity of self-defense as a defense to a charge that one had violated the concealed-weapons statute. The court responded that the statute does not really prohibit self-defense; rather, it simply limits the right to select a particular *type* of weapon for self-defense (and to carry it). (For the argument that the right of self-defense entails the right to procure the means for self-defense, including so-called junk guns—inexpensive handguns that are a frequent target of gun control advocates—see Victoria Dorfman and Michael Koltonyuk, *When the Ends Justify the Reasonable Means: Self-Defense and the Right to Counsel*, 3 Texas Review of Law and Politics 381 [1999].)

City of Salina v. Blaksley
83 P. 619 (Kan. 1905)

[Justice Greene delivered the opinion of the court.]

James Blaksley was convicted in the police court of the city of Salina, a city of the second class, of carrying a revolving pistol within the city while under the influence of intoxicating liquor. . . .

The question presented is the constitutionality of section 1003 of the General Statutes of 1901, which reads: "The council may prohibit and punish the carrying of fire arms or other deadly weapons, concealed or otherwise, and may arrest and imprison, fine or set at work all vagrants and persons found in said city without visible means of support, or some legitimate business."

Section 4 of the Bill of Rights is as follows: "The people have the right to bear arms for their defense and security; but standing armies, in time of peace, are dangerous to liberty, and shall not be tolerated, and the military shall be in strict subordination to the civil power." The contention is that this section of the Bill of Rights is a constitutional inhibition upon the power of the Legislature to prohibit the individual from having and carrying arms, and that section 1003 of the General Statutes of 1901 is an attempt to deprive him of the right guarantied by the Bill of Rights, and is therefore unconstitutional and void. The power of the Legislature to prohibit or regulate the carrying of deadly weapons has been the subject of much dispute in the courts. The views expressed in the decisions are not uniform, and the reasonings of the different courts vary. It has, however, been generally held that the Legislatures can regulate the mode of carrying deadly weapons, provided they are not such as are ordinarily used in civilized warfare. To this view, there is a notable exception in the early case of *Bliss v. Commonwealth*, 2 Litt. (Ky.) 90 . . . where it was held, under a constitutional provision similar to ours, that the act of the Legislature prohibiting the carrying of concealed deadly weapons was void, and that the right of the citizen to own and carry arms was protected by the Constitution, and could not be taken away or regulated. While this decision has frequently been referred to by the courts of other states, it has never been followed. . . . In view of the disagreements in the reasonings of the different courts by which they reached conflicting conclusions, we prefer to treat the question as an original one.

The provision in section 4 of the Bill of Rights "that the people have the right to bear arms for their defense and security" refers to the people as a collective body. It was the safety and security of society that was being considered when this provision was put into our Constitution. It is followed immediately by the declaration that standing armies in time of peace are dangerous to liberty and should not be tolerated, and that "the military shall be in strict subordination to the civil power." It deals exclusively with the military. Individual rights are not considered in this section. The manner in which the people shall exercise this right of bearing arms for the defense and security of the people is found in article 8 of the Constitution, which authorizes the organizing, equipping, and disciplining of the militia, which shall be composed of "able-bodied male citizens between the ages of twenty-one and forty-five years. . . ." The militia is essentially the people's army, and their defense and security in time of peace. There are no other provisions made for the military protection and security of the people in time of peace. In the absence of constitutional or legislative authority, no person has the right to assume such duty. In some of the states where it has been held, under similar provisions, that the citizen has the right preserved by the Constitution to carry such arms as are ordinarily used in civilized warfare, it is placed on the ground that it was intended that the people would thereby become accustomed to handling and using such arms, so that in case of an emergency they would be more or less prepared for the duties of a soldier. The weakness of this argument lies in the fact that in nearly every state in the Union there are provisions for organizing and drilling state militia in sufficient numbers to meet any such emergency.

That the provision in question applies only to the right to bear arms as a member of the state militia, or some other military organization provided for by law, is also apparent from the second amendment to the federal Constitution, which says: "A well regulated militia, being necessary to the security of a free state, the right of the people to keep and bear arms shall not be infringed." Here, also, the right of the people to keep and bear arms for their security is preserved, and the manner of bearing them for such purpose is clearly indicated to be as a member of a well-regulated militia, or some other military organization provided for by law. . . .

DISCUSSION NOTES

1. *Blaksley* was the first holding by a court adopting the "collective right" argument that individuals have no right under the Second Amendment to possess firearms. (See David B. Kopel, *The Second Amendment in the Nineteenth Century*, 1998 Brigham Young University Law Review 1359, 1510–12 [1998].) Kopel argues that none of the sources cited by the Kansas Supreme Court supports the collective right theory. As a matter of textual interpretation, is *Blaksley* persuasive? If the Kansas right-to-arms provision simply restates a prerogative of the Kansas government, why is the provision in the Kansas Bill of Rights?

2. The court states in its opinion that the state militia is "the people's army" and that it alone is responsible for the people's "defense and security in time of peace." The court continued: "In the absence of constitutional or legislative authority, no [other] person has the right to assume such duty." Does this foreclose an individual's ability to engage in

self-defense? (Perhaps the court's statement was influenced by memories of "Bloody Kansas" in the days preceding the Civil War, when private armies of free-soilers and pro-slavery settlers invaded the state in an effort to influence the outcome of the vote over whether Kansas would allow slavery. See generally, James M. McPherson, *Battle Cry of Freedom* 145–69 [New York: Oxford University Press, 1988]; Kopel, *The Second Amendment in the Nineteenth Century, supra*, at 1441–44.)

3. In 1979 the Kansas court struck down a local gun control ordinance, holding that it was "overbroad" (a legal term of art originally used in First Amendment law and subsequently by several state supreme courts in decisions holding that gun control laws violated state constitutional rights to arms). (See *Junction City v. Mevis*, 601 P. 2d 1145 [Kans. 1979]). Should *Junction City* be considered a tacit repudiation of *Blaksley*? To what extent can First Amendment or other constitutional principles be useful in analyzing right-to-arms issues?

4. In the penultimate paragraph of *United States v. Miller*, Justice McReynolds wrote: "In the margin some of the more important opinions and comments by writers are cited" (*Miller*, 307 U.S. at 182). In the attached footnote *Miller* lists, without comment, five state court opinions that treat the Second Amendment or its state analogue as an individual right and that uphold particular gun controls: *Fife v. State*, 31 Ark. 455 (1876) (Second Amendment does not apply to the states; state right to arms not violated by ban on brass knuckles); *People v. Brown*, 253 Mich. 537, 235 N.W. 245 (1931) (Michigan state constitutional right to arms applies to all citizens, not just militiamen; right is not violated by ban on carrying blackjacks); *Aymette v. State*, 21 Tenn. (2 Hum.) 154 (1840) (Tennessee state constitutional right to arms and U.S. Second Amendment right belong to individual citizens, but right includes only the types of arms useful for militia service); *State v. Duke*, 42 Tex. 455 (1874) (Second Amendment does not directly apply to the states; Texas Constitution protects "arms as are commonly kept, according to the customs of the people, and are appropriate for open and manly use in self-defense, as well as such as are proper for the defense of the State"); *State v. Workman*, 35 W. Va. 367 (1891)(protecting individual right only to weapons "such as swords, guns, rifles, and muskets—arms to be used

in defending the State and civil liberty—and not to pistols, bowie-knives, brass knuckles, billies, and such other weapons as are usually employed in brawls, street-fights, duels, and affrays, and are only habitually carried by bullies, blackguards, and desparadoes, to the terror of the community and the injury of the state"). But the same *Miller* footnote also cites the *Blaksley* decision, which is directly contrary, holding that the right to arms in Kansas belongs only to the state government. What do you think Justice McReynolds intended by listing such contradictory cases together? Was he just providing a list of cases, without endorsing their content?

STATE V. KESSLER

614 P. 2d 94 (Ore. 1980)

[Justice Lent delivered the opinion of the court.]

The defendant in this case was convicted of "possession of a slugging weapon." . . . We allowed review to consider his claim that the legislative prohibition of the possession of a "billy" . . . violates Article I, section 27, of the Oregon Constitution. That provision states: "The people shall have the right to bear arms for the defence (sic) of themselves, and the State, but the Military shall be kept in strict subordination to the civil power."

. . . The scope of Article I, section 27, has not previously been analyzed by Oregon courts. The decisions construing the second amendment to the United States Constitution are not particularly helpful because the wording of the second amendment differs substantially from our state provision. . . . The wording of Oregon's right to bear arms provision also differs from many other state constitutional provisions.

. . . We are not unmindful that there is current controversy over the wisdom of a right to bear arms, and that the original motivations for such a provision might not seem compelling if debated as a new issue. Our task, however, in construing a constitutional provision is to respect the principles given the status of constitutional guarantees and limitations by the drafters; it is not to abandon these principles when this fits the needs of the moment. . . .

II. The Oregon Right to Bear Arms

A. "Defense of themselves and the state"

We have noted that Oregon's constitutional right to bear arms provision
. . . was taken verbatim from the Indiana constitutional provision drafted
in 1816 [, which, in turn,] was most likely taken from the Kentucky provision in its 1799 constitution, or the Ohio provision in its 1802 constitution. The phrase "for defense of themselves and the state" appears in
the present day constitutions of Oregon, Indiana, and six other states.
The language is subject to varying interpretations. It has been suggested
that the language includes three separate justifications for a state constitutional right to bear arms: (a) The preference for a militia over a standing army; (b) the deterrence of governmental oppression; and (c) the
right of personal defense.

The language "the right to bear arms . . . for defense of . . . the state"
more likely refers to the historical preference for a citizen militia rather
than a standing army as outlined above. . . .

The phrase "the right to bear arms in defense of themselves" has a suggested purpose which is closely related to the preference for citizen militias. That suggested purpose is the deterrence of government from op-
pressing unarmed segments of the population. . . .

"Defense of themselves" has also been said to include an individual's
right to bear arms to protect his person and home. . . . Self-defense has
been recognized as a privilege in both civil and criminal law since about
1400 in England and at all times in the United States. Although the right
to bear arms for self protection does not appear to have been an important development in England, the justification for a right to bear arms in
defense of person and home probably reflects the exigencies of the rural
American experience. . . .

B. The Meaning of the Term "Arms"

The term "arms" is also subject to several interpretations. In the colonial
and revolutionary war era, weapons used by militiamen and weapons
used in defense of person and home were one and the same. . . .

Therefore, the term "arms" as used by the drafters of the constitutions probably was intended to include those weapons used by settlers for both personal and military defense. The term "arms" was not limited to firearms, but included several hand-carried weapons commonly used for defense. The term "arms" would not have included cannon or other heavy ordnance not kept by militiamen or private citizens.

The revolutionary war era ended at a time when the rapid social and economic changes of the so-called Industrial Revolution began. The technology of weapons and warfare entered an unprecedented era of change. . . . Firearms and other hand-carried weapons remained the weapons of personal defense, but the arrival of steam power, mechanization, and chemical discoveries completely changed the weapons of military warfare. The development of powerful explosives in the mid-nineteenth century, combined with the development of mass-produced metal parts, made possible the automatic weapons, explosives, and chemicals of modern warfare.

These advanced weapons of modern warfare have never been intended for personal possession and protection. When the constitutional drafters referred to an individual's "right to bear arms," the arms used by the militia and for personal protection were basically the same weapons. Modern weapons used exclusively by the military are not "arms" which are commonly possessed by individuals for defense, therefore, the term "arms" in the constitution does not include such weapons.

If the text and purpose of the constitutional guarantee relied exclusively on the preference for a militia "for defense of the State," then the term "arms" most likely would include only the modern day equivalents of the weapons used by colonial militiamen. The Oregon provision, however, guarantees a right to bear arms "for defense of themselves, and the State." The term "arms" in our constitution therefore would include weapons commonly used for either purpose, even if a particular weapon is unlikely to be used as a militia weapon.

The constitutional guarantee that persons have the right to "bear arms" does not mean that all individuals have an unrestricted right to carry or use personal weapons in all circumstances. . . . The courts of many states have upheld statutes which restrict the possession or manner of carrying personal weapons. The reasoning of the courts is generally that a regulation is valid if the aim of public safety does not frustrate the guarantees of the state constitution. For example many courts have upheld statutes prohibiting the carrying of concealed weapons . . . ; and statutes prohibiting possession of firearms by felons. . . .

III. The Present Case

We now turn to the facts of the present case. The defendant was involved in an off and on verbal argument with his apartment manager in the course of the day on November 13, 1978. The dispute escalated into name calling, colorful words, and object throwing. At one point the defendant kicked the elevator door in the apartment building. The police were called and arrested the defendant. The defendant asked the police to get his coat from his apartment. The officers found two "billy clubs" in the defendant's apartment.

The defendant was charged with disorderly conduct . . . and possession of a slugging weapon. . . . The matter went to trial without a jury [and the defendant] . . . was found guilty as charged on both counts.

The defendant appealed to the Court of Appeals, [which] . . . held that [the statute banning "slugging weapons"] was within the reasonable exercise of the "police power" of the state to curb crime. . . .

The defendant contends that his conviction for possession of a billy club violates his right to possess arms in his home for personal defense. [W]e hold . . . the Oregon Constitution includes a right to possess certain arms for defense of person and property. The remaining question is whether the defendant's possession of a billy club in this case is protected by Article I, section 27.

The club is considered the first personal weapon fashioned by humans. . . . The club is still used today as a personal weapon, commonly carried by the police. . . .

The statute in this case, ORS 166.510, prohibits the mere possession of a club. The defendant concedes that the legislature could prohibit carrying a club in a public place in a concealed manner, but the defendant maintains that the legislature cannot prohibit all persons from possessing a club in the home. The defendant argued that a person may prefer to keep in his home a billy club rather than a firearm to defend against intruders.

Our historical analysis of Article I, section 27, indicates that the drafters intended "arms" to include the hand-carried weapons commonly used by individuals for personal defense. The club is an effective, hand-carried weapon which cannot logically be excluded from this term. We hold that the defendant's possession of a billy club in his home is protected by Article I, section 27, of the Oregon Constitution.

The defendant's conviction . . . for possession of a slugging weapon is reversed.

DISCUSSION NOTES

1. Note the similar wording of the Oregon and Kansas constitutional provisions; yet the courts reached different conclusions. Do you find one or the other court's reasoning more persuasive?

2. The 1980 *Kessler* decision contrasts sharply with many nineteenth-century right-to-bear-arms cases in that it recognizes that the "arms" protected by the guarantee encompassed more than military-style weapons such as those that might be borne by militia members on active service. (Compare *Aymette v. State*, 21 Tenn. (2 Hum.) 154, 1840 WL 1554 at * 3 [1840]: "As the object for which the right to keep and bear arms is secured is of general and public nature . . . so the arms the right to keep which is secured are such as are employed in civilized warfare, and that constitute ordinary military equipment.") Might this be an indication that the self-defense rationale for the modern existence of the right has moved to the forefront, as opposed to the tyranny-opposing or the anti-militarist elements predominant in eighteenth- and nineteenth-century discussions of both the Second Amendment and its state analogues? Consider the *Kessler* court's comment that "advanced weapons of modern warfare have never been intended for personal possession and protection," and thus "the term 'arms' . . . does not include such weapons." The court goes on, however, to offer protection for weapons that may be useful for self-defense, even if such weapons are not and were not part of a militia member's kit. Hence, the court concludes that a billy club is protected if kept in the home for self-defense. Should weapons that have little militia use but that are useful for personal protection have con-

stitutional protection? Does it depend on the particular wording of the constitutional provision?

ARNOLD V. CITY OF CLEVELAND
616 N.E. 2d 163 (Ohio 1993)

[Justice Douglas delivered the opinion of the court.]

The underlying issue in this appeal concerns the constitutionality of an ordinance which bans the possession and sale of "assault weapons" in the city of Cleveland. Appellants . . . contend that the ordinance is an overbroad restriction on their constitutional right to bear arms and defend themselves and, thus, is in violation of Sections 1 and 4, Article I of the Ohio Constitution. . . .

Right to Bear Arms in Ohio

The language of Section 4, Article I of the Ohio Constitution is clear. . . . [It] secures to every person a fundamental *individual* right to bear arms for "their *defense and security*. . . ." This clause was obviously implemented to allow a person to possess certain firearms for defense of self and property. . . .

The right of defense of self, property and family is a fundamental part of our concept of ordered liberty. To deprive our citizens of the right to possess any firearm would thwart the right that was so thoughtfully granted by our forefathers and the drafters of our Constitution. For many, the mere possession of a firearm in the home offers a source of security. Furthermore, given the history of our nation and this state, the right of a person to possess certain firearms has indeed been a symbol of freedom. . . .

However . . . the people of our nation, and this state, cannot have unfettered discretion to do as we please at all times. Neither the federal Bill of Rights nor this state's Bill of Rights, implicitly or explicitly, guarantees unlimited rights.

[The court then gave examples of rights contained in both the federal and Ohio constitutions that are nevertheless subject to limits.]

Therefore, based on the foregoing, we find that . . . the Ohio Constitution confers upon the people of Ohio the fundamental right to bear arms. However, this right is not absolute.

Police Power

The authority to regulate or limit constitutional guarantees has been commonly referred to as the police power. . . . [T]he Ohio Constitution, which provides that: "Municipalities shall have authority to exercise all powers of local self-government and to adopt and enforce within their limits such local police, sanitary and other similar regulations, as are not in conflict with general laws."

This court has, on numerous occasions, stated the standards a court must follow in review of an enactment under the police power. . . .

"Laws or ordinances passed by virtue of the police power which limit or abrogate constitutionally guaranteed rights must not be arbitrary, discriminatory, capricious or unreasonable and must bear a real and substantial relation to the object sought to be obtained, namely, the health, safety, morals or general welfare of the public." . . .

This court has established that firearm controls are within the ambit of the police power. . . .

In [*Mosher v. Dayton*] this court concluded that an ordinance, which required individuals having or acquiring handguns to possess an identification card issued by the city of Dayton, was not violative of either Section 4, Article I or the Second Amendment. The court reasoned that neither the federal nor the state constitution states that the right to bear arms is supreme over the authority of a municipality under the police power. . . . The court further observed that the public purpose of the ordinance was to safeguard the public from the dangers of illegal weapons and, therefore, such weapons were a proper subject for reasonable regulation. . . .

Here, the question is whether the legislation is a reasonable regulation, promoting the welfare and safety of the people of Cleveland.

. . . [W]e believe that the ordinance, while admittedly broad in its scope, is a reasonable exercise of the municipality's police power. The ultimate objective of the legislation appears to be public safety. To reach this end, the municipality is attempting to limit the accessibility of certain generally recognized dangerous firearms.

Appellants and various *amici curiae* have presented numerous materials and statistical data, urging that the instant gun control legislation is not needed. However, even if the statistics presented are accurate, this does not diminish the public safety threat of assault weapons, or demonstrate that the ordinance is unreasonable or arbitrary. The prohibition of a harmful act need not be postponed until it occurs. . . .

Any form of gun control legislation is destined to attract much attention. That does not change the fact that there must be some limitation on the right to bear arms to maintain an orderly and safe society while, at the same time, moderating restrictions on the right so as to allow for the practical availability of certain firearms for purposes of hunting, recreational use and protection. In our opinion, appellee has, under the present legislation, properly balanced these competing interests.

Appellants concede that appellee may regulate, within reason, the manner in which firearms are purchased or used. Appellants insist, however, that the ordinance under review goes beyond regulating the manner of acquisition and use and, instead, acts as a prohibition on the right to possess firearms, which is beyond the scope of the police power.

Appellants' contention lacks merit. This court has commented that the police power includes the power to prohibit. . . .

The ordinance at issue affects a class of firearms. Clearly, the city would have exceeded its authority under Section 3, Article XVIII, and would have violated Section 4, Article I if it had banned *all* firearms. For this reason, we are not persuaded by appellants' argument that by banning certain firearms "there is no stopping point" and legislative bodies will have "the green light to completely ignore and abrogate an Ohioan's right to bear arms."

[Judge Hoffman, Concurring in Part and Dissenting in Part]

The majority correctly recognizes that Sections 1 and 4, Article I of the Ohio Constitution confer upon the citizens of Ohio the fundamental right to bear arms and that such right is an individual one. Conceded to the majority is the fact that, although fundamental, such right is not absolute.

It is undisputed that legislative concern for public health and safety is a proper police power objective. This court has recognized as constitutional gun control legislation which has regulated the manner in which a weapon may be borne. . . . However, the Cleveland ordinance goes beyond mere regulation. It is a total prohibition of possession of certain types of arms.

The majority adopts the position that as long as the legislation is enacted to promote public health and safety it need only be reasonable to pass constitutional muster, even though it interferes with a personal or collective liberty. Such standard is appropriate when analyzing legislative restrictions on nonfundamental rights. However, I believe a stricter standard must be utilized when the legislation places restrictions upon fundamental rights, particularly where the legislation prescribes an outright prohibition of possession as opposed to mere regulation of possession. A "strict scrutiny" test, i.e., whether the restriction is *necessary* to promote a *compelling governmental interest,* as opposed to the less demanding "reasonable" or "rational relationship" test, ought to be applied. . . . Under the strict scrutiny analysis, a law which impinges upon a fundamental right is presumptively unconstitutional unless a compelling governmental interest justifies it. . . . Furthermore, any such infringement must be drawn with "precision." . . . Exercise of the police power may not be achieved by a means which sweeps unnecessarily broadly. . . . The majority candidly recognizes that the Cleveland ordinance is broad in its scope.

Whether the city of Cleveland's objective in enacting the subject ordinance is necessary to promote a compelling governmental interest and whether the legislation enacted to accomplish that objective sweeps unnecessarily broadly are questions which are not yet ripe for review by this court in light of the procedural posture of this case. . . .

The briefs of the parties and respective amici filed herein are replete with statistics and reports collected throughout the country regarding the impact of guns and their relationship to criminal behavior. The majority makes reference to these materials but concludes that even if accurate, they could not diminish the public safety threat of "assault weapons" or demonstrate that the ordinance is unreasonable or arbitrary. Though the majority's position may ultimately be proven correct, the parties have been precluded from establishing their record in the courts below.

Few would question the wisdom of banning "assault weapons." However, use of the term "assault weapons" generates emotional responses and inherent bias. Whether the weapons banned by the Cleveland ordinance are primarily antipersonnel or whether they are equally suitable for defensive or sporting purposes has yet to be demonstrated. All weapons are antipersonnel and assaultive by nature. The mere declaration by Cleveland Council that it finds the primary purpose of assault weapons to be antipersonnel and any civilian application or use of those weapons is merely incidental to such primary antipersonnel purpose, coupled with its declaration that the proliferation and use of said assault weapons pose a serious threat to the health, safety, welfare and security of the citizens of Cleveland is, standing alone, insufficient to satisfy the government's burden when such legislation infringes upon a fundamental right. When challenged, the government must be allowed to demonstrate this claim and the challenger must be afforded an opportunity to demonstrate otherwise. Both sides have been precluded from doing so in this case.

I would reverse the decision of the appellate court, and remand the matter to the trial court for further proceedings in accordance with this opinion and the law.

DISCUSSION NOTES

1. *Arnold* holds that an individual's right to keep and bear arms is guaranteed by the Ohio Constitution, yet it also upholds Cleveland's "assault weapons" ban. Why?

2. What is the test that the court employs when weighing Cleveland's assault weapons ban, which was passed under its police power, against the individual's right to keep and bear arms, which the majority opinion characterizes as "fundamental"?

3. Note that, despite all the technical analysis of the right to bear arms versus the police power of municipalities, the court's ultimate decision depended on a very simple test of whether the court viewed the ban on

assault weapons as "reasonable." Do you think, ultimately, that is the standard that should be used to evaluate the legality of gun control restrictions, regardless of whether constitutional arms provisions are construed as protecting an individual or a collective right? Observe that none of the state court decisions discussed in this section took the position that all restrictions on guns are unconstitutional. Once one concedes that not all restrictions on guns are unconstitutional, is the question of what is and what is not constitutional necessarily reduced—implicitly if not expressly—to an evaluation of reasonableness? Who should determine reasonableness? Do you think "reasonable people" can have "reasonable disagreements" as to what is "reasonable"? If so, are reasonableness tests, which are common in the law, devoid of substantive content? Do they leave it to judges or juries to decide cases however they want to? Do you think bans on assault weapons are reasonable? (For an analysis of three state court cases upholding assault weapons bans in Ohio, Oregon, and Colorado, see Kopel, Cramer, and Hattrup, *A Tale of Three Cities, supra.*) Federal courts, and most state courts apart from Ohio, apply a stricter standard than mere reasonableness when evaluating legislative infringements of either the Bill of Rights or other rights deemed fundamental. When subjected to so-called strict scrutiny, laws generally need to further an important or compelling governmental interest and be narrowly tailored to achieve that interest. Is the right to bear arms a "fundamental" right? Recall from early in the chapter that the U.S. Supreme Court has never held the Second Amendment to be a fundamental right so as to make it binding on the states through the Fourteenth Amendment due process clause.

4. In his partial dissent, Judge Hoffman suggests that the Cleveland ordinance sweeps too broadly in banning an entire class of weapons that may or may not play a role in the crime that the city is rightfully trying to suppress. He argues that the court should have heard evidence about whether assault weapons really are especially dangerous or especially likely to be used in crime. Is this a valid critique?

5. What of Judge Hoffman's point about the use of the term *assault weapons?* He claims that the mere use of the term begs the question "What *is* an assault weapon?" He argues that the challenger ought to have been allowed to present evidence that the weapons posed no threat

to public safety sufficient to justify a total ban on their ownership. Later, the U.S. Court of Appeals for the Sixth Circuit struck down a similar ordinance, due in part to the fact that the term *assault weapon* was vague and overbroad. (See *People's Rights Organization, Inc. v. Columbus*, 152 F. 3d 522, 535–39 [6th Cir. 1998]; see also *Springfield Armory, Inc. v. Columbus*, 29 F. 3d 250, 254 [6th Cir. 1994], striking down earlier version of the law.) Do you think it is possible to define "assault weapon" in a statute with adequate precision? In 1994, Congress banned the manufacture of new semiautomatic "assault weapons" (18 *U.S. Code* § 921[a][30], defining assault weapons; § 922[v][1], banning manufacture of assault weapons). Congress took an interesting approach to defining "assault weapons." In addition to a general definition, the legislation lists several specific brands and models of guns that are banned, while also including a lengthy list of more than six hundred specific brands and models of semiautomatic rifles and shotguns that are not banned. Does this approach cure the definitional problem? Because the ban defines "assault weapons" solely on the basis of characteristics unrelated to the gun's firepower (e.g., whether the gun has a bayonet lug, where the magazine is inserted into the gun), many gun manufacturers have been able to make cosmetic changes to their products, avoiding application of the statute without altering the firearm's internal operations. (For analysis of the 1994 federal statute, see David B. Kopel, *Rational Basis Analysis of "Assault Weapon" Prohibition*, 20 Journal of Contemporary Law 381 [1994]; Kopel, *Assault Weapons*, in *Guns: Who Should Have Them?* ed. David B. Kopel [Buffalo: Prometheus Books, 1995].)

CHAPTER 5

GUNS AND IDENTITY

Race, Gender, Class, and Culture

Firearms have a definite but different impact on individuals and groups of different races, genders, classes, and cultures. This impact is marked by wide disparities in the levels of gun violence and gun ownership and in the varying perceptions of guns among different sexes and races.

With respect to race, personal firearms were used by Minutemen on the greens of Lexington and Concord to help win the Revolutionary War, and some state militias included men of all races—but militias in the South were also used to prevent or stop potential slave revolts. As seen in this chapter, one commentator suggests the real purpose of the Second Amendment was to assure Southern states that the new federal government would not undermine the South's principal instrument for suppressing "domestic insurrection." Two other commentators suggest that firearms offer minorities living in urban high-crime areas an affordable tool for defending themselves when police protection fails. The data in this chapter also show that criminal use of firearms takes a disproportionately heavy toll on minorities in the inner city, particularly young blacks. Do minorities have more to gain or lose from firearms?

The gender debate revolves around whether guns are a "great equalizer" that enable women to defend themselves against physically stronger men or a machismo instrumentality used to perpetuate violence against women. The firearms industry began a controversial campaign to market guns to women in the mid-1980s. Should efforts by the firearms industry to target women consumers be viewed positively, as an advancement of women's empowerment, or cynically, as an effort by a male-dominated industry to exploit the fears of women? This chapter offers starkly different viewpoints on the issue.

The class and cultural implications of firearms policy are deeply entwined with race and sex issues. Demographic factors closely associated with gun ownership include being white, male, and affluent, whereas factors associated with being injured by a firearm include being black, male, and poor. Socioeconomic class affects personal security in numerous ways. Persons of higher socioeconomic status, in addition to being able to afford better and more guns for self-defense, can take refuge in safer neighborhoods, purchase security systems, gate their communities, even hire private security guards to patrol their streets. To the contrary, persons who rank low on the economic ladder are often forced to live in crime-ridden neighborhoods where even the police may fear to tread. While the rich can afford electronic security systems that automatically dial for help, the poor may not even have adequate locks on their doors and windows. For the poor, a firearm may be the only means of affordable protection in some situations. By contrast, introducing more firearms into already violent neighborhoods may increase the overall risk of violence in the community. Despite the potential self-defense benefits of firearms, polling data consistently show blacks favor greater restrictions on guns at higher percentages than whites. This chapter presents conflicting viewpoints on whether firearms prevalence is the cause of the crime problem or the cure.

Cultural differences also play a role in gun violence. Why, as one commentator asks in this chapter, is the homicide rate for white men in Mississippi so much higher than the rate for white men in Minnesota? Are we a nation of distinct subcultures of lethal violence?

A. RACE

This section begins with excerpts from two law review articles expressing conflicting views on the benefit of firearms for blacks, both as a means for overcoming a legacy of oppression and as a modern tool for self-protection in the face of inadequate police protection. It moves next to excerpts from a lawsuit filed by the National Association for the Advancement of Colored People (NAACP) against more than one hundred gun manufacturers, claiming that the firearms industry has negligently marketed its products in ways that disproportionately harm African Americans. An editorial response to this lawsuit raises, in provocative fashion, the age-old bumper-sticker debate over whether "guns kill people" or "people kill people."

THE SECOND AMENDMENT: TOWARD AN AFRO-AMERICANIST RECONSIDERATION
(80 Georgetown Law Journal 309 [1991])

Robert J. Cottrol and Raymond T. Diamond

Many of the issues surrounding the Second Amendment debate are raised in particularly sharp relief from the perspective of African-American history. With the exception of Native Americans, no people in American history have been more influenced by violence than blacks. Private and public violence maintained slavery. The nation's most destructive conflict ended the "peculiar institution." That all too brief experiment in racial egalitarianism, Reconstruction, was ended by private violence and abetted by Supreme Court sanction. Jim Crow was sustained by private violence, often with public assistance.

If today the memories of past interracial violence are beginning to fade, they are being quickly replaced by the frightening phenomenon of black-on-black violence, making life all too precarious for poor blacks in inner city neighborhoods. Questions raised by the Second Amendment, particularly those concerning self-defense, crime, participation in the security of the community, and the wisdom or utility of relying exclusively on the state for protection, thus take on a peculiar urgency in light of the modern Afro-American experience.

This article explores Second Amendment issues in light of the Afro-American experience. . . .

Arms and Race in Colonial America

. . . Britain's American colonies were home to three often antagonistic races: red, white, and black. For the settlers of British North America, an armed and universally deputized white population was necessary not only to ward off dangers from the armies of other European powers, but also to ward off attacks from the indigenous population which feared the encroachment of English settlers on their lands. An armed white population was also essential to maintain social control over blacks and Indians who toiled unwillingly as slaves and servants in English settlements.

This need for racial control helped transform the traditional English right [to bear arms] into a much broader American one. If English law had qualified the right to possess arms by class and religion, American law was much less concerned with such distinctions. Initially all Englishmen, and later all white men, were expected to possess and bear arms to defend their commonwealths, both from external threats and from the internal ones posed by blacks and Indians. The statutes of many colonies specified that white men be armed at public expense. In most colonies, all white men between the ages of sixteen and sixty, usually with the exception of clergy and religious objectors, were considered part of the militia and required to be armed. Not only were white men required to perform traditional militia and posse duties, they were also required to serve as patrollers, a specialized posse dedicated to keeping order among the slave population, in those colonies with large slave populations. . . .

One year after the ratification of the Second Amendment and the Bill of Rights, Congress passed legislation that reaffirmed the notion of the militia of the whole and explicitly introduced a racial component into the national deliberations on the subject of the militia. The Uniform Militia Act called for the enrollment of every free, able-bodied white male citizen between the ages of eighteen and forty-five into the militia. The act further specified that every militia member was to provide himself with a musket or firelock, a bayonet, and ammunition. . . .

The Southern Antebellum Experience: Control of Arms as a Means of Racial Oppression

[The authors discuss how Southern states passed laws to tightly control the ability of blacks, both free and slave, to possess firearms as a means of suppressing rebellion. As one example, in 1833, Florida passed a statute authorizing white citizen patrols to seize arms found in the homes of slaves and free blacks and provided that blacks without a proper explanation for the presence of the firearms be summarily punished.]

The Northern Antebellum Experience: Use of Firearms to
Combat Racially Motivated Deprivations of Liberty

[The authors detail several terroristic attacks against blacks in the North.] . . . Awareness of racial hostility generally, and of incidents like these, made blacks desirous of forming militia units. The firing of the weapon in Providence in 1831 that sparked the mob to violence illustrated that blacks were willing to take up arms to protect themselves, but also illustrated the potentially counterproductive nature of individual action. The actions of the white militia in Providence and Philadelphia, as well as those of the police and fire units in Boston, proved the strength of collective armed action against mob violence. Moreover, the failure of police to take action in Providence in 1824 illustrated the vulnerability of the black community to mob violence, absent protection.

Though the Uniform Militia Act of 1792 had not specifically barred blacks from participation in the state organized militia, the northern states had treated the act as such, and so the state organized militia was not an option. Blacks could nonetheless form private militia groups that might serve to protect against racial violence, and did so. Free blacks in Providence formed the African Greys in 1821. Oscar Handlin tells of an attempt by black Bostonians in the 1850s to form a private militia company. . . .

It is not clear whether private black militia groups ever marched on a white mob. But that they may never have been called on to do so may be a measure of their success. The story of the July 1835 Philadelphia riot is illustrative. Precipitated when a young black man assaulted a white one, the two day riot ended without resort to military intervention when a rumor reached the streets that "fifty to sixty armed and determined black men had barricaded themselves in a building beyond the police lines."

Undoubtedly, the most striking examples of the salutary use of firearms by blacks in defense of their liberty, and concurrently the disastrous results from the denial of the right to carry firearms in self-defense, lie in the same incident. In Cincinnati, in September 1841, racial hostility erupted in two nights of assaults by white mobs of up to 1500 people. On the first evening, after destroying property owned by blacks in the business district, mobs descended upon the black residential section, there to be repulsed by blacks who fired into the crowd, forcing it out of the area. The crowd returned, however, bringing with it a six-pound cannon, and the battle ensued. Two whites and two blacks were killed, and more than a dozen of both races were wounded. Eventually, the militia took control, but on the next day the blacks were disarmed at the insistence of whites, and all adult black males were taken into protective custody. On the second evening, white rioters again assaulted the black residential district, resulting in more personal injury and property damage. . . .

The 1841 Cincinnati riot represents the tragic, misguided irony of the city's authorities who, concerned with the safety of the black population, chose to disarm and imprison them—chose, in effect, to leave the black population of Cincinnati as southern authorities left the black population in slave states, naked to whatever indignities private parties might heap upon them, and dependent on a government either unable or unwilling to protect their rights. . . .

Arms and the Postbellum Southern Order

[The authors discuss how Southern states in the post–Civil War era passed "black codes" as a way to continue the suppression of blacks after their emancipation from slavery. Included in these codes were prohibitions against blacks carrying firearms without licenses, a requirement to which whites were not subjected. The black codes prompted fear among Northerners that the South was trying to reinstitute slavery, which fed the determination of Northern Republicans to enforce the Bill of Rights against state action.

The post–Civil War adoption of the Fourteenth Amendment, the authors here assert, was intended to make the Bill of Rights applicable to state action. They argue that the U.S. Supreme Court weakened the effectiveness of the Second Amendment and other provisions of the Bill of Rights in late-nineteenth-century cases such as *United States v. Cruikshank*. In *Cruikshank*, the federal government brought charges against William Cruikshank and others for violating the rights of two black men peaceably to assemble and to bear arms. The Supreme Court held that the federal government does not have the lawful power to protect citizens against private action that deprives them of constitutional rights, and that the First and Second Amendments restrict federal action only. For protection against private criminal action, citizens must look to state governments.]

The rest of the story is all too well known. The Court's denial of an expanded role for the federal government in enforcing civil rights played a crucial role in redeeming white rule. The doctrine in Cruikshank, that blacks would have to look to state government for protection against criminal conspiracies, gave the green light to private forces, often with the assistance of state and local governments, that sought to subjugate the former slaves and their descendants. Private violence was instrumental in driving blacks from the ranks of voters. It helped force many blacks into peonage, a virtual return to slavery, and was used to force many blacks into a state of ritualized subservience. With the protective arm of the federal government withdrawn, protection of black lives and property was left to largely hostile state governments. In the Jim Crow era that would follow, the right to possess arms would take on critical importance for many blacks. This right, seen in the eighteenth century as a mechanism that enabled a majority to check the excesses of a potentially tyrannical national government, would for many blacks in the twentieth century become a means of survival in the face of private violence and state indifference.

Arms and Afro-American Self-Defense in the Twentieth Century: A History Ignored

[The authors trace a continued pattern of violence and repression of blacks after the Civil War, including formation of the Ku Klux Klan (KKK). Between 1882 and 1968, the KKK lynched 3,446 black citizens, mostly in the South. On occasion, blacks were able to defend themselves with firearms, although usually not with success.]

. . . Although individual efforts of blacks to halt violence to their persons or property were largely unsuccessful, there were times that blacks succeeded through concerted or group activity in halting lynchings. In her autobiography, Ida Wells-Barnett reported an incident in Memphis in 1891 in which a black militia unit for two or three nights guarded approximately 100 jailed blacks who were deemed at risk of mob violence.

When it seemed the crisis had passed, the militia unit ceased its work. It was only after the militia unit left that a white mob stormed the jail and lynched three black inmates.

A. Philip Randolph, the longtime head of the Brotherhood of Sleeping Car Porters, and Walter White, onetime executive secretary of the National Association for the Advancement of Colored People, vividly recalled incidents in which their fathers had participated in collective efforts to use firearms to successfully forestall lynchings and other mob violence. As a thirteen-year-old, White participated in his father's experiences, which, he reported, left him "gripped by the knowledge of my own identity, and in the depths of my soul, I was vaguely aware that I was glad of it." After his father stood armed at a jail all night to ward off lynchers, Randolph was left with a vision, not "of powerlessness, but of the 'possibilities of salvation,' which resided in unity and organization."

The willingness of blacks to use firearms to protect their rights, their lives, and their property, alongside their ability to do so successfully when acting collectively, renders many gun control statutes, particularly of Southern origin, all the more worthy of condemnation. This is especially so in view of the purpose of these statutes, which, like that of the gun control statutes of the black codes, was to disarm blacks. . . .

[The authors discuss more incidents of violence against blacks up through the Civil Rights movement of the 1960s.]

It struck many, then, as the height of blindness, confidence, courage, or moral certainty for the civil rights movement to adopt nonviolence as its credo, and to thus leave its adherents open to attack by terrorist elements within the white South. Yet, while nonviolence had its adherents among the mainstream civil rights organizations, many ordinary black people in the South believed in resistance and believed in the necessity of maintaining firearms for personal protection, and these people lent their assistance and their protection to the civil rights movement.

Daisy Bates, the leader of the Little Rock NAACP during the desegregation crisis, wrote in her memoirs that armed volunteers stood guard over her home. Moreover, there are oral histories of such assistance [including stories] of black Mississippi citizens with firearms who followed civil rights workers in order to keep them safe.

Ad hoc efforts were not the sole means by which black Southern adherents of firearms protected workers in the civil rights movement. The Deacons for Defense and Justice were organized first in 1964 in Jonesboro, Louisiana, but received prominence in Bogalusa, Louisiana. The Deacons organized in Jonesboro after their founder saw the Ku Klux Klan marching in the street and realized that the "fight against racial injustice include[d] not one but two foes: White reactionaries and police." Jonesboro's Deacons obtained a charter and weapons, and vowed to shoot back if fired upon. The word spread throughout the South, but most significantly to Bogalusa, where the Klan was rumored to have its largest per capita membership. There, a local chapter of the Deacons would grow to include "about a tenth of the Negro adult male population," or about 900 members, although the organization was deliberately secretive about exact numbers. What is known, however, is that in 1965 there were fifty to sixty chapters across Louisiana, Mississippi, and Alabama. In Bogalusa, as elsewhere, the Deacons' job was to protect black people from violence, and they did so by extending violence to anyone who attacked. This capability and willingness to use force to protect blacks provided a deterrent to white terroristic activity. . . .

Blacks in the South found the Deacons helpful because they were unable to rely upon police or other legal entities for racial justice. This provided a practical reason for a right to bear arms: In a world in which the legal system was not to be trusted, perhaps the ability of the system's victims to resist might convince the system to restrain itself.

Conclusion: Self-Defense and the Gun Control Question Today

. . . Throughout American history, black and white Americans have had radically different experiences with respect to violence and state protection. Perhaps another reason the Second Amendment has not been taken very seriously by the courts and the academy is that for many of those who shape or critique constitutional policy, the state's power and inclination to protect them is a given. But for all too many black Americans, that protection historically has not been available. Nor, for many, is it readily available today. If in the past the state refused to protect black people from the horrors of white lynch mobs, today the state seems powerless in the face of the tragic black-on-black violence that plagues the mean streets of our inner cities, and at times seems blind to instances of unnecessary police brutality visited upon minority populations. . . .

The history of blacks, firearms regulations, and the right to bear arms should cause us to ask new questions regarding the Second Amendment. These questions will pose problems both for advocates of stricter gun controls and for those who argue against them. Much of the contemporary crime that concerns Americans is in poor black neighborhoods and a case can be made that greater firearms restrictions might alleviate this tragedy. But another, perhaps stronger case can be made that a society with a dismal record of protecting a people has a dubious claim on the right to disarm them. Perhaps a re-examination of this history can lead us to a modern realization of what the framers of the Second Amendment understood: that it is unwise to place the means of protection totally in the hands of the state, and that self-defense is also a civil right.

DISCUSSION NOTES

1. In tracking the history of violence and oppression against blacks in America, the authors point out that much of this oppression was able to occur only because whites were armed and blacks were disarmed. The authors make laudatory references to instances where blacks formed armed militias to defend themselves against white violence. They appear to be suggesting that blacks in modern times arm themselves, even to the extent of forming armed militias, for protection from white violence and black-on-black violence. Is that a good idea? Who would regulate such militias? Do you favor unregulated militia groups of any race? How would modern black militias be compared to the historical black militia groups referred to in the Cottrol-Diamond article? What, if any, are the differences between genuine militias and street gangs such as the Bloods and the Crips?

2. Many early gun control laws were passed for the express purpose of keeping blacks disarmed. A 1639 Virginia law required the arming of white men at public expense, whereas the very first mention of blacks in Virginia law was a 1644 statute preventing free blacks from owning firearms. The "Black Codes" adopted by several Southern states after the Civil War denied the newly freed slaves many rights enjoyed by whites,

including the right to bear firearms. Illustrative is this Mississippi statute: "Be it enacted . . . [t]hat no freedman, free negro or mulatto, not in the military . . . and not licensed to do by the board of police of his or her county, shall keep or carry fire-arms of any kind, or any ammunition . . . and all such arms or ammunition shall be forfeited" (1866 Mississippi Laws ch. 23 [1865]).

Some commentators have suggested that even modern gun control laws are motivated by a racist intent. (See Clayton E. Cramer, *The Racist Roots of Gun Control*, 4 Kansas Journal of Law and Public Policy 17 [1995].) Journalist Robert Sherrill asserted that the Gun Control Act of 1968, the centerpiece of federal gun control legislation, "was passed not to control guns but to control blacks" (Robert Sherrill, *The Saturday Night Special* 280 [1973]). If Saturday night specials or "junk guns" are the only guns poor people can afford for self-protection, are laws regulating or banning such guns unfair? (See T. Markus Funk, *Gun Control and Economic Discrimination: The Melting-Point Case-in-Point*, 85 Journal of Criminal Law and Criminology 764 [1995].) What about laws that give police chiefs broad discretion about who may carry or own a gun?

3. In the years before the Civil War, anti-slavery lawyer and activist Lysander Spooner used the Second Amendment to argue that slavery was unconstitutional:

> These provisions [the Second Amendment] obviously recognize the natural right of all men "to keep and bear arms" for their personal defence; and prohibit both Congress and the State governments from infringing the right of "the people"—that is, of any of the people—to do so; and more especially of any whom Congress have power to include in their militia. The right of a man "to keep and bear arms," is a right palpably inconsistent with the idea of his being a slave. Yet the right is secured as effectually to those whom the States presume to call slaves, as to any whom the States condescend to acknowledge free.

> Under this provision any man has a right either to give or sell arms to those persons whom the States call slaves; and there is no constitutional power, in either the national or State governments, that can punish him for so doing; or that can take those arms from the slaves; or that can make it criminal for the slaves to use them, if, from the inefficiency of

the laws, it should become necessary for them to do so, in defence of their own lives or liberties; for this constitutional right to keep arms implies the constitutional right to use them, if need be, for the defence of one's liberty or life. (Lysander Spooner, *The Unconstitutionality of Slavery* 66 [1860; reprint, Burt Franklin, 1965].)

As Kopel has observed, Spooner's argument that slavery was unconstitutional was not very persuasive in light of article 4, section 2 of the Constitution, providing for the return of fugitives "held to Service or Labour." The provision shows that the Constitution contemplated that persons in the United States could be slaves. (See David B. Kopel, *The Second Amendment in the Nineteenth Century,* 1998 Brigham Young University Law Review 1359, 1437 [1998]. See also Randy E. Barnett, *Was Slavery Unconstitutional before the Thirteenth Amendment? Lysander Spooner's Theory of Interpretation,* 28 Pacific Law Journal 977 [1997], detailing Spooner's life and analyzing his theory that slavery was unconstitutional.) Spooner argued that, although the Founders clearly intended the Constitution to protect slavery, the text of the Constitution never mentions the words *slave* or *slavery,* and the text should be interpreted according to natural justice rather than original intent. Thus, the clause about persons "held to Service or Labour" would be read to apply only to indentured servants. Was Spooner's legal position reasonable?

RACE, RIOTS, AND GUNS
(66 Southern California Law Review 1365 [1993])

Carl T. Bogus

On May 14, 1992, the New York Times ran a disturbing lead article. "In the aftermath of the Los Angeles riots," it reported, "Californians are buying firearms at the highest rate since the state began keeping records 20 years ago, and other states are reporting similar surges in gun sales." The article continued:

> In large part, the rush to buy guns in California can be attributed to one of the more frightening messages to come out of the two days of arson, looting and violence in South-Central Los Angeles. That message, that

fear, is that the police might not be able to defend people during an outbreak of civil unrest.

. . . Even before the riot, some scholars suggested that gun control had racial implications.

In December 1991 Professors Robert J. Cottrol and Raymond T. Diamond . . . presented what they called an Afro-American reconsideration of the Second Amendment to the Constitution, which contains the provision referring to the right to bear arms. Cottrol and Diamond trace how guns were used by white colonialists to subjugate blacks and Indians in early America and by Southern whites to enforce the Jim Crow system after the Civil War. They explain that, at least in the South, gun control laws were originally designed to disarm blacks, and suggest that these statutes helped the Ku Klux Klan (KKK) lynch thousands of African-Americans. "[A] society with a dismal record of protecting a people has a dubious claim on the right to disarm them," Cottrol and Diamond write. They conclude that "it is unwise to place the means of protection totally in the hands of the state, and that self-defense is also a civil right"—a judgment, some would argue, that has been corroborated by the L.A. riots.

This article challenges that conclusion. It argues that an examination of the interrelationships among race, riots, and guns in America properly leads to the conclusion that African-Americans have been particularly victimized by guns and the so-called "right to bear arms." The lesson to be drawn from both history and contemporary experience is not that blacks should be armed, but that all citizens should be subject to stricter gun control regulations. . . .

[The author describes the development of slavery in the New World and discusses how guns were used to enforce white control.]

The historical record . . . suggests that the Second Amendment may have been inspired as much by a desire to maintain a form of tyranny as to provide a means of resisting tyranny. George Mason of Virginia worried that Congress might render the state militias useless by "disarming them"—as he put it, Congress might "neglect to provide for arming and disciplining the militia." Virginia proposed amending the new federal Constitution to provide "[t]hat each state respectively shall have the power to provide for organizing, arming, and disciplining its own militia, whenever Congress shall omit or neglect to provide for the same." Why the fear about Congress disarming the militia? Congress could presumably be trusted to be diligent about national defense. But contrary to the desires of the anti-Federalists, Congress had been granted both the power to organize the militia and to maintain an army and navy. Congress might, therefore, rely on a federal standing army instead of the state militia. Northern states would control Congress, and the North was finding slavery increasingly obnoxious. Intentionally or unintentionally, Congress might subvert the slave system by allowing the militia to decay.

History should not be read too simply. . . . [S]trong evidence suggests that the Southern states' concerns about maintaining the militia for slave control, and the Northern states' desires to relieve the Southern states' anxiety on the matter, were significant forces behind the Second Amendment. From this perspective, the Second Amendment appears to be a remnant from an era that ended in 1865 when the Thirteenth Amendment was enacted and slavery was abolished.

Contemporary Perspectives

[The author recounts brutal attacks by Klansmen on nonviolent civil rights protesters in Birmingham, Alabama, which the police ignored. In one incident, carloads of armed blacks came to the aid and rescue of a group of besieged pacifist protesters.]

. . . Do experiences such as these demonstrate that minorities should be armed? Do they, to quote Cottrol and Diamond again, teach that "it is unwise to place the means of protection totally in the hands of the state, and that self-defense is also a civil right"? Gun control opponents argue that they do. Their argument is neatly capsulized in the image of Bull Connor—a chief of police in cahoots with a rapacious mob. How can citizens be asked to rely exclusively on the state for self-protection when the state is Bull Connor? . . .

Cottrol and Diamond suggest that a revitalized Second Amendment would protect groups [of armed blacks] like the Deacons for Defense and Justice, which was organized to protect blacks and civil rights workers in the South during the civil rights movement. But there is no way to

sanction protective activity by responsible groups and simultaneously restrict irresponsible ones. Moreover, Americans reject the idea that it is
sometimes better for private parties to take the law into their own hands.

The specter of vigilantism haunts us always, yet it is far from our most
serious gun-related problem. The biggest problem is not a potential
tragedy, it is actual tragedy. It is the stream of death and injury that flows
continuously in our society, particularly within our inner cities. There
are, in Los Angeles alone, about one thousand murders, two thousand
rapes, 40,000 robberies and 47,000 aggravated assaults (many of which
result in serious injury) per year. A disproportionate amount of violent
crime occurs in the black community. In just the neighborhood around
Vermont and Vernon Avenues, where the riot in South-Central began,
there are, during a typical week, between three and four murders, five
rapes, and more than a dozen robberies. For residents, this is tantamount
to living in a war zone, but worse because there is no reprieve, no hope
for an end to the war.

Guns fuel this violence. More than sixty-six percent of all murders are
committed with firearms. No other type of weapon is used nearly as
often; knives, for example, are used only 15.8% of the time and blunt instruments only 5% of the time. . . .

Historian Roger Lane has described the interrelationship among guns,
crime, and racism for urban blacks. As Lane traces the history, during the
late 1800s white gangs often attacked blacks, and blacks increasingly carried handguns for self-protection. Guns, therefore, were increasingly on
hand during moments of rage or recklessness, which made the black
community even more dangerous and, in turn, intensified the cycle. As
Lane puts it, "the historically justified fear of white violence, and the ten-
sions created by living, involuntarily, in districts full of wired-up
strangers looking for action, encouraged the habit of carrying weapons,
which were then all too handy during routine arguments with family and
acquaintances." Meanwhile, the white urban population was being
transformed by the industrial revolution. For whites there were jobs in
the skilled trades, in offices, in factories. Life became regimented, a powerful work ethic developed, and it became increasingly important to keep
one's nose clean. Lane writes: "These effects are shown in the relatively
rapid decline in homicide rates among Irish and Italian immigrants, two

other ethnic groups with high levels of preindustrial violence, as their integration into the industrial work force demanded levels of sober, disciplined, orderly behavior, which carried over into their private lives."

Urban blacks did not share these opportunities. Blacks were excluded from blue-collar jobs, from clerical jobs, from civil service jobs, even from factory jobs. These barriers were finally removed during World War II, but this change occurred too late to prevent the entrenchment of a terrible cycle. Today guns and drugs continue to plague the black community. In the United States today, murder by gunshot is the leading cause of death among black males between the ages of fifteen and nineteen. This history helps us to appreciate better the role that guns play in the life of the inner city. Poverty is commonly identified as a cause of urban riots, but we are less mindful about how constant violence contributes to pent-up frustration and rage—as well as a willingness to ventilate those feelings through violence, including rioting. Although perhaps unverifiable through empirical study, it is reasonable to assume that one of the long-term, underlying causes of the Los Angeles riot was the constant violence generated by guns.

Guns also played a role in triggering the riot. Many feel that the acquittal of the police officers who beat Rodney King was not the only cause of pre-riot rage. The King verdict followed another case, involving a Korean shopkeeper, who shot and killed a fifteen-year-old black girl whom she accused of shoplifting, received a sentence of only probation. Many felt that the combination of these two verdicts sparked the riot. Rigorous gun control might have kept that gun out of the shopkeeper's hands.

It is likely, moreover, that effective gun control would have made the riot less severe. At least thirty-nine of the fifty-four people who died in the riot were shot to death. Most were gunned down in the street for no reason, the victims of random shootings. Race did not matter:

The death toll included twenty-two blacks, eighteen Hispanics, eleven whites, two Asians, and one corpse so badly burned that the victim's race could not be determined. Snipers were one of the worst problems, as in the riots of the 1960s. Not only are snipers directly responsible for many of the deaths, but they hinder rescue efforts by firefighters and police. Moreover, innocent bystanders get killed in shootouts between police and snipers. . . .

Members of minority communities understand their predicament. In significantly higher numbers than do whites, blacks and other non-whites believe that possession of handguns by civilians should be banned. . . .

Conclusion

An African-American reconsideration of the Second Amendment casts the militia and the right to bear arms in a new light. It appears that the Second Amendment was, at least in part, adopted to assure the southern states that they could maintain armed militia to control their slaves. To the extent that this is the case, the amendment became moot when slavery was abolished by the Thirteenth Amendment.

It would be a mistake to interpret the Second Amendment as conferring rights on private individuals rather than on the states. This is not to deny that there will be times or circumstances when we mistrust public authorities. We live in an imperfect world—as cynics are fond of saying—and problems are inevitable. However, we will live in a far more imperfect world if private groups are armed and ready to defend "the security of a free state" as they themselves see fit.

Throughout our history, race, riots, and guns have been strangely enmeshed with one another. There is one lesson we should have learned by now: More guns will not improve matters. It is understandable that many urban blacks started carrying guns in the nineteenth century, but in the long run guns have not made the black community more secure. Guns will not make other communities safer either.

DISCUSSION NOTES

1. Do minorities have more to fear from the right to bear arms than they stand to gain? Statistics show that blacks, both male and female, suffer much higher rates of firearm homicide than whites (see Table 8).
2. John Lott, whose study on the positive effects of concealed-weapons laws in reducing crime has had a substantial influence on the national gun control debate, argues that blacks and others living in urban areas have the most to gain from being able to defend themselves with guns. He

TABLE 8 U.S. Rates of Firearm Homicide by Age, Race, and Sex: 1995
(Death Rate per 100,000 Population)

Item	5–14 yrs. old	15–24 yrs. old	25–34 yrs. old	35–44 yrs. old	45–54 yrs. old	55–64 yrs. old	65–74 yrs. old	75–84 yrs. old
White Males	0.9	13.6	9.8	6.3	4.0	2.8	1.5	0.8
Black Males	4.1	121.0	80.7	38.3	24.6	15.9	10.8	(B)
White Females	0.4	2.2	2.3	1.8	1.2	0.8	0.7	0.8
Black Females	1.2	11.8	10.2	6.7	3.4	2.3	(B)	(B)

Source: Bureau of the Census, U.S. Department of Commerce, *Statistical Abstract of the United States*: 1998, 108 table 149. (B) does not meet standard of reliability or precision.

cites survey data showing that black, central-city residents were almost twice as likely as whites to believe that the police did not provide them with adequate protection, and six times more likely to report they had considered moving because the police failed to provide adequate protection in their neighborhoods (John R. Lott Jr., *More Guns, Less Crime* 69 [1998]). If minority communities cannot rely on the police for protection, do residents have any alternative but to resort to private action?

3. A 1999 Associated Press poll found blacks were much more likely than whites to support gun control. Eighty-three percent of blacks supported tougher restrictions on firearms, compared to 52 percent of whites (Will Lester, *Men, Women Differ Widely on Gun Control in AP Poll*, San Diego Union-Tribune, Sept. 8, 1999, at A8). This disparity is consistent with prior polling results. A study of black perceptions of guns and violence found that 84 percent of blacks believed guns are too easy to obtain. However, 62 percent also believed that having a gun in the home would help protect them. (James H. Price et al., *African-American Adults' Perceptions of Guns and Violence*, 86 Journal of the National Medical Association 426 [1994].) Do you think that support for gun control is in the interest of all blacks? Some blacks?

4. Do you believe most white gun owners are desirous of blacks owning more guns? Most white non–gun owners? Bogus notes that one researcher has tied gun ownership among whites to racial prejudice and a desire to punish, rather than defend oneself from, criminals. (See Robert Louis Young, *Race, Sex, and Guns: A Social Psychology of Firearms Ownership* [1982], available from UMI Dissertation Service, Ann Arbor, Michigan.) Other researchers, though, have found no strong personality

differences between gun owners and the general population—perhaps because gun owners comprise such a significant share of the total population. (See James D. Wright et al., *Under the Gun* 120–22 [Hawthorne, NY: Aldine de Gruyter, 1981], summarizing various studies.)

5. Bogus argues that armed organizations such as the Deacons for Defense "take the law into their own hands." If the organizations engage in only legal activities (e.g., owning guns in accordance with state law, using them in lawful self-defense, etc.), are they "taking the law into their own hands"? What if an organization goes further, by holding trials and/or imposing punishment on alleged lawbreakers? (The Deacons did not do this, but the vigilantes of the nineteenth-century west did. For more on vigilantism, see Richard Maxwell Brown, *The American Vigilante Tradition*, in *Violence in America: Historical and Comparative Perspectives*, ed. Hugh Davis Graham and Ted Robert Gurr [New York: Praeger, 1969]; Thomas J. Dimsdale, *The Vigilantes of Montana: Being a Correct and Impartial Narrative of the Case, Trial, Capture, and Execution of Henry Plummer's Notorious Road Agent Band* [Norman: University of Oklahoma Press, 1977 3d ed.]; David B. Kopel, *The Samurai, the Mountie, and the Cowboy* 323–29 [Amherst, NY: Prometheus Books, 1992].)

6. For a more fully developed version of Professor Bogus's argument that, in large part, the Second Amendment was written to assure the South that the federal government could not undermine the slave system by disarming the state militia, see Carl T. Bogus, *The Hidden History of the Second Amendment*, 31 University of California Davis Law Review 309 (1998). Kopel responds that there were many motives for the Second Amendment—including self-defense, national defense, and civic virtue. He notes that even some of the prominent Virginians, who were among those most concerned about preserving the militia to suppress slave insurrections, also expressed concern about preserving a widespread right to arms so that white Virginians could resist enslavement by a potentially tyrannical federal government. For example, George Mason told the Virginia Constitutional Ratifying Convention: "Forty years ago, when the resolution of enslaving America was formed in Great Britain, the British Parliament was advised by an artful man [Sir William Keith], who was governor of Pennsylvania, to disarm the people; that it was the best and most effectual way to enslave them; but that they should not do

it openly, but weaken them, and let them sink gradually, by totally dis-
using and neglecting the militia" (June 14, 1788). (See David B. Kopel,
The Second Amendment in the Nineteenth Century, 1998 Brigham Young
University Law Review 1359, 1515–29 [1998].) Is the Second Amendment
irrelevant or illegitimate in the twenty-first century if one of its motives
was preventing slave revolt? If slave revolt were the only motive?

NATIONAL ASSOCIATION FOR THE ADVANCEMENT OF COLORED PEOPLE v. A. A. ARMS, INC., ET AL.

[In July 1999, the National Association for the Advancement of Colored
People (NAACP) sued 110 gun manufacturers, alleging they have engaged in negligent manufacturing, marketing, and distribution practices
that have a disproportionate harmful impact on blacks. The lawsuit does
not seek money damages but rather injunctive relief that, if granted,
would require gun manufacturers to effect substantial changes in how
they market and distribute their products. (The lawsuit is similar in
many respects to the more than thirty lawsuits filed against the gun industry by various cities, counties, and states. These lawsuits are discussed extensively in chapter 6.) Here are some brief excerpts from the
fifty-one-page complaint (the legal document that initiates a lawsuit)
filed by the NAACP.]

Complaint

Plaintiffs National Association for the Advancement of Colored People
(hereinafter "NAACP"), on behalf of themselves, their individual members, and those whose interests they represent, by way of Complaint
against the defendants, and each of them, allege as follows:

1. Plaintiff, NAACP, brings this action for equitable relief against the
    defendants seeking changes to the marketing, distribution and sales
    practices of the defendants—practices which have led to dispro-
    portionate numbers of injuries, deaths and other damages among
    those whose interests the plaintiff represents.

2. Handguns designed, manufactured, imported, marketed, distributed and sold by the defendants kill and seriously injure tens of thousands of people in the United States every year. Many of those who are injured, killed or placed at risk by the defendants' handguns are children, including the children of members of the NAACP, and other children whose interests and welfare the NAACP represents and endeavors to protect.

3. These handgun-related injuries and deaths are the result of the defendants' conduct in failing to regulate, supervise and otherwise exercise reasonable control over the marketing, distribution and sale of their handguns, resulting in an oversupply of illegal handguns in the United States.

4. For years the handgun industry comprising the defendants has negligently distributed handguns and by doing so has flooded and saturated the lawful handgun market so as to create, maintain and supply an unlawful, unregulated and underground handgun market. Defendants knew, or reasonably should have known and foreseen, that they were producing, marketing and distributing handguns far in excess of the reasonable legitimate demand from responsible and legal consumers in the lawful handgun market, but they have failed and refused to take any meaningful steps to regulate and control the marketing and distribution of their handguns. . . .

128. Plaintiff NAACP is particularly concerned about the level of handgun violence in the African-American communities, as well as other minority communities. . . . The human cost suffered by victims of handgun violence, their families and communities is disproportionately borne by African-Americans. According to a 1990 study by the Federal Centers for Disease Control ("CDC"), homicide is the leading cause of death for black males aged 15–17 and handguns were involved in 78% of these homicides. According to the same CDC study, a young African-American male is nine (9) times more likely to be murdered than a young white male. . . . Despite overall decreases in handgun-related crimes, according to a 1998 Uniform Crime Report compiled by the Department of Justice ("DOJ"), the

only demographic which did not indicate a decrease in handgun-related homicides was that of black males between the ages of 14 and 24. The National Center for Health Statistics, DOJ *Crime Statistics Report for 1998*, revealed that two-thirds of homicide victims are non-white. . . .

[The complaint proceeds to set forth lengthy allegations that the gun industry has failed to take steps to manufacture safer guns, intentionally targets sales to women and juveniles, and markets and distributes guns in ways that increase the risk that they will end up in the hands of criminals.

The complaint concludes by asserting that the defendants are negligent in manufacturing, marketing, and distributing their products. The plaintiff asks for injunctive relief focusing primarily on the defendants' distribution practices. More specifically, plaintiff seeks a court order requiring defendants to exercise much greater control over the sales methods of their distributors and retailers as a way to reduce the numbers of guns going to criminals.]

GUNS DON'T KILL BLACK PEOPLE, OTHER BLACKS DO
(Salon.com, Aug. 16, 1999, at http://www.salon.com/news/
col/horo/1999/08/16/naacp)

David Horowitz

When the National Association for the Advancement of Colored People announced plans recently to file an injunctive class-action suit "to force [gun manufacturers] to distribute their product responsibly," the NAACP president, Kweisi Mfume, noted that gun violence takes a disproportionately high toll among young black males.

According to an NAACP press release, African-American males between the ages of 15 and 24 are almost five times more likely to be injured by firearms than are white males in the same age group. "Firearm homicide has been the leading cause of death among young African-American males for nearly 30 years," it stated.

Am I alone in seeing this as an absurd act of political desperation by the civil rights establishment? . . .

[W]ho makes guns shoot in ways that victimize blacks more than whites? . . .

The fact is that while blacks make up only 12 percent of the population, they account for 46 percent of total violent crime and 90 percent of the murders of other blacks. It is they, not whites or gun manufacturers, who are responsible for the disproportionate gun deaths of young black males.

Firearms don't kill people. Sociopaths do. It takes a human brain to pull the trigger. If young black males abuse firearms in an irresponsible and criminal fashion, why should the firearm industry be held accountable? Why not their parents? Why not themselves? . . .

The myth of racial oppression, invoked to explain every social deficit of blacks, is an exercise in psychological denial. Crying racism deflects attention from the actual causes of the problems that afflict African-American communities. Its net result is to deprive people and communities who could help themselves of the power to change their fate. . . .

If the NAACP and other black leaders want to end the terrible scourge of gun violence committed by young inner-city blacks, they should launch a campaign to promote marriage and family formation in the African-American community; they should issue a moral plea to the community to stigmatize fathers who abandon their children and parents who have more children than they can afford. Instead of waging war against law enforcement agencies and supporting destructive racial demagogues like Al Sharpton, they should support the Rudy Giulianis and other champions of public safety, whom they now attack. They should campaign for a tripling of police forces in inner-city areas to protect the vast majority of inhabitants who are law-abiding and who are the true victims of the predators among them.

But to take these remedial steps would require rejecting the bogus charge of white oppression. It would mean abandoning the ludicrous claim that white America and firearms manufacturers are the cause of the problems afflicting African-Americans. It would mean taking responsibility for their own communities instead.

DISCUSSION NOTES

1. The Horowitz article, though strident, raises legitimate questions for discussion, questions that are often left unasked and unanswered because of discomfort with the topic. But we cannot hope to solve complex social problems if we are afraid to talk about all aspects of them. Why is the firearm death rate and overall homicide rate so much higher for blacks than for whites? In 1994 the FBI reported an overall murder rate of 9 persons per 100,000 U.S. residents. The rate for black men the same year was 65.1 per 100,000. The rate for black men between the ages of fifteen and twenty-four was 157.6 per 100,000. Although blacks constitute roughly 12 percent of the population, the black homicide rate since 1980 has accounted for 46 percent of the U.S. total. Firearms are the leading cause of death for black males aged fifteen to twenty-four. To what do you attribute these dire statistics? Is it because of guns? Poverty? Drugs? Unstable families? Police and societal indifference? An underclass revolution? Something else? As an exercise, make a list of the ten factors you believe contribute most to firearms violence. Order the list from most important to least important. Does your list change if the question is not "firearms violence" in general but "firearms violence in black communities"? (For psychological and sociological theories on the causes of crime, see Thomas Gabor, *The Prediction of Criminal Behaviour* 27–70 [1986]; Harold J. Vetter and Ira J. Silverman, *The Nature of Crime* 305–31 [1978]; *The Psychology of Crime*, ed. Hans Toch, 147–236 [1971].)

2. Is the NAACP lawsuit frivolous? Is it a misguided attempt to shift responsibility from guilty criminals to innocent product makers? Is the suit an overall assault on the gun industry, dressed up in the language of race, or is there a legitimate racial component to the claims? (Chapter 6 analyzes many of the gun manufacturing, marketing, and distribution changes sought in litigation against the gun industry, including those sought in the NAACP suit.)

3. One curious racial disparity in the inventory of firearms violence concerns mass-shooting incidents, virtually all of which are carried out by white males (including Martin Bryant, who killed thirty-five people in Port Arthur, Australia, in 1996; Thomas Hamilton, who killed sixteen

schoolchildren in Dunblane, Scotland, in 1996; George Hennard, who killed twenty-three people in a cafeteria in Killeen, Texas, in 1991; Gene Simmons, who killed sixteen family members and others in Russellville, Arkansas, in 1987; and James Oliver Huberty, who killed twenty-one people in a McDonald's in San Ysidro, California, in 1984). Moreover, all the recent mass school shootings in this country have been carried out by white male students (Littleton, Colorado: fifteen dead, including assailants, and twenty-three injured; Conyers, Georgia: six injured; Springfield, Oregon: two dead and twenty-two injured; Jonesboro, Arkansas: five dead and eleven injured; Paducah, Kentucky: three dead and five injured; Pearl, Mississippi: two dead and seven injured). Among this nation's prominent mass-shooting incidents, only one has been carried out by a member of a minority: in December 1993, Colin Ferguson, a black man, killed five and wounded eighteen others on a crowded commuter train in Long Island, New York. Can you think of explanations for this lopsided racial difference in mass-shooting episodes?

B. Gender

This section features the contrasting views of two feminist commentators concerning whether gun ownership by women promotes or hinders the cause of feminism. As you read the following materials, keep in mind the central dispute between the authors: do women individually and/or societally benefit more or suffer more from the ownership, possession, and proliferation of firearms?

Why Annie Can't Get Her Gun: A Feminist Perspective on the Second Amendment
(University of Illinois Law Review 467 [1996])

Inge Anna Larish

Violent crime against women has reached epidemic proportions in the United States, and the trend shows no signs of abating. Three out of four women will be victims of at least one violent crime in their lifetimes.

While violent crime against young males decreased from 1974 to 1987, violent crime against women increased nearly fifty percent. Ninety percent of the 4,693 women murdered in 1991 were slain by males (only one out of eight males murdered in 1991 were slain by females) and every fifteen seconds a woman is battered.

Statistics on forcible rape are even more staggering. An estimated one in five women will be raped at some point in their lives. Federal Bureau of Investigation (FBI) statistics show that the rape rate has risen four times faster than the overall crime rate in the United States. According to the most conservative estimate, women reported 106,593 rapes to authorities in 1991 (an estimated 83 of every 100,000 females in the country reported being raped)—a three percent increase over the record-breaking 1990 volume and a thirteen percent increase since 1987. Based on the 1990 and 1991 reports, men rape or attempt to rape over twelve women each hour and close to three hundred every day. . . .

Gun control proponents use this frightening trend of increasing violence toward women in their rhetoric espousing gun control legislation as a solution to the increase in violent crime, arguing that gun control will stop or reverse the trend. Control rhetoric rarely mentions the empirical evidence that, although violent crime towards women has escalated, gun use in assault and robbery has decreased. Further, gun control rhetoric generally ignores empirical evidence indicating that guns play a small role in the escalation of violent crimes against women. For example, the data available from reported rapes reveals that only nine percent of rapists have guns at the time of attack or attempted attack. Gun control rhetoric also argues that decreasing the number of guns by decreasing civilian gun availability or banning civilian gun use will make "everyone" safer. Control proponents commonly quote studies concluding that a handgun kept in the home is more likely to be used against family members than against an intruder. They fail to disclose, however, the critiques of the methodology of these studies. These studies falsely portray gun ownership as harmful to women—a false picture of actual gun use which may be life-threatening for women. For example, a staggering number of the homicides counted by the studies are actually instances of domestic abuse. Finally, control rhetoric generally ignores the evidence that crime against the physically weaker members of society (women, children, the elderly, or the disabled) increases where guns are less available. . . .

The exclusion of women's concerns in the gun control debate ignores that women are most in need of guns for self-defense. All else being held equal, women are physically weaker than men and will continue to be victimized by men whether or not men have guns. Moreover, unlike men, women use guns primarily for defensive purposes—most often as a last resort. Repeated reports have shown that police are incapable of responding to women's protection needs. . . .

Gun control proponents . . . argue that the need for private gun ownership is obsolete because the police will protect people from crime. However, the courts have repeatedly held that the function of the police is to deter crime in general, not to protect the individual citizen. For example, police have no duty to, and do not, protect citizens who are under death threat. This principle derives from both legal history and practical necessity. . . .

Practically, the complete displacement of citizen self-protection by police is not feasible. Current statistics on the inadequacy of police resources and responses to violent crime provide a glaring rebuttal to the proposal that the need for citizen self-defense has become obsolete. Simple calculations make it painfully obvious that even if all of the 553,733 total police officers in America were on patrol at the same time, they could not protect 244 million citizens from more than 1.9 million unpredictable violent crimes. . . . As a further problem, average police response times vary from ten to fifteen minutes, with police often arriving on the scene to find the crime well in progress or already committed. . . .

The Impact of Control Measures on Women

Men and women are not created equal in physical strength and, thus, guns not only equalize the differences between men, but also eliminate the disparity in physical power between the sexes. The available information on civilian restriction of gun ownership indicates that one of the groups most harmed by restrictions on private gun ownership will be women. Yet, control legislation and the surrounding political rhetoric fail to consider the effects of such legislation on the ability of women to defend themselves. In fact, some control proponents use rhetoric portraying women as too emotional to use guns. They cite the statistic that the overwhelming majority of murders committed by women are of male relatives or acquaintances—creating the inference that women are more likely to become irrational and kill their lovers, spouses, or boyfriends. Although it specifically targets women, this argument is framed as a justification for keeping guns out of the hands of citizens. Such rhetoric fails to mention that, in the overwhelming majority of actual cases in which a woman used a gun against a spouse or boyfriend, she did so as a last resort to fend off a male threatening her life. The rhetoric similarly fails to mention that control measures which would remove the gun from the domestic violence arena may take away the woman's best means for self-defense. Control proponents refer to surveys portraying women in favor of gun control to help stop violent crime. While women are in favor of stopping violence, however, and guns are often linked with violence, no evidence exists that banning guns will result in less violence against women. The available evidence even suggests that if guns are banned, women may become more frequent targets of violent crime.

Waiting Periods

Control proponents tout waiting periods as an effective way to prevent gun homicide both because such controls allow states without the capability for instant checks the time to check an individual's record and because waiting periods reduce "heat of passion" crimes by allowing time for the purchaser of the gun to "cool off." Again, the impact on women's defensive uses of guns is largely ignored.

To begin with, the evidence shows that killings that fit the profile of those sought to be prevented through waiting periods are extremely rare. Further, although proponents argue that waiting periods have merit for saving lives, they may also cost lives—women's lives. Depending on how long the period is, women in abusive situations may be deprived of ready access to guns—which are the most effective protection available to them. The lack of appeal provisions and the poor mechanisms for correcting errors also may hamper ready access to guns by women who may need to obtain a gun quickly. . . .

Carry Permits

Carry permits are often issued based on "need" and are discretionary. In many states, "need" is found for financial or status reasons. In Illinois, for example, provisions allow employees of banks and other financial institutions to carry guns. In New York, the standard of "unique need" has resulted in permits to the rich and the influential. Criticism of the New York system includes that it grants celebrities and the economic/social elite permits while denying permits to working-class individuals who must operate in crime-ridden areas as part of their daily jobs.

Major metropolitan and urban areas which have the greatest proportion of violent crime against women, as well as the greatest likelihood of woman-headed households, also have the most restrictive gun control measures. . . .

Other cities, such as New York, have special permit/licensing systems which allow private citizens to own guns for personal protection. These licenses discriminate against the economically disadvantaged—the "need" criteria most often accepted is protection of property.

Women are particularly disadvantaged because they tend on average to hold lower-paying and lower-status jobs than men and because they are at an inherent physical disadvantage. Such laws appear to ignore the incredible violent crime aimed especially at women, as well as the statistics showing that women desire to carry guns primarily for defensive purposes. The high restriction areas in major metropolitan centers also tend to have the largest resource problems—seriously affecting their ability to provide adequate police protection to private citizens.

Women's Use of Self-Defense Weapons

The statistical evidence on defensive gun use shows that women have good reasons for seeking to use guns for self-defense. Defense with guns results in 17.4% fewer injuries to the defender than alternatives. For example, in 40.3% of instances where the defender uses a knife, he or she is injured. Similarly, the aggressor injures the defender 22% of the time when the defender uses some weapon other than a knife or gun, 50.8%

of the time when the defender uses physical force, and 34.9% of the time when the defender uses evasion. Analysts repeatedly find that guns are the surest and safest method of protection for those who are most vulnerable to "vicious male predators." Guns are thus the most effective self-defense tools for women, the elderly, the weak, the infirm, and the physically handicapped. . . .

Analysis

A problem with gender-neutral law is its assumption that such laws concern themselves with women's interests, when, a closer examination reveals that, the interpretation, discussion, and application of the law often ignores women. . . . [T]here is no discussion of the effectiveness (or ineffectiveness) of the police and how such inadequacies affect the women who comprise over half of the citizens of the United States. Because police have been so ineffective in preventing the crimes which greatly and disproportionately affect women, such as sexual assault and domestic violence, and which remain on the rise, the exclusion of women's needs from the debate results in subtle—but real—discrimination. . . .

Current control proponents subsume women's needs and rights under the rubric of all citizens. Similarly, gun control laws and self-defense standards are largely written in gender-neutral terminology. Under liberal or traditional equality theory, women will by definition be guaranteed the same rights under the Second Amendment as long as state laws use the same standards to restrict gun ownership, possession, and use for women as for men. According to such an analysis, concealed carry permits do not discriminate against women to the extent that they set "need" as their neutral standard [for] granting a permit. However, standards using a monetary minimum or social status for granting permits reflect an inherent male bias. Women often do not hold jobs in which they must carry money because women still lag behind men in achieving job parity in those fields. The criteria of money itself as opposed to dangerousness of occupation is discriminatory. The night nurse at the city hospital has an equally valid reason to carry a gun as the proprietor carrying a payroll exceeding X amount of dollars, or the politician, or the wealthy businessman—why should New York allow Donald Trump to protect himself, but not a woman living in an area of high crime? Even in jurisdictions where the criteria is not based on monetary sum carried, an even more insidious discrimination occurs when categories of work are perceived as dangerous enough to be worthy of concealed carry permits; these categories do not generally encompass traditionally female work. In jurisdictions that allow discretion in applying criteria (as do most), the perception that women are irrational, emotional, and incapable of handling guns makes it difficult for women to obtain permits—even though their situations may otherwise warrant it (i.e., if a man applied and all else were equal, he would get the permit).

Criteria which use need for protection of property or status as a basis for issuing carrying permits for guns are male-oriented. If the state banned all guns, women would lose because they could not physically fight off men and the viability of alternate methods of self-defense is questionable. However, a gun ban—if effective—would benefit men because criminal violation of property and affronts on status would decrease. Men on average could better defend themselves in hand-to-hand combat, and would not face the physical difficulties confronted by women. Men would lose only to the extent that a complete gun ban is virtually impossible; and criminals would still have access to guns. But men who perpetuate violent crime against women—rape and assault, especially—would greatly benefit from civilian gun bans. Women who previously had the option of legally possessing guns would have to choose between committing the crime of possessing a gun and self-defense. For most women, men's fists are lethal force. Even with high degrees of self-defense combat training, women have a definite disadvantage in street fights. More insidiously, society would send women the message that they should not use force to defend themselves—a message society is already sending in denying women the defense of self-defense. . . .

DISCUSSION NOTES

1. Larish focuses on the need for women living in abusive relationships to have firearms for their protection, stating that guns are "the most effec-

tive protection available to them." Do you agree? Are guns a more effective and desirable response to domestic violence than calling the police? Leaving the relationship? Seeking safe shelter? Or are guns a supplement to these steps? Do you believe that introducing a firearm into a violent domestic abuse situation is likely to improve the situation or cause it to degenerate further? Does it depend on whether the gun is in the hands of the abuser or the victim?

2. Many states now have laws that require the police to make an arrest when responding to a domestic abuse call. Some states have adopted "no drop" or "no dismissal" policies in domestic abuse cases, which require offenders to be prosecuted regardless of whether the victim wishes to "drop the charges," a common obstacle to punishing domestic abusers. Is enhanced emphasis on prosecuting abusers likely to be a more effective deterrent to domestic abuse than arming women with firearms? Even if you believe the answer is yes, do more arrests obviate the need for guns?

3. One of the author's main points is that gun control laws that are gender-neutral on their face might have the effect of discriminating against women. She offers mandatory waiting periods to purchase firearms as one example. Do waiting periods discriminate against women? On March 5, 1991, Bonnie Elmasri, worried that her estranged husband might violate a restraining order to keep away from her, telephoned a firearms instructor to inquire about obtaining a handgun. The instructor explained to her that Wisconsin has a forty-eight-hour waiting period for purchasing handguns. Elmasri's husband murdered her and her two children that night. (See David B. Kopel, *Background Checks and Waiting Periods*, in *Guns: Who Should Have Them?* 61–65 ed. David B. Kopel ed. [1995], discussing several incidents where he asserts that waiting periods may have contributed to women being harmed by attackers.) Do you think that possessing a firearm would enable a victiom of domestic abuse to repel or defeat her attacker? In what percentage of cases? Do you have concerns that the same reason raised in support of women arming themselves against domestic abusers—the superior physical strength of men—could enable some domestic abusers to disarm women of their firearms and use the weapons against

them? Proponents of waiting periods argue that they provide a "cooling-off" time during which assailants might change their minds about carrying out an attack. Do you think the cooling-off rationale has merit? Do you think that (choose one) all/most/some/a few domestic abusers will simply wait until the waiting period expires to obtain possession of their firearms and use them against their victims?

On November 30, 1998, the national five-day waiting period for handgun purchases imposed by the Brady bill expired, replaced by a computerized instant background-check system. Several states, however, impose their own waiting periods of varying lengths. Which side do you think has the better argument with respect to waiting periods? On balance, do you view them as a desirable and effective cooling-off period or as an unfair obstruction to a person needing a handgun for self-protection?

Should there be waiting periods for abortion? Are the arguments in favor of a waiting period for abortion stronger or weaker than those for waiting periods for gun purchases? (For an examination of the similarities between abortion rights and gun rights constitutional and policy arguments, see Nicholas J. Johnson, *Principles and Passions: The Intersection of Abortion and Gun Rights*, 50 Rutgers Law Review 97 [1997].)

4. What about the argument that discretionary "right-to-carry" laws discriminate against women? Larish complains that New York's concealed-weapon law protects only "celebrities and the economic/ social elite." She asks, "[W]hy should New York allow Donald Trump to protect himself, but not a woman living in an area of high crime?" Why not use Madonna as an example and ask why the state should protect her but not a man living in an area of high crime? Do you believe that laws which give the police wide discretion in deciding who may carry a firearm have a disparate impact on women?

In a dramatic turnabout from just a few years ago, thirty-three states have passed what are known as "shall issue" right-to-carry laws, which require the issuance of a concealed-handgun permit to any person who meets certain nondiscretionary requirements, which usually consist of passing a background check and completing a firearms training course. Twenty-one of these state laws have been adopted since 1995. Do you think women will be safer if they carry concealed handguns on their persons?

5. Larish touts firearms as an instrument that furthers the cause of feminism. What should a feminist think of the following advice to firearms retailers on "equipping ladies" with purses designed to carry concealed weapons? "Be sure to have a variety of purses on hand or catalogs your customer can order from. A woman considers her purse a part of her wardrobe and may want to own purses in several styles and colors. Having a large selection means bigger sales for you" (Lisa Parsons, *Equipping Ladies for Firearms Training Is Smart Business*, 39 Shooting Industry 22 [Aug. 1994]).

6. In 1996, Congress enacted the "Lautenberg Amendment" to the Gun Control Act of 1968, which makes it illegal for any person who has been convicted of a misdemeanor crime of domestic violence to possess a firearm (18 *U.S. Code* § 922[g][9]). Does encouraging potential victims of domestic abuse to arm themselves run contrary to the purpose of the Lautenberg Amendment to remove firearms from the homes of domestic abusers? Or is it consistent with the Lautenberg Amendment that victims be better armed than perpetrators?

7. Is the real problem that men are more violent than women? If so, is it a desirable solution to, in effect, encourage women to also resort to violence, or should we seek other societal solutions to the issues of violence against women? Can you think of any?

Why Packing a Pistol Perpetuates Patriarchy
(8 Hastings Women's Law Journal 351 [1997])

Alana Bassin

This essay argues . . . that for women, the handgun is not a source of empowerment. Instead, the handgun is a serious detriment to women and our communal interest in safety. Specifically, this essay demonstrates that: (1) Guns are a source of male domination; (2) Guns foster violence in society and against women; (3) Women who endorse the theory that the gun is an equalizer are victims of the NRA and gun industry marketing campaigns exploiting our nation's violence; and (4) Women advocating gun use have misdiagnosed societal violence and ignored the communal interest in gun control as a result. . . .

Guns Are a Source of Male Domination

Firearms are a source of male domination—a symbol of male power and aggression. First, the gun is phallic. Just as sex is the ultimate weapon of patriarchy used to penetrate and possess women, the gun's sole purpose is to intrude and wound its victim. Historically, men have used guns to conquer and dominate other peoples. . . .

The Second Amendment itself disregards women. Most notably, the language legitimizing the right to bear arms refers specifically to a "well regulated militia," an institution that did not include women. Additionally, the Second Amendment was ratified by men at a time when women had no legitimate voice in society. In interpreting the Constitution, scholars and judges often rely on the framers' intent. Because none of the framers were women, women's views and voices were never heard. As a result, the absence of a female view during the creation of the right to bear arms critically impacts society. . . .

For victims of domestic violence, the freedom to purchase a gun also can be lethal. In the United States, domestic violence is the leading cause of injury for women between the ages of 15–44. Between 2–4 million incidents of domestic violence occur each year. Of those, an estimated 150,000 are gun-related. Where there is a gun at home, women subjected to one incident of physical abuse at home are almost five times more likely to be murdered or fatally shot in a later instance of physical abuse. An Atlanta study about domestic violence involving guns found that death was twelve times as likely to occur. Overwhelmingly, it was women who died. . . .

Women Who View Guns as an "Equalizer" Are Victims of the NRA and the Gun Industry's Marketing Campaigns and Fear Tactics

The NRA and gun manufacturers have capitalized on the violence in the United States, and although some women perceive buying guns as empowering, these women have actually become victims of marketing campaigns and fear tactics. First, in the late 1980s, the gun industry, realizing the male gun market was saturated, focused on women as a new focus group. In the name of feminism and motherhood, the gun industry and the NRA aggressively pursued their new consumers: women, aged 25–40, mostly professionals, with a median income of $55,000.

Then, in February 1989, Smith and Wesson produced the Lady Smith™, a handgun designed for women. According to them, it is elegant yet practical. Soon after, a large number of gun advertisements focused on societal violence toward women, most often "stranger danger." Advertisements headlined phrases such as: "Things that go bump in the night aren't always your imagination. . . ."; "You thought no one could fit in your back seat. . . ."; and "Self-protection is more than your right . . . it's your responsibility," with a picture of a mother tucking her child into bed. The NRA's advertisements were similar, with headlines such as: "Should you shoot a rapist before he cuts your throat?" and "He's followed you for two weeks. He'll rape you in two minutes. Who Cares?" The gun industry capitalized on women's fears by stressing the danger of rapists, stalkers, and burglars. Yet violence against women is generally not committed by "strangers in the night" but by known acquaintances. More than twice as many women are shot and killed by their husbands or lovers than by strangers, leaving only a small percentage of violent crime victims who successfully use a gun to defend themselves against strangers.

Ironically, while gun advertisements emphasized the need for a woman to have a gun for safety, gunmakers gave little concern to ensure safe gun use. In a qualitative analysis examining 125 gun magazines and twenty advertisements, statistics showed that none of the advertisements expressly mentioned any need for a woman to seek training in how to use a gun and only 20–25% discussed safety features or safety equipment. Nothing in the advertisements emphasized a need for women to learn safe gun posture, how to load and unload ammunition, or how to operate a gun and store it. [See Debra Burke et al., *Women and Guns: Legal and Ethical Implications for Marketing Strategy*, 12 St. Louis University Public Law Review 393, 395–96 (1993).] Unfortunately, research among women shows that they feel secure simply from gun ownership. There is little concern for learning proper gun care. Considering the lethal nature of a gun and the high number of accidents occurring because of improper gun use, it is peculiar that the gun industry, which purports to be an advocate for women's safety, does not advertise the need for education in gun operation and use.

In addition, the NRA and the gun industry have misled the general public in the statistics they cite concerning the increase in women gun owners over the past decade. During the 1980s, Smith and Wesson hired the Gallup organization to determine the potential number of women gun buyers for a study which was never intended to be published. At the end of the study, Gallup identified approximately 15.6 million women who could buy guns, but only 900,000 women who were likely buyers. In 1989, Smith and Wesson reported that 15.6 million women were potential buyers. Within only a few years, the media turned potential buyers into actual owners, quoting the number of actual women gun owners in the United States to be 15–20 million. Typically, statistics quoted by the media and the NRA state that 17–20% of women own guns, and these statistics soar to as high as 43.5%. However, the General Social Surveys, conducted by the National Opinion Research Center at the University of Chicago, indicate that during 1980–94, the number of women gun owners has remained static at about 11.6%. Yet Smith and Wesson, the NRA, and other gun manufacturers continue to misquote the number of women gun owners in the United States and continue to let the media mislead the public. They have effectively created a perception of "everybody is doing it—you should too." The only problem, however, is that not everybody is doing it.

Women Advocating Gun Use Have Misdiagnosed Societal Violence and Ignored the Communal Interest in Gun Control

Most people would agree that a handgun often provides a person with a sense of security. Unarmed, anyone could fall victim to an assault. But, while gun ownership may provide some protection in the short term, it fails to address the deep-rooted problems of gun violence in society and will only perpetuate violence in the long term.

Women who are buying into the patriarchy need to examine the impact of guns on all levels of society. . . .

Unfortunately, women often perceive the norm in society according to "white, middle class, heterosexual, able-bodied, and otherwise privileged" standards and ignore realities concerning other women. Not surprisingly, women who are most interested in gun ownership are privileged women and not subject to inner city gun violence. Women, however, who pack pistols have more to consider than personal empowerment. Guns in society are taking a heavy toll on lower-income, often non-white, communities. Packing a pistol may promote personal safety, but it does not end the violence in these areas. Women who have fought to have a voice in society have a responsibility to address gun oppression on women and people of all races and incomes. Ignoring the impact of gun violence in the inner cities affronts the entire premise of liberty for which women have been fighting.

Nevertheless, even if the impact of guns on inner city communities does not trouble gun-toting women, endorsing broad individual gun ownership is detrimental to society as a whole. A gun is only an effective self-defense tool if the attacker is not armed. If society accepts that gun ownership is necessary for survival, eventually everyone will possess a gun. The gun will no longer be an equalizer. It will be a lethal weapon accessible to any frustrated person.

Moreover, the doctrine supporting gun ownership for survival is, in essence, supporting vigilantism. Should women encourage people to take the law into their own hands? In the case of domestic violence, some women are forced to take the law into their own hands to survive (and their actions are not being judged by this author's remarks). Advocating gun use as self-defense, however, creates an opportunity for unjustifiable aggression without preventing violence in the first instance.

Women do not have to surrender to the existing societal structure where the white male norm is status quo and violence against women is not a serious concern. Instead, women have a choice: they can support individual gun ownership like many of their male counterparts do and give in to the patriarchal world, or they can seek radical changes to end the violence. . . .

DISCUSSION NOTES

1. The Larish article promotes firearms as a source of empowerment for women to be more equal to men. The Bassin article asserts that women who purchase firearms are victims of an exploitation campaign by the firearms industry and National Rifle Association, designed to prey on their fears. Which argument is more persuasive? Why?

2. The author states that supporting gun ownership for women amounts to supporting "vigilantism." Why not "self-defense"? What is the difference? (A dictionary defines "vigilante" as being a member of a "vigilance committee," which is defined as "an extralegal group of citizens that summarily punishes criminals" [*Random House College Dictionary* 1467 (1975)].)

3. Do you believe the police are willing or able to effectively protect individual women from physical attack? Always? Usually? Sometimes? Consider the case of *Thurman v. City of Torrington*, 595 F. Supp. 1521 (D. Conn. 1984). For more than eight months, Tracey Thurman made numerous calls to the Torrington, Connecticut, police, notifying them of repeated threats by her estranged husband, Charles Thurman, against Tracey and her child, Charles, Jr. The pleas were ignored. When Charles used force to remove Charles Jr. from the home of a friend, the police refused to accept a complaint for trespassing. In November 1982, a police officer stood on the street watching as Charles screamed threats at Tracey, arresting him only after he broke the windshield on her car. Charles was convicted of breach of peace and ordered to stay away from Tracey. In December 1982, Charles confronted Tracey and once again threatened her. The police ignored a request to arrest him for violating the court's order. Finally, in June 1983, Charles attacked Tracey, stabbing her in the neck, throat, and chest. Upon arrival of a police officer, Charles dropped the bloody knife and kicked Tracey in the head. He went inside and returned with Charles Jr., whom he dropped on top of the wounded Tracey. He then kicked her in the head a second time. Even after several other officers had arrived on the scene, Charles was permitted to wander about the crowd continuing to threaten Tracey. He was arrested only as he approached her while she was lying on a stretcher.

Tracey Thurman filed a lawsuit alleging that the City of Torrington denied equal protection of the law to victims of domestic abuse by affording them less protection than other victims of violent crime. The city's motion to dismiss the complaint for failing to state a valid cause of action was denied, meaning the suit was permitted to go forward. According to a lawyer for the plaintiff, the lawsuit was settled on appeal for $2 million (telephone interview with Burton Weinstein, Nov. 1, 1999).

The Thurman case is unusual. Most lawsuits against cities or the police for failing to protect citizens from crime are dismissed without trial. As a general rule, the police have no legal duty under tort law or constitutional law to protect individuals from criminal attack, even when a clear, identifiable threat exists. (See, e.g., *Riss v. New York*, 240 N.E. 2d 860 [N.Y. Ct. App. 1968]): police had no duty under tort law to protect a woman who was the subject of repeated threats by a rejected suitor and who had sought police help without success on several occasions.)

If men are bigger, stronger, and more violent than women, and the police are unable or unwilling to protect women, should women rely on firearms for protection? Should the law be changed to impose a legal duty on the police to protect individual citizens from attack? In all cases or only where there is a clearly indentifiable threat? What problems might result from the creation of such a duty?

4. In what ways do you modify your daily activities to avoid being the victim of a sexual assault? Do you think your answer might be different if you were of the other sex? One of the editors' colleagues routinely asks students in her classes how many of them modify their conduct on a daily basis to avoid rape. Virtually all female students, but no male students, raise their hands. Does this additional fear provide greater justification for women to arm themselves? Or are there better safety alternatives to carrying guns?

5. The author suggests that women should set aside their personal safety concerns in favor of the larger communitarian interest in having fewer guns. Accepting for the purpose of argument that fewer guns would lead to an overall lower rate of gun violence, is it asking too much of a person to sublimate her personal safety to promote some abstract benefit to society?

Women may be more willing than men to sacrifice personal safety goals for broader community interests. One theory of feminism, derived from the work of psychologist Carol Gilligan in her groundbreaking book *In a Different Voice* (Cambridge, MA: Harvard University Educational Review 1977), is that women view the world from a relational perspective. This means they are more likely than men to consider the needs of children, spouses, friends, and even the community in making decisions. The result is that a woman may reject the presence of a gun in the household, even if it might benefit her personally, as too dangerous to others with whose safety she is concerned.

6. Men are indisputably more violent than women. Although women comprise half of the U.S. population, men commit at least 85 percent all homicides. (See Arthur L. Kellermann and James A. Mercy, *Men, Women, and Murder: Gender-specific Differences in Rates of Fatal Violence and Victimization*, 33 Journal of Trauma 1 [1992], citing data that men committed 85.3 percent of the 215,273 homicides occurring between 1976 and 1987.) Suppose that, in place of the complete gun prohibition proposed by some gun control advocates, a law were passed allowing only women to possess guns. Such a law would probably run afoul of the equal protection clause of the Fourteenth Amendment, and perhaps of the Second Amendment as well. But assume *arguendo* that such a law would be valid. In other words, imagine an American society in which women, rather than men, possessed most of the legally owned firearms. How might this shift be expected to affect violent crime? How could it alter traditional sex roles?

Two researchers studied the social perception of women who own guns (Nyla R. Branscombe and Susan Owen, *Influence of Gun Ownership on Social Inferences about Women and Men*, 21 Journal of Applied Social Psychology 1567 [1991]). They hypothesized that, because owning a gun is "an aggressive cue" and because it is more socially acceptable for men to behave aggressively, gun ownership by women would cause them to be perceived as "masculinized" and defying stereotypical female roles. They conducted two studies (a survey of college students and a community sampling) that supported their hypothesis. Women handgun owners were perceived as being more male in physical appearance, as possessing more stereotypical positive (e.g., independent) and negative (e.g., reckless) male traits, as possessing fewer positive stereotypical female traits (e.g., understanding of others), as being more likely to occupy traditionally male occupational roles, and as being less likely to occupy traditional female occupational roles.

7. Do gun manufacturers have a duty to ensure that buyers of their products receive training on how to use a firearm properly, beyond including a manual with every gun sold? Three law professors conducted a survey of women gun buyers and firearms retailers in Asheville, North Carolina. The survey found that 34.5 percent of women handgun buyers had completed a training program in firearm use. Sixty-seven percent of the retailers surveyed stated they do not believe their female customers know how to use a firearm at the time of purchase. (See Debra Burke et al., *Women, Guns, and the Uniform Commercial Code,* 33 Willamette Law Review 219, 236 [1997].) Do manufacturers of other products, such as cars, boats, or skis, have obligations to ensure that their customers are trained? To do more than include a manual with their product? (Chapter 6 discusses lawsuits against gun manufacturers which assert that they have a legal duty to exercise greater care in the marketing of their products.)

8. There are references in some feminist literature to guns as "penis symbols" or "phallic symbols." Do you see guns as symbols of power? Domination? Do concerns about phallic symbols also suggest that men or women should not swing baseball bats, shoot pool, or play electric guitars? Are these good analogies?

9. The percentage of women owning guns is a matter of dispute. The media routinely portray the number of women gun owners as rising dramatically. *Time* magazine called the rising figures a "gender revolution." Other articles describe the figures as "soaring" or refer to a "boom" or "surge" in women purchasing guns. A Smith & Wesson survey found that gun ownership among women increased by 53 percent from 1983 to 1986. A Smith & Wesson/Gallup survey reported that there were 15.6 million potential women gun buyers in 1989, and that this number was 100 percent higher than in 1983.

A study of media reporting on firearms purchasing trends among women found that twenty-eight of thirty-three newspaper and magazine articles discussing the issue used figures supplied by the National Rifle Association or Smith & Wesson, a prominent gun manufacturer.

The study found that media-reported estimates of women gun ownership varied dramatically, from a low of 15 percent to a high of 43 percent. Analyzing data from the General Social Surveys conducted by the National Opinion Research Center, University of Chicago, the study concluded that no statistically significant trend in increased firearms ownership occurred for either men or women from 1980 to 1994. The study estimates that 11.6 percent of women own firearms. (See Tom W. Smith and Robert J. Smith, *Changes in Firearms Ownership among Women, 1980-1994*, 86 Journal of Criminal Law and Criminology 133 [1995].) More recent surveys show middle-class rural married women to be the fastest-growing group of female gun owners.

10. Survey data consistently show that women favor gun control restrictions by much higher percentages than men. A 1999 survey commissioned by the Associated Press found that 66 percent of American women favor tougher gun laws, compared to 45 percent of men. (Will Lester, *Men, Women Differ Widely on Gun Control in AP Poll*, San Diego Union-Tribune, Sept. 8, 1999, at A8.) Why do you think this is so?

11. Nadine Strossen, president of the American Civil Liberties Union, notes that people who want to outlaw pornography claim that enjoyment of sexually oriented entertainment is contrary to a woman's true nature, and that women who do enjoy such entertainment are dupes of a male-dominated industry. Strossen observes that the arguments against women's choice to consume sexually explicit entertainment are very similar to the arguments made against gun ownership by women: in both cases, the arguments assume there is only one true form of womanhood, and that women need to be protected from making choices. Do you agree with Strossen?

C. Class and Culture

How do class and culture affect gun violence in America? Note that class and culture are closely aligned with race and gender in our society. To the extent that socioeconomic status dictates class standing, white males clearly come out on top. Despite economic progress for women and minorities, white males continue to earn more. (Differences become smaller if education and workforce participation are accounted for.) The median annual income of white households in 1996 was $37,161, compared to $23,482 for black households and $24,906 for Hispanic households. Only 11.2 percent of whites lived below the poverty level in 1996, compared to 28.4 percent of blacks and 29.4 percent of Hispanics. Regarding gender, the median annual income for single-person male households was $27,266, compared to $16,398 for single-person female households. Males fell below the poverty level at a rate of 11.2 percent, compared to 24.2 percent for females. The average annual earnings of year-round, full-time workers in the United States are $42,077 for men and $28,363 for women. (*Statistical Abstract of the United States: 1998*, 471 table 743, 476 table 754, 477 table 756, 480 table 762.)

Consider the following article excerpt, identifying three subcultural groups that the author asserts play a disproportionate role in inflicting lethal violence.

Submission Is Not the Answer: Lethal Violence, Microcultures of Criminal Violence and the Right to Self-Defense
(69 University of Colorado Law Review 1029 [1998])

Robert J. Cottrol

Culture . . . must be part of any discussion of comparative crime or violence rates whether that comparison is cross-national, or a contrasting of groups or sub-groups within a particular nation, or even a comparison of one nation's or one group's experience over time. A simple look at contemporary American society readily confirms this point. Why, for example, is the homicide rate among Americans of African descent so extraordinarily high while the rate among Americans of Japanese descent is so incredibly low? Certainly a simple instrumentality theory fails to account for the differences. Firearms and other lethal instruments are certainly not less readily available to Asian Americans than they are to black Americans. Clearly we must search for some other explanation. A number of researchers in recent years have tried to revive social science theories rooted in biological and pseudo-biological views of inherent racial differences. Many have offered these theories as explanations for group differences in criminal behavior. But these explanations . . . leave too many unanswered questions. They won't, for example, explain why white men in Minnesota have a homicide rate significantly lower than the national average, while white men in Mississippi have one that is significantly above the national average. . . .

Culture clearly plays a significant role in influencing national homicide rates as well as the homicide rates of particular subcultures within nations. But to say that by no means simplifies matters. Culture is an elusive concept. It is concerned with complex patterns of behavior, attitudes, and at times even learned reflexes that help define groups and subgroups within particular societies. The essence of a culture or subculture is rarely caught with great accuracy by the kinds of shorthands that we usually employ to describe individuals and groups. Although it is, thus, common to describe people by race, ethnicity, geographic origin, sex, or religious or political affiliation, the prudent analyst realizes that within these broad categories lies a wide array of subcultures and even microcultures all of which can exert and do exert profound "cultural" influences on individual behavior.

Culture can also be a difficult concept to grapple with because the boundaries between cultural influences on individual behavior and other influences are frequently imprecise and overlapping. In almost every society and subculture, men tend to be more violent than women, and the young more prone to commit homicide than the elderly. Should these differences be simply attributed to differences in physical strength? Do men and women, or the young and the elderly, form different subcultures even when they come from the same national or religious or ethnic communities? Dealing rigorously with such a concept poses significant difficulties.

Culturally based explanations for group differences in crime, or indeed other forms of behavior, run another risk. They can be seen as, and sometimes unfortunately are intended to be, occasions for engaging in negative stereotypings. They can appear to be a condemnation of a culture's or subculture's mores to point out that it has a disproportionately high level of homicides—our concern in this discussion. . . .

Let me suggest that three cultural or subcultural groups in the United States have historically played and continue to play a disproportionate role in the story of lethal violence in American society. The first group, immigrants, is not an ongoing group. Different immigrant populations have migrated to the United States from various world regions at different times in American history. They have come from often widely varying cultural backgrounds. Despite these differences, there have often been certain commonalities in the immigrant experience, particularly at the initial stages of a group's immigrant experience, that could lead to disproportionate levels of crime, particularly violent crime. These include disproportionately high numbers of single young men in immigrant populations, overrepresentation of immigrant labor in low-paying undesirable jobs, and often strained or difficult relations between immigrants and law enforcement authorities. All of these attributes have contributed to disproportionately high levels of violent crime in some immigrant communities. At least some of the differences between homicide in the United States and other advanced industrial societies should be attributed to the fact that immigrants historically and at present account for a greater percentage of the United States population.

White southerners are another group that has been identified as having disproportionately high levels of violence including homicide. There is a substantial body of social science literature debating the issue of a southern subculture of violence. Although this is not the place to enter that debate, a number of points should be made. Historically, much of the violence associated with American society has taken place in the South. Indeed much of what we think of as nineteenth-century frontier violence was more southern than western in character. Much of white southern violence was racial. Historically, white southern violence was, of course, spurred on by the presence of a large racially subordinate black population whose victimization at the hands of whites was rarely addressed by the law. It should also be added that southern law exhibited a wider degree of tolerance for private violence among whites than was generally the case in other regions of the country. . . .

Any discussion of violence in southern culture inevitably leads to the topic of race and violence, and more specifically to the issue of black homicide. Historically, the Afro-American experience has been a southern experience. It is still rare to find an Afro-American in any region of the country without southern relatives including a parent or grandparent who was a native of the South. It was in the South that much of what we have come to regard as black culture developed. Some researchers, with considerable justification, have even contended that the problem of black homicide is really a subset of the larger issue of the southern subculture of violence.

Whether or not the issue of contemporary black homicide should be linked to the historic Afro-American experience in the South, several points regarding the connection should be made. First, it is probably valuable to regard the historic South as a region shared by two overlapping yet distinguishable subcultures, a superordinate white subculture and a subordinate black subculture. The superordinate white subculture was dominant, although the transmission of habits and mores was by no means entirely asymmetrical. For our purposes, certain aspects of southern culture may have played a particularly significant role in helping to develop the modern inner-city problem of black homicide. The southern legacy of resorting to private violence as a means of resolving disputes raises critical questions concerning the link between culture and homicide. . . .

Firearms Ownership by Class and Culture

Firearms ownership varies widely according to demographic factors related to class and culture.

Gender

Male firearms owners far outnumber women (42.3 percent of men; 9.8 percent of women). (Tom W. Smith, *1998 National Gun Policy Survey of the National Opinion Research Center: Research Findings*, National Opinion Research Center, University of Chicago, May 1999 Report [hereafter NORC Survey].)

Marital Status

Firearms are more likely to be found in married households than in divorced or separated households (48.7 percent for married; 25.7 percent for divorced; 29.8 percent for separated). (NORC Survey.)

Education Level

Education level is not strongly associated with different gun ownership rates (23.9 percent of persons with less than a high school education own guns; 28.5 percent of persons with high school education; 23.9 percent of persons with college education; 25.6 percent of persons with higher than college education). (NORC Survey.)

Income Level

Persons with higher incomes are more likely to own firearms, although the percentage tapers off at the highest income level (21.8 percent of persons with an annual income of less than $9,999 have a gun in the household; 25.4 percent for incomes $10,000–$19,999; 35.5 percent for incomes $20,000–$29,999; 41.8 percent for incomes $30,000–$39,999; 46.4 percent for incomes $40,000–$49,999; 50.9 percent for incomes $50,000–$59,999; 46.8 for incomes $60,000–$79,999; and 36.7 percent for incomes exceeding $80,000). (NORC Survey.)

Age

The highest percentage of firearms owners are middle-aged (19.5 percent of persons younger than thirty years old own guns; 22.1 percent of persons thirty to thirty-nine; 25.2 percent of persons forty to forty-nine; 35.8 percent of persons fifty to sixty-five; 26.5 percent of persons over sixty-five). (NORC Survey.)

Race

Although the data vary, several studies have found that white households are more likely to contain firearms than are minority households. A 1994 study of gun ownership in Pennsylvania found that white households were three times more likely to contain firearms than were black households (Samuel N. Forjuoh et al., *Firearm Ownership and Storage Practices in Pennsylvania Homes*, 2 Injury Prevention 278 [1996]). A 1990 New Mexico study found firearms present in 44 percent of white households, 33 percent of Hispanic households, and 39 percent of "other" households (Stefan Z. Wiktor et al., *Firearms in New Mexico*, 161 Western Journal of Medicine 137 [1994]). A survey of parents at pediatric clinics in urban, suburban, and rural areas at various locations around the country found that 36.3 percent of white households own firearms, 15 percent of black households, 8.8 percent of Asian households, and 8.3 percent of Hispanic households (Yvonne D. Senturia et al., *Children's Household Exposure to Guns: A Pediatric Practice-based Survey*, 93 Pediatrics 469 [1994]). An older nationwide survey found that 51.3 percent of white households contained guns, compared to 37.3 percent of nonwhite households (Robert E. Markush and Alfred A. Bartolucci, *Firearms and Suicide in the United States*, 74 American Journal of Public Health 123 [1984]).

Rural versus Urban Households

Firearms are more likely to be present in rural households (54.7 percent) than in urban (23.3 percent) or suburban (32.2 percent) households. (Senturia et al., *Children's Household Exposure to Guns, supra*). Other studies have reached the same conclusion.

Region

Gun ownership varies widely by region. Two researchers estimated regional gun ownership patterns based on data derived from the National Opinion Research Center's General Social Surveys from 1989–91. Breaking the country down into the nine geographic regions used by the U.S. Census Bureau, the study found gun ownership ranged from a low of 38.6 percent of households with firearms in New England to a high of 70 percent in the East South Central United States, a region made up of Alabama, Kentucky, Mississippi, and Tennessee. Here are the nine regional divisions and the percentages of households with firearms within each region:

New England (Connecticut, Maine, Massachusetts, New Hampshire, Rhode Island, Vermont): 38.6 percent

Middle Atlantic (New Jersey, New York, Pennsylvania): 38.9 percent

East North Central (Illinois, Indiana, Michigan, Ohio, Wisconsin): 54.6 percent

West North Central (Iowa, Kansas, Minnesota, Missouri, Nebraska, North Dakota, South Dakota): 60.9 percent

South Atlantic (Delaware, District of Columbia, Florida, Georgia, Maryland, North Carolina, South Carolina, Virginia, West Virginia): 58.8 percent

East South Central (Alabama, Kentucky, Mississippi, Tennessee): 70.0 percent

West South Central (Arkansas, Louisiana, Oklahoma, Texas): 67.87 percent

Mountain (Arizona, Colorado, Idaho, Montana, Nevada, New Mexico, Utah, Wyoming): 56.7 percent

Pacific (Alaska, California, Hawaii, Oregon, Washington): 48.3 percent

See Mark S. Kaplan and Olga Geling, *Firearm Suicides and Homicides in the United States: Regional Variations and Patterns of Gun Ownership*, 46 Social Science Medicine 1227, 1232 (1998).

Lethal Violence Victimization by Class and Culture

Who dies by lethal violence in America by class and culture? Here is some of what is known.

Gender

A study of 215,273 homicides occurring between 1976 and 1987 showed that 77 percent of the victims were men and 23 percent were women. Firearms were the most common method of death. More than twice as many women were fatally shot by their husbands or by intimate acquaintances than were killed by strangers by any method. Sixty percent of the homicides committed by women were against spouses or other intimate acquaintances, whereas 80 percent of homicides committed by men were committed against strangers or other nonintimate acquaintances. (Arthur L. Kellermann and James A. Mercy, *Men, Women, and Murder: Gender-*

specific Differences in Rates of Fatal Violence and Victimization, 33 Journal of Trauma 1 [1992].)

Age

Since 1990, the highest homicide rate by age group has been for persons aged fifteen through twenty-four. In 1995, homicides accounted for 21 percent of all deaths for persons in this age group. (Lois Fingerhut et al., *Homicide Rates among US Teenagers and Young Adults*, 280 Journal of the American Medical Association 423 [1998].) Gun homicides as a percentage of total homicides peak at ages seventeen to nineteen (victim's age), with 76 percent of homicides for that age group being gun homicides. For under one year, the percentage of homicides committed with guns is 4 percent; age 5, 28 percent; age 10, 47 percent; age 13, 61 percent; age 27, 70 percent; age 35, 65 percent; age 45, 62 percent; age 55, 55 percent; age 65, 45 percent; age 75, 32 percent; age 85, 21 percent; and age 90, 17 percent. (Bureau of Justice Statistics, U.S. Department of Justice, *Homicide Trends in the United States: Weapons Used* [2001].) Why do you think that eighteen-year-old murder victims are likely to be murdered with a gun, while small children and the elderly are likely to be murdered in some other way?

Race

The firearm death rate for blacks is significantly higher than for whites. (See Table 8 on page 251 for detailed information.)

Rural versus Urban Location

For teens and young adults, data regarding firearms victimization by rural or urban location show, not surprisingly, that firearm homicide rates are substantially higher in urban than in rural areas. In 1995 firearm death rates for persons fifteen to twenty-four years of age ranged from 6.5 victims per 100,000 residents in nonmetropolitan counties to 33.5 per 100,000 in counties containing a city of more than 1 million residents. The death rate was 9.6 victims per 100,000 in fringe counties to cities of more than 1 million residents and 13.3 per 100,000 in medium-sized metropolitan areas. (Fingerhut et al., *supra*.)

Region

Southern states have significantly higher homicide rates than states in the North. The homicide rate in western states also tends to be higher than in the North, although there is greater fluctuation from state to state than in the South. Here are the homicide rates for 1996 (per 100,000 residents for each state):

> Southern states: Alabama, 10.4; Arkansas, 8.7; Florida, 7.5; Georgia, 8.6; Kentucky, 5.9; Louisiana, 17.5; Mississippi, 11.1; North Carolina, 6.5; South Carolina, 9.0; Tennessee, 9.5; Texas, 7.7; Virginia 7.5
>
> Northern states: Connecticut, 4.8; Delaware, 4.3; District of Columbia, 73.1; Maine, 2.0; Maryland, 11.6; Massachusetts, 2.6; New Hampshire, 1.7; New Jersey, 4.2; New York, 7.4; Pennsylvania, 5.7; Rhode Island, 2.5; Vermont, 1.9; West Virginia, 3.8
>
> Midwestern states: Illinois, 10.0; Indiana, 7.2.; Iowa, 1.9; Kansas, 6.6; Michigan, 7.5; Minnesota, 3.6; Missouri, 9.1; Nebraska, 2.9; North Dakota, 2.2; Ohio, 4.6; Oklahoma, 6.9; South Dakota, 1.2; Wisconsin, 4.0
>
> Western states: Alaska, 7.4; Arizona, 8.5; California, 9.1; Colorado, 4.7; Hawaii, 3.4; Idaho, 3.6; Montana, 3.9; Nevada, 13.7; New Mexico, 11.5; Oregon, 4.0; Utah, 3.2; Washington, 4.6; Wyoming, 3.3

(*Statistical Abstract of The United States: 1998, supra,* at 211 table 337. The District of Columbia is the homicide capital of the United States, with a 1996 murder rate of 73.1 per 100,000 residents.)

DISCUSSION NOTES

1. Having now read the Cottrol excerpt regarding cultural violence differences and the statistics concerning gun ownership and lethal violence victimization, can you draw any conclusions that might explain the

various differences? Divide the class into groups. Assign each group (or individual if it's a small class) one of the categories detailed under the headings "Firearms Ownership by Class and Culture" (gender, marital status, education level, income level, age, race, rural versus urban household, and region) and "Lethal Violence Victimization by Class and Culture" (gender, age, race, rural versus urban location, and region). Instruct each group of students to study the gun ownership or victimization statistics given for the group's assigned category with a view towards coming up with hypotheses that might explain the various statistical differentials within the category. Have each group present its conclusions to the class for discussion and feedback.

2. Some of the broad correlations and the contrasts between gun ownership and lethal violence victimization (most of which occurs by firearms), include:

   • Whites own more guns, but blacks die by guns at a much higher rate per capita.

   • Firearms are more likely to be present in rural homes than in urban homes, but firearms homicide rates are much higher in urban areas.

   • Men own roughly 90 percent of all guns and commit about 85 percent of all homicides.

   • Southerners own more guns and also have the highest homicide rates.

   Can you think of reasons that help explain these correlations?

3. Studies have shown that black homicide rates do not vary between the North and South but that white homicide rates vary substantially between the two regions, suggesting there may be something about white Southern culture that is responsible for the difference. (See Dov Cohen, *Culture, Social Organization, and Patterns of Violence*, 75 Journal of Personality and Psychology 408 [1998].) Can you think of any explanations? Some researchers have attributed the difference to a "culture of honor" existing in the South, in which insults and threats to reputation, self, home, or family are deemed to justify a violent response. In sociological experiments, Southerners show more politeness than Northerners unless insulted, in which case they respond more aggressively than Northerners.

4. Laws of self-defense in the South and West are more lenient in allowing people to use force to protect their property or themselves. Cohen argues that the culture of honor arose out of frontier conditions: "Without effective law enforcement and without the stabilizing forces of social order in the South and West, men had to rely on themselves for protection and let it be known that they were not to be trifled with. Thus, the importance of honor and the legitimization of violence in response to provocations great and small emerged." (Cohen, *supra*, at 417.) Do you give credence to this theory? Is there a similar "culture of honor" in some inner cities today, in which being "disrespected" demands a lethal response?

CHAPTER 6

GUNS AND CIVIL LIABILITY

More than any area of law except criminal and constitutional law, tort law has infiltrated the consciousness of mainstream America. Even laypersons have opinions about the tort system, although these opinions are often based on incomplete and distorted reporting of cases. Torts are civil wrongs for which the law provides a remedy, usually in the form of money damages. Tort law is better known to laypersons as "personal injury" law, and indeed, most of tort law is concerned with physical injuries suffered by the plaintiff as result of the defendant's conduct.

The most controversial field of tort law is the area known as "products liability." Pick up a newspaper on any given day and the chances are good you will find articles about lawsuits against the manufacturers and sellers of products alleged to have caused injury to users. The well-publicized lawsuits against the tobacco industry, asbestos manufacturers, breast-implant makers, and tire manufacturers all involve products liability claims. Products liability is at the center of the "tort reform" movement, a nationwide battle waged—with the support of insurance, medical and industry groups—to restrict tort liability and damages rules.

Recently, firearms have moved to the forefront of the tort controversy, spurred primarily by a series of lawsuits filed by cities, counties, and states seeking damages and changes in the way the gun industry manufactures, markets, and distributes its products. Lawsuits against gun manufacturers are not a new development. In the last three decades, victims of firearms injuries have filed dozens of suits against gun makers. Plaintiffs routinely lost these lawsuits in cases involving properly working firearms. The sole exception was a 1985 Maryland case, subsequently overruled by the state legislature. The usual reasoning offered by courts is that a properly working firearm is not a "defective product" for purposes of products liability law, and that issues involving firearms regulation are appropriately left to legislatures to decide.

Two modern developments might reinvigorate the tort arena with regard to firearms: (1) a shift in legal theories to new claims alleging that guns can be made safer and that gun manufacturers have acted negligently in the manner in which they distribute and market their products; and (2) the initiation of public plaintiff litigation by government entities, in a manner similar to the tobacco litigation.

Are firearms lawsuits a legitimate effort to hold gun manufacturers accountable for the harm inflicted by their products, or politically motivated "litigation terrorism" designed to drive lawful gun companies out of business? Because the tort system is adversarial and involves parties strongly motivated by both moral conviction and high financial stakes, it presents many of the fundamental issues concerning firearms regulation in unusually stark relief. This chapter examines the different legal theories invoked in lawsuits against gun makers and closes with a discussion of the wave of suits filed by government entities.

A. Are Guns Defective Products on the Theory That Their Risk to Society Outweighs Their Usefulness?

Not all of products liability is controversial. When a product fails to perform as intended by the manufacturer because of a defect occurring during the manufacturing process, the product is "defective" in a popularly understood sense. When this occurs, the manufacturer is "strictly liable" for injuries caused by the defect; the plaintiff can recover without having to prove negligence or other fault on the part of the manufacturer. Thus, if a gun manufacturer produced a handgun that discharged even while the safety was engaged, a person injured because of the defect could sue the manufacturer and recover damages with little fanfare. (See, e.g., *Caveny v. Raven Arms Co.*, 665 F. Supp. 530, 531 [S.D. Ohio 1987], stating plaintiffs may recover under strict liability when a firearm malfunctions; *Armijo v. Ex Cam, Inc.*, 656 F. Supp. 771, 773 [D. N.M. 1987], explaining in a dictum that strict liability would be appropriate if a gun functions improperly.)

Manufacturing defect cases are relatively easy to adjudicate because we have a built-in comparative standard for determining the existence of a defect: the manufacturer's own properly made products of the same type. When one unit of the product fails to perform like others of its kind, it is not difficult to brand the malfunctioning product as defective.

Much more problematic than cases involving manufacturing flaws are those involving product risks resulting from conscious design choices by the manufacturer. In "design defect" cases, the product comes off the assembly line precisely as intended by the manufacturer. Unlike the situation with manufacturing flaws, no ready standard exists for determining if a design is defective. In design cases the plaintiff is alleging that the manufacturer should have designed the product differently to minimize some risk presented by the product. The difficult, often intractable, problem for the tort system is attempting to answer the question "How safe is safe enough?"

Many products can be made safer, but only at great cost. These costs include the actual financial cost of making the product safer, as well as costs to society and to consumers that can result from changing designs in ways that impair the usefulness of products for their intended purposes. For example, automobiles would be safer in rollover collisions if they had roll bars installed. A roll bar, however, would add several hundred dollars to the cost of a car, might impair the aesthetics of the product, and might create other risks. Should the tort system brand ordinary passenger cars without roll bars as defectively designed? Autos would also be safer if designed to travel at top speeds of thirty-five miles per hour, but would society's interests be served by rendering cars incapable of traveling at normal highway speeds?

Most courts address design defect cases by applying a "risk-utility" test that requires the jury to balance the risk of the product design against the feasibility of a proposed safer alternative design. Feasibility of the alternative takes account of factors such as the cost of the alternative design, whether it is technologically feasible, whether it will impair the usefulness of the product for its intended purpose, and whether the new design will create other risks.

But what about products than cannot be made safer at any cost? Many products present risks of injury, often very dangerous risks, that cannot be eliminated. Indeed, in many instances, the risk is essential to the proper functioning of the product: matches burn; saws and knives cut; alcohol causes intoxication. To eliminate these risks would destroy the intended utility of the product. To a large extent, firearms are such a product. Although modern lawsuits allege that guns can be made safer by incorporating locks or so-called smart-gun technology, the fact remains that firearms are, by design and function, extremely dangerous. When they discharge a metal projectile at high velocity, they are fulfilling their intended purpose.

Should risk-utility analysis be applied to some dangerous products on the theory that, even accepting that they cannot be made safer, their overall risk to society outweighs their utility to society? Numerous early lawsuits against gun manufacturers asserted this claim. The following early essays on the issue debate the theory.

Handguns as Products Unreasonably Dangerous Per Se
(13 University of Arkansas at Little Rock Law Journal 599 [1991])

Andrew J. McClurg

The narrow legal issue involved in this debate is whether a well-made handgun is in a "defective condition unreasonably dangerous" when used for its intended or foreseeable purpose so as to subject the manufacturer to strict liability. . . .

As the name implies, risk-utility balancing requires that the risk of the product be weighed against the utility of the product to determine whether it is in a defective condition unreasonably dangerous. Underlying this approach is the recognition that all products have some risk and some utility. If every product which presented a risk of harm were deemed to be defective, every product would be defective. Therefore, the only way to meaningfully evaluate whether the product is unreasonably dangerous is to weigh the risk of the product against the product's usefulness to the user and to society. . . .

A central theme in products liability law is that, as a threshold to imposing strict liability, there must be "something wrong" with the product. Otherwise, the argument goes, all product related injuries would result in liability to the manufacturer. However, as applied to handguns and other products which are unreasonably dangerous per se, this simply begs the question. Under risk-utility balancing, there is "something wrong" with the product if the risk presented by the product outweighs its utility. This conclusion is strengthened where substitute products exist which satisfy the same needs as the unreasonably dangerous product.

Contrary to argument, this is not the same as saying that all products which cause injury are defective. The examples usually offered in connection with this argument—e.g., automobiles, knives, matches—are not defective because their utility outweighs their risk. . . . Automobiles, knives and matches have substantial utility apart from causing harm. Handguns do not. Were it declared that beginning at sunrise tomorrow we could not use our automobiles, knives, or matches, society would be paralyzed. On the other hand, were it declared that handguns could no longer be used, society would continue to function with little disruption. . . .

Handguns are perhaps the paradigmatic case of a product unreasonably dangerous per se. As discussed below, they present tremendous risk and have low utility. Accordingly, manufacturers should be strictly liable for handgun inflicted deaths and injuries. . . .

The risk to human life presented by handguns in terms of both the severity of the risk and the probability of it occurring is almost unparalleled. Of all the millions of products marketed in the United States, only automobiles surpass handguns as a cause of unnatural death. Handguns kill 22,000 people each year and injure probably another 100,000.

A telling contrast in how our society treats dangerous products can be found by examining the case of lawn darts. In 1990, the Consumer Product Safety Commission banned the sale of lawn darts based upon a finding that they "present an unreasonable risk of injury." The commission arrived at this conclusion by applying a risk-utility analysis quite similar to that which would be used to determine whether lawn darts are an unreasonably dangerous product for purposes of strict products liability.

The commission described the degree and nature of the risk as being the "puncture of the skulls of children caused by lawn darts being used by children," but mentioned that the total ban on lawn darts would also eliminate other types of puncture wounds, lacerations, fractures, and other injuries associated with the use of lawn darts. With respect to the probability of the risk occurring, the commission estimated that 670 lawn dart injuries occurred each year and found that three children had been killed by lawn darts since 1970.

This risk was seen as outweighing the utility of lawn darts: i.e., the "recreational enjoyment" they provided to the more than one million consumers who purchased lawn darts annually. This conclusion was bolstered by the commission's determination that substitute recreational enjoyment can be obtained from other products. The commission did not specify any particular type of recreational product which would replace the enjoyment of launching steel tipped missiles across the yard into a hoop. Apparently, the commission deemed recreational products to be fungible. Horseshoes, for example, might be deemed an adequate substitute for lawn darts.

. . . Compare the three children killed in twenty years by lawn darts to the 22,000 annual handgun deaths, or even to the 365 children under age fifteen killed in accidental handgun shootings every year. Compare the 670 lawn dart injuries that the commission estimated were occurring each year to the estimated 100,000 yearly handgun injuries. Then ask: what is wrong with this picture? . . . [Note the firearms injury figures in this essay were accurate when written but have changed. See chapter 2 for more recent data.]

The answer lies in the exaggerated utility attached to handguns. . . .

The utility of handguns in modern society is twofold: (1) they have recreational utility in the form of hunting and target shooting; and (2) they have the utility of self-protection. While I do not attach as much importance to these utilities as do gun owners, I do not reject them as insignificant. I appreciate that many people get substantial enjoyment from hunting and target shooting, and also that many people believe handguns afford them effective protection from criminals.

However, the utility of handguns is outweighed by the tremendous risk they pose to society, particularly in light of the availability of a substitute product which serves the same needs as a handgun: i.e., a long gun. . . . The availability of rifles and shotguns substantially dilutes the utility of handguns. Long guns have almost the same utility and present less risk because they are not easily concealable.

As to recreational use, long guns are obviously superior in their utility for hunting because of their greater accuracy. This would seem to make them superior for target shooting as well. Some sportsmen might insist that they are fond of shooting at targets with rifles and pistols, but this is where risk-utility balancing comes into play. The marginal utility in the smidgeon of extra pleasure derived from plinking a target with a handgun as opposed to a rifle is outweighed by the greatly increased risk of handguns. . . .

[McClurg argues that faith in guns as insurers of personal security is out of proportion to reality. See chapter 1 for thorough analysis of the utility of guns for personal defense.]

[A]ccepting that in some cases a gun offers an effective means of defending one's self, long guns fulfill that purpose almost as well. If a homeowner feels more secure with a loaded gun in the house while he sleeps, he should not feel any less secure because the weapon is a long gun rather than a handgun. Indeed, I would think that confronting a burglar with a 12-gauge shotgun would be much more intimidating and effective than a handgun. A large, visible weapon is more likely to deter the criminal, thereby eliminating the need to actually use deadly force. If the use of such force becomes necessary, accuracy counts. However, most people are not expert pistol shooters, particularly in a dark house when they are under tremendous stress. With a shotgun, simply firing the weapon in the general direction of the target offers a reasonable chance of making contact. Moreover, shotgun pellets which miss their target are not likely to penetrate the walls of a dwelling and kill innocent persons outside. That possibility exists as to missed shots fired from a high-powered handgun.

I concede there are situations where a long gun, because it is not small and easily concealable, will not be as effective as a handgun in defending persons or property. A liquor store owner, for example, may have a hard time withdrawing a long gun from beneath the counter to defend against a robber. However, this is another instance where risk-utility balancing dictates that long guns be viewed as an adequate substitute product. This marginal degree of enhanced utility of handguns attributable to their small size is outweighed by the vastly greater risk presented by handguns because of the same feature.

It is the easy concealability of handguns which makes them unreasonably dangerous as compared with long guns. [McClurg wrote his essay at a time when few states had laws liberally allowing people to carry concealed handguns. Thirty-three states now have such laws. See chapter 1.]

Roughly seventy-five percent of all firearm homicides are committed with handguns. Handguns are what our children are carrying to school, not hunting rifles. Handguns are what armed robbers use to gun down store clerks. Handguns are what felons use to shoot police officers during routine traffic stops. While rifles and shotguns are very dangerous, they are not unreasonably dangerous because their greater utility for most legitimate purposes outweighs their reduced risk as compared to handguns. . . .

DISCUSSION NOTES

1. What do you think of the argument that a court should declare handguns to be legally defective products for purposes of tort recovery on the theory that their risk to society outweighs their utility to society? No court has accepted the argument, although one court came close. In *Kelley v. R. G. Industries, Inc.*, 497 A. 2d 1143 (Md. 1985), an assailant shot the plaintiff in the chest with a small, inexpensive handgun during a robbery of a convenience store. The plaintiff sued the manufacturer of the gun. The Court of Appeals of Maryland held that strict liability could properly be imposed against manufacturers of so-called Saturday Night Specials, which the court described as cheap, easily concealable handguns used in criminal activity. The legal reasoning offered in support of the decision was murky. Essentially, the court reasoned that liability was appropriate "as a matter of public policy." While the court purported to reject liability under a risk-utility analysis, close scrutiny of the opinion reveals that risk-utility balancing played a crucial role in the decision. In justifying its different treatment of Saturday Night Specials as a matter of public policy, the court essentially argued that such weapons present an unusually high risk of being used for criminal activity and have low utility for most legitimate purposes.

2. The Maryland legislature effectively overruled *Kelley* by passing legislation prohibiting the imposition of strict liability for gun sellers. The statute provides that "a person or entity may not be held strictly liable for damages of any kind resulting from injuries to another person sustained as a result of the criminal use of any firearm by any third person" (*Md. Code Ann., Crimes and Punishments* § 36-I[h][I]). Several

states have passed statutes expressly barring products liability claims grounded in risk-utility analysis against gun manufacturers. (See *Cal. Civ. Code* § 1714.4: "In a products liability action, no firearm or ammunition shall be deemed defective in design on the basis that the benefits of the product do not outweigh the risk of the injury posed by its potential to cause serious injury, damage, or death when discharged.") Do you view such statutes as a proper exercise of legislative authority to restrict illegitimate lawsuits, or an unfair denial of access to the courts to victims of firearms violence? When courts deny these claims, are the denials more or less fair than legislative denials?

3. Most courts rejecting liability for harm caused by handguns have done so on the basis that when a handgun causes harm it is functioning properly and therefore lacks a "defect" upon which to predicate a products liability claim. Typical is the reasoning offered in *Delahanty v. Hinckley*, 686 F. Supp. 920 (D. D.C. 1986), a suit filed by victims of John Hinckley's assassination attempt against President Ronald Reagan. In denying tort claims, including a strict liability risk-utility claim, against the manufacturer of the handgun Hinckley used in the assassination attempt, the court said that "there was no argument in this case that the handgun was defective, or that it did not operate as intended. The gun proved to be highly accurate, as is clear from the fact that the intended target, the President of the United States, was struck twice, and the plaintiffs were wounded." The decision was affirmed on appeal. (*Delahanty v. Hinckley*, 900 F. 2d 368 [D.C. Cir. 1990].) What do you think of this reasoning? Suppose a criminal used a properly functioning knife to kill someone, and a court, denying a tort claim, described how well the knife cut. Would the court's reasoning be more or less valid, or the same, as the *Delahanty* court's? If a criminal used a properly functioning automobile to commit a murder, should the manufacturer be liable? Are these analogies apt, given the intended nonlethal uses of knives and autos?

4. Should the fact that guns are intended to kill work for or against imposing liability against gun manufacturers? Consider the following:

> Every day in this country, courts routinely shift the cost of personal injuries to the manufacturers of useful and benign products such as lad-

ders, football helmets, space heaters, small aircraft, playground equipment, hair dryers, water skis, lawnmowers, nuts, bolts, just about anything except for handguns. All too often the only "defect" in these products is the failure to warn of risks that most people would consider to be obvious or the giving of a warning which, in hindsight, a jury concludes could have been marginally improved by adding or changing a few words.

But we are told a different result is commanded for the makers of a product which has as its only purpose the infliction of exactly what the tort system is designed to prevent: injury to human beings. . . .

Compare handguns to asbestos, that most hated and dreaded of all products known to tort law. Asbestos is a natural fiber with certain unique, desirable properties: high tensile strength, flexibility and resistance to temperature and corrosive chemicals. These properties make it an excellent thermal and acoustic insulator for buildings, homes, and ships. Asbestos once was hailed as a "'miraculous mineral' and a boon to mankind." It is estimated that eighty percent of the buildings constructed in the United States before 1979 contain asbestos. Unfortunately, while asbestos fulfills important societal needs as an insulator, it presents a collateral, unintended risk to human health when airborne fibers from the product become lodged in a person's lungs.

Despite the fact that asbestos is a beneficial product that admirably fulfills its intended purpose, and even though it cannot be made any safer, asbestos manufacturers are sued and held strictly liable more often than the manufacturers of any other product in the world. There are almost 90,000 asbestos cases pending in state and federal courts. Asbestos manufacturers have been held strictly liable even where courts accept that the risks of asbestos were unknown and scientifically unknowable at the time the product was manufactured and distributed.

How does one explain wreaking tort liability havoc upon the makers of asbestos and other universally used, socially beneficial products which present unintended risks of harm while rejecting liability for the manufacturers of a product intended to be deadly? (Andrew J. McClurg, *The Tortious Marketing of Handguns: Strict Liability Is Dead, Long Live Negligence*, 19 Seton Hall Legislative Journal 777, 793–95 [1995].)

If the utility of a product lies in its capacity to harm, should that insulate the product from liability for causing that harm?

Was it right for courts to allow lawsuits against asbestos makers? Was the Consumer Product Safety Commission right to ban lawn darts?

5. Suppose a safety advocate made the following argument: "The lawn dart ban was a good first step, but it did not go far enough. Toys and games which have small pieces have led to many more child deaths, via choking, than have lawn darts. Indeed, more small children are killed by toys than by gun accidents. Toy manufacturers include warning labels that toys or games with small parts are not suitable for children under three. But since some adults ignore safety warnings, choking deaths do occur. Therefore, all toys and games with small pieces should be outlawed. Alternatively, any time a child is injured by a small toy, the manufacturers should be liable in a lawsuit." In what ways does this argument resemble or differ from the argument for banning or imposing liability on a particular type of gun or on all guns? Are comparisons between products intended for nonlethal uses and products intended for lethal uses valid or invalid?

6. The Consumer Product Safety Commission (CPSC) has administrative authority over most consumer products, but the congressional statute that created the CPSC specifically forbids the commission to regulate or ban certain especially controversial products, such as tobacco and firearms. Should administrative agencies be given the power to ban the manufacture and sale of products that they determine to be unreasonably dangerous, or should that power reside only with legislatures? Would it be feasible and efficient for Congress to investigate and weigh the dangers of all of the millions of consumer products, or can that job be performed better through administrative mechanisms? Should administrative agencies be allowed to make recommendations but only Congress allowed to outlaw products?

Since article 1 of the U.S. Constitution gives "[A]ll legislative powers herein granted" to the Congress, some scholars argue that Congress cannot delegate lawmaking power to executive branch agencies such as the CPSC. For an argument that allowing Congress to delegate law-making to administrative agencies allows Congress to dodge tough decisions, see

David Schoenbrod, *Power without Responsibility: How Congress Abuses the People through Delegation* (New Haven: Yale University Press, 1993).

7. Regardless of what you think of the risk-utility theory generally, might it be appropriate to apply it to particular firearms such as small inexpensive handguns, sometimes called Saturday Night Specials (SNSs) or junk guns? The *Kelley* court defined SNSs as "generally characterized by short barrels, light weight, easy concealability, low cost, use of cheap quality materials, poor manufacture, inaccuracy and unreliability" (497 A. 2d at 1153–54). In the aftermath of Senator Robert Kennedy's assassination with an inexpensive European-made .22 caliber revolver, Congress passed the Gun Control Act of 1968, which set minimum safety and size standards for imported handguns but exempted domestically produced handguns. (See Eva H. Shine, *The Junk Gun Predicament: Answers Do Exist*, 30 Arizona State Law Journal 1183 [1998].) Part of the reason that the Gun Control Act, a compromise measure, passed was that domestic firearms manufacturers wanted protection from low-priced imports. Many domestic manufacturers also quietly supported President George H. W. Bush's 1989 ban (using administrative power granted under the Gun Control Act) on the import of so-called assault weapons—mainly rifles that were priced below the cost of most American-made rifles.

Although most guns, including most small handguns, are never used in a crime, small handguns are used in crime in numbers far disproportionate to other types of guns. In 1995, the Bureau of Alcohol, Tobacco and Firearms determined that eight of the ten firearms most frequently traced to crime scenes were SNSs (Shine, *The Junk Gun Predicament*, *supra*, at 1183–84).

For arguments that BATF gun traces do not reveal useful information about gun crime in general, see Gary Kleck, *BATF Gun Trace Data and the Role of Organized Gun Trafficking in Supplying Guns to Criminals*, 18 St. Louis University Public Law Review 23 (1999); David B. Kopel and Paul H. Blackman, *Firearms Tracing Data from the Bureau of Alcohol, Tobacco and Firearms: An Occasionally Useful Law Enforcement Tool, but a Poor Research Tool*, 11 Criminal Justice Policy Review 44 (2000); David B. Kopel, *Clueless: The Misuse of BATF Firearms Tracing Data*, 1999 Law Review of Michigan State University Detroit College of

Law 171 (1999). Kleck, Kopel, and Blackman argue that the small fraction of guns that BATF traces is not representative of crime guns. For example, the BATF almost always refuses to trace older guns. When one compares the BATF traces within a particular city to the complete inventory of guns seized by the police, gun types that are very common in BATF traces may be very rare in the complete inventory.

Inexpensive handguns, which tend to be smaller than more expensive models, have lower utility for legitimate uses than other handguns because of their poorer quality. The *Kelley* court quoted this testimony about SNSs given before the Senate Judiciary Committee:

> "Saturday night specials," because of their poor construction and low quality, are extremely dangerous weapons, not only to intended targets and bystanders, but also to the user himself. They misfire, fire accidentally, and backfire with some degree of regularity. They are notoriously inaccurate at even short distances. Furthermore, the low-grade components used in these weapons, in addition to the fact that many of the parts are foreign-made at reduced labor costs, result in their mass production and extremely low retail prices. (*Kelley v. R. G. Industries, Inc.,* 497 A. 2d at 1153–54 n. 9.)

Some argue that claims about the low quality of inexpensive handguns are exaggerated. They point out that police officers sometimes carry such guns as backups, often in ankle holsters. If the guns really do malfunction frequently, should police be allowed to carry them? Would they want to carry them? Also, while many smaller guns (such as those from Jennings, Raven, and Bryco) are relatively inexpensive, selling for less than a hundred dollars, others are not. Beretta, for example, makes some small handguns that sell for several hundred dollars (the typical price range for handguns) and whose high quality is undisputed. Some laws regulating "junk guns" apply to all small handguns, regardless of quality, while others attempt to single out less-expensive guns by focusing on features such as the melting point of the guns' metal. (Less expensive guns often incorporate alloys that melt at a lower temperature than steel.) Given the evidence about risk and utility, would it be appropriate for courts to hold manufacturers of small, inexpensive guns liable under a risk-utility analysis?

8. Can you spot the problems that would arise from singling out small and/or inexpensive handguns for liability or prohibition? Consider what the *Delahanty* court had to say in rejecting liability:

> The definition of Saturday Night Special as used in the theory is unclear. The effect of the theory would be, presumably, to discourage the manufacture and sale of cheap handguns, but the result would be to impose liability on some manufacturers, while not imposing liability on others even though the handguns manufactured or sold by all may be used for criminal purposes. In short, it would seem to be better for a potential victim to be shot or injured by cheap gun, than by an expensive one because in the case of the former, the victim could sue the manufacturer which no doubt would have a deeper pocket. Also, this Court wonders whether the theory discriminates against those law abiding citizens, who purchase a handgun for self defense, but who cannot afford a $200 or $300 weapon and who must resort to the purchase of a cheap handgun. (*Delahanty v. Hinckley*, 686 F. Supp. at 928.)

Would courts be able successfully to distinguish Saturday Night Specials from other guns? Would imposing liability on SNS manufacturers discriminate against poor people who cannot afford higher-priced guns? If persons can afford a $70 gun but not a $300 gun, have we made it impossible for them to buy guns? (See T. Markus Funk, *Gun Control and Economic Discrimination: The Melting-Point Case-in-Point*, 85 Journal of Criminal Law and Criminology 764 [1995].) Or do you believe that if persons view a particular consumer product as important enough, they will find a way to save the money for it? How long should a person threatened by crime be expected to save in order to buy a handgun? Half a year? More? Less?

9. What if criminals like John Hinckley turned to larger guns, which tend to be more accurate (longer barrels), easier to shoot (bigger grips and larger frames to absorb recoil), and more powerful (since small guns tend to come in the small calibers of .22, .25, and .32)? Had Hinckley been using a bigger, better gun, would the consequences of his attack have been worse? In contrast, while larger handguns are concealable, they are less concealable than smaller handguns, and some impecunious criminals might not be able to afford moderately priced guns. Who

should decide the trade-offs about what kinds of guns should be available? Courts? Administrative agencies? Legislatures? None of these, in deference to the Second Amendment (see chapter 4)?

REJECTING THE "WHIPPING-BOY" APPROACH TO TORT LAW: WELL-MADE HANDGUNS ARE NOT DEFECTIVE PRODUCTS

(14 University of Arkansas at Little Rock Law Journal 1 [1991])

Philip D. Oliver

The merits vel non of gun control need not be evaluated in order to determine that judicially-imposed strict liability for gun suppliers is a very bad idea, indeed. . . . The most fundamental objection is that courts should defer to legislative bodies to resolve competing policy choices, within constitutional limits. Both action and inaction by legislative bodies lead to the inescapable conclusion that they have uniformly rejected strict liability for gun suppliers. . . .

Tenth-grade civics students learn that the proper role of legislative bodies is to make law, while that of courts is interpretation. . . .

Even "activist" courts generally defer to legislative determinations. Courts recognize that their legitimacy derives from the supposition that they are applying and interpreting constitutions, statutes, regulations, and common-law precedent, and not purely applying their ideas of good policy. . . .

While the primary argument of liability proponents is that legislative bodies have not spoken, leaving courts free to do what they think best, the proponents offer two additional, and quite revealing, lines of argumentation on this issue. One group of liability proponents argues that legislative bodies have been intimidated by the "gun lobby"—principally, the National Rifle Association. They argue that legislative bodies, particularly Congress, have kowtowed to the gun lobby, and thus have failed to enact gun control legislatively, disregarding popular support for gun control. Assuming *arguendo* that these proponents are correct concerning public opinion, this attitude suggests a fundamental misunderstanding of how the political branches of government are supposed to work.

We do not use the New England town-meeting system, much less government by public opinion poll. It is to be expected that in a representative government, those individuals to whom an issue is particularly important will exercise influence disproportionate to their numbers. This is the case not only regarding gun control but also with respect to almost all issues arising before any legislative body. . . . This open society, with its freedom of speech and press, affords advocates of gun control the opportunity to seek a reversal of policy by legitimate means—by taking its case not to the courts, but to the public and its elected officials. . . .

[Oliver asserts that courts would find it impossible to limit the effect of strict liability to specified types of guns.]

. . . Whatever classification might be chosen by a court, the chances are great that it would prove unstable. For example, suppose a court imposed strict liability for certain types of handguns, such as "Saturday Night Specials" or "snubbies." If common-law courts imposed strict liability against one of these types of handguns, there is no particular reason to think that the matter would stop there. Victims shot with other types of handguns are just as appealing, just as worthy of compensation, and the defendants just as deep-pocketed. It would be difficult for a court to hold that someone shot with a concealed "snubby" could recover, for example, yet deny recovery to the next victim who was shot with a concealed handgun having a slightly longer barrel.

Professor McClurg and other liability proponents would have us believe that courts could impose liability with respect to all handguns, but no long guns, while even at present, calls are made for liability against suppliers of some long guns. Once a court rejected the common-sense notion that there must be something wrong with a gun before it is defective, why would it stop at handguns? Or at assault weapons? The victim of a criminal wielding a sawed-off shotgun is appealing, as are innocent victims of criminals using other types of firearms, such as rifles and unmodified shotguns. Each time, the incremental difference in cases would be very small, and the slope might prove irresistibly slippery. . . .

Imposition of strict liability on gun suppliers would constitute a radical departure from the principles governing products liability law. Courts and legislatures alike, all over the country, have recognized this. As a result, after a decade of determined litigation all over the country, no jurisdiction in the country (including Maryland) imposes strict liability on gun suppliers. In the face of this overwhelming rejection, liability proponents nevertheless assert, incorrectly, that their proposals are consistent with, and flow logically from, existing tort law. . . .

Under the Restatement [of Torts] and under the law in every jurisdiction, a prerequisite to the imposition of strict liability is that the product be defective. . . .

[T]he gravamen of liability proponents' complaint about guns is that they are not defective. If a gun gave its user no more deadly force than a water pistol, it would be defective, but liability proponents would be the last to complain. Instead, gun suppliers provide precisely what is requested and expected—an instrument that can intimidate, injure, and kill. . . .

Professor McClurg's argument that handguns are defective products because long guns can fulfill substantially the same function, but more safely, merits discussion. This argument is much closer to traditional analysis concerning alternative design. Here, the substitute design, or substitute product, obviously is available; millions of long guns have been manufactured for five centuries.

For several reasons, however, this argument also must be rejected. First, and most fundamentally, it is by no means clear that long guns are safer than handguns; indeed, the contrary is more likely true. Second, as Professor McClurg concedes, handguns are preferable for some important purposes, such as for police use and defense of business premises. Third, Professor McClurg's advice to homeowners that they could better defend their homes with a shotgun will not withstand analysis.

Finally, Professor McClurg simply overlooks one of the most important self-defense uses of handguns: self-protection outside the home or place of business. In many parts of our cities, law-abiding people are simply scared to leave home unarmed. Professor McClurg and I both wish that were not the case, but tort law should not be based on wishful thinking. A long gun is not a reasonable alternative to carry along to the grocery store. . . .

Those who favor sweeping gun control should take their arguments to people who can act on them legitimately. . . . Representative democracy may be slow and cumbersome, and frequently wrong, but it is our legitimate system of government.

DISCUSSION NOTES

1. Oliver identifies several problems with allowing courts to impose strict liability for well-made handguns. Would courts be able to rationally limit liability to handguns? Should "assault weapons" also be included? What about rifles and shotguns? They can be used to kill just as effectively as handguns—perhaps even more effectively, since they are more powerful. Would courts be able to draw viable lines between which weapons should be subject to strict liability and which should not?

2. If courts were willing to impose tort liability for well-made handguns on the theory that their risk to society outweighs their utility, would such action open the door for similar lawsuits against the makers of other dangerous products? Tobacco and alcohol both cause tremendous harm and offer a utility that some people consider to be an illicit pleasure. Should courts declare these products to be defective on the ground that their risks outweigh their utility?

3. In rejecting products liability for properly functioning handguns, numerous courts have agreed with Oliver's main point: that the decision to impose gun control, either directly or indirectly through tort litigation, is a major policy decision that should be left to elected representatives. (See *Miles v. Olin Corp.*, 922 F. 2d 1221, 1225 [5th Cir. 1991]—decision whether a properly functioning shotgun is a defective product should be left to legislature; *Delahanty v. Hinckley*, 686 F. Supp. 920, 930 [D.C. 1986]—attempts to impose tort liability on gun makers amount to indirect gun control, which should be left to legislatures to determine.) Is Oliver correct? Selling, buying, and possessing long guns is legal everywhere in the United States, and handguns are legal almost everywhere. Valid arguments exist on both sides of the debate as to whether guns should be more stringently regulated; but who should make these heavily value-laden decisions? Legislators or judges and juries? Are courts, in effect, "making legislation" if they impose tort liability on manufacturers of properly functioning, legally sold firearms?

4. If the legislative process appears "broken" regarding an issue, does that strengthen the case for a judicial response? Can you think of major policy issues in our nation's history where you believe courts acted properly in stepping in to fill the vacuum when legislators failed to act? Where

courts just imposed their political views without a good basis in law? (For some cases that have attracted both criticism and praise as instances of judges imposing their own policy views, see *Roe v. Wade*, 410 U.S. 113 [1973]: the Constitution restricts government regulation of abortion; *Gideon v. Wainwright*, 372 U.S. 335 [1963], recognizing a Sixth Amendment right to court-appointed counsel for indigent criminal defendants in the face of state inaction on the issue; *Brown v. Board of Education*, 347 U.S. 483 [1954]: racial segregation in government schools is unconstitutional; *Schenck v. United States*, 249 U.S. 49 [1919], holding that the First Amendment allowed punishment of people who, during wartime, mailed leaflets telling young men that the draft is unconstitutional [the leaflets were said to have presented "a clear and present danger" of hindering the war effort]; *Scott v. Sandford*, 60 U.S. 393 [1856]: free blacks were held not to be citizens, although the Constitution is silent on the subject, and Congress had enacted no law against black citizenship.)

The U.S. Supreme Court in *Gideon* expressly based its decision mandating appointed counsel to indigent felony defendants in part on the failure of states to take adequate measures to provide counsel. The U.S. Supreme Court in *Dred Scott* may have believed that the legislative branches had been remiss in failing to act to strip citizenship rights from free blacks. The U.S. Supreme Court in *Roe* may have believed that state legislatures had been remiss in not repealing laws against abortion. The Maryland Supreme Court in *Kelley* (see page 295) may have believed the state legislature had been remiss in not regulating Saturday night specials. In which of the above cases do you think the judicial activism was proper? Does your answer depend on something other than your own policy preferences? The *Gideon*, *Brown*, and *Roe* courts were acting to enforce constitutional rights. Do courts have a greater basis for policy-making activism in constitutional cases than in tort or other civil law cases?

5. A second theory of strict liability, or liability without fault, frequently employed in early firearms litigation is that the manufacturing and marketing of handguns constitutes an "abnormally dangerous activity" within the meaning of sections 519–20 of the Restatement (Second) of Torts (an influential treatise of tort law). Section 519 provides strict liability for "one who carries on an abnormally dangerous activity" and

makes him liable "for harm to the person, land or chattels of another resulting from the activity, although he has exercised the utmost care to prevent the harm." The rationale behind this doctrine is that some activities, though having sufficient social utility that it is not negligent merely to engage in them, present such unusual risks of danger that they should pay their own way in society. Activities subject to strict liability under this doctrine include blasting with dynamite, using toxic chemicals, and hazardous waste disposal. Abnormally dangerous activities (also called "ultrahazardous activities") do not include the manufacture and sale of dynamite or of chemicals, nor the industrial processes that create hazardous waste.

Section 520 of the Restatement lists six factors to be considered in determining whether an activity is abnormally dangerous: (a) the existence of a high risk of harm; (b) a likelihood that the resulting harm will be great; (c) the inability to use reasonable care to eliminate the risk; (d) the extent to which an activity is not a matter of common usage; (e) the inappropriateness of the activity to the locality; and (f) the extent to which the danger of the activity outweighs its usefulness to the community.

Plaintiffs have argued that the manufacturing and marketing of handguns constitutes an abnormally dangerous activity under these factors, but courts have uniformly rejected the theory. The principal judicial rationale was articulated in *Perkins v. F.I.E. Corp.*, 762 F. 2d 1250 (5th Cir. 1985). The mother of a murder victim shot with a .38 caliber handgun manufactured by the defendant Charter Arms sued Charter. The trial court held the case could go forward under the Restatement's abnormally dangerous activity theory. The Fifth Circuit Court of Appeals reversed. The court rejected liability on the basis that the marketing of a handgun, as distinguished from its use, is not an abnormally dangerous activity. The court said only activities that are dangerous "in and of themselves and that can directly cause harm" are encompassed by the doctrine. Several other courts have agreed with this rationale.

Other courts have rejected abnormally dangerous activity claims against gun manufacturers by focusing on the doctrine's historical tie to land-related activities. These courts hold that only dangerous land-based activities that threaten neighboring landowners qualify for treatment under the doctrine. Still other courts have concluded that the widespread marketing of handguns fails the Restatement requirement that the activity not be a matter of common usage.

Do you think courts made a mistake in rejecting this theory? Study the legal test for strict liability under the abnormally dangerous activities doctrine described above. Does it strike you as an appropriate legal theory for imposing liability on gun manufacturers? (For more in-depth analysis, see Andrew O. Smith, *The Manufacture and Distribution of Handguns as an Abnormally Dangerous Activity*, 54 University of Chicago Law Review 369 [1987]; Donald E. Santarelli and Nicholas E. Calio, *Turning the Gun on Tort Law: Turning to Courts to Take Product Liability to the Limit*, 14 St. Mary's Law Journal 471 [1983].)

B. Are Guns Defective Products If They Can Be Made Safer?

Early tort litigation against gun manufacturers proceeded on the premise that guns are inherently dangerous instrumentalities that cannot be made safer. That has changed, however. Modern suits against gun manufacturers, including most of the suits filed by governmental entities, claim that guns are defective in design for failing to incorporate safety devices, such as personalized gun technology intended to disable guns to all but authorized users. The following article excerpt addresses ways for changing the design of guns to make them safer.

A Public Health Approach to Regulating Firearms as Consumer Products
(148 University of Pennsylvania Law Review 1193 [2000])

Jon S. Vernick and Stephen P. Teret

. . . Design standards are at the heart of regulating firearms in the same manner as other consumer products. Unfortunately, left to themselves, firearm manufacturers have not uniformly incorporated feasible safety technologies into the design of handguns. In fact, the general trend in handgun design has been to increase lethality rather than safety. Recently, for example, there has been a shift among manufacturers toward the production of semiautomatic pistols rather than revolvers. Most pistols can hold more ammunition in their magazine or clip than revolvers hold in their rotating cylinder, thereby increasing the opportunity for multiple wounds. In addition, there has been a trend toward higher caliber handguns. Other things being equal, higher caliber ammunition can produce more serious injuries than lower caliber ammunition. Other factors, such as the widespread availability of and media attention given to laser sighting devices, may also increase the overall lethality of handguns.

This trend toward increased firearm lethality can be reversed. There are design changes to firearms that can actually reduce the risks they pose to both individuals and society. For example, a personalized gun is designed to be operable only by an authorized user. Sometimes also called "smart guns," these firearms have been patented, though generally not manufactured, for many years. Recently, however, SigArms has developed a new gun that uses personalization technology, which the company expects to market in the near future. The new gun has a built-in key pad requiring the authorized user to enter a personalized identification number. The gun can be set so that it will not operate unless the user enters the correct code, and includes a timer that can be programmed to re-lock the gun after a certain period of time has elapsed. Additional ways to personalize guns are also being developed, including guns that will identify the fingerprints of their authorized user(s).

Personalized guns might prevent several different kinds of firearm-related deaths and injuries. Such technology can prevent firearm suicides or unintentional deaths in which the person pulling the trigger, for example a juvenile, is not the gun's owner or authorized user. In addition, if personalized guns are not readily operable by criminals who might steal them, even some homicides may be prevented.

Other design features intended to prevent certain unintentional shootings are included on some, but not all, handguns. A loaded-chamber indicator is a device designed to indicate to a user or observer if the gun contains ammunition ready to be fired. Because semiautomatic pistols may retain one ammunition round in the firing chamber after the ammunition magazine has been removed, this device can prevent accidental shootings where the shooter mistakenly believes that the gun is not loaded. A magazine safety, sometimes called a magazine disconnect safety, is also designed to prevent some of these shootings by automatically preventing the pistol from firing when its ammunition magazine has been removed, even if one round remains in the firing chamber. Despite the lifesaving potential of these devices, they are available on only about ten percent of new pistol models. . . .

Consumer-product regulation of firearms, like that outlined above, can save lives. Although the effectiveness of personalized guns, loaded chamber indicators, and magazine safeties has not been fully quantified—in part because firearm manufacturers have not yet widely implemented the technology—they can be expected to prevent some firearm-related deaths and injuries. In 1997, more than 1200 people aged ten to nineteen committed suicide with a gun. Another 142 children aged fourteen and younger were unintentionally killed by firearms. Personalized guns might prevent at least some of these deaths caused by unauthorized users, such as juveniles. A personalized gun would also not be operable by the criminal who disarms a police officer. From 1987 to 1996, more than seventy police officers were shot and killed with their own weapons.

There are no reliable estimates of the number of shootings caused by persons mistakenly believing a gun is unloaded. In one survey, however, more than one-third of respondents did not know that a pistol can still be fired even if its ammunition magazine has been removed. A study performed by the U.S. General Accounting Office ("GAO") examined the potential benefits of loaded chamber indicators. After examining a series of 107 accidental shootings that occurred in 1988–1989, the GAO concluded that twenty-three percent might have been prevented by a loaded chamber indicator. Extrapolating to the number of accidental deaths in the United States at that time, the study concluded that 345 lives might have been saved by loaded chamber indicators.

The absence of effective firearm-injury surveillance systems makes it difficult to determine more precisely the likely effects of various safer gun designs. However, public health professionals can draw on the lessons learned from the implementation of safety standards for other products. For example, motor vehicles have been subject to numerous federal safety standards since the late 1960s. Since then, motor vehicle–related fatalities have declined dramatically. Certainly other factors have also contributed to the decline in motor vehicle deaths, but safe design standards have played an important role. Standards requiring childproof designs for cigarette lighters and aspirin bottles have also been associated with declines in accidental deaths.

Several studies suggest that banning particularly dangerous firearm designs will reduce the likelihood that guns incorporating those designs will be used in crime. Maryland is one of seven states that has banned Saturday night specials, and in Baltimore, these banned guns make up a much smaller proportion of the guns used in crime than in other cities that do not ban them. Similarly, since federal law banned certain semi-automatic assault weapons, these guns, though never a significant share of the crime problem, are even less frequently involved in crime. Some jurisdictions, such as Washington, D.C. and Chicago, have chosen to ban all handguns. An evaluation of Washington's law concluded that it was associated with an approximately twenty-five percent decline in firearm-related homicides and suicides between 1976 and 1987.

Tort litigation can be an important complement to effective regulation. By providing manufacturers with economic incentives to make their products safer, litigation can serve a public-health purpose. When manufacturers or regulators fail to keep up with innovations in design, litigation allows individual citizens or municipalities to force manufacturers to design or market their products more safely. Although a cause and effect relationship is difficult to prove, shortly after the first verdict against firearm manufacturers finding liability for negligently marketing their products, one major manufacturer required its dealers to adhere to a new code of conduct. Examples in other product-related areas include litigation against motor vehicle manufacturers who failed to provide air bags and against alcoholic beverage providers who served intoxicated persons who then injured others (called dram-shop liability). . . .

DISCUSSION NOTES

1. Should guns be considered defective products if the manufacturer fails to implement personalized (also called "smart-gun") technology? More than one hundred patents have been issued for devices designed to allow

guns to be fired only by authorized users. Advocates of personalized technology argue that it would reduce accidental shootings by children, suicides by unauthorized users, and criminal misuse of stolen guns. One technology currently being tested requires the user to wear a transponder embedded in a ring, badge, belt buckle, or other item worn on the person. The transponder sends a radio signal allowing the gun to "know" that it is being operated by an authorized user. Do you see practical problems with this technology? (More advanced technologies are also being developed. Smith & Wesson is investing in biometrics, a technology that employs digital scanners to recognize the authorized user's fingerprint. As discussed below, Smith & Wesson has entered into a settlement agreement with the City of Boston in which Smith & Wesson agrees to incorporate personalized technology into all new model handguns within three years, if feasible.)

2. Do you think an unauthorized user determined to defeat personalized technology would be able to do so? What about authorized users who did not want the technology—similar to automobile owners who found ways to defeat the seat-belt interlock? (In the gun industry, efforts by the owner to defeat the personalization are called "chip twigglies." Among the methods that might be attempted, depending on the particular personalization device, are removing the personalization equipment; removing the battery; allowing the battery to die; destroying the magnetic images; cooking the unloaded gun to expose it to extreme heat, which might destroy a computer chip but not the metal of the gun itself; and gluing a lock button to keep the gun in the unlocked position. Since personalized guns have not yet been introduced into the market on a widespread basis, it is unknown whether any of these methods would be successful.)

3. Personalized technology will increase the cost of firearms. Is that a relevant consideration? How much would you be willing to see gun prices rise to implement personalized technology? One hundred dollars per gun? Two hundred? Five hundred? If all gun manufacturers were required to implement personalized technology, would you expect the price to decline over time through competition and advances in technology? (Prototype automobile air bags cost $20,000; now they cost about $200.) Would higher-priced smart guns discriminate against

poor people living in high-crime areas who wish to own a gun for self-protection?

4. Do you have concerns about the reliability of personalized firearms? As with all inventions, the more "bells and whistles" that are added, the greater the chance of a malfunction. None of the firearm personalized safety technologies currently available have been adapted for police firearms or for other guns made primarily for defensive purposes.

Would you feel comfortable relying on a gun for self-defense that might not work when needed because, for example, a fingerprint sensor was smudged, or a battery for it ran down, or a ring the user needed to wear in order to fire the gun was in another room? Would it be prudent to stake one's life on a product that functions properly 99 percent of the time? Ninety percent? Do you have faith that technological advances could "work the bugs out" of possible reductions in firearms reliability attributable to personalized technology? Can you think of other mechanical safety devices that work reliably enough that you feel comfortable relying on them? If you are old enough to remember, would you have felt comfortable relying on an airbag twenty years ago? Fifteen years ago? Ten years ago? Today?

5. In December 2000, Smith & Wesson (S&W) entered into a settlement agreement with the City of Boston, one of the governmental entities that has sued the gun industry. As part of the settlement agreement, S&W agreed that within two years, all handguns will incorporate an internal locking device that can be unlocked only by key or combination unique to the particular gun. S&W further agreed to commit 2 percent of its annual sales revenues to the development of personalized technologies and agreed to use its best efforts to incorporate personalized technologies in all new handgun designs within three years. Does the fact that S&W agreed to these provisions suggest that the technology to make personalized guns is either currently available or close at hand? If S&W does produce such guns, and they prove reliable, should the tort system impose similar requirements on other gun makers? Again assuming *arguendo* that the technology exists and would be reliable, do you think the failure of a gun manufacturer to incorporate personalized technology should render its products legally "defective" under tort law?

6. Should firearms manufacturers be held liable for failing to incorporate other safety features into their products, such as magazine-disconnect safeties, chamber-load indicators or childproofing technology? The first two devices are intended to prevent accidental shootings by persons who may not realize that a semiautomatic pistol can be loaded and discharged even when the magazine is removed. Only 14 percent of 1998 pistol models contained a magazine-disconnect safety, and only 11 percent contained a chamber load indicator. (See Jon S. Vernick et al., *I Didn't Know the Gun Was Loaded: An Examination of Two Safety Devices That Can Reduce the Risk of Unintentional Firearm Injuries,* 20 Journal of Public Health Policy 427, 433 [1999].) Opponents of such requirements argue that the above features are available to consumers who want them, and most consumers do not. They contend that a magazine disconnect could prevent a gun from firing in an emergency, and a chamber-load indicator undermines the safety rule that one should treat *every* gun as loaded unless one has personally inspected the gun, including the firing chamber. To what extent should courts require companies to incorporate product features that many consumers do not want? That may make the product more dangerous in some respects, even though safer in others? Should auto manufacturers be permitted to dispense with seat belts if some buyers prefer not to use them and do not want to pay for them? Should automobile manufacturers be sued for not installing regulators on cars to prevent them from exceeding seventy-five miles per hour, or ignition interlocks designed to prevent drunk driving that would require a Breathalyzer test every time the ignition is turned on? Whose job is it to decide what safety devices a product should have: the (state or federal) legislature, (state or federal) executive branch agencies, or the (state or federal) judiciary? A combination of these branches of government? Or consumers and producers in a free market? Who should win when different entities want different levels of regulation or product accessories?

7. *Dix v. Beretta U.S.A. Corp.,* No. 750681-9 (Alameda County, Calif. Superior Ct.), was a lawsuit by the parents of fifteen-year-old Kenzo Dix, who was accidentally shot and killed by a friend with a 9 mm Beretta semiautomatic pistol. The gun belonged to the friend's father, who kept

it loaded in a camera bag in his unlocked bedroom. Dix's friend got out the gun, removed a loaded magazine, and replaced it with an empty one. Unaware that one ammunition cartridge remained in the gun's firing chamber, the boy pointed the gun at Dix and pulled the trigger. The gun discharged, killing Dix. His parents sued Beretta, alleging the gun was defective for failing to include an internal lock to prevent unauthorized use and because the gun's "load indicator" was insufficient to inform unknowledgeable users that a round of ammunition was present in the chamber. At trial, Beretta argued that the plaintiff's proposed internal lock would have made the gun less reliable and would encourage owners to leave loaded firearms accessible to children, a practice contrary to the advice in Beretta's product manual that firearms and ammunition should be stored separately out of the reach of children. Beretta argued the death was attributable solely to the negligence of the shooter and his father. The jury returned a verdict in defendant's favor. (See *Defense Verdict in Suit against Manufacturer of Semi-Automatic Pistol,* Verdicts, Settlements and Tactics, Jan. 1999, at 27.) If you were on the jury, would you have voted for the plaintiff or defendant Beretta?

8. Should gun makers be held liable for failing to "childproof" guns by, for example, including a locking device, strengthening the trigger pull, or increasing the size of the grip? Kopel asserts that childproofing guns would increase, rather than decrease, the risk of guns to children:

> Any company that markets a "childproof" gun—and any public policy expert who urges mandates for such guns—must recognize that such guns will be left around children more often. After all, if the gun is really "childproof," there is no risk in leaving it near children. No one, however, would seriously propose treating a gun so casually because no one would risk a child's life on a commercial claim that a product is totally childproof. Moreover, despite the rhetoric about "childproof" guns, it is doubtful that a truly childproof device can ever be made. At best, a "childproof" device of any type could only reliably be expected to deter children under age six or thereabouts who would have neither the strength nor the ingenuity to defeat a safety device. Design-standard modifications would be of little benefit in reducing

the more common type of childhood gun accident, involving preteen and older boys. (David B. Kopel, *Treating Guns like Consumer Products*, 148 University of Pennsylvania Law Review 1213, 1234–36 [2000].)

9. Do you favor civil liability for gun owners who store guns accessible to children when accidents result? (Several courts have imposed liability. See, e.g., *Jacobs v. Tyson*, 407 S.E. 2d 62 [Ga. Ct. App. 1991]: twelve-year-old retrieved loaded pistol from unlocked dresser drawer; *Valence v. State*, 282 So. 2d 517 [La. 1973]: four-year-old accessed loaded pistol in glove compartment; *Kuhns v. Brugger*, 135 A. 2d 395 [Pa. 1957]: twelve-year-old obtained loaded pistol from drawer in grandfather's cottage; *Mendola v. Sambol*, 71 A. 2d 827 [Pa. 1950]: eleven-year-old retrieved .22 caliber rifle from behind door in living room; *Stanley v. Joslin*, 757 S.W. 2d 328 [Tenn. Ct. App. 1987]: fourteen-year-old obtained rifle and cartridges from gun rack. Studies of firearm storage practices show that roughly 50 percent of the nation's handguns are stored unlocked and that millions of children live in homes with unlocked, loaded firearms. See Andrew J. McClurg, *Armed and Dangerous: Tort Liability for the Negligent Storage of Firearms*, 32 Connecticut Law Review 1189, 1190–1200 [2000], reviewing numerous gun storage studies showing that high percentages of guns are stored unlocked, and that millions of guns are stored loaded and unlocked.)

10. Vernick and Teret argue in their article that firearms be administratively regulated for product safety, like other consumer products. Should they? While there are some laws addressing gun design, such as the federal assault-weapon ban, the Consumer Product Safety Commission, the federal agency charged with regulating the safety of most consumer products, is prohibited by statute from regulating firearms. (See 15 *U.S. Code* § 2052[a][1][E] [1994], excluding firearms from the definition of consumer products.) In the words of an oft-quoted sound bite, the commission has the authority to regulate toy guns but not real ones. Does it make sense to you that the Consumer Product Safety Commission should be charged with the job of regulating the product safety of toasters, hair dryers, space heaters, and most other products, but not firearms? Why or why not? If a legislature determines that a certain control should not be imposed on a product, should appointed

administrators have the authority to impose the control anyway? What if, as in most cases, the legislature has not expressly considered whether a particular product safety measure is appropriate or necessary? (Kopel wrote a counterpoint to Vernick and Teret. See David B. Kopel, *Treating Guns like Consumer Products*, 148 University of Pennsylvania Law Review 1213 [2000].)

11. Some states have imposed design and manufacturing safety standards on guns. In 1997, the Massachusetts attorney general imposed sweeping regulations that define as "an unfair or deceptive trade practice" the sale of handguns that (a) lack a tamper-resistant serial number; (b) fail integrity standards such as firing and drop tests; (c) lack locking mechanisms such as key or combination locks; (d) can be fired by an average five-year-old child; and (e) have a barrel of shorter than three inches, unless disclosures are made to the consumer regarding the accuracy of the gun. (See 940 *Code Mass. Regs.* § 16.00 et seq.) Several gun makers and firearm trade associations filed suit to block implementation of the regulations, asserting that the attorney general exceeded his authority in promulgating them. Although this claim succeeded in the trial court, the Massachusetts Supreme Court rejected the claim and upheld the regulations. (See *American Shooting Sports Council, Inc. v. Attorney General*, 711 N.E. 2d 899 [Mass. 1999].) In 1999, California passed laws patterned after the Massachusetts regulations. (See *Cal. Penal Code* §§ 12125–133.) Maryland has passed legislation requiring that all guns sold in the state beginning January 1, 2003, be equipped with internal-locking devices (*Md. Ann. Code* Art. 27 § 442C). Do you see the dilemma such legislative action by a small number of states presents to gun makers? Unless they are willing and able to avoid selling noncomplying guns in these states, they will be forced to retool all their products to conform to the standards. Are the California and Maryland restrictions more legitimate than the Massachusetts regulations because they were enacted by legislatures, rather than imposed by aggressive interpretation of a statute prohibiting "deceptive" trade practices?

12. The Second Amendment and similar state constitutional restrictions aside, is it constitutionally permissible for states to impose safety standards on manufacturers of firearms? Earlier, it was mentioned that the

Congress forbade the Consumer Product Safety Commission from regulating or banning guns. Does this represent a policy choice on Congress's part that such products should be regulated only by Congress and by the Bureau of Alcohol, Tobacco and Firearms? Or does it represent an example of Congress bending to pressure from the NRA and other gun rights supporters? Is there a difference?

Under the doctrine of "preemption," states are not allowed to enact statutes that conflict with those enacted by Congress. (See U.S. Constitution art. 6, sec. 2: "This Constitution, and the Laws of the United States which shall be made in Pursuance thereof . . . shall be the supreme Law of the Land.") A congressional statute need not express an intended preemptive effect explicitly; preemption may be implied. (See, e.g., *Crosby v. Nat'l Foreign Trade Counsel*, 120 S. Ct. 2288 [2000]: congressional sanctions aimed at Burma preempted state law attempting to impose greater restrictions on companies doing business with Burma; *United States v. Locke*, 120 S. Ct. 1135 [2000]: congressional statute preempted state safety regulations imposing standards on oil tankers operating within state waters; Boris I. Bittker, *Bittker on the Regulation of Interstate and Foreign Commerce* § 5.06 [New York: Aspen Law and Business, 1999 and supp.], describing preemption doctrine.)

Even in the absence of congressional action, states are forbidden to pass legislation that discriminates against or otherwise burdens "interstate commerce," which Congress is permitted to regulate under article 1, section 8 of the Constitution. Under the "dormant Commerce Clause doctrine," federal courts have struck down state attempts to regulate interstate commerce where the state regulations might subject interstate commercial actors to conflicting obligations should different states pass different standards. (See, e.g., *Southern Pac. Co. v. Arizona*, 325 U.S. 761, 782 [1945], voiding Arizona law regulating the length of trains: "[N]ationwide control . . . is essential to the maintenance of an efficient transportation system, which Congress alone can provide"; *Bibb v. Navajo Freight Lines, Inc.*, 359 U.S. 520 [1959], striking down state statute that prescribed a particular type of mudguard for interstate trucks traveling within the state; *Kassel v. Consolidated Freightways Corp.*, 450 U.S. 662 [1981], striking down state regulation of the length of tractor trailers; *American Library Ass'n v. Pataki*, 969 F. Supp. 160

[S.D.N.Y. 1997], invalidating state "cyberporn" law on grounds that Web site operators would be subject to potentially contradictory state regulatory schemes.) This rule derives from an 1851 case, *Cooley v. Board of Wardens*, 53 U.S. 299 (1851), in which the Court held that if subjects that states wanted to regulate were "national" subjects or "admit only of one uniform system, or plan of regulation," then Congress alone could prescribe regulations.

The dormant Commerce Clause doctrine also prohibits a state from attempting to regulate conduct that occurs beyond its borders. (See, e.g., *Healy v. Beer Institute*, 491 U.S. 324 [1989], striking down "price-affirmation" statutes prohibiting the sale of beer in state at prices greater than those at which beer was offered in surrounding states; *Brown-Forman Distillers Corp. v. New York St. Liquor Auth.*, 476 U.S. 573 [1986], applying the same for liquor.)

Do you think states should have the right to impose safety standards on guns sold within their jurisdictions? Or would the potential of fifty separate state safety regimes place an unacceptable burden on manufacturers, or force them to conform to the most stringent regime, thus allowing that state to, in effect, legislate for the entire country? Are gun accessories (or gun regulation in general) a subject that requires a "national" solution?

13. Do you think Congress and state legislatures are "held hostage" by the NRA? Are organizations such as the American Association of Retired Persons, the National Education Association, and the Sierra Club—all of which have large grassroots membership bases and a great deal of political influence—holding legislatures hostage? Do you think these organizations wield more, less, or about the same influence on legislative policy decisions affecting their constituencies as the NRA?

Proponents of judicial action against gun makers sometimes argue that the legislative process cannot be trusted in this area because of the NRA's effective lobbying efforts. Does the legislative and regulatory activity described above suggest that the democratic process, contrary to the claims of some control advocates, is working? Or is the process not working because the restrictions will not really improve safety? Does the legislative process only "work" when it achieves the results one wants?

C. Have Gun Manufacturers Negligently Marketed Guns to Criminals?

With the failure of strict liability, plaintiffs in gun litigation have fallen back on the more traditional but often overlooked theory of common-law negligence. This movement was spurred in part by a 1995 law review article written by Andrew J. McClurg, in which he suggested that plaintiffs in gun cases abandon strict liability claims and "go back to basics" (See Andrew J. McClurg, *The Tortious Marketing of Handguns: Strict Liability Is Dead, Long Live Negligence*, 19 Seton Hall Legislative Journal 777 [1995]).

For more than a century, negligence law has placed a duty on actors to exercise reasonable care to reduce unreasonable, foreseeable risks of harm presented by their conduct. Most recent lawsuits against gun manufacturers, including most of the lawsuits filed by public plaintiffs such as cities and counties, include negligent distribution and marketing claims. Among other things, the lawsuits claim that gun makers have negligently failed to monitor and control their retailers to prevent them from supplying the criminal gun-trafficking market.

The plaintiffs rely in part on gun-tracing data generated by the BATF. In 1999 the BATF released a tracing analysis of seventy-six thousand guns confiscated at crime scenes in twenty-seven cities. The study found that 50 percent of the guns came from "straw purchases," transactions in which a legal purchaser buys guns, often in large numbers in a single transaction, with the intent of transferring them to the criminal market. Other BATF data show that 1 percent of dealers accounted for 57 percent of crime guns traced back to their original source. In 1998, 1,020 of the nation's 83,272 licensed gun dealers were the source of at least ten traced guns used in crime; 132 dealers were linked to fifty or more traced crime guns. (For more information, see http://www.ATF.treas.gov/firearms/index.htm.)

Plaintiffs in the gun suits argue that manufacturers have a duty to train dealers to recognize illegal sales and to track dealer inventory to identify—and terminate—unscrupulous dealers who engage in illegal transactions. Gun manufacturers respond that they are selling a heavily regulated lawful product, that every consumer transaction by a licensed dealer requires a background check through the FBI's National Instant Check System, and that they have no duty or practical ability to monitor what happens to their products after they sell them to distributors or dealers.

Some negligent distribution and marketing claims raise what has become known as the "oversupply" argument. The gist of this claim is that gun makers supply retailers with guns at volumes they know, or should know, oversupply the legitimate relevant geographical market, then close their eyes as large numbers of these guns are siphoned off to criminals. The oversupply argument has undergone one courtroom test. In *Hamilton v. Beretta U.S.A. Corp.*, the families of seven New York shooting victims went to trial in federal court against twenty-five handgun manufacturers on a claim that the defendants negligently oversupplied Southern states that have weak gun laws, fostering an underground market of guns illegally transported to cities with strict gun laws, such as New York. Plaintiffs produced expert testimony that 90 percent of the handguns used in crime in New York come from states with lenient gun laws (compared to New York's very strict laws). Statisticians also testified that the defendant gun manufacturers must have known they were oversupplying those states with less restrictive gun laws; that is, they were selling far more guns to dealers in the suspect states than could reasonably be used by residents of those areas. The jury returned a complex verdict that was hailed as a victory by both sides. Only one of the shooting victims was awarded damages, against three gun manufacturers deemed to be a proximate cause of his injuries. The jury did decide, however, that fifteen of the twenty-five manufacturers had negligently marketed their handguns.

On appeal, the U.S. Court of Appeals for the Second Circuit "certified" to the Court of Appeals of New York the question of whether gun manufacturers owe a duty to gun-violence victims under negligence law to exercise reasonable care in the marketing and distribution of their products. (This certification process is a legal mechanism by which a federal court can ask a state's high court to resolve important questions of state law that have not previously been ruled upon.) The New York Court of Appeals ruled in favor of the defendants, holding that gun manufacturers owe no such duty under New York law (*Hamilton v. Beretta U.S.A. Corp.*, 750 N.E. 2d 1055 [N.Y. Ct. App. 2001]).

Among the reasons cited by the court in support of its "no duty" ruling were: (1) a reluctance to impose liability on gun manufacturers for their failure to control the conduct of others; (2) the remoteness of the causal connection between the defendants' conduct and victims of gun violence; (3) the failure of the one plaintiff who recovered damages to show where the gun that injured him came from (the gun was never found); (4) the failure of all the plaintiffs to prove that a change in the defendants' marketing practices would have prevented their injuries; (5) the belief that the marketing changes sought by plaintiffs would have the effect of eliminating a significant number of lawful sales by "responsible" federal firearms licensees to "responsible" buyers; and (6) the fear that recognition of a duty would open gun manufacturers to limitless liability.

DISCUSSION NOTES

1. Do you think gun manufacturers should have a duty under tort law to monitor and regulate their retailers if they know that large numbers of their guns are entering the criminal trafficking market directly from the legitimate market? Should automobile manufacturers be responsible for monitoring their dealers to make sure they do not sell cars to persons with bad driving records? Should alcohol manufacturers be liable for failing to monitor liquor stores to ensure they do not sell alcohol to minors or alcoholics? Are these apt analogies, or can they be distinguished?

2. If a relatively small number of licensed dealers are responsible for a disproportionate number of guns entering the criminal market, would a better answer be for law enforcement to crack down on those dealers? Is it possible the sales figures are partly attributable to large stores having a major share of the retail firearms business? Only 13 percent of federal firearms licensees (licensed gun dealers) sell over one hundred guns a year, and they account for 88 percent of all retail sales. (Garen J. Wintemute, *Relationship between Illegal Use of Handguns and Handgun Sales Volume*, 284 Journal of the American Medical Association 566, 567 [2000].) By judicial interpretation in most federal courts, straw purchases have been a federal felony since the Gun Control Act of 1968.

(See, e.g., *United States v. Moore*, 109 F. 3d 1456 [9th Cir. 1997] [en banc]; *United States v. Straach*, 987 F. 2d 965 [5th Cir. 1993].) Sellers who can be proved to have knowingly participated in straw transactions can be prosecuted for "aiding and abetting" the buyer's false statement on the federal gun purchase form.

The BATF has the equivalent of about two hundred full-time agents to monitor roughly eighty-thousand nonmanufacturer firearms licensees. Should the BATF's powers and resources to monitor firearms dealers be expanded? Does it depend on what the additional resources would be used for? Cracking down on illegal dealers, or prosecuting honest dealers for paperwork errors? (For background on current laws that impose restrictions on the BATF's search and seizure powers, see David T. Hardy, *The Firearms Owners' Protection Act: A Historical and Legal Perspective*, 17 Cumberland Law Review 585 [1986–87].) The NRA has been criticized for arguing that better law enforcement is the best response to illegal gun sales while at the same time opposing expansion of BATF resources or power.

3. Multiple handgun sales contribute to the criminal trafficking market. One gun trafficker helped arm the streets of Philadelphia by traveling to Ohio and purchasing 135 handguns during a six-month period in ten visits to the same gun store. Another trafficker purchased 132 handguns in Florida between September 1992 and December 1992 in three visits to the same Florida gun dealer, during which he bought, respectively, 34, 66, and 32 handguns. (See Mark D. Polston, *Civil Liability for High Risk Gun Sales: An Approach to Combat Gun Trafficking*, 19 Seton Hall Legislative Journal 821 [1995], documenting these cases and explaining how sellers can spot many illegal purchases.)

Federal law does not limit multiple handgun sales, although licensed firearms dealers must file a multiple-sales report with the BATF and the state or local police when a person buys two or more handguns in a five business-day period (18 *U.S. Code* § 923[g][3][A]). Some states have adopted "one gun a month" laws. (See *Va. Code. Ann.* 18.2–308.2:2Q, making it a misdemeanor for any person who is not a licensed firearms dealer to purchase more than one handgun within a thirty-day period but making exceptions for qualified collectors and situations where a gun has been lost or stolen.) Are one-gun-a-month restrictions reasonable, or do they unreasonably infringe on the right to keep and bear arms? If the government can ration sales to one per month, can it ration sales to one per year? Even further? Should it? Should gun manufacturers have a legal duty to monitor multiple sales by their dealers?

4. Gun control advocates argue that manufacturers should track the sales of their dealers and study BATF criminal traces, and that if they did, they could identify and terminate dealers who are supplying the criminal market. David Kairys asserts that the BATF has conducted approximately eight hundred thousand criminal gun traces in the last five years, each involving a direct contact between the BATF and a particular gun manufacturer. Based on these data, he estimates that communications from the BATF to manufacturers regarding guns traced to crime occur "at the rate of more than one per minute, on average, during every workday for the last five years." He characterizes these contacts as "an extraordinary level of direct notice" to gun manufacturers. (David Kairys, *The Origin and Development of the Governmental Handgun Cases*, 32 Connecticut Law Review 1163, 1166 [2000].) (See pages 299–300 for a brief discussion of whether the BATF tracing data accurately reflect the criminal gun market.)

Should tracking dealers be the manufacturers' obligation? What if the manufacturer, like most major U.S. firearms manufacturers, never sells directly to retailers but instead distributes through wholesalers? Should a wholesaler be expected to recognize when a retailer who has a valid federal firearms license from the BATF is selling guns at retail illegally?

5. With regard to the oversupply argument, should gun manufacturers be held responsible for crimes in one state based on guns they lawfully sold in other states? Should liquor manufacturers be held liable for "oversupplying" retail liquor outlets in college towns if they know, or should know, that a large number of underage drinkers are illegally purchasing their products? Is this a good analogy?

6. Should third parties be held legally responsible under tort law for the criminal acts of others? What if the criminal act is a foreseeable consequence of the defendant's conduct which is alleged to be negligent? A leading source of tort law, the Restatement (Second) of Torts, states:

An act or omission may be negligent if the actor realizes or should realize that it involves an unreasonable risk of harm to another through the conduct of the other or a third person which is intended to cause harm, even though such conduct is criminal. (Restatement [Second] of Torts § 302B [1965].)

Courts, however, traditionally have been reluctant to impose duties to protect against criminal attack in the absence of a special relationship between the defendant and the victim, in part because of the potentially large burden such a duty would exact on the defendant. (Compare *Romero v. Nat'l Rifle Ass'n*, 749 F. 2d 77 [D.C. Cir. 1984], rejecting liability for a criminal attack committed with a gun stolen from NRA headquarters, with *Pavlides v. Niles Gun Show, Inc.*, 637 N.E. 2d 404 [Ohio Ct. App. 1994], imposing liability on the operator of a gun show for a criminal attack committed with guns stolen from the gun show by minors.)

7. Gun manufacturers take the position that, as long as they are complying with applicable laws and regulations regarding firearms distribution, they should be immune from tort liability. Do you agree? It is textbook tort law that compliance with laws and regulations, while sometimes admissible to show "due care," is never conclusive as to the issue of due care. Is compliance with applicable laws good evidence of due care when the relevant laws are especially comprehensive or strict? What if, as gun control advocates assert, the relevant laws are lax?

One controversial private suit took the negligent marketing theory a step further and deserves detailed examination. In *Merrill v. Navegar, Inc.* the plaintiffs alleged that Navegar, the manufacturer of the TEC-DC9 semiautomatic pistol, was negligent in manufacturing a weapon that appealed primarily to criminals and in marketing the weapon in ways that increased the risk it would be used by criminals. The lawsuit arose from a 1993 San Francisco law-firm mass shooting.

On July 1, 1993, Gian Luigi Ferri entered 101 California Street, a high-rise office building in San Francisco, armed with two TEC-DC9s manufactured and distributed by Navegar, as well as a .45-caliber semiautomatic pistol. He attacked a law firm against which he held a grudge and opened fire, killing eight men and women and wounding six others before fatally shooting himself in a stairwell. Survivors of some of those who died brought suit against Navegar, asserting common-law negligence and other theories of recovery. The trial court granted Navegar's motion for summary judgment. The plaintiffs appealed this ruling. A California appellate court reversed the judgment, concluding that "Navegar owed appellants a duty to exercise reasonable care not to create risks above and beyond those inherent in the presence of firearms in our society" (*Merrill v. Navegar, Inc.*, 89 Calif. Rptr. 2d 146 [Calif. Ct. App. 1999]).

On appeal, the California Supreme Court reversed the intermediate appellate court, striking yet another blow to those who favor using the civil tort system against gun manufacturers. In a five to one decision, the California Supreme Court ruled that a California statute precluded the lawsuit (*Merrill v. Navagar, Inc.*, 110 Calif. Rptr. 2d 370 [Calif. 2001]). The statute, *Cal. Civil Code* § 1714.4, states that a gun manufacturer may not be held liable "[i]n a products liability action . . . on the basis that the benefits of [its] product do not outweigh the risk of injury posed by [the product's] potential to cause serious injury, damage, or death when discharged." Plaintiffs sought to avoid the effect of the statute by framing their case in terms of negligent distribution and marketing, rather than as a strict-liability design-defect "products liability action." The court said, however, that no matter how plaintiffs characterized their claim, it still amounted to a risk-utility-based design-defect products liability claim. "[C]ontrary to the assertion of the plaintiffs and the dissent," the majority stated, "the record demonstrates that plaintiffs do, in fact, seek to hold Navegar liable precisely because, as the trial court stated, the TEC-9/DC9's 'potential for harm substantially outweighs any possible benefit to be derived from [it].'" Thus, the court held that the statute barred the lawsuit.

Below we have set forth excerpts from the majority and dissenting opinions issued in the case by the California Court of Appeals (which ruled in favor of plaintiffs), rather than excerpts from the California Supreme Court's opinion (which reversed the Court of Appeals), because the Court of Appeals more squarely addressed the interesting policy issues raised by the case.

MERRILL V. NAVEGAR, INC.
(89 Calif. Rptr. 2d 146 [Calif. Ct. App. 1999], *reversed,*
110 Calif. Rptr. 2d 370 [Calif. 2001])

Majority Opinion

The intensive discovery in this case focused upon the characteristics of the TEC-DC9. Appellants' experts provided deposition testimony and declarations establishing that the TEC-DC9 is a "military-patterned weapon" of the type "typically issued to specialized forces such as security personnel, special operations forces, or border guards." Even though it is nominally a semiautomatic, the standard 32-round magazine "can be emptied in seconds." According to the undisputed testimony of police chief Leonard J. Supenski, a nationally recognized firearms expert, the TEC-DC9 differs from conventional handguns in several ways. A large capacity detachable magazine, "designed to deliver maximum firepower by storing the largest number of cartridges in the smallest . . . space," provides a level of firepower "associated with military or police, not civilian, shooting requirements." The TEC-DC9 has a "barrel shroud," also peculiar to military weapons, which disperses the heat generated by the rapid firing of numerous rounds of ammunition and allows the user to grasp the barrel and hold the weapon with two hands, which facilitates spray-firing. The barrel is threaded, allowing the attachment of silencers and flash suppressors, which are restricted under federal law and are primarily of interest to criminals. The threaded barrel also permits the attachment of a barrel extension, enabling the weapon to be fired with higher velocity and at greater distances, while still allowing it to be broken down into smaller concealable parts. The weapon comes with a "sling swivel" that permits it to be hung from a shoulder harness, known as a "combat sling," when firing rapidly from the hip. The sling device also permits the rapid firing of two weapons simultaneously, as was done by Ferri in this case. The relatively compact size of the TEC-DC9 allows a shooter to transport maximum firepower with relative ease, and with far greater concealability than almost any other weapon having similar firepower. . . .

Chief Supenski stated that the TEC-DC9 is "completely useless" for hunting, is never used by competitive or recreational shooters and "has no legitimate sporting use." The weapon is designed to engage multiple targets during rapid sustained fire. It has no practical value for self-defense and is hazardous when used for that purpose due to its weight, inaccuracy, and firepower, he stated. . . .

Supenski directed research for an association of police chiefs of large American cities in 1992 which showed that the TEC-9 was "far and away" the leading assault weapon seized by law enforcement agencies in such cities in 1990 and 1991, "accounting for 24% of all assault weapons seized, and 42% of all assault pistols seized." . . .

Supenski validated an analysis of BATF [Bureau of Alcohol, Tobacco and Firearms] data in 1988 and 1989 by Cox Newspapers, which also reported that due to its unsurpassed firepower, concealability and low price (then about $380), the TEC-9 was the most favored weapon of the most dangerous criminals, particularly violence prone drug gangs in large metropolitan areas. . . .

The record includes evidence Navegar deliberately targeted the marketing of the TEC-9 and TEC-DC9 to certain types of persons attracted to or associated with violence. . . .

Navegar's advertising targeted "militarists" and "survivalists" by advertising the TEC-DC9 in magazines they favored, such as Soldier of Fortune, SWAT, Combat Handguns, Guns, Firepower, and Heavy Metal Weapons. . . . According to Solodovnick, the substance of Navegar's advertising and its other promotional activities was deliberately calculated to attract "military-type thinking people" likely to use the weapon offensively by referring to the TEC-DC9, for example, as an "assault-type pistol." Navegar's advertisements emphasized the "paramilitary" appearance of the weapon, including references to "[m]ilitary non-glare" finish and "combat-type" sights. Among the advertising methods employed for the TEC-DC9 were using the slogan, "tough as your toughest customer," in promotional materials sent to dealers and distributors, but accessible to the general public, and pointing out that the surface of the weapon had "excellent resistance to fingerprints." Solodovnick acknowledged that people who were not knowledgeable about fingerprints could interpret the latter representation as meaning fingerprints would not be left on this weapon. [Fingerprints from the gun can be read as easily as from any other gun. The TEC-DC9 has a coating that reduces the finish's vulnerability to natural oils in human hands.] . . .

Solodovnick was aware that news reports of the TEC-DC9 being used in a sensational murder or other crime, and condemnation of the weapon by law enforcement and other government officials, invariably helped sales. He acknowledged having been correctly quoted in a 1992 New York Times article, as follows: "I'm kind of flattered," Mr. Solo[dovnick] said when he was asked about condemnations of the TEC-9. "It just has that advertising tingle to it. Hey, it's talked about, it's read about, the media write about it. That generates more sales for me. It might sound cold and cruel, but I'm sales oriented." He also acknowledged saying, with reference to an assault at a school in Stockton, that "whenever anything negative has happened, sales have gone tremendously high." . . .

[I]mplicit in appellants' claim of ordinary negligence is that the manner in which Navegar manufactured and marketed the TEC-DC9 and made it available to the general public created risks above and beyond those citizens may reasonably be expected to bear in a society in which firearms may legally be acquired and used and are widely available. Appellants' complaint can best be understood as presenting a theory of negligence based on Navegar's breach of a duty to use due care not to increase the risk beyond that inherent in the presence of firearms in our society. . . .

Dissenting Opinion

[T]he majority has become the first appellate court anywhere in this land to declare that, in an ordinary negligence action, a gun manufacturer owes a duty of care to persons injured and the survivors of others killed by the criminal misuse of its product by a remote purchaser. In so doing, I sadly conclude, it has undertaken what I believe to be an egregious exercise in judicial legislation. . . .

There is one final weakness in the majority's generalized "duty not to increase risks": we are never told, indeed never even given a hint, as to how it is to be applied. . . . For example, and confining myself for the moment to the record before us, would it or would it not apply to the manufacturer of the Norinco .45, also used with such deadly effect by Ferri on the day in question? [Ferri killed or wounded six of his fourteen victims with this pistol.] Would it apply to the Glock semi-automatic 9mm gun Ferri so carefully considered in April 1993 if, hypothetically, he had chosen it for one of his weapons on July 1? Would it apply to the many other semi-automatic assault weapons, similar to the TEC-DC9 . . . ? Would it apply to assault weapons generally (assuming that such are susceptible to judicial definition)? . . .

[The dissent discusses the fact that courts have overwhelmingly rejected the imposition of a duty under negligence law on gun manufacturers.]

I submit that a major reason so many courts have declined to impose a duty in similar cases and, rather, have deferred to their respective legislatures is the problem of line-drawing. . . .

I suggest there is—and should be—overwhelming doubt as to the competence of the judiciary to develop and then apply criteria such as marketing tactics, appearance and design of a gun, language in the promotional material, and legitimacy of usage for civilian purposes, to distinguish between guns as to which either a generalized "duty not to increase risks" (the majority) or a specific "duty not to sell to the general public" (appellants) exists and those as to which it does not. And, I suggest, that is precisely the reason every other court which has considered this issue has declined to embark on such a perilous journey. . . .

[A]ppellants could not, other than by an "impermissibly speculative" path, show that Navegar's marketing of its TEC-DC9 was the legal cause of Ferri's purchase and later lethal use of it. "Only a series of unsupportable assumptions could lead a jury to conclude: first, that Ferri saw a Navegar advertisement; second, that that advertisement caused Ferri to purchase its assault firearms; and third, that the advertisements further caused Ferri to use those firearms at 101 California Street to inflict such incomprehensible destruction." . . .

The conclusion to be drawn from all of this is, I submit, obvious: Ferri was going to buy some gun to commit his planned carnage; he did not commit it because he had two TEC-DC9s as opposed to some other model of weapon. Put another way, clearly neither the identity of the gun nor the gun manufacturer was a critical matter to him.

The terrible tragedy of July 1, 1993, in San Francisco will not soon be forgotten, nor should it be. But something else which needs to be kept in mind is the whole issue of responsibility, a concept too often minimized in some contemporary legal discourse. . . . "[T]he responsibility for tortious acts should lie with the individual who commits those acts; absent facts which clearly give rise to a legal duty, that responsibility should not be shifted to a third party."

Gian Luigi Ferri organized and executed every aspect of the tragedy underlying this litigation. He—and he alone—planned for at least six months, down to such exquisite detail as combat slings, Hell Fire triggers [a trigger attachment that makes a gun feel but not fire like a machine gun], satchels in which to carry the guns, etc. [No one at Navegar], no matter how appalling their judgment or callous their sensitivities, pulled a trigger at 101 California Street on July 1, 1993. . . .

This veritable hailstorm of value judgments [in the majority opinion] calls to mind a quotation from Justice Felix Frankfurter: "It is not easy to stand aloof and allow want of wisdom to prevail, to disregard one's own strongly held view of what is wise in the conduct of affairs. But it is not the business of this Court to pronounce policy. It must observe a fastidious regard for limitations on its own power, and this precludes the Court's giving effect to its own notions of what is wise or politic. That self-restraint is of the essence in the observance of the judicial oath." . . .

DISCUSSION NOTES

1. Although subsequently reversed by the California Supreme Court, *Merrill v. Navegar* was the first appellate court decision ever to hold that a gun manufacturer can be sued for negligence for marketing and distributing a properly functioning firearm. Do you agree with the majority or the dissent? The dissent argues it is impossible to draw meaningful and reliable legal lines to single out one model of firearm for liability. Do you agree? Does the TEC-DC9 stand in a class by itself?

2. Navegar argued that imposing tort liability for marketing and distributing its pistols would amount to a judicially imposed ban on their sale. Do you agree? The majority's opinion disagreed:

> Appellants are not asking that any of Navegar's commercial activities be enjoined, nor could they; they are simply asking that a jury, after trial,

award them damages for the consequences of conduct—which included affirmative acts, not just acts of omission—that increased the risk of the harm they suffered. "Making an activity tortious forces the people who derive benefit from it to internalize the costs associated with it, thereby making sure that the activity will only be undertaken if it is desired by enough people to cover its costs. It does not proscribe it altogether. As a result, very different policy considerations go into the decision of whether to forbid something and the decision of whether to find a duty that permits liability for the harm it causes." [Quoting *McCarthy v. Olin Corp.*, 119 F. 3d 148, 169–170 (2d Cir. 1997) (Calabresi, J., dissenting).]

The court also conceded, however, that "limitless liability" might force Navegar out of business or to reorganize under bankruptcy laws. Would that be a positive or pernicious effect of the tort system? Is there any difference between driving a company into bankruptcy and banning its products? (Navegar did indeed go out of business in 2001, in part due to legal fees.)

3. Were Navegar's TEC-DC9s a "cause" of the harm to Ferri's victims? An essential element of any negligence claim, which the plaintiff must prove by a "more likely than not" standard, is that the defendant's allegedly negligent conduct was a "proximate" or "legal" cause of the plaintiff's injury. This entails proving both that the defendant's conduct was a "substantial factor" in causing the injury and also that the injury was foreseeable, at least in a general way. Was a mass criminal assault a foreseeable consequence of Navegar's marketing practices? Did Navegar's marketing of the TEC-DC9 play a substantial role in Ferri's decision to carry out the attack? An expert psychological witness for the plaintiff testified that Navegar's promotional activities emphasizing the military assault features of its weapon "likely emboldened Ferri to undertake mass killings without fear of failure." How reliable is such testimony? Ferri—the only person with firsthand knowledge concerning what influenced his decisions—committed suicide during the assault. Would Ferri have carried out the attack even in the absence of Navegar's marketing tactics? Would he have simply used a different type of weapon had the TEC-DC9 not been available? A fundamental difficulty

of proving causation is that it requires jurors to apply a "hypothetical alternative" test under which they must hypothesize what would have happened if the defendant had acted differently. Unfortunately, we often cannot know with any degree of reliability what would have happened under a different set of circumstances. Plaintiffs' alternative causation claim was that the results of Ferri's attack would have been less severe had he been forced to rely on a weapon with less firepower. But given plaintiffs' own expert testimony about the TEC-DC9's inaccuracy and its vulnerability to jamming and misfires, it is not necessarily clear that a different gun would have resulted in lower casualties. The legal element of causation is likely to be a problem for plaintiffs in many cases against gun manufacturers. Can a plaintiff ever successfully prove that a gun manufacturer's conduct was a substantial factor in a criminal acquiring and misusing one of the manufacturer's products?

4. Does the TEC-DC9 have any social utility? The court pinned its holding on the marketing practices of Navegar, but much of the court's opinion appears focused on the point that the TEC-DC9 lacks usefulness for legitimate purposes and is used disproportionately for criminal purposes. Does this amount to reconstituting under the rubric of negligence law the same risk-utility balancing analysis that courts rejected under a strict products liability theory? (There is little theoretical difference in the legal analysis between a negligence analysis and a strict-liability risk-utility analysis. The Restatement [Second] of Torts, in § 291, defines an unreasonable risk under negligence law as one that "is of such magnitude as to outweigh what the law regards as the utility of the act or of the particular manner in which it is done.") A Congressional Research Study found that about 2 percent of TEC-9 guns (very similar to the TEC-DC9) have been traced to a crime (See K. Bea, *"Assault Weapons": Military-style Semiautomatic Firearms: Facts and Issues* [Washington, D.C.: Congressional Research Service, May 13, 1992; Technical Revisions, June 4]). Much of the market for the Navegar guns appears to be "Walter Mitty" types and people who enjoy "plinking" (informal target shooting), but not competitive target shooters.

5. Negligence claims against firearms retailers for selling guns to persons whom the retailer allegedly knew, or should have known, would misuse the gun are less controversial than claims against manufacturers.

Plaintiffs have been successful in several cases: see, for example, *Cullum and Boren-McCain Mall, Inc. v. Peacock*, 592 S.W. 2d 442 (Ark. 1980) (negligence claim arising from sale to customer who told retailer he wanted a gun that could make "a big hole in a man"); *Kitchen v. K-Mart Corp.*, 697 So. 2d 1200 (Fla. 1997) (upholding $11.5 million verdict for selling gun to intoxicated customer who used it to shoot estranged girlfriend); *Diggles v. Horwitz*, 765 S.W. 2d 839, 841 (Tex. Ct. App. 1989) (fact issue as to whether it was negligent for pawn shop to sell gun to mental patient who acted strangely while purchasing gun and subsequently used it to commit suicide). Do you see why it is easier to establish negligence in these cases than in cases against gun manufacturers?

D. GOVERNMENT PLAINTIFF LITIGATION

Equipped with information concerning the most prominent legal theories employed in tort suits against the gun industry, we are now prepared to consider a dramatic recent development in the arena of firearms litigation: massive lawsuits filed by government entities against the gun industry, seeking hundreds of millions of dollars in damages and court-ordered changes in the way gun makers manufacture, distribute, and market their products.

More than thirty cities and counties, the District of Columbia, and the state of New York have filed suit against the gun industry. Several of the lawsuits have been dismissed (those of Bridgeport, Chicago, Cincinnati, Gary, Miami, and Philadelphia, among others). Some have made it past the initial hurdle of pretrial dismissal and have entered the discovery phase of litigation, including a group of consolidated cases filed by twelve California cities and counties.

Events are moving quickly in this area, and by the time you read this, many changes are likely to have occurred. More suits may be dismissed. Other cities and states may file additional suits. Whether additional suits are filed will probably depend on what happens to the first wave of suits. Some potential plaintiffs are following a wait-and-see approach.

In the meantime, the lawsuits have already had significant consequences. About two dozen states have passed laws barring cities and counties within those states from suing the gun industry. More may follow. Similar bills have been introduced in Congress to prohibit suits against the gun industry.

An important event occurred in April 2000, when the nation's largest handgun manufacturer, Smith & Wesson, entered into a comprehensive settlement agreement with many of the government plaintiffs in which it agreed to numerous restrictions regarding the way it manufactures, distributes, and markets firearms. Although this agreement subsequently fell apart over disputes regarding its scope (particularly over whether the agreement would control how Smith & Wesson authorized dealers sold firearms made by other companies), Smith & Wesson subsequently entered into a similar settlement with the City of Boston. Settlements between Smith & Wesson and other individual government plaintiffs could follow, although some cities, such as Chicago, have said that they will not settle unless Smith & Wesson pays the city a substantial amount of money.

The public plaintiff suits against the gun industry raise a variety of legal claims. As is common practice in novel civil litigation, lawyers representing the plaintiffs have taken an "everything but the kitchen sink" approach in deciding what claims to include. A review of more than thirty complaints in the city/county gun suits finds the following legal claims being raised: assault, breach of warranty, conspiracy, defective product design (both negligence-based and strict liability), failure to warn (both negligence-based and strict liability), fraudulent concealment, intentional interference with economic advantage, negligent distribution and marketing, negligent misrepresentation, public nuisance, unjust enrichment, and a variety of claims grounded in alleged violations of state and local consumer and business-practices laws.

Despite the shotgun approach, the lawsuits focus on two basic theories already discussed in this chapter: first, that guns are defective in design for failing to incorporate personalized gun technology or other safety devices; and second, that gun manufacturers have failed to take reasonable steps to reduce the likelihood that criminals will acquire their products.

A unique legal aspect of the governmental lawsuits is the introduction of a new claim to the fray known as "public nuisance." "Public nuisance" is a tort claim available only to public authorities. It exists when a defendant's conduct constitutes a substantial and unreasonable interference with public rights and the defendant fails to take reasonable measures to ameliorate the harm. Traditionally, it has been applied to abate nuisance conditions such as the keeping of diseased animals or the operation of establishments devoted to illegal activities, such as prostitution, gambling, or drug sales. The usual remedy for public nuisance is abatement of the nuisance. Damages can be awarded only if the plaintiff suffers a harm different from the public in general.

Although "public nuisance" is a distinct legal claim, the factual basis for the public-nuisance claims in the government lawsuits is the same as that for the negligent distribution and marketing claims previously discussed: that gun makers have acted unreasonably in failing to take steps to keep guns out of the hands of criminals. For example, the first government lawsuit to raise the public-nuisance claim was that filed by the City of Chicago. Chicago's public-nuisance claim was based on a version of the oversupply argument. The complaint accused gun manufacturers of knowingly oversupplying gun shops outside the city limits as a way to circumvent the city's tough gun restrictions, which make it illegal to possess handguns within the city limits. The lawsuit asserted that the gun manufacturers market guns this way knowing that the firearms will be sold to criminals who will bring them into the city illegally. The Chicago suit was dismissed by a trial court judge in September 2000. City officials have appealed the dismissal.

The public plaintiff gun suits are frequently compared to the lawsuits against the tobacco companies that, in 1998, led to a nationwide $246 billion settlement between the industry and forty-six states; however, the tobacco and gun lawsuits are different in several respects.

First, the legal claims are different. The state tobacco suits involved claims that the defendants knew nicotine is an addictive ingredient, intentionally manipulated the nicotine content in cigarettes, and fraudulently concealed this information from the American public. The principal claims in the gun suits are that manufacturers have failed to incorporate personalized technology in guns and that they have failed to take reasonable steps in distributing and marketing their guns to keep them out of the hands of criminals.

The second major difference between the tobacco and gun cases involves the element of causation. In the tobacco cases, there is a direct connection between the injury (smoking-related illnesses and diseases) and proper use of the product. In gun cases, the intervening act of a criminal misuser often comes into play as the direct harm-causing agent, raising the question of whether or not gun manufacturers should be held responsible for the actions of criminal misusers over whom they lack control.

Third, the damages in the gun suits are less concrete than those in the tobacco suits. In the latter, states were seeking to recoup the Medicare payments they paid out to treat smoking-related illnesses. A federal statute at least arguably authorizes such recoupment. Most of the governmental gun suits seek to recover the costs of certain public services incurred in connection with gun violence, such as police and emergency services.

There is one key similarity between the state tobacco suits and the gun suits: in both sets of cases, the plaintiffs are government entities rather than private individuals. This aspect dramatically alters the scope of the litigation by allowing plaintiffs to present "the big picture" case against tobacco or guns, rather than the narrow claim of a particular individual. For example, in a private lawsuit against a gun manufacturer, the complaint (the initial pleading that begins a lawsuit) might allege something to the effect that "on X date, one of the defendant's products was used to injure or kill the plaintiff." Complaints filed in the city/county/state suits, however, paint with a much broader brush. Instead of alleging that a particular manufacturer's product was used to kill or injure a particular person, they join all major gun makers as defendants and detail the overall costs of guns to society. The government plaintiff lawsuit complaints read more like policy manifestos than traditional legal complaints. They include quotations from newspapers, statistical studies, and other advocacy-type information. The following excerpt sets forth the legal and policy arguments against the governmental gun suits.

MUNICIPAL FIREARM LITIGATION: ILL CONCEIVED FROM ANY ANGLE
(32 Connecticut Law Review 1277 [2000])

Anne Giddings Kimball and Sarah L. Olson

[The government plaintiff lawsuits against the gun industry constitute] an unprecedented governmental effort to use civil litigation to achieve uniquely legislative ends. Through these suits, cities and counties have

sought imposition of specific design criteria; heightened regulation of firearm distribution; a shift in the cost of providing public services from the tax-funded government sector to the private sector; and enforcement of sweeping restrictions on the manufacturers' lawful commercial enterprises in other jurisdictions. . . .

While the stated social goal of this effort—a reduction or elimination of violent injury and death—is blameless, it is plain that, as a matter of both law and policy, these complaints are ill conceived when examined from any angle. . . .

The first and most obvious difference between municipal firearms suits and traditional tort-claims rests on the nature of the parties involved. Municipal and county governments are simply not the legal equivalent of individuals, though in certain circumstances they may be treated as "persons" under the law. Municipal corporations cannot be shot and county governments cannot be murdered. From this simple fact flows an equally obvious conclusion: city and county governments stand in a different relationship to injuries inflicted by use of firearms than do their injured citizens. That difference deprives the city and county governments of the capacity to proceed in this type of litigation. . . .

In every case, cities and counties seek compensatory damages sufficient to reimburse them for the cost of certain public services they have provided in the past or will provide in the future, in response to violence or the threat of violence perpetrated with firearms, including costs of 911 services, ambulance, police, police pensions, emergency response teams, medical examiner and forensic services, jail, prosecution, judicial, medical, workers compensation, and other expenditures. In one case, a city has explicitly sought to recover the operating costs of its police department allegedly "attributable to gun violations," totaling "approximately $75,700,260 for 1997." Some cities seek compensation for the costs of security in the public schools or public housing. A number of cities also seek compensatory damages for a purported "loss of substantial tax revenues due to lost productivity, decreased property values and loss of population." . . . Almost every complaint also seeks punitive damages.

In those cases in which plaintiffs have pled unjust enrichment, "disgorgement" or "restitution" is sought in the form of a monetary award based on defendants' profits from the marketing and sale of firearms. In one complaint, a city seeks the imposition of a constructive trust as an apparent vehicle for disgorgement of past and future profits.

Many complaints also seek unprecedented injunctive relief, including some or all of the following components:

- Requiring manufacturers to create and implement "standards and training regarding [defendants'] own distribution of firearms, as well as the conduct of the gun dealers and distributors to whom they distribute firearms, for the purpose of eliminating or substantially reducing the illegal secondary market [in firearms in a particular city]";

- Requiring manufacturers to "monitor the sales of dealers through which they distribute their firearms to ensure that they are being sold legally and responsibly, and to terminate shipments of firearms to dealers who do not enforce standards and practices to prevent sales to persons whom the dealer has direct or constructive notice will not use them lawfully and responsibly";

- Requiring manufacturers to stop making or selling all firearms "without appropriate safety devices and warnings, including devices designed to prevent unauthorized use," including firearms sold without "adequate warnings relating to the risk of handguns and the proper storage thereof";

- Prohibiting the sale of firearms "in a manner which causes such firearms to inappropriately enter" the state or city in question;

- Prohibiting the sale of firearms "under circumstances that place the defendants on direct or constructive notice that the firearms will not be used for the purchaser's personal use or otherwise will not be used for legal purposes." . . .

The suits brought by cities and counties against firearms manufacturers are ill conceived because they are barred by a number of principles fundamental to tort law in every state: (1) plaintiffs must be injured themselves and cannot recover for remote injuries to third parties; (2) cities and counties cannot recover the costs of providing ordinary public services to their citizens; and (3) there are limits to the extent to which city and county governments may impose extraterritorial edicts— whether through ordinance or litigation—in an effort to restrict lawful commercial conduct in other states or to restrain interstate commerce. Furthermore, the substantive tort law of each state precludes these suits.

The Cities' Claims Are Too Remote to Permit Recovery

The first fundamental bar to municipal firearm suits is the simple proposition that a plaintiff cannot recover for injuries to third parties, absent a statutory basis to do so. For over one hundred and fifty years, this "doctrine of remoteness" has been accepted and applied by American courts as an appropriate limitation on recovery in tort. . . .

[T]he causes and the consequences of actions can theoretically stretch forever and encompass many more players than the direct wrongdoer. The concepts of proximate cause and actual injury are utilized by courts to limit responsibility for the consequences of actions which would otherwise expose individuals and companies alike to unacceptable risk. Both the concepts of proximate cause and actual injury have traditionally required that there be "some direct relation between the injury asserted and the injurious conduct alleged." . . .

The government plaintiffs' complaints against firearm manufacturers seek damages and injunctive relief for injuries that are clearly derivative and too remote to permit recovery as a matter of law. In every case, plaintiffs seek to recover costs of public services which were allegedly necessitated because of the use or threat of use of firearms against or by the plaintiffs' citizens. Although postured as "direct" and "independent" injuries, in fact each city or county plaintiff seeks reimbursement of expenses which arise only because of the use of firearms to injure or threaten injuries to plaintiffs' residents. Indeed, it is plaintiffs' underlying assumption that in the absence of firearms from within their boundaries, firearm-related injuries would decrease, and these costs would either not be incurred or not be as great.

All three of the recent decisions [Bridgeport, Cincinnati, Miami] dismissing municipalities' suits against firearm manufacturers have clearly analyzed plaintiff's complaints in light of the remoteness doctrine, and have rested their dismissals in part on this well-established basis. As elaborated by the court's December 10, 1999 opinion dismissing Bridgeport:

The result of these [suits by states against tobacco companies] is that states that sued tobacco companies have been promised more than $200 billion over a twenty-five year period. When conceiving the complaint in this case, the plaintiffs must have envisioned such settlements as the dawning of a new age of litigation during which the gun industry, liquor industry, and purveyors of "junk" food would follow the tobacco industry in reimbursing government expenditures and submitting to judicial regulation.

[Yet t]he tobacco litigation by the states, has not succeeded in eradicating the rules of law on proximate cause, remoteness of damages and limits on justiciability. . . .

However the cities' suits against firearm manufacturers are dressed, their basis remains derivative and their claims remain remote from those who have sustained actual injury. . . .

Cities May Not Recover the Cost of Public Services

City and county suits against firearm manufacturers fail for a second, independent reason: political subdivisions cannot recover the costs of providing public services, the very reason for their existence, in the absence of clear statutory authority. Every jurisdiction to have squarely addressed this issue has adopted the common law rule that "public expenditures made in the performance of governmental functions are not recoverable," absent a specific authorizing statute. . . .

District of Columbia v. Air Florida, Inc. . . . arose from the tragic crash of an Air Florida airplane into the Potomac River. In the wake of this crash, the District of Columbia brought suit in negligence against Air Florida, seeking reimbursement of emergency and clean-up costs totaling over three quarters of a million dollars. The city contended that it was entitled to seek reimbursement on the basis that a "tort theory of rational cost allocation" supported the shift of costs of providing public services to the airlines and its passengers "rather than those distressed municipalities fortuitously located in the path of crashes." In this way, the District argued, the cost of responding to accidents could be underwritten by the party most able economically to avoid the risk or to spread the costs to an acceptable degree.

. . . [T]he Court of Appeals for the District of Columbia rejected this argument, noting that the court was:

> especially reluctant to reallocate risks where a governmental entity is the injured party. It is critically important to recognize that the government's decision to provide tax-supported services is a legislative policy determination. . . . Furthermore, it is within the power of the government to protect itself from extraordinary emergency expenses by passing statutes or regulations that permit recovery from negligent parties. In other words, the city clearly has recourse to legislative initiative to eliminate or reduce the economic burdens of accidents such as the Air Florida crash.

As the Air Florida decision points out, the prohibition against government recovery of the cost of public service stems from the very nature of our system of government, one significant function of which is to even-handedly provide public services without consideration to sources of reimbursement. . . .

A system in which costs are charged to those responsible for their being incurred contains tremendous disadvantages which are obvious upon brief reflection. Litigation would follow every "chargeable event," necessitating elaborate allocation schemes based on the contribution of every conceivable party. . . .

In cases discussing this principle, courts have carefully left one avenue—and only one avenue—open to cities which seek recovery of the costs of providing public services. That exception requires the existence of a municipal ordinance or state or federal statute which specifically authorizes the municipal or county government to seek recoupment of the particular costs in question. . . .

In an effort to evade the claim-barring impact of the cost-recovery rule, government plaintiffs in firearm litigation have argued to limit the rule to single catastrophic events such as plane crashes or train derailments. . . . The rationale for forbidding such cost recovery in catastrophic situations supports the same prohibition even more strongly in ordinary, daily public life. Having funded government with tax dollars, the public has a right to obtain government services without consideration for whose fault created the need for them, and without receiving another bill.

The Cities' Claims Are an Unconstitutional Effort to Restrict Lawful Interstate Commerce in Firearms through Litigation

The scope of the remedies sought by the government plaintiffs clearly reflects the nature of this litigation as regulation-in-disguise. In the guise of traditional tort suits, governmental subdivisions are using both extraordinary compensatory and punitive damage requests and wide-ranging injunctive relief in an attempt to impose extremely broad new regulations on the design, manufacture, and interstate distribution of firearms, outside of the appropriate legislative context. . . .

If successful, these damage claims can only result in—and indeed, are deliberately intended to result in—an alteration of the lawful commercial practices of every firearm manufacturer, domestic or foreign, which sells its products in the United States. . . .

Not only do the extraordinary compensatory and punitive damages sought here amount to government regulation, but the injunctive relief claimed expressly seeks regulation of the firearm manufacturing industry as well. In public proclamations, mayors and plaintiffs' counsel in these suits have likewise acknowledged the regulatory goals of this litigation. Thus, it is clear that the government plaintiffs seek to achieve in a judicial forum what they have been unwilling or unable, in large measure, to obtain in their own legislatures and through law enforcement efforts: limits on the numbers, locations, and types of firearms sold, and a shift in the responsibility for violence response costs from cities to the private sector.

As various commentators have noted, one consequence of this end-run around the legislature is a wholly predictable erosion of the separation of powers of the various branches of government, with potentially long-lasting negative results. . . . "The doctrine of separation of powers prohibits courts from exercising a legislative function by engaging in policy decisions and making or revising rules or regulations." Thus, when the judiciary attempts to legislate or to regulate conduct rather than resolving specific justiciable controversies, it commits an unconstitutional encroachment under the separation of powers doctrine expressed or inherent in the state and federal constitutions. . . .

Democratically elected legislatures at every level of government have hotly debated and enacted laws concerning precisely these issues over the last decade. Regularly over the last decade, firearm control proposals have also been addressed in national and state administrative and regulatory bodies. Through their complaints, the plaintiff cities and counties seek to bypass these appropriate forums. . . .

The government plaintiffs' complaints against firearm manufacturers expressly and implicitly seek to prohibit, restrict, or limit lawful commercial conduct taking place entirely within other states. Typically, plaintiffs do not allege any conduct by manufacturers within the city or county in question, much less any unlawful conduct. Rather, many complaints expressly seek an end to extraterritorial or interstate commerce in firearms. Further, by virtue of the enormous compensatory and punitive damages sought, and more importantly because of the types of injunctive relief requested, these complaints in practical effect would require manufacturers of lawful firearms to curtail or cease all lawful commercial trade in those firearms in the jurisdictions in which they reside—almost uniformly outside of the states in which these complaints are brought—to avoid potentially limitless liability. There is little question that the express goal and the practical effect of these complaints is precisely to stop—not just burden—interstate commerce in firearms. As such, these complaints seek remedies in violation of the United States Constitution. . . .

Conclusion

When viewed from any angle, the recent city and county lawsuits against firearm manufacturers are rampant with legal flaws. Whether the prism of analysis is proximate cause, municipal powers, the nature of injury, the nature of damages, or the substance of any given tort cause of action, these claims are generally unsupported by the law of any state.

The genesis of these deficiencies is simple: the plaintiff cities and counties are seeking overtly or implicitly legislative and regulatory results from a judicial system not formulated to produce them. The solution is likewise simple. These complaints are grossly insufficient as a matter of law on many fronts; they deserve dismissal.

DISCUSSION NOTES

1. Do you support or oppose the concept of tort litigation by public authorities against lawfully operated industries that sell dangerous products? Which industries? Tobacco? The firearms industry? Alcohol producers? Fast-food producers? Automobile manufacturers? All of these industries produce products that, when misused, harm health and therefore impose health care costs, at least indirectly, on the government. Do you feel more comfortable relying on courts or on legislatures to "do the right thing" in setting policy, directly or indirectly, regarding dangerous products? If you choose courts, have you forsaken faith in representative government? If so, why?

2. Do you agree with Kimball and Olson that the governmental gun suits constitute an attempt to achieve judicial regulation of the gun industry in violation of the doctrine of separation of powers? If a court determines an automobile or an airplane (both of which are subject to federal design regulations) to be a defective product because of a design problem, which they have done frequently, does it infringe on separation of powers? Do courts infringe on separation of powers whenever they impose liability for defective products, any of which could be regulated by legislatures? What's different about the government gun suits? Is it simply that government entities are the plaintiffs?

3. Does unrestricted tort litigation against gun manufacturers risk infringing on the Second Amendment right to keep and bear arms? Kopel and Richard E. Gardiner argued in a law review article that tort litigation threatens to chill Second Amendment rights by driving gun manufacturers out of business, and that courts should extend constitutional protection to gun manufacturers from "abusive common law tort suits" (David B. Kopel and Richard E. Gardiner, *The Sullivan Principles: Protecting the Second Amendment from Civil Abuse*, 19 Seton Hall Legislative Journal 737 [1995]). They analogize the situation to the U.S. Supreme Court's decision in *New York Times v. Sullivan*, 376 U.S. 254 (1964), which imposed constitutional restrictions on libel lawsuits to protect

First Amendment freedom of speech, and argue that Second Amendment rights should also be protected from abusive litigation. Do you agree with this analogy? Why or why not?

4. Are the gun suits being used illegitimately to extort concessions from the gun industry or to drive gun producers out of business? Attorneys' fees and other litigation costs are expensive. The gun industry does not have the same "deep pockets" as the tobacco industry; it generates about $1.5 billion in annual U.S. sales, compared to $45 billion in annual domestic sales for the tobacco industry. Government gun litigation is having a detrimental effect on gun makers, and several manufacturers of small, inexpensive guns have filed for bankruptcy. One of these manufacturers was Lorcin Engineering Co. Lorcin advertised its products as "The World's Most Affordable Handguns." The Lorcin L-25 semiautomatic pistol cost only $10 to produce, for both parts and labor, and sold wholesale for $28 and retail for $69 in 1997. (See Sharon Walsh, *The Cheapest Handgun Was Loaded with Profit; For Pistol Firm, Heavy Sales, Then Bankruptcy Protection*, Washington Post, Aug. 26, 1999, at A01.) Lorcin handguns regularly place near the top of lists of guns used most frequently in crime. The 1999 BATF gun-tracing study of seventy-six thousand crime guns from twenty-seven cities found that the Lorcin 9 mm pistol had the shortest "time-to-crime" span of any firearm (meaning it traveled fastest from an initial retail sale by a federally licensed firearms dealer to recovery at a crime scene). Is the bankruptcy of Lorcin a desirable effect of tort litigation or an illicit use of our compensation system? Is it desirable to have inexpensive handguns so that poor people can better afford them? Or does the fact that poor people are most often the victims of cheap handguns refute that argument?

5. Are the injuries asserted by the governmental plaintiffs too remote from the alleged conduct of the defendant gun manufacturers?

6. Most of the governmental lawsuits are seeking, in addition to injunctive relief, damages for the increased cost of police and emergency services due to gun violence. Should government entities be permitted to collect the costs of services they are obligated to provide to the public? What if they can prove that a defendant is responsible for substantially increasing such costs?

7. One important response to the public plaintiff gun suits has been the passage in some states of laws rendering the gun industry immune from governmental suits. Two dozen states have passed laws banning or restricting city and county lawsuits against the gun industry. Some of these laws are intended to have retroactive effect on city lawsuits already filed. The Louisiana statute, passed after New Orleans became the first city to sue the gun industry, is representative. It states in part: "The governing authority of any political subdivision or local or other governmental authority of the state is precluded and preempted from bringing suit to recover against any firearms or ammunition manufacturer, trade association or dealer for damage for injury, death, or loss or to seek other injunctive relief resulting from or relating to the lawful design, manufacture, marketing, or sale of firearms or ammunition" (*La. Rev. Stat. Ann.* § 1799). Statutes designed to restrict tort litigation against various industries exist in some other contexts. Colorado, for example, limits the kinds of lawsuits injured skiers can bring (*Colo. Rev. Stats.* § 33-44-112). Should states ever pass laws to protect or immunize particular industries from lawsuits? Should states have the power to do so retroactively? (A trial court declared the Louisiana statute unconstitutional, ruling it was impermissible for the state to pass a retroactive law designed to benefit a certain class of private citizens. On appeal, the Louisiana Supreme Court reversed the trial court and upheld the statue, ruling that legal protections against retroactive legislation apply only to individual citizens, not local governmental entities. The City of New Orleans sought review of this decision in the U.S. Supreme Court, but in October 2001, the nation's high court refused, without comment, to hear the case. This means that the Louisiana Supreme Court's ruling upholding the statute stands, although the U.S. Supreme Court's decision to deny review does not set any Supreme Court precedent on the issue.)

The Smith & Wesson Settlement

An important development in the government plaintiff gun litigation occurred when Smith & Wesson (S&W), the nation's largest gun manufacturer by market share, entered into a settlement agreement in April 2000 as a means of escaping many of the lawsuits. In return for an agreement to dismiss the lawsuits, S&W agreed to numerous conditions regarding how the company designs and sells its products. This agreement subsequently dissolved over a dispute between the parties as to whether the sales restrictions it imposed on S&W's distributors and dealers applied to all firearms sold by those distributors and dealers or only to S&W firearms. The government plaintiffs argued that the restrictions applied to all firearms; S&W argued that they applied only to S&W products.

In December 2000, S&W entered into a similar settlement agreement with the City of Boston, one of the government plaintiffs that has sued the gun industry. The Boston agreement, although similar to the defunct national agreement, clarifies many of the original settlement terms. The most important change is that the Boston agreement clearly specifies that the sales restrictions it imposes on S&W's distributors and dealers apply only to S&W products.

Because the settlement terms encapsulate the type of injunctive relief the plaintiffs are seeking in the government lawsuits, it is worthwhile to consider the restrictions in some detail. S&W's concessions fall into two groups: restrictions pertaining to design and manufacture and those pertaining to distribution and marketing. (It should be noted that S&W was complying with many of the provisions prior to the settlement agreement.)

As you peruse the following list, try to figure out the motivation behind each restriction and consider whether it will or will not help reduce firearm deaths and injuries.

Safety and Design

With respect to safety and design, S&W agreed to the following terms:

- External trigger locks shall be furnished with each handgun sold. (Major U.S. handgun manufacturers have been doing so since 1998.)
- Within two years, each handgun shall be equipped with an internal lock that can be operated only by a key, combination, or other mechanism unique to the particular gun.
- S&W shall commit 2 percent of annual firearm sales revenues to the

development of personalized technology that would permit only authorized users to fire a handgun. Within three years, S&W will use its best efforts to incorporate personalized technology into all new handgun designs. If it is not feasible to incorporate personalized technology within three years, S&W will continue to commit 2 percent of annual revenues to the development of such technology.

- New guns will bear both a visible serial number (already required by federal law) and a second serial number that is not susceptible to eradication (such as inside the barrel).

- Within one year, all handguns shall be designed so that they cannot be readily operated by an average five-year-old child. This can be accomplished by measures such as strengthening the trigger pull, altering the firing mechanism so it cannot be operated by a child's small hands, or requiring multiple motions to fire the gun.

- Handguns shall be subject to minimum size requirements unless smaller weapons can meet specified accuracy requirements.

- Each handgun shall pass a performance test in which the gun must be fired six hundred times without generating any hairline cracks or other signs of material failure.

- Each handgun must pass a "drop test" (intended to ensure the integrity of guns against accidental discharge).

- Within one year, all pistols shall have a chamber load indicator that allows users to know if a cartridge is already loaded in the chamber or a magazine-disconnect device that prevents the pistol from being fired when the magazine is detached.

- New pistol models shall not be able to accept magazines with more than a ten-round capacity.

- Within six months, the packaging for handguns shall include warnings concerning the necessity for safe storage, including warnings that each year more than two hundred thousand firearms are stolen from residences and that more than one thousand teenagers and children commit suicide and hundreds more die in accidental shootings.

- Firearms shall be designed so that they cannot be easily converted to illegal fully automatic weapons (a long-standing requirement of federal law) and shall not be designed to be resistant to fingerprints.

Sales and Distribution

The stated purpose of the settlement restrictions on sales and distribution practices is to commit S&W "to a standard of conduct to make every effort to eliminate sales of firearms that might lead to illegal possession and/or misuse by criminals, unauthorized juveniles, and other prohibited persons ('suspect firearms sales'). Suspect firearms sales include sales made to straw purchasers, multiple sales of handguns without reasonable explanation (excluding sales to FFLs), and sales made to any purchaser without a completed background check." (Straw purchases and sales without a background check are illegal under federal law. Federal law requires that multiple handgun sales must be reported to the BATF and the local police. See pages 322–23.) S&W bound itself to sell its products only to distributors and dealers who agree in writing to:

- Possess a valid federal firearms license and certify annually that they are in compliance with all applicable local, state, and federal firearms laws (required by current federal law).
- Where available, carry a minimum of $1 million in liability insurance.
- Make no sales of S&W firearms at gun shows unless all sales by *any* seller at the gun show are conducted only on completion of a background check.
- Within two years, maintain an inventory tracking plan for sales of S&W guns that includes: (1) a record of the make, model, caliber, serial number, and acquisition and disposition date for each gun; (2) an inventory check prepared once each month; (3) retention on the premises of all BATF firearm transaction records; (4) a provision that if inventory audits reveal S&W firearms are not accounted for, the dealer is subject to termination.
- Implement a plan for the secure storage of S&W firearms, including firearms in transit. Display cases must be kept locked during business hours except when removing firearms to show a customer. Firearms must be secured in a locked vault during nonbusiness hours. Firearms must be stored separately from handgun ammunition.
- Prohibit persons under age eighteen to handle a S&W firearm un-

less under direct supervision of both an employee and a parent or guardian.

- Not sell S&W magazines capable of holding more than ten rounds.
- Not sell S&W semiautomatic "assault weapons," regardless of date of manufacture. (Congress banned the manufacture of new assault weapons in 1994; however, sales of the guns manufactured prior to that date remain legal.)
- Participate in and comply with all monitoring of firearms distribution by S&W or law enforcement; provide S&W with access to any documents related to the acquisition or distribution of S&W firearms.
- Keep records of all trace requests of S&W firearms initiated by the BATF and report those trace requests monthly to S&W.
- Require employees to receive training (which shall be developed by S&W in consultation with the BATF) covering: laws governing firearm transfers; how to recognize straw purchasers and other attempts to purchase firearms illegally; how to recognize indicators that firearms may be diverted for later transfer to illegal possessors; how to respond to illegal purchase attempts; and safe handling and storage practices.
- Require employees to pass a comprehensive written exam covering the above matters.
- Not transfer S&W firearms to a federal firearms licensee without verifying the validity of tranferee's license against a BATF database.
- Transfer S&W firearms only: (1) to persons who have completed a certified firearms safety training course or passed a certified firearms safety training examination; (2) after demonstrating to the purchaser how to load, unload, and safely store the firearm; (3) after providing the purchaser with a copy of the BATF Disposition of Firearms Notice; and (4) after providing the purchaser with a written record containing identifying information regarding the firearm, to enable the purchaser to describe it accurately to law enforcement in the event it is lost or stolen.
- Agree to terms and procedures that authorize their termination as S&W distributors or dealers if they violate the terms of the settlement agreement.

- Not engage in sales of S&W firearms that a dealer knows or has reason to know are being made to straw purchasers.
- With regard to multiple handgun sales of S&W firearms, allow a purchaser to take only one gun on the date of sale and wait fourteen days to pick up additional guns.

The settlement agreement also obligates S&W to: (1) provide the BATF with quarterly sales data; (2) implement stringent security measures to protect against gun thefts both at manufacturing facilities and during shipment; (3) encourage its distributors and dealers to consent to up to three unannounced BATF compliance inspections each year (federal law currently limits such inspections to one per year, unless there is particular evidence of a crime); (4) terminate or investigate any distributor or dealer on receiving notice that it has violated the agreement or has (according to a formula to be established by the BATF) sold a disproportionate number of crime guns; (5) designate an executive-level manager to serve as compliance officer for the agreement; (6) cooperate fully with law enforcement to eliminate illegal firearm sales and possession; (7) if technologically feasible, fire each firearm before sale and enter a digital image of its casing, along with the weapon's serial number, into a system compatible with the National Integrated Ballistics Identification Center (for the purpose of facilitating the tracing of crime guns); and (8) work to support legislative efforts to reduce firearm misuse and the development of personalized technology.

DISCUSSION NOTES

1. Can you figure out the reason behind each restriction in the settlement agreement? Identify which restrictions you think would be most likely to reduce gun deaths and injuries and which ones you think would be least likely to accomplish that result.
2. Do the provisions in the S&W settlement agreement pose a threat to the rights of law-abiding citizens to own firearms? Identify which specific provisions, in any, you believe present such a threat.
3. Some seemingly obscure provisions may have more importance than is readily apparent. For example, the settlement agreement binds S&W to

deal only with distributors and dealers who adhere to safe gun-storage procedures and obligates S&W to implement strict security procedures to prevent thefts at their manufacturing facilities and during shipping. Thefts are a significant source of guns used in crime. BATF data show that, during fiscal years 1996 and 1997, federal firearms licensees filed 5,041 gun theft reports involving 24,697 guns. During the same two-year period, interstate carriers filed 1,872 theft reports involving 4,842 guns. (See *1997 BATF Annual Report* 19 [1997].) It is suspected that more thefts occur than are reported. By definition, all stolen guns go directly to criminals. Although manufacturers and sellers of all products have a financial interest in not having their inventory stolen, should gun sellers, manufacturers, and interstate shippers of guns be required to take extra steps to display, store, and ship guns in a manner designed to reduce the risk of theft? What if these steps entail substantial expense?

4. Many of the sales and distribution restrictions imposed on S&W dealers are aimed at cutting into the criminal gun-trafficking market by reducing straw and other illegal purchases. Do you think the settlement agreement provisions are likely to accomplish that purpose? Can gun manufacturers control what happens to their products after they leave their manufacturing facility? Can they take reasonable steps to reduce the risk of criminal purchases?

5. When S&W entered into its initial nationwide settlement agreement (before it fell apart), the government plaintiffs encouraged law enforcement officials around the country to give preference to S&W when purchasing handguns. The status of this initiative is now in doubt. Do you think it is a good or bad policy for government entities to give preference to S&W in buying firearms as a "reward" for entering the settlement? S&W has lost a share of its consumer business as a result of the agreement, due to a boycott initiated by Gun Owners of America. Moreover, some distributors and dealers have decided it is not worth the extra expense and effort that will be required of them under the agreement to sell S&W guns. Are these justifications for government entities to give S&W gun-purchasing preferences? (Some state and local governments have laws requiring that government procurement be based solely on the best product at the best price, and not on any form of preference. Also,

some police unions have objected to their members being forced to use S&W guns, as opposed to guns preferred by the officers.)

6. Do you agree with the movement among some gun owners to boycott S&W? Why or why not?

7. Do S&W's concessions encourage more lawsuits against the gun industry? Against other industries? Kopel takes the position that the settlement "has legitimated frivolous lawsuits against financially vulnerable businesses, and has thereby encouraged the victimization of many other businesses by abusive lawyers and prohibition groups" (See David B. Kopel, *Smith & Wesson's Faustian Bargain, Part I*, at http://www.nationalreview.com/comment/comment032000b.html; and *Faustian Bargain, Part II*, at http://www.nationalreview.com/comment/comment032100a.html.) Do you agree? Does your opinion depend on whether you agree with Kopel that the lawsuits are frivolous? Kopel is concerned that if the settlement terms are enforced against smaller gun companies, they could be forced out of business because they will not have the resources to produce products that measure up to the settlement terms, particularly the development of personalized technology. He suggests that even Glock, a large and successful handgun manufacturer, could be threatened because Glock made a business decision not to invest in the development of personalized technology (mainly because Glock does not believe it will ever be reliable enough). Does that concern you? If it turns out that personalized technology is feasible, did Glock simply make a bad business decision? If you had to make a prediction, would you predict that ten years from now, all new guns will come equipped with personalized technology? Or do you think personalized technology will prove to be a "flash in the pan" that never comes into widespread use? Or will it be an available option that appeals to some but not all consumers?

8. One option for more efficient monitoring and control of gun sales at the retail level would be for manufacturers to implement a marketing structure for their products known as "vertical integration forward," by which manufacturers would manage and control their own retail outlets. Thus, the Smith & Wesson or Glock store might be located next to the Sprint PCS store. Would this be a desirable change in gun market-

ing? Would consumers lose the benefit of dealers who carry many different brands, and who can explain the relative advantages of each one? Is convenient shopping a reason not to adopt a distribution system that would give gun manufacturers greater control over the distribution of their dangerous products?

The Future

Events in the public plaintiff litigation are unfolding at a rapid pace. A crystal ball would be required to predict the ultimate resolution and impact of the governmental lawsuits. This litigation, along with possible class-action suits by private persons, ultimately may play a more prominent role than legislation in determining firearms policy in the United States. Whether you believe this is a good or a bad development may be tied to your broader views on the gun debate. In any event, interested observers would do well to stay tuned to the news for future developments.

PERMISSIONS

Grateful acknowledgment is made to the following for use of copyrighted materials:

Bassin, Alana. *Why Packing a Pistol Perpetuates Patriarchy.* 8 Hastings Women's Law Journal 351 (1997) by permission of University of California, Hastings College of Law.

Bogus, Carl T. *Race, Riots, and Guns.* 66 Southern California Law Review, 1365–1388 (1993) reprinted with the permission of the Southern California Law Review.

Clarke, Stevens H. *Firearms and Violence: Interpreting the Connection.* 65 Popular Government 3 (Winter 2000) reprinted by permission of the Institute of Government, University of North Carolina at Chapel Hill.

Cook, Philip J., Jens Ludwig, and David Hemenway. *The Gun Debate's New Mythical Number: How Many Defensive Uses per Year?* 16 Journal of Policy Analysis and Management 463 (1997). Reprinted by permission of John Wiley & Sons, Inc.

Cornell, Saul. *Commonplace or Anachronism: The Standard Model, the Second Amendment, and the Problem of History in Contemporary Constitutional Theory.* 16 Constitutional Commentary 221 (2000).

Cottrol, Robert J. *Submission Is Not the Answer: Lethal Violence, Microcultures of Criminal Violence and the Right to Self-Defense.* 69 University of Colorado Law Review 1029 (1998). Reprinted with permission of the University of Colorado Law Review.

Cottrol, Robert J., and Raymond T. Diamond. *The Second Amendment: Toward an Afro-Americanist Reconsideration.* 80 Georgetown Law Journal 309 (1991).

Henigan, Dennis. *Arms, Anarchy and the Second Amendment.* 26 Valparaiso Law Review 107 (1991) reprinted by permission.

Horowitz, David. *Guns Don't Kill Black People, Other Blacks Do,* Salon.com, August 16, 1999. This article first appeared in Salon.com, at http://www.salon.com. Reprinted with permission.

Kates, Don B. *Public Health Pot Shots.* Reprinted with permission, from April 1997 issue of *Reason* magazine. Copyright 2001 by the Reason Foundation, 3415 S. Sepulveda Blvd, Suite 400, Los Angeles, CA 90034. www.reason.com.

Kimball, Anne Giddings, and Sarah L. Olson. *Municipal Firearm Litigation: Ill Conceived from Any Angle,* 32 Connecticut Law Review 1277 (2000) reprinted by permission.

Kleck, Gary. *Point Blank: Guns and Violence in America.* Hawthorne, NY: Aldine de Gruyter. Copyright 1991.

Kleck, Gary. *Targeting Guns: Firearms and Their Control.* Hawthorne, NY: Aldine de Gruyter. Copyright 1997.

Kleck, Gary, and Marc Gertz. *Armed Resistance to Crime: The Prevalence and Nature of Self-Defense,* 86 Journal of Criminal Law and Criminology 153 (1995) reprinted by permission.

Kopel, David B. *The Samurai, the Mountie, and the Cowboy.* Amherst, NY: Prometheus Books. Copyright 1992. Reprinted by permission of the publisher.

Kopel, David B. *The Second Amendment in the Nineteenth Century,* Brigham Young University Law Review 1359 (1998) reprinted by permission.

Larish, Inge Anna. *Why Annie Can't Get her Gun: A Feminist Perspective on the Second Amendment.* University of Illinois Law Review 467 (1996) reprinted by permission.

Locke, John. *Locke: Two Treatises on Government.* Edited by Peter Laslett. Cambridge: Cambridge University Press. 1988. Reprinted by permission of Cambridge University Press.

Lott Jr., John R. *More Guns, Less Crime: Understanding Crime and Gun-Control Laws.* Chicago and London: University of Chicago Press. Copyright 1998.

McClurg, Andrew J. *The Tortious Marketing of Handguns: Strict Liability Is Dead, Long Live Negligence.* 19 Seton Hall Legislative Journal 777 (1995) reprinted by permission.

McClurg, Andrew J. *Armed and Dangerous: Tort Liability for the Negligent Storage of Firearms.* 32 Connecticut Law Review 1189 (2000) reprinted by permission.

McClurg, Andrew J. *Handguns as Products Unreasonably Dangerous Per Se.* 13 University of Arkansas at Little Rock Law Journal 599 (1991) reprinted by permission.

McClurg, Andrew J. *"Lotts" More Guns and Other Fallacies Infecting the Gun Control Debate.* 11 Journal on Firearms and Public Policy 139 (1999) reprinted by permission.

McClurg, Andrew J. *The Public Health Case for the Safe Storage of Firearms: Adolescent Suicides Add One More "Smoking Gun."* 51 Hastings Law Journal 953 (2000).

Oliver, Philip D. *Rejecting the "Whipping-Boy" Approach to Tort Law: Well-made Handguns Are Not Defective Products.* 14 University of Arkansas at Little Rock, Law Journal 1 (1991) reprinted by permission.

Reynolds, Glenn Harlan. *A Critical Guide to the Second Amendment.* A full text of this article was published originally at 62 Tennessee Law Review 461 (1995), and this edited version appears here by permission of the author and the Tennessee Law Review Association, Inc.

Smith, Adam. *An Inquiry into the Nature and Causes of the Wealth of Nations.* © Oxford University Press 1976. Reprinted from *Adam Smith: An Inquiry into the Nature and Causes of the Wealth of Nations,* edited by R. H. Campbell, A. S. Skinner, and W. B. Todd (Oxford: Oxford University Press, 1976) by permission of Oxford University Press.

Vernick, Jon S., and Stephen P. Teret. *A Public Health Approach to Regulating Firearms as Consumer Products.* 148 University of Pennsylvania Law Review 1193 (2000) reprinted by permission.

Wright, James D., and Peter H. Rossi. *Armed and Considered Dangerous: A Survey of Felons and Their Firearms.* New York: Aldine de Gruyter. Copyright 1994.

INDEX

ABOUT THE EDITORS

Andrew J. McClurg is Professor of Law at Florida International University College of Law. He has also taught at the University of Arkansas at Little Rock, Wake Forest University, the University of Colorado, and Golden Gate University. McClurg has won several awards both for his teaching and academic publications. He is the author of numerous law review articles in the areas of tort law and firearms policy that have been cited by many courts and in more than 100 different law reviews. He has been quoted as an expert on gun-related issues by the *New York Times, Washington Post,* National Public Radio, *Time, U.S. News & World Report,* and many other sources. McClurg is also a noted legal humorist. His Web site is www.lawhaha.com.

David B. Kopel is Research Director of the Independence Institute in Golden, Colorado, and a fellow with the Cato Institute, in Washington, D.C. He is the author of ten books and numerous law review articles on constitutional law, firearms, criminal justice, antitrust, technology, and environmental policy. Kopel also is a columnist for *National Review Online* and the *Sunday Denver Post/Rocky Mountain News.* Previously, he served as an assistant attorney general for Colorado. In 1998–99, he served as an adjunct professor of law at New York University. His Web site is www.davekopel.org.

Brannon P. Denning is Assistant Professor of Law at Southern Illinois University. Denning has published many articles on the Second Amendment and its interpretation by lower courts, as well as articles on militias and the National Guard. Denning graduated magna cum laude from the University of the South with a B.A. He received his J.D., magna cum laude, from the University of Tennessee. After two years in private practice, Denning served as a Research Associate and Senior Fellow at Yale Law School and received his LL.M. from Yale in 1999. His e-mail address is bdenning@siu.edu.

CPSIA information can be obtained at www.ICGtesting.com
Printed in the USA
BVOW031148291012

304197BV00003B/13/P